普通高等教育"十一五"国家级规划教材

21世纪英语专业系列教材

新编美国文学选读

SELECTED READINGS OF AMERICAN LITERATURE

（第5版）

(The 5th Edition)

主编 胡亚敏 李公昭

编者（按姓氏音序排序）

陈礼珍 谷 伟 胡亚敏 黄 川 李梦雨

陆志阳 石平萍 夏 辉 张运恺

西安交通大学出版社
XI'AN JIAOTONG UNIVERSITY PRESS

国家一级出版社
全国百佳图书出版单位

图书在版编目（CIP）数据

新编美国文学选读：汉文、英文 / 胡亚敏，李公昭主编. —5版. —西安：西安交通大学出版社，2022.8（2023.1重印）
ISBN 978-7-5693-2573-7

Ⅰ.①新… Ⅱ.①胡…②李… Ⅲ.①英语—阅读教学—高等学校—教材 ②文学—作品—介绍—美国 Ⅳ.①H319.4：Ⅰ

中国版本图书馆CIP数据核字（2022）第068252号

书　　名	新编美国文学选读（第5版）
	XINBIAN MEIGUO WENXUE XUANDU
主　　编	胡亚敏　李公昭
责任编辑	蔡乐芊　庞钧颖
出版发行	西安交通大学出版社
	（西安市兴庆南路1号 邮政编码710048）
网　　址	http://www.xjtupress.com
电　　话	（029）82668357　82667874（市场营销中心）
	（029）82668315（总编办）
传　　真	（029）82668280
印　　刷	西安五星印刷有限公司
开　　本	787mm×1092mm　1/16　印张　25.5　字数　585千字
版次印次	2022年8月第5版　2023年1月第2次印刷
书　　号	ISBN 978-7-5693-2573-7
定　　价	59.80元

如发现印装质量问题，请与本社市场营销中心联系调换。
订购热线：（029）82665248　（029）82667874
投稿热线：（029）82665371

版权所有　侵权必究

第 5 版前言

Preface to the 5th Edition

《新编美国文学选读》(第4版)出版至今已有五年,到了该对教材进行修订的时候。根据我国高等教育的改革需求、教材的使用情况,以及教师和学生们提出的意见和建议,我们在《新编美国文学选读》(第5版)中进行了如下修订。

第一,新版教材中新增了科马克·麦卡锡和唐·德里罗这两位当代美国作家的介绍和代表作。同时,由于教材篇幅的限制,不得不忍痛删除了亨利·华兹华斯·朗费罗、华莱士·史蒂文斯、舍伍德·安德森、威廉·卡洛斯·威廉姆斯、鲍勃·迪伦和司格特·莫马戴的相关内容,并根据教材使用的实际情况,对部分选文和内容进行了不同程度的调整和更新。

第二,我们补充和更新了部分选文后的思考题,旨在启发学生洞察文学作品蕴含的思想价值和精神内涵,体会人类共同情感和全人类共同价值,引导学生在评析美国文学作品、开展跨文化比较和研究时,能够坚持马克思主义世界观和方法论,既坚持文化自信,也展现国际视野,提升思辨能力。

第三,我们对之前教材出现的错误也进行了更正。

另外,需要说明的是,《新编美国文学选读》(第5版)保留了之前各版的主要特色,在作品后提供"简评"或"解读举例",以扩展学生的思路和视野。

参加此次教材修订工作的有战略支援部队信息工程大学洛阳校区(原解放军外国语学院)的(按姓氏音序)谷伟、胡亚敏、黄川、李梦雨、陆志阳、石平萍、夏辉、张运恺和杭州师范大学外国语学院的陈礼珍。胡亚敏和李公昭负责审定全书,并统稿润色。需要指出的是,本教材是在先前四个版本的基础上完成的,没有之前各版作者的辛勤努力，是不可能有《新编美国文学选读》（第5版）的，在此再向他们表示感谢。另外，研究生刘可心参与了新版教材的校对工作，在此一并表示感谢。

最后要感谢西安交通大学出版社和负责《新编美国文学选读》（第5版）编辑工作的蔡乐芊、庞钧颖女士为本教材付出的辛勤努力。

编　者
2022年8月

第 1 版前言

Preface to the 1st Edition

《新编美国文学选读》(以下简称《新编》)是一套适合大学英语本科高年级美国文学课需要的,编排方法更为新颖、合理、实用的美国文学选读课本。《新编》在研究、参考了国内外同类型教材的基础上,针对我国本科英语专业美国文学课教学的实际情况,精选了美国文学各重要时期的代表作家共 30 名,以及他们的作品选篇,反映了美国文学的大致轮廓。除了借鉴其他教材的特色(如各重要时代的背景介绍、作家简介、作品题解、作品注解和思考题等)外,《新编》还有如下三个特色。

首先,重要作品后附解读举例,有若干种可能的解读方法供学生参考,以拓宽学生的思路。对不适合做多种解读的作品则提供简评,以起抛砖引玉之作用。

其次,每位作家及其作品后附加带评注的推荐书目,以供对该作家或作品感兴趣的学生进一步研究使用(如要作本科毕业论文的学生)。

最后,在全书末尾附上美国历史、文学的大事记年表,将美国文学置于美国历史与文化的大背景下,简约地勾勒出美国文学的发展线索。除原著与问题外,其余均用中文编写,以扩大读者面。

另外,需要说明以下两点。

第一, 个别作家如亨利·詹姆斯、埃兹拉·庞德、T. S. 艾略特等先后为英美两国公民,本应同时选入《新编英国文学选读》和《新编美国文学选读》,但考虑篇幅,我们把艾略特、詹姆斯、庞德分别放到了《新编英国文学选读》和《新编美国文学选读》中,以避免重复。

第二,"背景介绍"和作品后的"推荐书目"一般推荐作者书目、传记、标准版本的作品集各一本,以及重要的作家、作品评论三四本,并以此顺序排列。评论则按作者姓氏的字母顺序排列。

参加《新编》编写工作的同志有（按姓氏音序）陈榕、高俊、胡亚敏、李公昭、刘向东、王岚、许德金、朱荣杰。李公昭最后对全书进行审定、统稿与润色。

编　者
1999 年 11 月

目 录

Contents

American Literature
Before the Civil War

Washington Irving	7
Rip Van Winkle	9
James Fenimore Cooper	24
The Last of the Mohicans	27
Ralph Waldo Emerson	38
Nature	40
The American Scholar	45
Nathaniel Hawthorne	49
The Minister's Black Veil	51
Edgar Allan Poe	64
The Raven	66
The Masque of the Red Death	71
Henry David Thoreau	78
Walden; or, Life in the Woods	79
Walt Whitman	87
Song of Myself	89
O Captain! My Captain!	98
Herman Melville	99
Moby Dick	101

Emily Dickinson ···· 113
    Because I Could Not Stop for Death ···· 114
    I Heard a Fly Buzz—When I Died ···· 116
    Tell All the Truth But Tell It Slant ···· 117

American Literature
Between 1865 and 1914

Mark Twain ···· 124
    The Adventures of Huckleberry Finn ···· 126
Henry James ···· 135
    Daisy Miller ···· 137
Kate Chopin ···· 151
    The Story of an Hour ···· 153
Stephen Crane ···· 157
    The Red Badge of Courage ···· 159

American Literature
Between the Two Wars: 1914–1945

Robert Frost ···· 176
    Mending Wall ···· 178
    The Road Not Taken ···· 181
    Stopping by Woods on a Snowy Evening ···· 182
Ezra Pound ···· 184
    In a Station of the Metro ···· 186
    L'Art, 1910 ···· 187
    The River-Merchant's Wife: A Letter ···· 188
F. Scott Fitzgerald ···· 191
    The Great Gatsby ···· 193
Eugene O'Neill ···· 208
    Long Day's Journey into Night ···· 210
Thomas Stearns Eliot ···· 224
    The Waste Land ···· 226
William Faulkner ···· 232
    A Rose for Emily ···· 234

Ernest Hemingway ··· 244
    The Killers ··· 246

Contemporary American Literature
1945–

Arthur Miller ··· 268
    Death of a Salesman ··· 269

J. D. Salinger ··· 283
    The Catcher in the Rye ··· 284

Joseph Heller ··· 292
    Catch-22 ··· 293

Flannery O'Connor ··· 303
    A Good Man Is Hard to Find ··· 304

Allen Ginsberg ··· 321
    Howl ··· 322

Toni Morrison ··· 324
    Beloved ··· 326

Philip Roth ··· 334
    Everyman ··· 336

Raymond Carver ··· 351
    So Much Water So Close to Home ··· 353

Maxine Hong Kingston ··· 361
    The Woman Warrior ··· 362

Cormac McCarthy ··· 374
    Blood Meridian, or the Evening Redness in the West ··· 376

Don DeLillo ··· 388
    White Noise ··· 390

American Literature
Before the Civil War

背景介绍

根据考古学家的推论，早在公元前数万年前，印第安人就开始在美洲大陆的土地上生活和耕作，并在这个过程中孕育出了丰富多彩的印第安文学。总的来说，印第安文学以口头文学为主，可以分为神话、典仪、曲词等不同的类别。印第安文明是部落文明，他们的神话是集体智慧的结晶，在部落中代代相传。印第安人用这些神话，解释自然中万物生息的规律，总结部落的历史，赞美英雄的英勇事迹。印第安文学的一个重要类别是典仪文学。印第安人在出征、狩猎、死亡等场合，常常要举行大型的典仪。典仪文学就是这种文化形式的产物。典仪文学是一种跨文类的文学形式，它融合了歌曲、叙述、表演等多种元素，人们在典仪上载歌载舞，边表演边吟唱，祈求身体、灵魂与自然之间的和谐共存。

曲词是印第安文学的另一重要类别。它内容广泛，反映了印第安人生活的各个方面。曲词形式如同短诗，长短错落，有很强的音韵美。其中德拉瓦尔人的《瓦拉姆·欧卢姆》(Walam Olum) 就是印第安曲词中的代表作，记载了德拉瓦尔人的历史和变迁，与欧洲文明中的史诗文学有异曲同工之处。可惜的是，进入17世纪之后，印第安文学传统出现了断裂。欧洲人的大规模殖民，对印第安部落文明造成了巨大的冲击，充满活力的印第安文学也逐步走向衰落，一直等到三百多年后进入20世纪下半叶，才出现了新的复兴。

与印第安文学的衰落同时发生的是以英语为书写语言的文学的兴起。1492年，意大利航海家哥伦布到达美洲大陆。这一划时代的地理大发现拉开了欧洲人向这片原先由印第安人定居的土地殖民的序幕。1630年，满载清教徒的"阿贝拉"号抵达美洲大陆前，后成为马萨诸塞殖民地首任总督的约翰·温思诺普 (John Winthrop, 1587—1649) 发表了著名的布道《基督徒仁慈的典范》("A Model of Christian Charity")，告诉即将踏上新大陆的清教徒们，他们建立的社会将是一座被世界瞩目的"山巅之城"(a city upon the hill)。温思诺普在布道中引用《圣经》中的"山巅之城"隐喻深入人心，对美国的民族文化和民族认同的形成产生了深远影响。

进入17世纪，随着大西洋沿岸贸易站的建立和"五月花"(Mayflower) 号的到来，欧洲人开始大规模向北美洲移民。欧洲人尤其是英国清教徒，不仅在这里定居，也带来了他们的文字和文学传统。不过，这一时期的文学并不算繁荣。由于清教文明排斥以娱乐为目的的虚构性文学，早期定居者的文学创作多以讲求实用的历史著作、日记、传记、赞美上帝的布道文、诗歌、散文等为主。科顿·马瑟 (Cotton Mather, 1663—1782) 的《耶稣在美洲的奇迹史》(Magnalia Christi Americana, 1702) 是传记中较好的一部。而自传的范本当首推本杰明·富兰克林 (Benjamin Franklin, 1706—1790) 的《自传》(Autobiography, 1771)。这些作品均以教诲他人为目的。18世纪60年代后的二三十年间，论战性文章和政论性小册子大量涌现，反映出清教作家们对如何将论述与宗教传统结合起来的浓厚兴趣。他们探讨个人权利、人的本质和政治权威等重大问题，给这一时期的美国文学抹上了浓厚的政治色彩。

18世纪中叶到19世纪初，美国出现了民族文学的萌芽。这种萌芽是伴随着美国独立运动和民族意识的高涨而出现的。美国人开始不甘于在政治上跟在宗主国英国后面亦步亦趋，他们追求独立的民族身份，然而在文化上，美国作家并没有能够彻底割断和宗主国的纽带。他们既憧憬新大陆的前程，又眷恋旧大陆的文明，而且在欧洲同行面前多少有些自卑，觉得美国没有什么可值得继承的文学遗产。在题材和写作方法上他们大多模仿英国的前辈或同代作家。此外，由于当时的美国尚无版权及版税法，因此出版商可以任意、廉价地翻印古典的或最新的英国作品，因而不愿出资来出版印数较低的美国作家的作品。这也是美国文学成熟比较缓慢的一个原因。1820年英国作家西德尼·史密斯(Sydney Smith, 1771—1845)曾轻蔑地说："普天之下有谁去读美国小说，看美国戏剧，欣赏美国绘画或雕塑呢？"

美国文学的依附地位，随着小说家华盛顿·欧文(Washington Irving, 1783—1859)的出现而发生了扭转。华盛顿·欧文的《纽约外史》(*A History of New York*, 1809)、《见闻札记》(*The Sketch Book*, 1819—1820)等作品为美国作家第一次赢得了国际声誉。尽管欧文的文学趣味明显带有英国文学的烙印，但在一些作品中他成功运用了美国题材，或把欧洲民间传说中的故事成功安置到美国场景中去。更重要的是，他在多种文学体裁中艺术性地展现了美国的田园生活和自然风光。

与欧文相比，有着"美国小说之父"美称的詹姆斯·费尼莫尔·库柏(James Fenimore Cooper, 1789—1851)则运用小说形式更为突出地表现了美国特色。他不仅在小说类别上多有独创，也是第一位大量采用民族题材、运用美国背景、反映美国人物的作家，因此被称为第一位"纯粹美国式"的小说家。他的"皮袜子故事集"(The Leatherstocking Tales)系列小说中的主人公奈蒂·邦普(Natty Bumpoo)在美国几乎成为家喻户晓的人物，对后来的美国小说，尤其西部小说(Western Fiction)产生了很大影响。此外库柏的作品在欧洲也拥有大量读者。至此，文学史家通常认为美国文学已经走上独立之路。这一时期美国民族文学的发展和繁荣同美国自身的发展，即西进运动和工业革命有着不可分割的联系。

独立战争以后，美国人为了寻求土地和财富，开始了从东部沿海向阿巴拉契亚山脉以西的大迁移。很多移民也加入了拓荒者的行列。交通运输业的发展极大地推动了西进运动。到内战结束时，美国已由1800年的16个州增加到36个州，人口增加了6倍，疆土从大西洋以西一直延伸到太平洋沿岸。所有这些不仅为美国工业化的发展提供了丰富的资源和市场，而且对美国民族价值观和民族特性的形成起到了至关重要的作用。这是一片忙碌、创新、渴望成功的土地，许多作家对西部和边疆产生了浓厚兴趣。库柏的边疆冒险小说就真实反映了这段重要时期的历史。社会与个人之间的矛盾、人类文明的进程与大自然的关系等成为后来美国文学的重要主题。西进运动中培育起来的乐观主义精神对浪漫主义文学的产生起到了重要的促进作用。

1793 至 1815 年英法战争期间，为了对抗封锁，美国政府实施了禁运法以刺激民族工业的发展。19 世纪中叶的美国工业在新英格兰地区已初具规模。尽管拉尔夫·沃尔多·爱默生 (Ralph Waldo Emerson, 1803—1882)、亨利·戴维·梭罗 (Henry David Thoreau, 1817—1862) 等作家对工业革命持批判态度，认为工业破坏了人的全面发展，但是谁也不能否定工业革命创造的财富使文化教育水平得到了极大提高。波士顿成为当时美国文化和出版业的中心。大批宗教理论家、文人和作家纷纷云集于此。他们的作品以崭新的内容和艺术形式塑造了美国和美国人的形象。19 世纪 20 年代以后的美国文学反映了当时国内强烈的民族主义情绪。哈佛大学教授兼评论家威廉·埃勒里·钱宁 (William Ellery Channing, 1780—1842) 曾撰文呼吁美国作家写自己的作品。爱默生也提出"我们要用自己的双脚走路，我们要用自己的双手劳动，我们要讲出自己的思想。"平民出身的杰克逊总统在任期间积极推行民主改革，国内的民主气氛和平等思想体现在文学中，产生了一大批以歌颂个人及个人主义为主题、富有浪漫主义气息的作品。这样，以欧文、库柏为先驱的美国浪漫主义文学进入了一个崭新的阶段。

美国浪漫主义文学的兴盛受到了欧洲浪漫主义运动，尤其是英国浪漫主义运动的较大影响。在要求摆脱 18 世纪传统的新古典主义的束缚、提倡发表个人见解、抒发个人情感、强调想象力、歌颂大自然等方面，美国浪漫主义文学和英国浪漫主义文学是基本一致的。然而，与英国浪漫主义传统不同的是，美国浪漫主义文学受到了新英格兰的超验主义 (Transcendentalism) 的影响。超验主义是美国 19 世纪 30 年代出现的一种哲学思潮。超验主义者聚集在工业发展较迅速的新英格兰，特别是距哈佛大学不远的康科德 (Concord)。他们中影响较大的有爱默生、梭罗、阿莫斯·布朗森·阿尔柯特 (Amos Bronson Alcott, 1799—1888)、玛格丽特·福勒 (Margaret Fuller, 1810—1850)、乔治·里普利 (George Ripley, 1802—1880) 等人。他们发起了一个"超验主义者俱乐部"，不定期地聚会，讨论神学、哲学、文学等问题，同时还出版了自己的刊物《日晷》(*The Dial*)，并积极从事社会改革，建立乌托邦式的布鲁克合作农场 (1840—1847)，支持废奴运动等。

早在 1838 年的《神学院献词》("The Divinity School Address") 中，超验主义的核心人物爱默生就提出了"人就是一切"的口号。超验主义在神学上反对加尔文教派的原罪说及命运先定论，认为人性可以通过自我修养和教化得到改善，人的本性是善良的，人同自然是统一的。他们还认为人可以依靠自己的直觉判断事物，分清是非。他们不为前人的知识与权威束缚，崇尚独立思考。

超验主义思想在神学、哲学和文学上都合乎美国独立后产生的社会需求，可谓是一种思想解放运动，其最深刻的影响表现在文学领域。超验主义者认为只有充满灵性的文艺作品才是优秀的作品。超验主义的影响巨大而深远，尤其在文学领域里，催生了相当数量的经典文学作品，其中包括爱默生和梭罗最出色的随笔，如《论自然》(*Nature*, 1836) 和《瓦尔登湖》(*Walden*, 1854)，以及沃特·惠特曼 (Walt Whitman, 1819—1892) 的初版《草叶集》(*Leaves of Grass*, 1855) 等。

在小说领域，19世纪内战前的美国文坛见证了美国最伟大的三位小说家的诞生。一位是纳撒尼尔·霍桑 (Nathaniel Hawthorne, 1804—1864)。他开创了"心理罗曼史"这一注重心理分析的小说类型。他是新英格兰清教传统的继承者兼批判者，既致力于探究人的内心，展示它的罪恶和黑暗，又对清教主义对人性的压抑提出了质疑，认为过度的压抑和罪恶感反而会滋生出扭曲的灵魂，成为罪恶的温床。在对人的罪恶本性的探讨及用寓言故事和象征手法揭示人物内心世界等方面，赫曼·麦尔维尔 (Herman Melville, 1819—1891) 深受霍桑影响。他的《白鲸》(*Moby Dick*, 1851) 融莎士比亚式的悲剧和浪漫主义小说为一体，表达了善与恶、生与死、理想与现实、人与自然、人与上帝等多重矛盾与冲突，成为美国文学的不朽杰作。遗憾的是直到他100周年诞辰时，人们才确立了他在文学史上的重要地位。而埃德加·爱伦·坡 (Edgar Allen Poe, 1809—1849) 则是这一时期杰出的短篇小说作家。他的短篇小说既有渲染气氛、展现人性黑暗的哥特小说，也有以缜密分析见长的侦探小说，是侦探小说这一文类的鼻祖。

在诗歌创作方面，惠特曼的《草叶集》是美国浪漫主义诗歌的里程碑。他认为作家是社会的预言家。富有创新精神的天才比依赖传统的大师更伟大。对于爱默生对自己的影响，他说道："我像是炉子上的水，在那里冒泡、冒泡、冒泡，爱默生使我沸腾起来。"《草叶集》热情地歌唱美国、时代、民族和普通人，其热情奔放的自由诗体开创了美国诗歌的新风格。

与霍桑、惠特曼几乎同时代的浪漫主义诗人还有亨利·华兹沃斯·朗费罗 (Henry Wadsworth Longfellow, 1807—1882) 和爱伦·坡。朗费罗是深受美国民众喜爱的另一位民族诗人，但他的诗有较多伤感情绪，在诗歌形式的革新和思想深度上要比惠特曼逊色。歌颂自然的浪漫主义诗人还有与朗费罗一起被称为"炉边诗人" (Fireside Poets) 的威廉·卡伦·布莱恩特 (William Cullen Bryant, 1794—1878)、詹姆斯·拉塞尔·洛威尔 (James Russel Lowell, 1819—1891) 等人。布莱恩特曾享有"美国华兹华斯"的美称。他们曾一度被认为是美国文学经典的组成部分，但随着时间的推移却几乎被人淡忘。与之相反的是坡。尽管当时他曾被同时代的爱默生贬为"叮当诗人",后来他的地位却不断提高。与爱默生不同,坡十分注重诗歌音韵和格律产生的美,并把音乐、图画、节奏、意境、题材和完整性较好地统一起来。他的诗歌理论和成就体现了美国的独创精神,并深受欧洲同行的赞赏,极大地影响到法国象征主义诗歌的发展。

最后值得一提的是 19 世纪前半叶美国妇女作家的大量涌现。这些被霍桑戏称为"涂鸦的女人们"(scribbling women) 敢于在以男性为中心的社会里发出自己的声音。具有代表性的作家有凯瑟琳·玛利亚·塞奇威克 (Catherine Maria Sedgwick, 1789—1867),她在风格典雅和清新明快这两个方面几乎超过了同时代的库柏;还有担任过《日晷》主编的超验主义者、女权运动的先驱玛格丽特·福勒 (Margaret Fuller 1810—1850);执意"以女性身份"写作并发表了 60 本诗集的女诗人莉迪亚·亨特利·西格尔尼 (Lydia Huntley Sigourney, 1791—1865),还有以写《小妇人》(*Little Women*, 1868&1869) 成名的露易莎·梅·阿尔科特 (Louisa May Alcott, 1832—1888) 和被称为"以一本书挑起一场战争"的哈丽雅特·比切·斯陀 (Harriet Beecher Stowe, 1811—1896)。哈丽雅特·比切·斯陀的《汤姆叔叔的小屋》(*Uncle Tom's Cabin*, 1852) 描写了南方黑奴遭受的迫害,一时轰动全国,对废奴运动起到了有力的推动作用。

总而言之,美国文学经过 19 世纪 20 年代到 60 年代的发展已完全独立,并日趋成熟。这一时期问世的《红字》(*The Scarlet Letter*, 1850)《白鲸》《瓦尔登湖》和《草叶集》等经典之作就是最好的证明。19 世纪上半叶的美国文坛,也因为它繁荣的景象,被盛赞为美国文学的第一次繁荣时期,或者说是"美国文艺复兴"。

Washington Irving
1783—1859

华盛顿·欧文是第一位获得国际声誉的美国作家。他创作的随笔、短篇小说、历史传奇和人物传记使他成为当时最负盛名的作家。他亦被称为美国文学的奠基人之一。

1783年，欧文出生于纽约一个殷实的商人家庭。他博览家中丰富的藏书，受兄长们的影响，积极投身于文化知识界的社交娱乐活动。他最初的作品是为哥哥彼得主办的《纪事晨报》(*The Morning Chronicle*) 撰写的文稿。这些署名为"老朽乔纳森"(Johnathan Oldstyle) 的作品幽默地讽刺了当时的纽约社会，尤其是当时的戏剧演出。1807年，欧文与哥哥威廉和纽约同乡鲍尔丁合作，创办了不定期出版的刊物《大杂烩》(*Salmagundi*, 1807—1808)。这个刊物共出了二十期，上面的小品文五花八门，但其中最有趣的是假托一位外国船长之名，以书信体形式写的政治和社会讽刺短文。欧文十分喜欢使用化名，例如威尔·威泽德(Will Wizard)、安东尼·埃弗格林(Anthony Evergreen) 等都是他用过的名字。1809年欧文创造了另一个化名狄德里希·尼克尔包克尔(Diedrich Knickerbocker)，以这位虚构作者的身份发表了《从世界开端到荷兰王朝结束时的纽约历史》(*A History of New York from the Beginning of the World to the End of the Dutch Dynasty, by Diedrich Knickerbocker*)，简称《纽约外史》。这部作品冗长的标题不仅暗示了它滑稽讽刺的特性，还表明了欧文对历史撰写的怀疑和攻击。这位尼克尔包克尔先生是个老单身汉，也是个性情古怪的历史学家，常常混淆事实和传说，不能明辨是非曲直。这给欧文提供了绝好的嘲弄历史的机会。他以挪揄讽刺的笔调描写荷兰殖民者在纽约的统治。作品情节荒唐，人物滑稽。与英国大讽刺家乔纳森·斯威夫特(Jonathan Swift, 1667—1745) 一样，欧文发现所谓人类光荣的业绩只不过是卑劣和野蛮的明证而已。愚蠢可笑的尼克尔包克尔先生的惯用手法——东拉西扯、感情用事、英雄崇拜和卖弄学识，欧文使用起来得心应手，以至尼克尔包克尔变成了一个自己并不察觉的滑稽小说家。《纽约外史》对当时的政界和包括托马斯·杰斐逊(Thomas Jefferson, 1743—1826) 在内的某些名人也进行了无情讽刺。此作出版后立即获得成功，很受美国读者的喜爱，被誉为美国的"第一部诙谐文学杰作"，"尼克尔包克尔"也变成了纽约人的绰号。因与欧文的偶然联系，以鲍尔丁为首的一批纽约作家也被称为"尼克尔包克尔"派作家。

　　欧文一生三次游历欧洲，第二次对他创作影响最大。1815年他乘船去利物浦，在英国、法国、德国、意大利和西班牙度过了十七年，遍访名胜古迹，研究当地风土人情，收集民间传说。1818年家族的商行破产，加上他离家期间母亲病故，哥哥彼得病重，这些变故给欧文带来沉重打击。为了摆脱痛苦，他提笔写成了《见闻札记》(*The Sketch Book*, 1819—1820)。这本包括33篇小品文和故事的作品在英国和美国出版后，立即引起轰动，被译成多种文字，流传甚广。欧文再次创造了一个化名人物——多愁善感、研究古物、一味崇拜英国的绅士杰弗里·克雷恩(Geoffrey Crayon)，让他充当大部分故事的作者。然而《见闻札记》中两篇最著名的故事，《瑞普·凡·温克尔》("Rip Van Winkle")和《睡谷的传说》("The Legend of Sleepy Hollow")，还是假托已故的尼克尔包克尔先生写的。这两篇故事都取材于德国民间传说，但欧文把它们成功地安置在美国哈德逊山谷(Hudson Valley)的背景中，并成功地表现了新世界的主题。后来欧文又发表了《布雷斯布里奇田庄》(*Bracebridge Hall*, 1822)、《旅客谈》(*Tales of a Traveller*, 1824)和《阿尔罕伯拉》(*Tales of the Alhambra*, 1832)等散文故事集。但这些作品总体上均未达到《见闻札记》的水平。欧文似乎也意识到了这一点。总的来说，他的创作风格有了明显变化。他开始愿意放弃那种自我防护的叙述距离和反讽手法，写出了《攻克格拉纳达》(*Chronicle of the Conquest of Granada*, 1829)、《哥伦布伙伴们的航行》(*Voyages and Discoveries of the Companions of Columbus*, 1831)和《征服西班牙的故事》(*Legends of the Conquest of Spain*, 1835)等一些"介于历史和传奇之间"的作品。1832年欧文回到美国以后，又创作了《草原游记》(*A Tour on the Prairies*, 1835)、《阿斯托里亚》(*Astoria*, 1836)和《博纳维尔队长历险记》(*The Adventures of Captain Bonneville*, 1837)等描写美国西部的作品。他对大自然的生动描绘，对古怪人物的刻画和对印第安人的同情给读者留下了深刻的印象。晚年，欧文呕心沥血创作了一部优秀的历史人物传记《乔治·华盛顿传》(*Life of George Washington*, 1855—1859)。

　　欧文继承了英国18世纪散文的传统，深受约瑟夫·艾迪生(Joseph Addison, 1672—1719)和奥利弗·哥尔德斯密斯(Oliver Goldsmith, 1730—1774)文风的影响，作品文笔流畅，风格典雅。他又吸收了19世纪初浪漫主义的一些手法，文章诙谐，使人浮想联翩。把现实与想象交融，把欧洲的传统与美国的风情完美结合是欧文创作中最突出的特色。他时常在作品中针砭时事，同时还流露出思古幽情。实际上，他的"尼克尔包克尔"式的夸张性模仿、讽刺和引用地方典故的手法对库柏、坡、霍桑等作家都有一定的影响。他的一些著作至今还是众多作家文学灵感的源泉。

Rip Van Winkle

【题解】

《瑞普·凡·温克尔》选自《见闻札记》。美国独立战争前，在哈德逊河畔的一个村子里，住着一个叫瑞普·凡·温克尔的人。他依靠耕种一小块贫瘠的土地养家糊口，无忧无虑，与世无争，乐于助人，对自己的家事几乎不管不问，而对于邻里之事却有求必应。他最不能忍受的就是妻子的唠叨和责骂。一天，他到山里打猎，不觉天色已晚。下山途中遇到一位老者，肩上扛着一只大酒桶，瑞普伸手相助，跟随老者来到一群陌生人当中。他们正在玩九柱戏。瑞普喝了他们的酒，一觉睡着了。"第二天"醒来后发现，他的狗不见了踪影，猎枪也生锈了。回到村里，他发现一切都变了，自己成了这里的陌生人。他的房屋已破落不堪。喋喋不休的妻子不见了。村里的老朋友们也不见了。他最爱去聊天的小酒馆变成了"合众国旅馆"，门前悬挂着星条旗，迎风招展。旅馆招牌上的画像也不再是英国国王乔治三世，而成了华盛顿将军。后来，终于有人认出了他。原来，他一觉睡了二十年，期间发生了美国独立战争。妻子去世了，儿子已长大，跟他的生活方式一模一样，女儿已成家。之后他回到女儿的家里，渐渐恢复了以前懒散自在的生活。

From Rip Van Winkle

Whoever has made a voyage up the Hudson must remember the Catskill Mountains. They are a dismembered branch of the great Appalachian family, and are seen away to the west of the river, swelling up to a noble height, and lording it over the surrounding country. Every change of season, every change of weather, indeed, every hour of the day, produces some change in the magical hues and shapes of these mountains, and they are regarded by all the good wives, far and near, as perfect barometers. When the weather is fair and settled, they are clothed in blue and purple, and print their bold outlines on the clear evening sky; but sometimes, when the rest of the landscape is cloudless, they will gather a hood of gray vapors about their summits, which, in the last rays of the setting sun, will glow and light up like a crown of glory.

At the foot of these fairy mountains the voyager may have descried the light smoke curling up from a village whose shingle roofs gleam among the trees, just where the blue tints of the upland melt away into the fresh green of the nearer landscape. It is a little village of great antiquity, having been founded by some of the Dutch colonists, in the early times of the province, just about the beginning of the government of the good Peter Stuyvesant[1] (may he rest in peace!), and there were some of the houses of the original settlers standing within a few years, with lattice windows, gable fronts surmounted with weathercocks, and built of small yellow bricks brought from Holland.

In that same village, and in one of these very houses (which, to tell the precise truth, was sadly time-worn and weather-beaten), there lived many years since, while the country was yet a province of Great Britain, a simple, good-natured fellow, of the name of Rip Van Winkle. He was a descendant of the Van Winkles who figured so gallantly in the chivalrous days of Peter Stuyvesant, and accompanied him to the siege of Fort Christina[2]. He inherited, however, but little of the martial character of his ancestors. I have observed that he was a simple, good-natured man; he was, moreover, a kind neighbor and an obedient, henpecked husband. Indeed, to the latter circumstance might be owing that meekness of spirit which gained him such universal popularity; for those men are most apt to be obsequious and conciliating abroad who are under the discipline of shrews at home. Their tempers, doubtless, are rendered pliant and malleable in the fiery furnace of domestic tribulation, and a curtain lecture[3] is worth all the sermons in the world for teaching the virtues of patience and long-suffering. A termagant wife may, therefore, in some respects, be considered a tolerable blessing; and if so, Rip Van Winkle was thrice blessed.

Certain it is that he was a great favorite among all the good wives of the village, who, as usual with the amiable sex, took his part in all family squabbles, and never failed, whenever they talked those matters over in their evening gossipings, to lay all the blame on Dame[4] Van Winkle. The children of the village, too, would shout with joy whenever he approached. He assisted at their sports, made their playthings, taught them to fly kites and shoot marbles, and told them long stories of ghosts, witches, and Indians. Whenever he went dodging about the village, he was surrounded by a troop of them, hanging on his skirts[5], clambering on his back, and playing a thousand tricks on him with impunity; and not a dog would bark at him throughout the neighborhood.

The great error in Rip's composition was an insuperable aversion to all kinds of profitable labor. It could not be from the want of assiduity or perseverance; for he would sit on a wet rock, with a rod as long and heavy as a Tartar's lance, and fish all day without a murmur, even though he should not be encouraged by a single nibble. He would carry a fowling piece[6] on his shoulder, for hours together, trudging through woods and swamps, and up hill and down dale, to shoot a few squirrels or wild pigeons. He would never even refuse to assist a neighbor in the roughest toil, and was a foremost man at all country frolics for husking Indian corn, or building stone fences. The women of the village, too, used to employ him to run their errands, and to do such little odd jobs as their less obliging husbands would not do for them; in a word, Rip was ready to attend to anybody's business but his own; but as to doing family duty, and keeping his farm in order, it was impossible.

In fact, he declared it was of no use to work on his farm; it was the most pestilent little piece of ground in the whole country; everything about it went wrong, and would go wrong, in spite of him. His fences were continually falling to pieces; his cow would either go astray or get among the cabbages; weeds were sure to grow quicker in his fields than anywhere else; the rain always made a point of setting in just as he had some outdoor work to do; so that though his patrimonial estate had dwindled away under his management, acre by acre, until there was little more left than a mere patch of Indian corn and potatoes, yet it was the worst-conditioned farm in the neighborhood.

His children, too, were as ragged and wild as if they belonged to nobody. His son Rip, an urchin begotten in his own likeness, promised to inherit the habits, with the old clothes of his father. He was generally seen trooping like a colt at his mother's heels, equipped in a pair of his father's cast-off galligaskins[7], which he had much ado to hold up with one hand, as a fine lady does her train[8] in bad weather.

Rip Van Winkle, however, was one of those happy mortals, of foolish, well-oiled dispositions, who take the world easy, eat white bread or brown, whichever can be got with least thought or trouble, and would rather starve on a penny than work for a pound. If left to himself, he would have whistled life away, in perfect contentment; but his wife kept continually dinning in his ears about his idleness, his carelessness, and the ruin he was bringing on his family. Morning, noon, and night, her tongue was incessantly going, and everything he said or did was sure to produce a torrent of household eloquence. Rip had but one way of replying to all lectures of the kind, and that, by frequent use, had grown into a habit. He shrugged his shoulders, shook his head, cast up his eyes, but said nothing. This, however, always provoked a fresh volley from his wife, so that he was fain to draw off his forces, and take to the outside of the house—the only side which, in truth, belongs to a henpecked husband.

Rip's sole domestic adherent was his dog Wolf, who was as much henpecked as his master; for Dame Van Winkle regarded them as companions in idleness, and even looked upon Wolf with an evil eye, as the cause of his master's so often going astray. True it is, in all points of spirit befitting an honorable dog, he was as courageous an animal as ever scoured the woods—but what courage can withstand the ever-during and all-besetting terrors of a woman's tongue? The moment Wolf entered the house his crest fell, his tail drooped to the ground, or curled between his legs; he sneaked about with a gallows air, casting many a sidelong glance at Dame Van Winkle, and at the least flourish[9] of a broomstick or ladle would fly to the door with yelping precipitation.

Times grew worse and worse with Rip Van Winkle as years of matrimony rolled on; a tart temper never mellows with age, and a sharp tongue is the only edged tool that grows keener by constant use. For a long while he used to console himself, when driven from home, by frequenting a kind of perpetual club of the sages, philosophers, and other idle personages of the village, which held its sessions on a bench before a small inn, designated by a rubicund portrait of his majesty George the Third. Here they used to sit in the shade, of a long lazy summer's day, talking listlessly over village gossip, or telling endless sleepy stories about nothing. But it would have been worth any statesman's money to have heard the profound discussions which sometimes took place, when by chance an old newspaper fell into their hands, from some passing traveler. How solemnly they would listen to the contents, as drawled out by Derrick Van Bummel, the schoolmaster, a dapper, learned little man, who was not to be daunted by the most gigantic word in the dictionary; and how sagely they would deliberate upon public events some months after they had taken place.

The opinions of this junto were completely controlled by Nicholas Vedder, a patriarch of the village, and landlord of the inn, at the door of which he took his seat from morning till night, just moving sufficiently to avoid the sun, and keep in the shade of a large tree; so that the neighbors could tell the hour by his movements as accurately as by a sun-dial. It is true, he was rarely heard to speak, but smoked his pipe incessantly. His adherents, however (for every great man has his adherents), perfectly understood him, and knew how to gather his opinions. When anything that was read or related displeased him, he was observed to smoke his pipe vehemently, and send forth short, frequent, and angry puffs; but when pleased, he would inhale the smoke slowly and tranquilly, and emit it in light and placid clouds, and sometimes taking the pipe from his mouth, and letting the fragrant vapor curl about his nose, would gravely nod his head in token of perfect approbation.

From even this stronghold the unlucky Rip was at length routed by his termagant wife, who would suddenly break in upon the tranquillity of the assemblage, and call the members all to nought; nor was that august personage, Nicholas Vedder himself, sacred from the daring tongue of this terrible virago, who charged him outright with encouraging her husband in habits of idleness.

Poor Rip was at last reduced almost to despair; and his only alternative, to escape from the labor of the farm and clamor of his wife, was to take gun in hand and stroll away into the woods. Here he would sometimes seat himself at the foot of a tree, and share the contents of his wallet[10] with Wolf, with whom he sympathized as a fellow-sufferer in persecution. "Poor Wolf," he would say, "thy mistress leads thee a dog's life of it; but never mind, my lad, while I live thou shalt never want a friend to stand by thee!" Wolf would wag his tail, look wistfully in his master's face, and if dogs can feel pity, I verily believe he reciprocated the sentiment with all his heart.

In a long ramble of the kind on a fine autumnal day, Rip had unconsciously scrambled to one of the highest parts of the Catskill Mountains. He was after his favorite sport of squirrel shooting, and the still solitudes had echoed and reëchoed with the reports of his gun. Panting and fatigued, he threw himself, late in the afternoon, on a green knoll, covered with mountain herbage, that crowned the brow of a precipice. From an opening between the trees he could overlook all the lower country for many a mile of rich woodland. He saw at a distance the lordly Hudson, far, far below him, moving on its silent but majestic course, the reflection of a purple cloud, or the sail of a lagging bark, here and there sleeping on its glassy bosom, and at last losing itself in the blue highlands.

On the other side he looked down into a deep mountain glen, wild, lonely, and shagged, the bottom filled with fragments from the impending cliffs, and scarcely lighted by the reflected rays of the setting sun. For some time Rip lay musing on this scene; evening was gradually advancing; the mountains began to throw their long blue shadows over the valleys; he saw that it would be dark long before he could reach the village, and he heaved a heavy sigh when he thought of encountering the terrors of Dame Van Winkle.

As he was about to descend, he heard a voice from a distance, hallooing, "Rip Van Winkle! Rip Van Winkle!" He looked around, but could see nothing but a crow winging its solitary flight across the mountain. He thought his fancy must have deceived him, and turned again to descend, when he heard the same cry ring through the still evening air: "Rip Van Winkle! Rip Van Winkle!"—at the same time Wolf bristled up his back, and giving a low growl, skulked to his master's side, looking fearfully down into the glen. Rip now felt a vague apprehension stealing over him; he looked anxiously in the same direction, and perceived a strange figure slowly toiling up the rocks, and bending under the weight of something he carried on his back. He was surprised to see any human being in this lonely and unfrequented place, but supposing it to be some one of the neighborhood in need of assistance, he hastened down to yield it.

On nearer approach, he was still more surprised at the singularity of the stranger's appearance. He was a short, square-built old fellow, with thick bushy hair, and a grizzled beard. His dress was of the antique Dutch fashion—a cloth jerkin strapped around the waist—several pair of breeches, the outer one of ample volume, decorated with rows of buttons down the sides, and bunches at the knees. He bore on his shoulders a stout keg, that seemed full of liquor, and made signs for Rip to approach and assist him with the load. Though rather shy and distrustful of this new acquaintance, Rip complied with his usual alacrity, and mutually relieving one another, they clambered up a narrow gully, apparently the dry bed of a mountain torrent. As they ascended, Rip every now and then heard long rolling peals, like distant thunder, that seemed to issue out of a deep ravine, or rather cleft between lofty rocks, toward which their rugged path conducted. He paused for an instant, but supposing it to be the muttering of one of those transient thunder showers which often take place in mountain heights, he proceeded. Passing through the ravine, they came to a hollow, like a small amphitheater, surrounded by perpendicular precipices, over the brinks of which impending trees shot their branches, so that you only caught glimpses of the azure sky and the bright evening cloud. During the whole time, Rip and his companion had labored on in silence; for though the former marveled greatly what could be the object of carrying a keg of liquor up this wild mountain, yet there was something strange and incomprehensible about the unknown that inspired awe and checked familiarity.

On entering the amphitheater, new objects of wonder presented themselves. On a level spot in the center was a company of odd-looking personages playing at ninepins[11]. They were dressed in a quaint, outlandish fashion: some wore short doublets[12], others jerkins, with long knives in their belts, and most had enormous breeches, of similar style with that of the guide's. Their visages, too, were peculiar: one had a large head, broad face, and small, piggish eyes; the face of another seemed to consist entirely of nose, and was surmounted by a white sugar-loaf hat set off with a little red cock's tail. They all had beards, of various shapes and colors. There was one who seemed to be the commander. He was a stout old gentleman, with a weather-beaten countenance; he wore a laced doublet, broad belt and hanger[13], high-crowned hat and feather, red stockings, and high-heeled shoes, with roses[14] in them. The whole group reminded Rip of the figures in an old Flemish painting, in the parlor of Dominie Van Schaick, the village parson, and which had been brought over from Holland at the time of the settlement.

What seemed particularly odd to Rip, was that though these folks were evidently amusing themselves, yet they maintained the gravest faces, the most mysterious silence, and were, withal, the most melancholy party of pleasure he had ever witnessed. Nothing interrupted the stillness of the scene but the noise of the balls, which, whenever they were rolled, echoed along the mountains like rumbling peals of thunder.

As Rip and his companion approached them, they suddenly desisted from their play, and stared at him with such fixed statue-like gaze, and such strange, uncouth, lack-luster countenances, that his heart turned within him, and his knees smote together. His companion now emptied the contents of the keg into large flagons[15], and made signs to him to wait upon the company. He obeyed with fear and trembling; they quaffed the liquor in profound silence, and then returned to their game.

By degrees, Rip's awe and apprehension subsided. He even ventured, when no eye was fixed upon him, to taste the beverage, which he found had much of the flavor of excellent Hollands[16]. He was naturally a thirsty soul, and was soon tempted to repeat the draught. One taste provoked another, and he reiterated his visits to the flagon so often, that at length his senses were overpowered, his eyes swam in his head, his head gradually declined, and he fell into a deep sleep.

On awaking, he found himself on the green knoll from whence he had first seen the old man of the glen. He rubbed his eyes—it was a bright sunny morning. The birds were hopping and twittering among the bushes, and the eagle was wheeling aloft and breasting the pure mountain breeze. "Surely," thought Rip, "I have not slept here all night." He recalled the occurrences before he fell asleep. The strange man with a keg of liquor—the mountain ravine—the wild retreat among the rocks—the woe-begone party at ninepins—the flagon—"Oh! that flagon! that wicked flagon!" thought Rip—"what excuse shall I make to Dame Van Winkle?"

He looked round for his gun, but in place of the clean, well-oiled fowling piece, he found an old firelock lying by him, the barrel incrusted with rust, the lock falling off, and the stock worm-eaten. He now suspected that the grave roysterers of the mountain had put a trick upon him, and having dosed him with liquor, had robbed him of his gun. Wolf, too, had disappeared, but he might have strayed away after a squirrel or partridge. He whistled after him, shouted his name, but all in vain; the echoes repeated his whistle and shout, but no dog was to be seen.

　　He determined to revisit the scene of the last evening's gambol, and if he met with any of the party, to demand his dog and gun. As he rose to walk, he found himself stiff in the joints, and wanting in his usual activity. "These mountain beds do not agree with me," thought Rip, "and if this frolic should lay me up with a fit of the rheumatism, I shall have a blessed time with Dame Van Winkle." With some difficulty he got down into the glen; he found the gully up which he and his companion had ascended the preceding evening; but to his astonishment a mountain stream was now foaming down it, leaping from rock to rock, and filling the glen with babbling murmurs. He, however, made shift to scramble up its sides, working his toilsome way through thickets of birch, sassafras, and witch-hazel, and sometimes tripped up or entangled by the wild grape vines that twisted their coils and tendrils from tree to tree, and spread a kind of network in his path.

　　At length he reached to where the ravine had opened through the cliffs to the amphitheater; but no traces of such opening remained. The rocks presented a high, impenetrable wall, over which the torrent came tumbling in a sheet of feathery foam, and fell into a broad, deep basin, black from the shadows of the surrounding forest. Here, then, poor Rip was brought to a stand. He again called and whistled after his dog; he was only answered by the cawing of a flock of idle crows, sporting high in air about a dry tree that overhung a sunny precipice; and who, secure in their elevation, seemed to look down and scoff at the poor man's perplexities. What was to be done? the morning was passing away, and Rip felt famished for want of his breakfast. He grieved to give up his dog and gun; he dreaded to meet his wife; but it would not do to starve among the mountains. He shook his head, shouldered the rusty firelock, and, with a heart full of trouble and anxiety, turned his steps homeward.

　　As he approached the village, he met a number of people, but none whom he knew, which somewhat surprised him, for he had thought himself acquainted with every one in the country round. Their dress, too, was of a different fashion from that to which he was accustomed. They all stared at him with equal marks of surprise, and whenever they cast their eyes upon him, invariably stroked their chins. The constant recurrence of this gesture induced Rip, involuntarily, to do the same, when, to his astonishment, he found his beard had grown a foot long!

　　He had now entered the skirts of the village. A troop of strange children ran at his heels, hooting after him, and pointing at his gray beard. The dogs, too, none of which he recognized for his old acquaintances, barked at him as he passed. The very village was altered: it was larger and more populous. There were rows of houses which he had never seen before, and those which had been his familiar haunts had disappeared. Strange names were over the doors—strange faces at the windows—everything was strange. His mind now began to misgive him; he doubted whether both he and the world around him were not bewitched. Surely this was his native village, which he had left but the day before. There stood the Catskill Mountains—there ran the silver Hudson at a distance—there was every hill and dale precisely as it had always been—Rip was sorely perplexed—"That flagon last night," thought he, "has addled my poor head sadly!"

It was with some difficulty he found the way to his own house, which he approached with silent awe, expecting every moment to hear the shrill voice of Dame Van Winkle. He found the house gone to decay—the roof fallen in, the windows shattered, and the doors off the hinges. A half-starved dog, that looked like Wolf, was skulking about it. Rip called him by name, but the cur snarled, showed his teeth, and passed on. This was an unkind cut[17] indeed—"My very dog," sighed poor Rip, "has forgotten me!"

He entered the house, which, to tell the truth, Dame Van Winkle had always kept in neat order. It was empty, forlorn, and apparently abandoned. This desolateness overcame all his connubial fears—he called loudly for his wife and children—the lonely chambers rung for a moment with his voice, and then all again was silence.

He now hurried forth, and hastened to his old resort, the little village inn—but it too was gone. A large rickety wooden building stood in its place, with great gaping windows, some of them broken, and mended with old hats and petticoats, and over the door was painted, "The Union Hotel, by Jonathan Doolittle." Instead of the great tree which used to shelter the quiet little Dutch inn of yore, there now was reared a tall naked pole[18], with something on the top that looked like a red nightcap[19], and from it was fluttering a flag, on which was a singular assemblage of stars and stripes—all this was strange and incomprehensible. He recognized on the sign, however, the ruby face of King George, under which he had smoked so many a peaceful pipe, but even this was singularly metamorphosed. The red coat was changed for one of blue and buff, a sword was stuck in the hand instead of a scepter, the head was decorated with a cocked hat, and underneath was painted in large characters, GENERAL WASHINGTON.

There was, as usual, a crowd of folk about the door, but none whom Rip recollected. The very character of the people seemed changed. There was a busy, bustling, disputatious tone about it, instead of the accustomed phlegm and drowsy tranquillity. He looked in vain for the sage Nicholas Vedder, with his broad face, double chin, and fair long pipe, uttering clouds of tobacco smoke instead of idle speeches; or Van Bummel, the schoolmaster, doling forth the contents of an ancient newspaper. In place of these, a lean, bilious-looking fellow, with his pockets full of handbills, was haranguing vehemently about rights of citizens—election—members of Congress—liberty—Bunker's Hill[20]—heroes of '76[21]—and other words, that were a perfect Babylonish jargon[22] to the bewildered Van Winkle.

The appearance of Rip, with his long grizzled beard, his rusty fowling piece, his uncouth dress, and the army of women and children that had gathered at his heels, soon attracted the attention of the tavern politicians. They crowded around him, eying him from head to foot, with great curiosity. The orator bustled up to him, and drawing him partly aside, inquired "on which side he voted?" Rip stared in vacant stupidity. Another short but busy little fellow pulled him by the arm, and raising on tiptoe, inquired in his ear, "whether he was Federal or Democrat."

Rip was equally at a loss to comprehend the question; when a knowing, self-important old gentleman, in a sharp cocked hat, made his way through the crowd, putting them to the right and left with his elbows as he passed, and planting himself before Van Winkle, with one arm akimbo, the other resting on his cane, his keen eyes and sharp hat penetrating, as it were, into his very soul, demanded, in an austere tone, "what brought him to the election with a gun on his shoulder, and a mob at his heels, and whether he meant to breed a riot in the village?" "Alas! gentlemen," cried Rip, somewhat dismayed, "I am a poor quiet man, a native of the place, and a loyal subject of the king, God bless him!"

Here a general shout burst from the bystanders—"A Tory! a Tory! a spy! a refugee! hustle him! away with him!" It was with great difficulty that the self-important man in the cocked hat restored order; and having assumed a tenfold austerity of brow, demanded again of the unknown culprit, what he came there for, and whom he was seeking. The poor man humbly assured him that he meant no harm; but merely came there in search of some of his neighbors, who used to keep about the tavern.

"Well—who are they?—name them."

Rip bethought himself a moment, and then inquired, "Where's Nicholas Vedder?"

There was silence for a little while, when an old man replied in a thin, piping voice, "Nicholas Vedder? why, he is dead and gone these eighteen years! There was a wooden tombstone in the churchyard that used to tell all about him, but that's rotted and gone, too."

"Where's Brom Dutcher?"

"Oh, he went off to the army in the beginning of the war; some say he was killed at the battle of Stony Point[23]—others say he was drowned in a squall, at the foot of Antony's Nose[24]. I don't know—he never came back again."

"Where's Van Bummel, the schoolmaster?"

"He went off to the wars, too, was a great militia general, and is now in Congress."

Rip's heart died away, at hearing of these sad changes in his home and friends, and finding himself thus alone in the world. Every answer puzzled him, too, by treating of such enormous lapses of time, and of matters which he could not understand: war—Congress—Stony Point!—he had no courage to ask after any more friends, but cried out in despair, "Does nobody here know Rip Van Winkle?"

"Oh, Rip Van Winkle!" exclaimed two or three, "Oh, to be sure! that's Rip Van Winkle yonder, leaning against the tree."

Rip looked, and beheld a precise counterpart of himself, as he went up the mountain: apparently as lazy, and certainly as ragged. The poor fellow was now completely confounded. He doubted his own identity, and whether he was himself or another man. In the midst of his bewilderment, the man in the cocked hat demanded who he was, and what was his name?

"God knows," exclaimed he, at his wit's end; "I'm not myself—I'm somebody else—that's me yonder—no—that's somebody else, got into my shoes—I was myself last night, but I fell asleep on the mountain, and they've changed my gun, and everything's changed, and I'm changed, and I can't tell what's my name, or who I am!"

The bystanders began now to look at each other, nod, wink significantly, and tap their fingers against their foreheads. There was a whisper, also, about securing the gun, and keeping the old fellow from doing mischief; at the very suggestion of which, the self-important man in the cocked hat retired with some precipitation. At this critical moment a fresh, likely woman pressed through the throng to get a peep at the gray-bearded man. She had a chubby child in her arms, which, frightened at his looks, began to cry. "Hush, Rip," cried she, "hush, you little fool, the old man won't hurt you." The name of the child, the air of the mother, the tone of her voice, all awakened a train of recollections in his mind. "What is your name, my good woman?" asked he.

"Judith Gardenier."

"And your father's name?"

"Ah, poor man, his name was Rip Van Winkle; it's twenty years since he went away from home with his gun, and never has been heard of since—his dog came home without him; but whether he shot himself, or was carried away by the Indians, nobody can tell. I was then but a little girl."

Rip had but one question more to ask; but he put it with a faltering voice:—

"Where's your mother?"

"Oh, she too had died but a short time since; she broke a blood vessel in a fit of passion at a New England peddler."

There was a drop of comfort, at least, in this intelligence. The honest man could contain himself no longer.—He caught his daughter and her child in his arms.—"I am your father!" cried he—"Young Rip Van Winkle once—old Rip Van Winkle now!—Does nobody know poor Rip Van Winkle!"

All stood amazed, until an old woman, tottering out from among the crowd, put her hand to her brow, and peering under it in his face for a moment, exclaimed, "Sure enough! it is Rip Van Winkle—it is himself. Welcome home again, old neighbor.—Why, where have you been these twenty long years?"

Rip's story was soon told, for the whole twenty years had been to him but as one night. The neighbors stared when they heard it; some were seen to wink at each other, and put their tongues in their cheeks; and the self-important man in the cocked hat, who, when the alarm was over, had returned to the field, screwed down the corners of his mouth, and shook his head—upon which there was a general shaking of the head throughout the assemblage.

It was determined, however, to take the opinion of old Peter Vanderdonk, who was seen slowly advancing up the road. He was a descendant of the historian of that name[25], who wrote one of the earliest accounts of the province. Peter was the most ancient inhabitant of the village, and well versed in all the wonderful events and traditions of the neighborhood. He recollected Rip at once, and corroborated his story in the most satisfactory manner. He assured the company that it was a fact, handed down from his ancestor the historian, that the Catskill Mountains had always been haunted by strange beings. That it was affirmed that the great Hendrick Hudson[26], the first discoverer of the river and country, kept a kind of vigil there every twenty years, with his crew of the Half-Moon[27], being permitted in this way to revisit the scenes of his enterprise, and keep a guardian eye upon the river, and the great city called by his name[28]. That his father had once seen them in their old Dutch dresses playing at ninepins in a hollow of the mountain; and that he himself had heard, one summer afternoon, the sound of their balls, like long peals of thunder.

To make a long story short, the company broke up, and returned to the more important concerns of the election. Rip's daughter took him home to live with her; she had a snug, well-furnished house, and a stout cheery farmer for a husband, whom Rip recollected for one of the urchins that used to climb upon his back. As to Rip's son and heir, who was the ditto of himself, seen leaning against the tree, he was employed to work on the farm; but evinced an hereditary disposition to attend to anything else but his business.

Rip now resumed his old walks and habits; he soon found many of his former cronies, though all rather the worse for the wear and tear of time; and preferred making friends among the rising generation, with whom he soon grew into great favor.

Having nothing to do at home, and being arrived at that happy age when a man can do nothing with impunity, he took his place once more on the bench, at the inn door, and was reverenced as one of the patriarchs of the village, and a chronicle of the old times "before the war." It was some time before he could get into the regular track of gossip, or could be made to comprehend the strange events that had taken place during his torpor. How that there had been a revolutionary war—that the country had thrown off the yoke of old England—and that, instead of being a subject of his Majesty, George III, he was now a free citizen of the United States. Rip, in fact, was no politician; the changes of states and empires made but little impression on him; but there was one species of despotism under which he had long groaned, and that was—petticoat government; happily, that was at an end; he had got his neck out of the yoke of matrimony, and could go in and out whenever he pleased, without dreading the tyranny of Dame Van Winkle. Whenever her name was mentioned, however, he shook his head, shrugged his shoulders, and cast up his eyes; which might pass either for an expression of resignation to his fate, or joy at his deliverance.

He used to tell his story to every stranger that arrived at Dr. Doolittle's hotel. He was observed, at first, to vary on some points every time he told it, which was, doubtless, owing to his having so recently awaked. It at last settled down precisely to the tale I have related, and not a man, woman, or child in the neighborhood but knew it by heart. Some always pretended to doubt the reality of it, and insisted that Rip had been out of his head, and this was one point on which he always remained flighty. The old Dutch inhabitants, however, almost universally gave it full credit. Even to this day they never hear a thunderstorm of a summer afternoon, about the Catskills, but they say Hendrick Hudson and his crew are at their game of ninepins; and it is a common wish of all henpecked husbands in the neighborhood, when life hangs heavy on their hands, that they might have a quieting draught out of Rip Van Winkle's flagon.

【注解】

1. Peter Stuyvesant: 彼得·斯特伊弗桑特 (1592?—1672)，当时荷兰在美洲的殖民行政官，曾任西印度公司荷兰分公司经理、荷属北美及加勒比海地区总督 (1645—1664)，建立新阿姆斯特丹 (即后来的纽约市) 市政府 (1653)。
2. Fort Christina: 克里斯蒂娜堡，瑞典在北美的第一个殖民地，后被荷兰人彼得·斯特伊弗桑特占领。
3. a curtain lecture：这里是古旧用法，指妻子对丈夫床帷内的训话。
4. Dame: 英国对爵士妻子、从男爵妻子、贵族妻女的尊称。这里指温克尔夫人，有挖苦之意。
5. skirts: (衣服的) 下摆。
6. fowling piece: 鸟枪，猎枪。
7. galligaskins: 宽大马裤；(谑) 马裤，男裤。
8. train: 裙裾，托裙。
9. flourish: 挥舞。
10. wallet: 行囊，旅行袋。
11. ninepins：九柱戏，一种保龄球游戏。
12. doublets: 紧身上衣。
13. belt and hanger: 带有匕首或短剑的皮带。
14. roses: 玫瑰花饰。
15. flagons: 酒壶。
16. Hollands: 荷兰杜松子酒。
17. cut: 伤人感情的言语或举动。
18. a tall naked pole: 相当于 the liberty pole, 自由旗杆。在顶端置一自由帽或共和国国旗的旗杆，作为自由的标志。
19. a red nightcap: 相当于 the liberty cap, 自由帽，18 世纪法国大革命时期被用作自由的标志。
20. Bunker's Hill: 邦克山，因邦克山战役而闻名。邦克山战役是美国独立战争期间最著名的战役之一，发生在 1775 年 6 月 17 日，是北美殖民地民兵与英军之间的第一次大规模武装冲突，双方死伤惨重。邦克山纪念碑建成于 1843 年，高 67 米，是美国最早的纪念碑之一，用以纪念邦克山战役。
21. '76: 1776 年。
22. Babylonish jargon: 就像巴别塔 (The Tower of Babel) 的故事一样，这里指 " 莫名其妙的话，令人费解的话 "。

23. Stony Point：斯托尼波因特，美国地名，位于纽约州哈德逊河西岸。1779 年，独立战争期间，美军将领安东尼·韦恩 (Anthony Wayne, 1745—1796) 曾率军攻克斯托尼波因特英军要塞。
24. Antony's Nose：位于美国纽约哈德逊河岸的一座山的名字。
25. the historian of that name：艾德里安·凡·德·邓克 (Adriaen van der Donck, 1618?—1655)，律师，著有《新尼德兰描述》(*A Description of New Netherland*, 1655)。
26. Hendrick Hudson：亨德里克·哈德逊 (1565—1611)，英国航海家、探险家，四次远航探寻通过北冰洋到达亚洲的航道，后因船员叛乱，被置一小船上漂流失踪。今天的哈德逊河、哈德逊湾等均以其姓氏命名。
27. Half-Moon:" 半月号 "，船的名字。
28. the great city called by his name：哈德逊市。

【思考题】

1. What is your comment on the image of Rip Van Winkle?
2. Compare the situations in the village before and after Rip's 20-year sleep.
3. What is Rip's opinion of the changes in his village after the American War of Independence? Do you agree with him?
4. What do you think of the image of Rip's wife?
5. What is the theme of the story?
6. With Rip's time traveling experience, "Rip Van Wrinkle" can be regarded as a kind of science fiction in modern sense. Discuss the functions of time travel in this story and those in many science fiction stories.

解读举例

1. 《瑞普·凡·温克尔》通过讲述一位普通美国人酒后一睡二十年的传奇故事，展示了二十年间美国社会发生的颠覆性变化，包括发生了美国独立战争，因此小说可被理解为一个历史的文本。

2. 《瑞普·凡·温克尔》开创了美国文学的" 逃遁 "主题 (escape motif)。瑞普离家出走，上山打猎，不仅仅是一种消极逃避，也是一种积极探索，代表对现实生活的不满和对理想生活的追求。这一逃遁主题对美国文学发展产生了重大影响。库柏的邦普、梭罗《瓦尔登湖》中的" 我 "、吐温笔下的哈克、塞林格的霍尔顿等都借鉴了瑞普这个角色。

3. 《瑞普·凡·温克尔》传达出对美国独立战争某种程度上的不理解或保留态度。美国独立战争发生期间，普通人瑞普"在睡觉"。他没有积极参与这场轰轰烈烈的革命斗争，对美国独立革命的背景、宗旨、过程、结果丝毫不知。对于美国革命带来的变化，他一无所知，甚至不能接受。唯一让他欣慰的是摆脱了妻子的唠叨，似乎这场史无前例的独立战争跟他并没有太大的关系。

4. 《瑞普·凡·温克尔》表达出一定的男权中心主义思想，同时也表现出一定的女性主义意识。小说的幽默建立在对瑞普太太的挖苦、嘲笑和贬低的基础上。在故事的结尾，瑞普解放了，但不是获得独立战争带来的政治自由，而是终于摆脱了妻子喋喋不休的训斥和抱怨，因为瑞普太太死了。但另一方面，读者发现，瑞普太太对丈夫的责备却事出有因。面对生活的不公，她迎难而上，耕种田地，料理家务，"总是把屋里收拾得井井有条"，担负起了养家糊口、教育子女的重担。她没有名字，被戏称为"温克尔夫人"(Dame Van Winkle)。然而她并没有得到村里其他妇女的同情。从一定意义上说，她是父权主义文化的受害者。

James Fenimore Cooper
1789—1851

作者简介

詹姆斯·费尼莫尔·库柏是美国第一位重要的小说家，出生于新泽西的伯林顿，后迁往纽约中部奥茨戈湖畔的库柏镇——一个由他父亲在奥茨戈湖畔建立起的边陲小镇。那里的迷人景色和丰富传说对库柏后来的创作产生了重大影响。1804年，15岁的库柏入读耶鲁大学，两年后因违纪被校方开除。在后来的五年中，库柏先后当过水手和海军军官学校学员，1811年解甲归田，娶妻生子，过上了乡绅的生活。

30岁那年，库柏突然心血来潮，向家人宣布要当一名小说家。经过一番努力，他于1820年自费出版了处女作《警惕》(Precaution)。这是一部模仿英国女作家简·奥斯汀(Jane Austen, 1775—1817)的写作风格，以英国上流社会为题材的消遣作品。这部作品出版后受到不少朋友的批评，他们认为库柏不应去写自己不熟悉的英国社会。库柏显然接受了这一忠告。第二年他创作了以美国独立战争为背景、反映美国人强烈爱国主义精神的长篇小说《间谍》(The Spy)，大获成功。这部作品为他今后的小说创作定下了基本框架，即以美国为写作背景，以美国人的生活为表现题材。从这个意义上说,库柏是第一位真正的美国作家。1823年,库柏创作出版了他的第三部长篇小说《拓荒者》(The Pioneers),故事以一个叫奈蒂·邦普的白人猎手为主人公,是美国文学史上首次详细描述北美边疆生活的作品。后来奈蒂·邦普的故事发展为一个由五本书组成的长篇小说系列——"皮袜子故事集"(The Leatherstocking Tales)。同年,库柏还创作出版了以他早期航海生活为题材的小说《舵手》(The Pilot)。库柏的这一创作变化不仅是为了猎取新奇,也是为了和苏格兰作家沃尔特·司各特爵士(Sir Walter Scott, 1771—1832)一年前发表的《海盗》(The Pirate)一比高低,因为库柏相信一个有过水手经历的作家创作的海上故事肯定比没有当过水手的作家创作得要好。

从1820到1823短短的几年中,库柏连续出版了四部长篇小说,开创了历史小说、边疆小说和海洋小说三种不同的小说类型,这使他声名大作。尤其是《拓荒者》,因反映了当时美国拓荒西部的现实生活而受到读者青睐。在这之后,库柏举家迁往纽约市,并在那里创立了"面包奶酪俱乐部"(Bread and Cheese Club),结交了许多作家、艺术家,他自己也成为当时美国文坛的中心人物。在成功的喜悦中,库柏制定了一个庞大的写作计划,即为当时十三个州各创作一部浪漫小说,但实际只完成了《利奥那·林肯》(Lionel Lincoln, 1825)一部。1826年库柏又重新开始创作以奈蒂·邦普为主人公的"皮袜子小说",并于当年发表了《最后的莫希干人》(The Last of the Mohicans)。1826年,正值文学事业如日中天之时,库柏渡海来到欧洲,先后游历了英国、法国、意大利等国。在法国巴黎期间,库柏创作出版了"皮袜子故事集"的第三部《草原》(The Prairie, 1827)。这一期间,库柏还连续创作了浪漫小说《红海盗》(The Red Rover, 1827)、《悲哀的希望》(The Wept of Wish-ton-Wish, 1829)、《水妖》(The Water-Witch, 1830),并针对司各特美化中世纪封建社会的历史小说创作了旨在打破封建桎梏,宣扬民主自由思想的三部曲《刺客》(The Bravo, 1831)、《教士》(The Heidenmauer, 1832)和《刽子手》(The Headsman, 1833),并因此获得了"美国司各特"的雅号。

1833年库柏回到美国。面对官场的腐败、道德的沦丧和权力的滥用,以及评论对他在欧洲发表的小说不公正的批评,库柏愤然写下了《告同胞书》(A Letter to His Countrymen, 1834),表达了他对美国世风日下、人心不古的痛心之情,并发誓从此不再创作小说。随后库柏又发表了寓言性讽刺作品《莫尼金斯》(The Monikins, 1835)、《欧洲拾零》(Gleanings in Europe, 1837—1838),以及阐述自己贵族式社会理想的《美国民主》(The American Democrat, 1838)、《归途》(Homeward Bound, 1838)和《重建家园》(Home as Found, 1838)。这些作品由于讽刺了美国上层社会的虚伪和愚昧而受到舆论的攻击，并引发了库柏和一些辉格党 (Whig Party)① 报纸的论战，最后甚至诉诸法律。然而这一切并没有影响库柏继续创作。1839 年他完成并出版了学术性的历史著作《美国海军史》(The History of the Navy of the United States of America)，但因其中对伊利湖战役 (The Battle of Lake Erie, 1813) 的不同见解，库柏又被卷入一场新的笔墨官司。1840 年，库柏放弃了自己六年前不再写小说的誓言，重新开始中断了十三年之久的"皮袜子故事集"系列的创作，先后发表了《探路者》(The Pathfinder, 1840) 和《猎鹿者》(The Deerslayer, 1841) 两部作品，完成了"皮袜子故事集"小说系列的全部创作。

"皮袜子故事集"按其叙述时间排列分别为《猎鹿者》(1744)、《探路者》(1750)、《最后的莫西干人》(1757)、《拓荒者》(1793) 和《草原》(1827)，描述了邦普作为一名勇士所必须经历的种种考验，体现了一种纯真浪漫的生活理想，生动地塑造出邦普作为"美国亚当"(American Adam) 的形象。《最后的莫西干人》表现的是 1757 年法印战争 (French and Indian War) 时期，正值中年的邦普帮助印第安人和英军，与法国殖民者及其印第安同盟做斗争的故事。《拓荒者》表现的是迈入老年的邦普与当地的坦普尔法官之间产生的矛盾与冲突。由于作品关注了自然的荒蛮状态与农业耕种文明之间的矛盾，因此有人将此看作是美国最早的一部生态小说。《草原》描写了邦普去世前的晚年生活。在上述作品中，邦普有着"皮袜子""鹰眼""捕兽人""探路者""猎鹿人"等不同绰号。通过库柏在这些作品中的精心打造，邦普这个人物变得家喻户晓，成为世界文学中著名的人物之一。

从《警惕》起，库柏以惊人的速度，在短短二十年里连续创作出版了 16 部长篇小说和一些政论、学术性著作。在此后的十年中，库柏以爆发式的精力，又创作发表了《卡斯蒂尔的默西迪斯》(Mercedes of Castile, 1840)、《两个舰队司令》(The Two Admirals, 1842)、《飞啊，飞》(Wing-and-Wing, 1842) 等 17 部作品。

在长达三十一年的创作生涯中，库柏总共创作发表的作品多达 33 部。这其中不少是没有经过深思熟虑，草草写成的作品，情节牵强，人物单薄，主要靠离奇、冒险和浪漫故事来赢得读者。因此尽管库柏是位十分多产的作家，但他真正为后人记住，并盛传不衰的只有《间谍》和"皮袜子故事集"等少数作品。然而他开创的美国战争文学、历史文学、海洋文学和边疆文学，他作品中表现出来的爱国主义精神和民主思想，塑造的哈维·柏契 (Harvey Birch) 和奈蒂·邦普等形象对他同时代和后来的美国作家都产生了深远的影响。

---

① 即美国共和党前身，美国自由党，建立于 1834 年，因仿效英国辉格党的政治纲领而得名。

American Literature Before the Civil War

The Last of the Mohicans

【题解】

《最后的莫希干人》是"皮袜子故事集"的第二部。1757年英、法殖民者为争夺印第安人的土地展开了激烈的战争。法国人在印第安易洛魁部落的帮助下围攻了纽约北部乔治湖附近的英军要塞。要塞司令芒罗的女儿考拉和爱丽丝在英军少校、爱丽丝的未婚夫邓肯·黑伍德的护送下赶往要塞与父亲会合。同行的还有一个休伦族(易洛魁部落的一支)的印第安人,名叫马古亚。他表面为英军服务,暗地却为法国人效力,并阴险狡诈地企图将考拉一行引入易洛魁人的地盘,然后将考拉据为己有。这一阴谋被在林中打猎的"鹰眼"(奈蒂·邦普)和他的印第安朋友——莫希干人钦格古克和他儿子昂卡斯发现。阴谋败露后,马古亚仓皇逃脱,但很快又纠集易洛魁部落的印第安人回来抓获了考拉姐妹。"鹰眼"再次赶来营救。然而在前往要塞的路上,他们再次被印第安人抓获。前来营救的"鹰眼"发现考拉和爱丽丝被分别关押在不同营地。黑伍德化装潜入休伦族人的营地,救出爱丽丝,与昂卡斯一同赶往关押考拉的特拉华营地,在那里见到了考拉与马古亚。根据特拉华印第安人的风俗,他们不便当面反对马古亚对考拉提出的要求。昂卡斯受命带队前云攻打休伦族人。在战斗中,马古亚临阵脱逃,昂卡斯跟踪其后,并因营救考拉牺牲,考拉亦惨遭杀害。这时赶来救援的"鹰眼"举枪击中马古亚,后者落崖身亡。故事最后,"鹰眼"仍然留在林中,而其他白人则回到文明社会。

以下章节选自《最后的莫希干人》第十二章,描写马古亚等人正要对被俘的考拉等人下毒手时,"鹰眼"和钦格古克父子赶来营救的惊险情节。

From The Last of the Mohicans

Chapter 12

"Clo. 'I am gone, sir,
And anon, sir,
I'll be with you again.'"

—*Twelfth Night*

The Hurons stood aghast at this sudden visitation of death[1] on one of their band. But as they regarded the fatal accuracy of an aim which had dared to immolate an enemy at so much hazard to a friend, the name of "La Longue Carabine[2]" burst simultaneously from every lip, and was succeeded by a wild and a sort of plaintive howl. The cry was answered by a loud shout from a little thicket, where the incautious party had piled their arms; and at the next moment Hawkeye, too eager to load the rifle he had regained, was seen advancing upon them, brandishing the clubbed weapon, and cutting the air with wide and powerful sweeps. Bold and rapid as was the progress of the scout, it was exceeded by that of a light and vigorous form which, bounding past him, leaped, with incredible activity and daring, into the very centre of the Hurons, where it stood, whirling a tomahawk, and flourishing a glittering knife with fearful menaces, in front of Cora. Quicker than the thoughts could follow these unexpected and audacious movements, an image, armed in the emblematic panoply of death, glided before their eyes, and assumed a threatening attitude at the other's side. The savage tormentors recoiled before these warlike intruders, and uttered, as they appeared in such quick succession, the often repeated and peculiar exclamation of surprise, followed by the well-known and dreaded appellations of:

"Le Cerf Agile! Le Gros Serpent!"[3]

But the wary and vigilant leader of the Hurons was not so easily disconcerted. Casting his keen eyes around the little plain, he comprehended the nature of the assault at a glance, and encouraging his followers by his voice as well as by his example, he unsheathed his long and dangerous knife, and rushed with a loud whoop upon the expecting Chingachgook. It was the signal for a general combat. Neither party had firearms, and the contest was to be decided in the deadliest manner—hand to hand, with weapons of offence and none of defence.

Uncas answered the whoop, and leaping on an enemy, with a single well-directed blow of his tomahawk cleft him to the brain. Heyward tore the weapon of Magua from the sapling, and rushed eagerly towards the fray. As the combatants were now equal in number, each singled an opponent from the adverse band. The rush and blow passed with the fury of a whirlwind and the swiftness of lighting. Hawkeye soon got another enemy within reach of his arm, and with one sweep of his formidable weapon he beat down the slight and inartificial[4] defences of his antagonist, crushing him to the earth with the blow. Heyward ventured to hurl the tomahawk he had seized, too ardent to await the moment of closing. It struck the Indian he had selected on the forehead, and checked for an instant his onward rush. Encouraged by this slight advantage, the impetuous young man continued his onset, and sprang upon his enemy with naked hands. A single instant was sufficient to assure him of the rashness of the measure, for he immediately found himself fully engaged, with all his activity and courage, in endeavoring toward the desperate thrusts made with the knife of the Huron. Unable longer to foil an enemy so alert and vigilant, he threw his arms about him, and succeeded in pinning the limbs of the other to his side with an iron grasp, but one that was far too exhausting to himself to continue long. In this extremity he heard a voice near him shouting:

"Exterminate the varlets! no quarter to[5] an accursed Mingo!"

At the next moment the breech of Hawkeye's rifle fell on the naked head of his adversary, whose muscles appeared to wither under the shock, as he sank from the arms of Duncan, flexible and motionless.

When Uncas had brained his first antagonist, he turned, like a hungry lion, to seek another. The fifth and only Huron disengaged at the first onset had paused a moment, and then seeing that all around him were employed in the deadly strife, he had sought, with hellish vengeance, to complete the baffled work of revenge. Raising a shout of triumph, he sprang towards the defenceless Cora, sending his keen axe as the dreadful precursor of his approach. The tomahawk grazed her shoulder, and cutting the withes which bound her to the tree, left the maiden at liberty to fly. She eluded the grasp of the savage, and, reckless of her own safety, threw herself on the bosom of Alice, striving, with convulsed and ill-directed fingers, to tear asunder the twigs which confined the person of her sister. Any other than a monster would have relented at such an act of generous devotion to the best and purest affection; but the breast of the Huron was a stranger to sympathy. Seizing Cora by the rich tresses which fell in confusion about her form, he tore her from her frantic hold, and bowed her down with brutal violence to her knees. The savage drew the flowing curls through his hand, and raising them on high with an outstretched arm, he passed the knife around the exquisitely moulded head of his victim with a taunting and exulting laugh. But he purchased this moment of fierce gratification with the loss of the fatal opportunity. It was just then the sight caught the eye of Uncas. Bounding from his footsteps, he appeared for an instant darting through the air, and descending in a ball, he fell on the chest of his enemy, driving him many yards from the spot, head long and prostrate. The violence of the exertion cast the young Mohican at his side. They arose together, fought, and bled, each in his turn. But the conflict was soon decided: the tomahawk of Heyward and the rifle of Hawkeye, descended on the skull of the Huron at the same moment that the knife of Uncas reached his heart.

The battle was now entirely terminated, with the exception of the protracted struggle between "Le Renard Subtil[6]" and "Le Gros Serpent". Well did these barbarous warriors prove that they deserved those significant names, which had been bestowed for deeds in former wars. When they engaged, some little time was lost in eluding the quick and vigorous thrusts which had been aimed at their lives. Suddenly darting on each other, they closed, and came to the earth, twisted together, like twining serpents, in pliant and subtle folds. At the moment when the victors found themselves unoccupied, the spot where these experienced and desperate combatants lay could only be distinguished by a cloud of dust and leaves, which moved from the centre of the little plain towards its boundary as if raised by the passage of a whirlwind. Urged by the different motives of filial affection, friendship, and gratitude, Heyward and his companies rushed with one accord to the place, encircling the little canopy of dust which hung above the warriors. In vain did Uncas dart around the cloud, with a wish to strike his knife into the heart of his father's foe; the threatening rifle of Hawkeye was raised and suspended in vain; while Duncan endeavored to seize the limbs of the Huron, with hands that appeared to have lost their power. Covered as they were with dust and blood, the swift evolutions of the combatants seemed to incorporate their bodies into one. The deathlike-looking figure of the Mohican and the dark form of the Huron gleamed before their eyes in such quick and confused succession that the friends of the former knew not where nor when to plant the succouring blow. It is true there were short and fleeting moments when the fiery eyes of Magua were seen glittering, like the fabled organs of the basilisk through the dusty wreath by which he was enveloped, and he read by those short and deadly glances the fate of the combat in the presence of his enemies; however, any hostile hand could descend on his devoted head, its place was filled by the scowling visage of Chingachgook. In this manner the scene of the combat was removed from the centre of the little plain to its verge. The Mohican now found an opportunity to make a powerful thrust with his knife; Magua suddenly relinquished his grasp, and fell backward, without motion, and seemingly without life. His adversary leaped on his feet, making the arches of the forest ring with the sounds of triumph.

"Well done for the Delawares![7] victory to the Mohican!" cried Hawkeye, once more elevating the butt of the long and fatal rifle; "a finishing blow from a man without a cross will never tell against his honour, nor rob him of his right to the scalp."

But at the very moment when the dangerous weapon was in the act of descending, the subtle Huron rolled swiftly from beneath the danger, over the edge of the precipice, and falling on his feet, was seen leaping with a single bound into the centre of a thicket of low bushes which clung along its sides. The Delawares, who had believed their enemy dead, uttered their exclamation of surprise, and were following with speed and clamour, like hounds in open view of the deer, when a shrill and peculiar cry from the scout instantly changed their purpose and recalled them to the summit of the hill.

"'Twas like himself," cried the inveterate forester, whose prejudices contributed so largely to veil his natural sense of justice in all matters which concerned the Mingoes— "a lying and deceitful varlet as he is. An honest Delaware now, being fairly vanquished, would have lain still, and been knocked on the head; but these knavish Maquas cling to life like so many cats-o'-the-mountain. Let him go—let him go; 'tis but one man, and he without rifle or bow, many a long mile from his French commerades[8]; and, like a rattler that has lost his fangs, he can do no further mischief until such time as he, and we too, may leave the prints of our moccasins over a long reach of sandy plain.—See, Uncas," he added in Delaware, "your father is flaying the scalps already. It may be well to go round and feel the vagabonds that are left, or we may have another of them loping through the woods, and screeching like a jay that has been winged."

So saying, the honest but implacable scout made the circuit of the dead, into whose senseless bosoms he thrust long knife, with as much coolness as though they had been so many brute carcasses. He had, however, been anticipated by the elder Mohican, who had already torn the emblems of victory from the unresisting heads of the slain.

But Uncas, denying his habits[9], we had almost said his nature, flew with instinctive delicacy, accompanied by Heyward, to the assistance of the females, and quickly releasing Alice, placed her in the arms of Cora. We shall not attempt to describe the gratitude to the Almighty Disposer of Events which glowed in the bosoms of the sisters, who were thus unexpectedly restored to life and to each other. Their thanksgivings were deep and silent— the offerings of their gentle spirits burning brightest and purest on the secret altars of their hearts, and their related and more earthly feelings exhibiting themselves in long and fervent, though speechless, caresses. As Alice rose from her knees, where she had sunk by the side of Cora, she threw herself on the bosom of the latter, and sobbed aloud the name of their aged father, while her soft, dove-like eyes sparkled with the rays of hope.

"We are saved! We are saved!" she murmured, "to return to the arms of our dear, dear father, and his heart will not be broken with grief. And you too, Cora, my sister—my more than sister, my mother—you too are spared. And Duncan," she added, looking round upon the youth with a smile of ineffable innocence, "even our own brave and noble Duncan has escaped without a hurt."

To these ardent and nearly incoherent words Cora made no other answer than by straining the youthful speaker to her heart, as she bent over her in melting tenderness. The manhood of Heyward felt no shame in dropping tears over this spectacle of affectionate rapture; and Uncas stood, fresh and blood-stained from the combat, a calm, and apparently an unmoved, looker-on, it is true, but with eyes that had already lost their fierceness, and were beaming with a sympathy that elevated him far above the intelligence, and advanced him probably centuries before the practices of his nation.

During this display of emotions so natural in their situation, Hawkeye, whose vigilant distrust had satisfied itself that the Hurons, who disfigured the heavenly scene, no longer possessed the power to interrupt its harmony, approached David[10], and liberated him from the bonds he had, until that moment, endured with the most exemplary patience.

"There," exclaimed the scout, casting the last withe behind him, "you are once more master of your own limbs, though you seem not to use them with much greater judgment than that in which they were first fashioned. If advice from one who is not older than yourself[11], but who, having lived most of his time in the wilderness, may be said to have experience beyond his years, will give no offence, you are welcome to my thoughts; and these are, to part with the little tooting instrument in your jacket to the first fool you meet with, and buy some useful weapon with the money, if it be only the barrel of a horseman's pistol. By industry and care, you might thus come to some prefarment[12]; for by this time, I should think, your eyes would plainly tell you that a carrion crow is a better bird than a mocking thresher. The one will at least remove foul sights from before the face of man, while the other is only good to brew disturbances in the woods, by cheating the ears of all that hear them.[13]"

. . .

When the foresters had made their selection, and distributed their prizes, the scout announced that the hour had arrived when it was necessary to move. By this time the song of Gamut had ceased, and the sisters had learned to still the exhibition of their emotions. Aided by Duncan and the younger Mohican, the two latter descended the precipitous sides of that hill which they had so lately ascended under so very different auspices, and whose summit had so nearly proved the scene off their massacre. At the foot, they found the Narragansetts[14] browsing the herbage of the bushes; and having mounted, they followed the movements of a guide, who, in the most deadly straits, had so often proved himself their friend. The journey was, however, short. Hawkeye, leaving the blind path that the Hurons had followed, turned short to his right, and entering the thicket, he crossed a babbling brook, and halted in a narrow dell, under the shade of a few water elms. Their distance from the base of the fatal hill was but a few rods, and the steeds had been serviceable only in crossing the shallow stream.

The scout and the Indians appeared to be familiar with the sequestered place where they now were; for, leaning their rifles against the trees, they commenced throwing aside the dried leaves, and opening the blue clay, out of which a clear and sparkling spring of bright, glancing water, quickly bubbled. The white man then looked about him, as though seeking for some object, which was not to be found as readily as he expected:—

"Them careless imps, the Mohawks, with their Tuscarora and Onondaga brethren, have been here slaking their thirst," he muttered, "and the vagabonds have thrown away the gourd! This is the way with benefits, when they are bestowed on such disremembering hounds! Here has the Lord laid his hand, in the midst of the howling wilderness, for their good, and raised a fountain of water from the bowels of the 'arth, that might laugh at the richest shop of apothecary's ware in all the colonies; and see! The knaves have trodden in the clay, and deformed the cleanliness of the place, as thought they were brute beasts, instead of human men."

Uncas silently extended towards him the desired gourd, which the spleen of Hawkeye had hitherto prevented him from observing, on a branch of an elm. Filling it with water, he retired a short distance to a place where the ground was more firm and dry; here he coolly seated himself, and after taking a long and apparently a grateful draught, he commenced a very strict examination of the fragments of food left by the Hurons, which had hung in a wallet on his arm.

"Thank you, lad," he continued, returning the empty gourd to Uncas; "now we will see how these rampaging Hurons lived when outlying in ambushments. Look at this! The varlets know the better pieces of the deer, and one would think they might carve and roast a saddle equal to the best cook in the land! But everything is raw, for the Iroquois are thorough savages. Uncas, take my steel and kindle a fire; a mouthful of a tender broil will give natur' a helping hand after so long a trail."

Heyward, perceiving that their guides now set about their repast in sober earnest, assisted the ladies to alight, and placed himself at their side, not unwilling to enjoy a few moments of grateful rest after the bloody scene he had just gone through. While, the culinary process was in hand, curiosity induced him to inquire into the circumstances which had led to their timely and unexpected rescue.

"How is it that we see you so soon, my generous friend," he asked, "and without aid from the garrison of Edward?"

"Had we gone to the bend in the river, we might have been in time, to rake the leaves over your bodies, but too late to have saved your scalps," coolly answered the scout. "No, no; instead of throwing away strength and opportunity by crossing to the fort, we lay by, under the bank of the Hudson, waiting to watch the movements of the Hurons."

"You were, then, witnesses of all that passed?"

"Not of all, for Indian sight is too keen to be easily cheated, and we kept close. A difficult matter it was, too, to keep this Mohican boy snug in the ambushment. Ah! Uncas, Uncas, your behaviour was more like that of a curious woman than of a warrior on his scent."

Uncas permitted his eyes to turn for an instant on the sturdy countenance of the speaker, but he neither spoke nor gave any indication of repentance. On the contrary, Hayward thought the manner of the young Mohican was disdainful, if not a little fierce, and that he suppressed passions that were ready to explode, as much in compliment to the listeners as from the deference he usually paid to his white associate.

"You saw our capture?" Heyward next demanded.

"We heard it," was the significant answer. "An Indian yell is plain language to men who have passed their days in the woods. But when you landed, we were driven to crawl like serpents beneath the leaves; and then we lost sight of you entirely, until we placed eyes on you again, trussed to the trees, and ready bound for an Indian massacre."

"Our rescue was the deed of Providence. It was neatly a miracle that you did not mistake the path, for the Hurons divided, and each band had its horses."

"Ay! There we were thrown off the scent, and might, indeed, have lost the trail, had it not been for Uncas. We took the path, however, that led into the wilderness; for we judged rightly, that the savages would hold that course with their prisoners. But when we had followed it for many miles, without finding a single twig broken, as I had advised, my mind misgave me, especially as all the footsteps had the prints of moccasins."

"Our captors had the precaution to see us shod like themselves," said Duncan, raising a foot and exhibiting the buskin he wore.

"Ay! 'twas judgmatical, and like themselves; though we were too expert to be thrown from a trail by so common an invention."

"To what, then, are we indebted for our safety?"

"To what, as a white man who has no taint of Indian blood, I should be ashamed to own; to the judgment of the young Mohican, in matters which I should know better than he, but which I can now hardly believe to be true, though my own eyes tell me it is so."

"'Tis extraordinary! Will you not name the reason?"

"Uncas was bold enough to say that the beasts ridden by the gentle ones," continued Hawkeye, glancing his eyes, not without curious interest, on the fillies of the ladies, "planted the legs of one side on the ground at the same time, which is contrary to the movements of all trotting four-footed animals of my knowledge, except the bear. And yet here are horses that always journey in this manner, as my own eyes have seen, and as their trail has shown for twenty long miles."

"'Tis the merit of the animal! They come from the shores of Narragansett Bay, in the small province of Providence Plantations, and are celebrated for their hardihood and the ease of this peculiar movement; though other horses are not unfrequently trained to the same."

"It may be—it may be," said Hawkeye, who had listened with singular attention to this explanation; "though I am a man who has the full blood of the whites, my judgment in deer and beaver is greater than in beasts of burden. Major Effingham has many noble chargers, but I have never seen one travel after such a sideling gait."

"True; for he would value the animals for very different properties. Still is this a breed highly esteemed, and, as you witness, much honoured with the burdens it is often destined to bear."

The Mohicans had suspended their operations about the glimmering fire to listen; and when Duncan had done, they looked at each other significantly, the father uttering the never-failing exclamation of surprise. The scout ruminated, like a man digesting his newly-acquired knowledge, and once more stole a curious glance at the horses.

"I dare to say there are even stranger sights to be seen in the settlements!" he said at length; "natur' is sadly abused by man when he once gets the mastery. But, go sidling or go straight, Uncas had seen the movement, and their trail led us on to the broken bush. The outer branch, near the prints of one of the horses, was bent upward, as a lady breaks a flower from its stem; but all the rest were ragged and broken down, as if the strong hand of a man had been tearing them. So I concluded that the cunning varmints had seen the twig bent, and had torn the rest to make us believe a buck had been feeling the boughs with his antlers."

"I do believe your sagacity did not deceive you; for some such thing occurred."

"That was easy to see," added the scout, in no degree conscious of having exhibited any extraordinary sagacity; "and a very different matter it was from a waddling horse! It then struck me the Mingoes would push for this spring, for the knaves well know the virtue of its waters!"

"Is it, then, so famous?" demanded Heyward, examining, with a more curious eye, the secluded dell, with its bubbling fountain, surrounded, as it was, by earth of a deep dingy brown.

"Few redskins who travel south and east of the great lakes but have heard of its qualities. Will you taste for yourself?"

Heyward took the gourd, and after swallowing a little of the water, threw it aside with grimaces of discontent. The scout laughed in his silent but heartfelt manner, and shook his head with vast satisfaction.

"Ah! you want the flavour that one gets by habit. The time was when I liked it as little as yourself; but I have come to my taste, and I now crave it as a deer does the licks[15]. Your high-spiced wines are not better liked than a redskin relishes this water, especially when his natur' is ailing." But Uncas has made his fire, "and it is time we think of eating, for our journey is long, and all before us."

Interrupting the dialogue by this abrupt transition, the scout had instant recourse to the fragments of food which had escaped the voracity of the Hurons. A very summary process completed the simple cookery, when he and the Mohicans commenced their humble meal with the silence and characteristic diligence of men who ate in order to enable themselves to endure great and unremitting toil.

When this necessary, and, happily, grateful duty had been performed, each of the foresters stooped and took a long and parting draught at that solitary and silent spring, around which and its sister fountains, within fifty years, the wealth, beauty, and talents of a hemisphere were to assemble in throngs, in pursuit of health and pleasure. Then Hawkeye announced his determination to proceed. The sisters resumed their saddles; Duncan and David grasped their rifles, and followed on their footsteps; the scout leading the advance, and the Mohicans bringing up the rear. The whole party moved swiftly through the narrow path, towards the north, leaving the healing waters to mingle unheeded with the adjacent brook, and the bodies of the dead to fester on the neighbouring mount. without the rites of sepulture; a fate but too common to the warriors of the woods to excite either commiseration or comment.

【注解】

1. this sudden visitation of death：" 死神的突然降临 "，指上一章末尾写到的突然飞来的一颗子弹导致一个休伦族人死亡这件事。
2. La Longue Carabine：法语，意为长枪，Hawkeye 的另一个绰号。
3. "Le Cerf Agile! Le Gros Serpent!"：法语，意为 " 飞腿鹿！大蟒蛇！"，分别为 Uncas 和 Chingachgook 的绰号。
4. inartificial：相当于 unskillful，拙劣的。
5. no quarter to：对……决不宽容。
6. "Le Renard Subtil"：" 狡猾的狐狸 "，是 Magua 的绰号。
7. Delawares：居住在特拉华地区的印第安人。
8. commerades：法语，相当于 comrades。
9. denying his habits：没有按习惯的做法，指印第安人战胜后剥死者头皮作为战利品的习惯。
10. David：大卫·噶姆 (David Gamut)，考拉等人在前往要塞途中遇到的一位音乐教师。
11. not older than yourself：此时奈蒂·邦普 (即 " 鹰眼 ")35 岁。
12. prefarment：相当于 preferment。
13. for by this time, I should think . . . the ears of all that hear them：此处指考拉等人沉醉于大卫的歌声而放松了警惕，因而遭到了敌人的袭击一事。
14. Narragansetts：纳拉甘西特，为产马地，此处指考拉姐妹的坐骑。
15. as a deer does the licks：像鹿去舔盐溪一样。"licks" 指森林中含盐的溪流。

【思考题】

1. Study the battle scene in this excerpt and comment on Cooper's description of combat.
2. Why did Magua suddenly relinquish his grasp and fall back motionless during the fierce fight with the Mohican?
3. When the Hawkeye is about to give a "finishing blow" to Magua, he calls himself "a man without a cross", and says his act will "never tell against his honor, nor rob him of his right to the scalp". What a man do you think the Hawkeye is, and what does he mean by saying what he says?
4. In Paragraph 12, Cooper writes, "He had, however, been anticipated by the elder Mohican, who had already torn the emblems of victory from the unresisting heads of the slain". What does "emblems of victory" here refer to?

5. At the end of the chapter, Cooper describes the different reactions of the Hawkeye and Major Heyward toward the water they drink. Cooper also makes the Hawkeye contrast the water with the "high-spiced wine" of the whites. What is Cooper's intention here?
6. What are the images of Indians in the novel? How is today's American racial relationship related to the early relationship between Indians and the white settlers?

【简评】

第十二章讲述的是作品中众多惊心动魄的战斗之一，从一开始就以扣人心弦的情节突出了"鹰眼"高超的枪法和他的迅捷勇猛。毫无疑问，"鹰眼"是库柏心目中的英雄。然而"鹰眼"的高超武艺和英勇善战只是他的一个方面。从他与印第安人的默契与友谊可以看出，在库柏心目中，不同肤色，不同种族的人本应该和谐相处。与英国军官黑伍德相比，"鹰眼"与钦格古克父子是真正的英雄。耶鲁大学 R.W.B. 刘易斯教授认为通过对奈蒂·邦普（即"鹰眼"）这一人物的描写，库柏塑造了一个自立、自足、自然、未受文明"污染"、天性纯真 (innocence) 的自然之子。他生活在深山密林，过着原始的生活，遵循着大自然的法则。文明社会的价值体系、道德习俗、法律规则对他一概不起作用，因此他又是一个社会的局外人 (social outsider)。然而尽管奈蒂·邦普不是一个社会异化的产物，他却与社会存在着不可调和的矛盾与冲突。作品中，库柏多次将钦格古克的儿子昂卡斯称为"最后一个莫西干人"，暗示以邦普和土著印第安人为代表的自然，虽极力抵御以白人为代表的社会与文明的入侵，最终却未能阻止白人社会的侵扰。作品，最后昂卡斯的死亡象征着自然生活的破坏和印第安人世界的没落。

Ralph Waldo Emerson
1803—1882

拉尔夫·沃尔多·爱默生出生于波士顿一个教师家庭，父亲早亡，家境贫寒。他先后就读于波士顿拉丁学校和哈佛大学。在大学里，他就意识到孤独和独立是他生命中最重要的追求，这也成为他以后作品中一个永恒的主题。毕业后，他先任教师，但 21 岁时决定专注于神学，担任波士顿第二教堂唯一一位神教的牧师。后因反对教义的一些呆板仪式，他于 1832 年辞去牧师职务，宣称"每一个真正的人都不能墨守成规",同年赴欧旅行。之后,他于1847年和1872年两度前往欧洲。旅欧期间,爱默生先后结识了英国浪漫主义诗人威廉·华兹华斯(William Wordsworth, 1770—1850)、塞缪尔·泰勒·柯勒律治(Samuel Taylor Coleridge, 1772—1834),并和史学家、哲学家托马斯·卡莱尔(Thomas Carlyle, 1795—1881)结为终生朋友。这次旅行中,爱默生深受欧洲浪漫主义和唯心主义哲学的影响,这对他以后的思想发展和形成具有重大意义。回国后,爱默生定居康科德,著书立说,公开演讲。1836年,他与梭罗、女权主义作家福勒、教育改革家阿尔柯特,以及教会改革家钱宁等几个志同道合的朋友组成一个非正式的"超验主义俱乐部"(The Transcendental Club),探讨哲学、神学问题,并出版刊物《日晷》(*The Dial*)。此后,爱默生不断完善自己的观点,成为这一时期超验主义运动的杰出代表和的精神领袖。他吸引并影响了同时代的许多作家,如梭罗、霍桑、麦尔维尔、惠特曼等。

爱默生最透彻地阐释了超验主义的观点。在被誉为超验主义宣言的《论自然》(*Nature*, 1836)中,他阐明了其基本哲学思想和对自然的态度。他推崇精神和直觉,坚信直觉是接近现实的唯一途径。他认为所有生活(生命)都是一种精神的幻觉,并主张人能超越感觉和理性直接认识真理。他认为所有人的灵魂都是相同、平等且神圣的,每个人都能爆发出永恒的火花,自身都拥有获得知识的方法。他鼓励人们回到自然之中,因为自然不仅揭示了物质真理,还能启示道德真理。

贯穿于爱默生作品里的一个永恒主题是探索个人之无限。他在《美国学者》("The American Scholar", 1837)和《神学院致辞》("The Divinity School Address", 1838)等重要作品中都强调了人的主观能动性,相信"人就是一切",人有潜力发展、完善自己。人应该了解个人在塑造自己的同时,也塑造了世界。爱默生总是鼓励人应该相信自己,依靠自己,他反对单纯的物质繁荣,坚持认为美德和天才孕育于物质的贫困之中。他倡导个性,推崇精神。他的作品为热情奔放、抒发个性的浪漫主义文学提供了思想基础,并代表了浪漫主义对当时金钱至上的物质文明的否定。

爱默生主张通过自然了解真理,他的思想为美国文学和文化的独立发展奠定了哲学基础。他帮助当时的美国摆脱传统神学的束缚,摒弃欧洲传统文化的限制。爱默生的哲学可以说是对诗人的期盼。他心目中的诗人负有担当精神革命领路人的责任。他指出诗人通过诗歌能比普通人更好地领会和传达自然的启示。他呼吁人摆脱传统的羁绊,直接发展具有美国本土特色的文化。他的这些观点对美国文艺复兴时期的文艺思想和创作产生了重大影响,除了梭罗和霍桑外,麦尔维尔、惠特曼和艾米莉·迪金森(Emily Dickinson, 1830—1886)也都受益于他。

爱默生的作品主要采用散文形式,大多收集在《随笔》(*Essays*, 1841)和《随笔:第二集》(*Essays: The Second Series*, 1844)中。文风气势磅礴,刚健活泼,形式不拘,既庄严宏伟，又别致生动，擅用形象的比喻来说明深奥的哲理，文笔优美简练，多见警句，故而广为传颂。但有时结构略显松散，系统性不强，这是因为他的作品大部分素材取自他的日记。

Nature

【题解】

《论自然》发表于1836年，是爱默生初次旅欧回国，受欧洲浪漫主义和唯心主义哲学的影响所作。尽管这部作品在发表后的最初十二年里仅售出500册，却详尽地阐述了超验主义的观点，被誉为新英格兰超验主义的宣言，也是美国浪漫主义运动的重要作品。全书强调自然是精神的象征，通过融入自然，人们能与心灵和精神对话。全书共分八章，"序言"短小别致，呼吁人们抛弃陈规旧律，与自然直接交流，捕捉灵性。"自然"与"物用"分别论述了大自然的深厚意蕴和它对人类生存的实用价值。"美"则从大自然本身的美、精神的美及自然和人结合的美三方面论述了自然能满足人类对美的追求。"语言"和"素养"进一步指出自然是思想的载体，能启迪我们的心智和直觉。"唯心主义"则传达了唯心主义的自然观。"精神"一章精练隽永，认为所有自然现象都是某种精神的象征，精神渗透于整个自然界中。"前景"则倡导人们正视自然，通过灵魂的解救来恢复世界原始之美，通过精神来寻找永恒。爱默生认为人只有远离喧嚣尘世，独自面对有形的自然时，才能感受到冥冥之中无形的自然。《论自然》一书的发表促进了美国浪漫主义文学运动的发展，并带来19世纪"美国文艺复兴"的繁荣。

下文节选自《论自然》中"序言"和"自然"两章。

From Nature

"Nature is but an image or imitation of wisdom, the last thing of the soul; nature being a thing which doth only do, but not know."

Plotinus[1]

Introduction

Our age is retrospective. It builds the sepulchres of the fathers. It writes biographies, histories, and criticism. The foregoing generations beheld God and nature face to face; we, through their eyes. Why should not we also enjoy an original relation to the universe? Why should not we have a poetry and philosophy of insight and not of tradition, and a religion by revelation to us, and not the history of theirs? Embosomed for a season in nature, whose floods of life stream around and through us, and invite us by the powers they supply, to action proportioned to nature, why should we grope among the dry bones of the past, or put the living generation into masquerade out of its faded wardrobe? The sun shines to-day also. There is more wool and flax in the fields. There are new lands, new men, new thoughts. Let us demand our own works and laws and worship.

Undoubtedly we have no questions to ask which are unanswerable. We must trust the perfection of the creation so far, as to believe that whatever curiosity the order of things has awakened in our minds, the order of things can satisfy. Every man's condition is a solution in hieroglyphic to those inquiries he would put. He acts it as life, before he apprehends it as truth. In like manner, nature is already, in its forms and tendencies, describing its own design. Let us interrogate the great apparition, that shines so peacefully around us. Let us inquire, to what end is nature?

All science has one aim, namely, to find a theory of nature. We have theories of races and of functions, but scarcely yet a remote approximation to an idea of creation. We are now so far from the road to truth, that religious teachers dispute and hate each other, and speculative men are esteemed unsound and frivolous. But to a sound judgment, the most abstract truth is the most practical. Whenever a true theory appears, it will be its own evidence. Its test is, that it will explain all phenomena. Now many are thought not only unexplained but inexplicable; as language, sleep, dreams, beasts, sex.

Philosophically considered, the universe is composed of Nature and the Soul[2]. Strictly speaking, therefore, all that is separate from us, all which Philosophy distinguishes as the NOT ME[3], that is, both nature and art, all other men and my own body, must be ranked under this name, NATURE. In enumerating the values of nature and casting up their sum, I shall use the word in both senses;—in its common and in its philosophical import. In inquiries so general as our present one, the inaccuracy is not material; no confusion of thought will occur. Nature, in the common sense, refers to essences unchanged by man; space, the air, the river, the leaf. Art is applied to the mixture of his will with the same things, as in a house, a canal, a statue, a picture. But his operations taken together are so insignificant, a little chipping, baking, patching, and washing, that in an impression so grand as that of the world on the human mind, they do not vary the result.

Chapter 1 Nature

To go into solitude, a man needs to retire as much from his chamber as from society. I am not solitary whilst I read and write, though nobody is with me. But if a man would be alone, let him look at the stars. The rays that come from those heavenly worlds, will separate between him and vulgar things. One might think the atmosphere was made transparent with this design, to give man, in the heavenly bodies, the perpetual presence of the sublime. Seen in the streets of cities, how great they are! If the stars should appear one night in a thousand years, how would men believe and adore; and preserve for many generations the remembrance of the city of God which had been shown! But every night come out these preachers of beauty, and light the universe with their admonishing smile.

The stars awaken a certain reverence, because though always present, they are always inaccessible; but all natural objects make a kindred impression, when the mind is open to their influence. Nature never wears a mean appearance. Neither does the wisest man extort all her secret, and lose his curiosity by finding out all her perfection. Nature never became a toy to a wise spirit. The flowers, the animals, the mountains, reflected all the wisdom of his best hour, as much as they had delighted the simplicity of his childhood.

When we speak of nature in this manner, we have a distinct but most poetical sense in the mind. We mean the integrity of impression made by manifold natural objects. It is this which distinguishes the stick of timber of the wood-cutter, from the tree of the poet. The charming landscape which I saw this morning, is indubitably made up of some twenty or thirty farms. Miller owns this field, Locke that, and Manning the woodland beyond. But none of them owns the landscape. There is a property in the horizon which no man has but he whose eye can integrate all the parts, that is, the poet[4]. This is the best part of these men's farms, yet to this their land-deeds give them no title.

To speak truly, few adult persons can see nature. Most persons do not see the sun. As least they have a very superficial seeing. The sun illuminates only the eye of the man, but shines into the eye and the heart of the child. The lover of nature is he whose inward and outward senses are still truly adjusted to each other; who has retained the spirit of infancy even into the era of manhood[5]. His intercourse with heaven and earth, becomes part of his daily food. In the presence of nature, a wild delight runs through the man, in spite of real sorrows. Nature says,—he is my creature, and maugre all his impertinent griefs, he shall be glad with me. Not the sun or the summer alone, but every hour and season yields its tribute of delight; for every hour and change corresponds to and authorizes a different state of the mind, from breathless noon to grimmest midnight. Nature is a setting that fits equally well a comic or a mourning piece. In good health, the air is a cordial of incredible virtue. Crossing a bare common, in snow puddles, at twilight, under a clouded sky, without having in my thoughts any occurrence of special good fortune, I have enjoyed a perfect exhilaration. Almost I fear to think how glad I am. In the woods too, a man casts off his years, as the snake his slough, and at what period soever of life, is always a child. In the woods, is perpetual youth. Within these plantations of God, a decorum and sanctity reign, a perennial festival is dressed, and the guest sees not how he should tire of them in a thousand years. In the woods, we return to reason and faith. There I feel that nothing can befall me in life,—no disgrace, no calamity, (leaving me my eyes) which nature cannot repair. Standing on the bare ground,—my head bathed by the blithe air, and uplifted into infinite space,—all mean egotism vanishes. I become a transparent eye-ball[6]. I am nothing. I see all. The currents of the Universal Being circulate through me; I am part or particle of God. The name of the nearest friend sounds then foreign and accidental. To be brothers, to be acquaintances,—master or servant, is then a trifle and a disturbance. I am the lover of uncontained and immortal beauty. In the wilderness, I find something more dear and connate than in streets or villages. In the tranquil landscape, and especially in the distant line of the horizon, man beholds somewhat as beautiful as his own nature.

The greatest delight which the fields and woods minister, is the suggestion of an occult relation between man and the vegetable. I am not alone and unacknowledged. They nod to me and I to them. The waving of the boughs in the storm, is new to me and old. It takes me by surprise, and yet is not unknown. Its effect is like that of a higher thought or a better emotion coming over me, when I deemed I was thinking justly or doing right.

Yet it is certain that the power to produce this delight, does not reside in nature, but in man, or in a harmony of both. It is necessary to use these pleasures with great temperance. For, nature is not always tricked in holiday attire, but the same scene which yesterday breathed perfume and glittered as for the frolic of the nymphs, is overspread with melancholy today. Nature always wears the colors of the spirit[7]. To a man laboring under calamity, the heat of his own fire hath sadness in it. Then, there is a kind of contempt of the landscape felt by him who has just lost by death a dear friend. The sky is less grand as it shuts down over less worth in the population.

【注解】

1. 《论自然》初版时，爱默生把罗马哲学家普罗提诺 (Plotinus, 204/5—270) 的这句话作为该书题词。1894 年再版时，他改用本人的一首诗 "Nature" 作为该书题词："A subtle chain of countless rings/ the next unto the fathers brings;/ the eye reads omens where it goes/ And speaks all languages the rose;/ and striving to be man, the worm/ Mounts through all the spires of form."。
2. The universe is composed of Nature and the Soul：宇宙由自然和灵魂组成。
3. NOT ME：非我。源自德国哲学，指除自我之外的其他事物。
4. the poet：爱默生认为，诗人的出现能指引漂泊的现代人重建美好的家园。爱默生在这里批判了当时社会的精神贫困，突出了其哲学的根本主题：拯救人类，重建精神家园。
5. retained the spirit of infancy even into the era of manhood：将儿童的精神保留到成年时期。超验主义深受英国浪漫主义诗歌的影响，推崇"婴孩的纯真"。
6. I become a transparent eye-ball：我变成了一个透明的眼球。此句体现了爱默生的超验思想和神秘主义，常被后人引用、延伸。
7. Nature always wears the colors of the spirit：自然总是染着精神的色彩。超验主义认为自然反映了人的精神。这一超验观点在《论自然》第四章"语言"，以及爱默生的《经验》("Experience") 一文中得到进一步发挥。

【思考题】

1. "Nature" is a key word in the book. What significance and profound implication does Emerson bestow on "nature"?
2. In "Introduction", what is Emerson's opinion about his age? How could people overcome the defects of his age?
3. Both Transcendentalism and Chinese culture emphasize the relationship between man and nature. What are the similarities and differences?
4. What kinds of transcendental view do you find in the above two chapters?
5. Emerson encouraged people to retain "the spirit of infancy even into the era of manhood". Try to find the connection between Emerson's thought and that of Wordsworth and Coleridge. What are the influences of the latter on the former? Comment on Emerson's tendency to Romanticism.

【简评】

《论自然》无论是从哲学角度去审视，还是用诗人的思维去欣赏，都是蕴涵深刻思想的作品。爱默生提倡人回归自然，回到能找回人类自信、发挥人类潜力的原始之地，因为自然才是人类灵感和力量的无穷源泉。此处节选的"序言"和"自然"

两章开宗明义地表达了爱默生的观点。它提倡不要因循守旧，囿于历史，而要用全新的目光来直接看待生机蓬勃的自然，因为"在这里，有新的天地，新的人，新的思想"。他认为宇宙是由自然和灵魂两部分构成，自然是精神的象征。只有人的精神和自然交融一体，和谐一致，才会产生真正的快乐。这也是浪漫主义思想的显著特征。他指出人类只有远离尘嚣，孤独不群，以不泯的童心去凝望自然时，他的精神才能与自然息息相通，感受到深奥的思想和美好的情感。这体现了爱默生的超验主义、神秘主义的观点。

The American Scholar

【题解】

《美国学者》是爱默生1837年发表的一篇著名演讲词。他认为真正的学者必须是一个"思想着的人"，而不仅仅是"冥想者"。他应该从自然、书籍中吸取营养，但又不能成为权威和书本的奴隶，而要通过自己的思考获得答案。同时，学者们应该行动起来，把他们获得的知识付诸行动。爱默生认为学者是世界的眼睛和心脏，应该传达并宣扬美好、崇高、圣洁的精神和诗章。为此，学者应信任自己，独立思考，不要为伟人的光辉、传统的习俗所慑服。爱默生在文中呼吁"我们要用自己的双脚走路；我们要用自己的双手劳动；我们要讲出自己的思想"。

爱默生的《美国学者》与其早前的《论自然》和稍后的《论自助》等著作中的观点一致，都强调思想和精神的独立和创新。他的思想不但影响了诸如梭罗、霍桑、麦尔维尔、惠特曼、迪金森等一大批重要的美国作家，推动了19世纪30至60年代的"美国文艺复兴"，而且对美国构建独立的民族文学和文化起到了重要的引导和推动作用，对美国文化影响深远。

下文选自该书的第二部分，讨论了学者应如何从书本中学习，而不拘泥于其中，批评了当时的美国没有"思考的人"，而只有以读书为职业的阶级。爱默生呼吁每一代人都应该创作自己的书。

The American Scholar

The next great influence into the spirit of the scholar, is, the mind of the Past, —in whatever form, whether of literature, of art, of institutions, that mind is inscribed. Books are the best type of the influence of the past, and perhaps we shall get at the truth—learn the amount of this influence more conveniently—by considering their value alone.

The theory of books is noble. The scholar of the first age received into him the world around; brooded thereon; gave it the new arrangement of his own mind, and uttered it again. It came into him, life; it went out from him, truth. It came to him, short-lived actions; it went out from him, poetry. It was dead fact; now, it is quick[1] thought. It can stand, and it can go. It now endures, it now flies, it now inspires. Precisely in proportion to the depth of mind from which it issued, so high does it soar, so long does it sing.

Or, I might say, it depends on how far the process had gone, of transmuting life into truth. In proportion to the completeness of the distillation, so will the purity and imperishableness of the product be. But none is quite perfect. As no air-pump can by any means make a perfect vacuum, so neither can any artist entirely exclude the conventional, the local, the perishable from his book, or write a book of pure thought that shall be as efficient, in all respects, to a remote posterity, as to contemporaries, or rather to the second age. Each age, it is found, must write its own books; or rather, each generation for the next succeeding. The books of an older period will not fit this.

Yet hence arises a grave mischief. The sacredness which attaches to the act of creation, —the act of thought, —is instantly transferred to the record. The poet chanting, was felt to be a divine man. Henceforth the chant is divine also. The writer was a just and wise spirit. Henceforward it is settled, the book is perfect; as love of the hero corrupts into worship of his statue. Instantly, the book becomes noxious. The guide is a tyrant. We sought a brother, and lo, a governor. The sluggish and perverted mind of the multitude, always slow to open to the incursions of Reason, having once so opened, having once received this book, stands upon it, and makes an outcry, if it is disparaged. Colleges are built on it. Books are written on it by thinkers, not by Man Thinking; by men of talent, that is, who start wrong, who set out from accepted dogmas, not from their own sight of principles. Meek young men grow up in libraries, believing it their duty to accept the views which Cicero, which Locke, which Bacon have given, forgetful that Cicero, Locke and Bacon were only young men in libraries when they wrote these books.

Hence, instead of Man Thinking, we have the bookworm. Hence, the book-learned class, who value books, as such; not as related to nature and the human constitution, but as making a sort of Third Estate[2] with the world and the soul. Hence, the restorers of readings, the emendators, the bibliomaniacs of all degrees.

This is bad; this is worse than it seems. Books are the best of things, well used;

abused, among the worst. What is the right use? What is the one end which all means go to effect? They are for nothing but to inspire. I had better never see a book than to be warped by its attraction clean out of my own orbit, and made a satellite instead of a system. The one thing in the world of value, is the active soul, —the soul, free, sovereign, active. This every man is entitled to; this every man contains within him, although in almost all men, obstructed, and as yet unborn. The soul active sees absolute truth; and utters truth, or creates. In this action, it is genius; not the privilege of here and there a favorite, but the sound estate of every man. In its essence, it is progressive. The book, the college, the school of art, the institution of any kind, stop with some past utterance of genius. This is good, say they, —let us hold by this. They pin me down. They look backward and not forward. But genius always looks forward. The eyes of man are set in his forehead, not in his hindhead. Man hopes. Genius creates. To create, —to create, —is the proof of a divine presence. Whatever talents may be, if the man create not, the pure efflux of the Deity is not his: —cinders and smoke, there may be, but not yet flame. There are creative manners. There are creative actions, and creative words; manners, actions, words, that is, indicative of no custom or authority, but springing spontaneous from the mind's own sense of good and fair.

On the other part, instead of being its own seer, let it receive always from another mind its truth, though it were in torrents of light, without periods of solitude, inquest and self-recovery, and a fatal disservice is done. Genius is always sufficiently the enemy of genius by over-influence. The literature of every nation bear me witness. The English dramatic poets have Shakespearized now for two hundred years.

Undoubtedly there is a right way of reading, —so it be sternly subordinated. Man Thinking must not be subdued by his instruments. Books are for the scholar's idle times. When he can read God directly, the hour is too precious to be wasted in other mens' transcripts of their readings. But when the intervals of darkness come, as come they must, —when the soul seethe not, when the sun is hid, and the stars withdraw their shining, — we repair to the lamps which were kindled by their ray to guide our steps to the East again, where the dawn is. We hear that we may speak. The Arabian proverb says, "A fig tree looking on a fig tree, becometh fruitful."

It is remarkable, the character of the pleasure we derive from the best books. They impress us ever with the conviction that one nature wrote and the same reads. We read the verses of one of the great English poets, of Chaucer, of Marvell, of Dryden, with the most modern joy, —with a pleasure, I mean, which is in great part caused by the abstraction of all time from their verses. There is some awe mixed with the joy of our surprise, when this poet, who lived in some past world, two or three hundred years ago, says that which lies close to my own soul, that which I also had well nigh thought and said. But for the evidence thence afforded to the philosophical doctrine of the identity of all minds, we should suppose some pre-established harmony, some foresight of souls that were to be, and some preparation of stores for their future wants, like the fact observed in insects, who lay up food before death for the young grub they shall never see.

I would not be hurried by any love of system, by any exaggeration of instincts, to underrate the Book. We all know, that as the human body can be nourished on any food, though it were boiled grass and the broth of shoes, so the human mind can be fed by any knowledge. And great and heroic men have existed, who had almost no other information than by the printed page. I only would say, that it needs a strong head to bear that diet. One must be an inventor to read well. As the proverb says, "He that would bring home the wealth of the Indies, must carry out the wealth of the Indies." There is then creative reading, as well as creative writing. When the mind is braced by labor and invention, the page of whatever book we read becomes luminous with manifold allusion. Every sentence is doubly significant, and the sense of our author is as broad as the world. We then see, what is always true, that as the seer's hour of vision is short and rare among heavy days and months, so is its record, perchance, the least part of his volume. The discerning will read in his Plato or Shakespeare, only that least part, —only the authentic utterances of the oracle, —and all the rest he rejects, were it never so many times Plato's and Shakespeare's.

Of course, there is a portion of reading quite indispensable to a wise man. History and exact science he must learn by laborious reading. Colleges, in like manner, have their indispensable office, —to teach elements. But they can only highly serve us, when they aim not to drill, but to create; when they gather from far every ray of various genius to their hospitable halls, and, by the concentrated fires, set the hearts of their youth on flame. Thought and knowledge are natures in which apparatus and pretension avail nothing. Gowns, and pecuniary foundations, though of towns of gold, can never countervail the least sentence or syllable of wit. Forget this, and our American colleges will recede in their public importance whilst they grow richer every year.

【注解】

1. quick：相当于 living，活着的。
2. as making a sort of Third Estate：法国大革命之前，西欧社会通常把人分为三个等级，第一、第二等级分别是贵族和僧侣，平民属于第三等级。

【思考题】

1. Emerson states that "Each age . . . must write its own books". What does he mean? Why does he say so?
2. Emerson points out, "instead of Man Thinking, we have the bookworm". He calls for the emergence of real American scholars. How does Emerson define a real American scholar?
3. According to Emerson, what is the right attitude towards books? How should one read books? What is the meaning of the Arabian proverb "A fig tree looking on a fig tree, becometh fruitful"?

Nathaniel Hawthorne
1804—1864

纳撒尼尔·霍桑是美国文学史上一位重要的浪漫主义作家，美国文艺复兴的领袖人物。他出生于马萨诸塞州塞勒姆市的一个清教徒世家。他的父亲是个海员，长期漂泊在外，在霍桑四岁的时候，客死他乡。霍桑一家只能靠母亲的亲戚接济度日。1821 至 1825 年霍桑就读于缅因州鲍登学院，在他的同班同学中有后来成为著名诗人的亨利·沃兹沃斯·朗费罗 (Henry Wadsworth Longfellow, 1807—1882) 和于 1853 至 1857 年间出任总统的富兰克林·皮尔斯 (Franklin Pierce, 1804—1859)。

霍桑 1825 年从鲍登学院毕业后，长期隐居塞勒姆，一边闭门苦读，一边从事写作。据霍桑自己的说法，他读完了塞勒姆图书馆的所有藏书，在自家的阁楼上涂涂写写。由于对自己的创作感觉不满，霍桑除了于 1828 年匿名发表了一部有关大学生活的小说《范肖》(Fanshawe) 以外，将这一时期的其余手稿均付之一炬。1837 年，在蛰居十二年之后，霍桑的名字才随着《重讲一遍的故事》(Twice-told Tales) 第一次与读者见面。这部短篇小说集受到了读者的好评，朗费罗称赞霍桑具有"天才的、诗一般的文风"。同时它也是霍桑在事业与生活上的一个转折。1839 年他与索菲亚·皮博迪 (Sophia Peabody) 订婚。由于要担当养家之任，仅靠发表作品收入甚微，所以他通过朋友在波士顿海关谋到煤盐计量员一职。此间他还写了 4 本篇幅不大的儿童历史读物，希望能增加收入。

1841 年他加入超验主义者在马萨诸塞州创建的乌托邦团体布鲁克农场 (Brook Farm Community)，一年后退出。后来在《福谷传奇》(*The Blithedale Romance*, 1852) 中，霍桑充分表达了他对超验主义的怀疑和反对态度。1842 年，扩编的《重讲一遍的故事》再版，尽管销路不如前版，却受到埃德加·爱伦·坡的高度赞誉。此后霍桑又创作出版了 20 多篇短篇小说，并于 1846 年以《古屋青苔》(*Mosses from an Old Manse*) 为名结集出版。他的短篇小说除一部分是历史传奇外，大多数是手法独特、效果强烈的寓言性故事，开创了现代短篇小说的先河。其中最著名、也经常被文学选集青睐的有《我的亲戚莫里纳少校》("My Kinsman Major Molineux", 1832)、《教长的黑面纱》("The Minister's Black Veil", 1836)、《年轻的布朗先生》("Young Goodman Brown", 1835)、《拉伯西尼医生的女儿》("Rappaccini's Daughter", 1844)、《胎记》("The Birth Mark", 1844) 等。

1846 年，霍桑依靠皮尔斯的关系被任命为塞勒姆海关督察员，1849 年因政治原因被解职。不久他的母亲去世。遭受双重打击的霍桑带着新的执着投身写作，仅用 7 个月就完成了长篇小说《红字》(*The Scarlet Letter*, 1850)，成为他二十五年来最成功的一部小说。《红字》被誉为美国浪漫主义的一部杰作。小说描写了一个受不合理婚姻约束的少妇海丝特因与情人相爱并生下女儿珠儿而犯了清教所严禁的通奸罪，被判监禁、示众、并被要求终生佩带代表"通奸罪"(Adultery) 的红字"A"。海丝特和情人迪明斯代尔牧师在受罪和赎罪的过程中逐渐获得了高贵的人格，而海丝特的丈夫罗杰医生则因一心复仇而变成了一个不可饶恕的恶魔。

在随后的几年中，霍桑接连发表了两部小说——《带有七个尖角阁的房子》(*The House of Seven Gables*, 1851) 和根据布鲁克农场经历写成的《福谷传奇》，三部儿童和青少年读物——《真实的历史和人物传记故事》(*True Stories from History and Biography*, 1851)、《奇异的书》(*Wonder Book for Girls and Boys*, 1851) 和《丛林传说》(*Tanglewood Tales for Girls and Boys*, 1853)，和一部新的短篇小说集《雪影和其他重讲一遍的故事》(*The Snow Image, and Other Twice Told Tales*, 1852)，以及一本为皮尔斯参加竞选写的传记。1853 年皮尔斯当选总统后，霍桑被任命为美国驻利物浦总领事，四年后离任，带领全家在罗马和佛罗伦萨度过两年，为今后的创作收集素材。1860 年他发表了以意大利为背景的《玉石雕像》(*The Marble Faun*)(又译《云石牧神》)，同年回国重返康科德过起隐居生活。1863 年霍桑出版了关于社会问题的小说《我们的老家》(*Our Old Home*)。1864 年，霍桑在新罕布什尔州去世。

霍桑在美国文学史上一直享有盛名。霍桑的小说和故事所表达的内容都是浪漫主义的重要主题：异化和孤独、自然和对自然的冲动、潜意识的想象和梦幻等。霍桑对爱默生所推崇的"人具有神性"的超验主义哲理表示怀疑，不相信空想社会主义通过改革改造社会的理想，他更倾向于把现实中的许多问题归结到"人的罪恶本性"之上。这或许和他出身清教世家的背景有关。当爱默生、梭罗等超验主义者歌颂人类灵魂升腾的高度时，霍桑却在他的笔下描写了人类内心世界的阴郁和黑暗。但他无意批判这种"罪恶感"，而是对它专心研究，以便发现其产生的原因、对人的影响及祛除它的可能。霍桑对人物内心的挖掘通常借助象征和隐喻的手法，使故事情节蒙上一层神秘的色彩。霍桑把自己的小说称为"心理罗曼史"。在《红字》的序言《海关》中他曾写道："假如一个人不能梦见奇怪的事物，并且使它们显得像是真的，他就永远不要去写罗曼史。"霍桑对想象和幻想的执着，以及对人在精神和道德方面失常心理的深入探索使他的作品经久不衰。他对美国文学最直接的影响在于他对心理现实主义的贡献。

The Minister's Black Veil

【题解】

《教长的黑面纱》中，一位年轻、受人爱戴的教长胡珀先生在一次布道时脸上挂了一层黑色的面纱，从此再也没有摘下。这层面纱使教民们既吃惊又恐惧。人们对它进行了种种猜测，怀疑他犯下了不可告人的罪过。教民与他疏远了。就连胡珀先生的未婚妻伊丽莎白也不能劝说他揭去面纱或讲出戴面纱的原因，因此他又失去了爱情。然而这层面纱的威力是巨大的，它使所有人对教长望而生畏。他成了教区最令人讨厌的人，但同时也成了最威严、最具声望的牧师。许多罪孽深重的人希望向他忏悔，许多垂死的人临终时叫喊着他的名字。胡珀先生恪尽职守，给别人解除心灵的痛苦，自己却被黑色的面纱隔绝在任何友情和幸福之外。当他孤独而漫长的一生即将结束之时，他依然拒绝揭去面纱，大声说道："我看看周围，每个人脸上都有一层黑色的面纱！"

霍桑十分喜欢用寓言和象征的表现手法。他通过黑面纱象征罪恶和人与人之间的隔阂。这篇故事也表现了他作品中常见的"意义含混"(ambiguity) 和"感情矛盾"(ambivalence) 两大特点。霍桑往往提出疑问和猜测，却从不明确表态，比如黑面纱究竟代表着谁的罪孽，是什么原因刺激胡珀教长带上了这面纱等。对于这些问题，霍桑没有给出答案，一切都留待读者细细体味与思考。

From The Minister's Black Veil

A Parable[1]

The Sexton stood in the porch of Milford meeting-house, pulling lustily at the bell-rope. The old people of the village came stooping along the street. Children, with bright faces, tripped merrily beside their parents, or mimicked a graver gait, in the conscious dignity of their Sunday clothes. Spruce bachelors looked sidelong at the pretty maidens, and fancied that the Sabbath sunshine made them prettier than on week-days. When the throng had mostly streamed into the porch, the sexton began to toll the bell, keeping his eye on the Reverend Mr. Hooper's door. The first glimpse of the clergyman's figure was the signal for the bell to cease its summons.

"But what has good Parson Hooper got upon his face?" cried the sexton in astonishment.

All within hearing immediately turned about, and beheld the semblance of Mr. Hooper, pacing slowly his meditative way towards the meeting-house. With one accord they started, expressing more wonder than if some strange minister were coming to dust the cushions of Mr. Hooper's pulpit.

"Are you sure it is our parson?" inquired Goodman Gray[2] of the sexton.

"Of a certainty it is good Mr. Hooper," replied the sexton. "He was to have exchanged pulpits with Parson Shute, of Westbury; but Parson Shute sent to excuse himself yesterday, being to preach a funeral sermon."

The cause of so much amazement may appear sufficiently slight. Mr. Hooper, a gentlemanly person, of about thirty, though still a bachelor, was dressed with due clerical neatness, as if a careful wife had starched his band, and brushed the weekly dust from his Sunday's garb. There was but one thing remarkable in his appearance. Swathed about his forehead, and hanging down over his face, so low as to be shaken by his breath, Mr. Hooper had on a black veil. On a nearer view it seemed to consist of two folds of crape, which entirely concealed his features, except the mouth and chin, but probably did not intercept his sight, further than to give a darkened aspect to all living and inanimate things. With this gloomy shade before him, good Mr. Hooper walked onward, at a slow and quiet pace, stooping somewhat, and looking on the ground, as is customary with abstracted men, yet nodding kindly to those of his parishioners who still waited on the meeting-house steps. But so wonder-struck were they that his greeting hardly met with a return.

"I can't really feel as if good Mr. Hooper's face was behind that piece of crape," said the sexton.

"I don't like it," muttered an old woman, as she hobbled into the meeting-house. "He has changed himself into something awful, only by hiding his face."

"Our parson has gone mad!" cried Goodman Gray, following him across the threshold.

A rumor of some unaccountable phenomenon had preceded Mr. Hooper into the meeting-house, and set all the congregation astir. Few could refrain from twisting their heads towards the door; many stood upright, and turned directly about; while several little boys clambered upon the seats, and came down again with a terrible racket. There was a general bustle, a rustling of the women's gowns and shuffling of the men's feet, greatly at variance with that hushed repose which should attend the entrance of the minister. But Mr. Hooper appeared not to notice the perturbation of his people. He entered with an almost noiseless step, bent his head mildly to the pews on each side, and bowed as he passed his oldest parishioner, a white-haired great-grandsire, who occupied an arm-chair in the centre of the aisle. It was strange to observe, how slowly this venerable man became conscious of something singular in the appearance of his pastor. He seemed not fully to partake of the prevailing wonder, till Mr. Hooper had ascended the stairs, and showed himself in the pulpit, face to face with his congregation, except for the black veil. That mysterious emblem was never once withdrawn. It shook with his measured breath, as he gave out the psalm; it threw its obscurity between him and the holy page, as he read the Scriptures[3]; and while he prayed, the veil lay heavily on his uplifted countenance. Did he seek to hide it from the dread Being[4] whom he was addressing?

Such was the effect of this simple piece of crape, that more than one woman of delicate nerves was forced to leave the meeting-house. Yet perhaps the pale-faced congregation was almost as fearful a sight to the minister, as his black veil to them.

Mr. Hooper had the reputation of a good preacher, but not an energetic one: he strove to win his people heavenward by mild, persuasive influences, rather than to drive them thither by the thunders of the Word[5]. The sermon which he now delivered was marked by the same characteristics of style and manner as the general series of his pulpit oratory. But there was something, either in the sentiment of the discourse itself, or in the imagination of the auditors, which made it greatly the most powerful effort that they had ever heard from their pastor's lips. It was tinged, rather more darkly than usual, with the gentle gloom of Mr. Hooper's temperament. The subject had reference to secret sin, and those sad mysteries which we hide from our nearest and dearest, and would fain conceal from our own consciousness, even forgetting that the Omniscient can detect them. A subtle power was breathed into his words. Each member of the congregation, the most innocent girl, and the man of hardened breast, felt as if the preacher had crept upon them, behind his awful veil, and discovered their hoarded iniquity of deed or thought. Many spread their clasped hands on their bosoms. There was nothing terrible in what Mr. Hooper said, at least, no violence; and yet, with every tremor of his melancholy voice, the hearers quaked. An unsought pathos came hand in hand with awe. So sensible were the audience of some unwonted attribute in their minister, that they longed for a breath of wind to blow aside the veil, almost believing that a stranger's visage would be discovered, though the form, gesture, and voice were those of Mr. Hooper.

At the close of the services, the people hurried out with indecorous confusion, eager to communicate their pent-up amazement, and conscious of lighter spirits the moment they lost sight of the black veil. Some gathered in little circles, huddled closely together, with their mouths all whispering in the centre; some went homeward alone, wrapt in silent meditation; some talked loudly, and profaned the Sabbath day with ostentatious laughter. A few shook their sagacious heads, intimating that they could penetrate the mystery; while one or two affirmed that there was no mystery at all, but only that Mr. Hooper's eyes were so weakened by the midnight lamp, as to require a shade. After a brief interval, forth came good Mr. Hooper also, in the rear of his flock. Turning his veiled face from one group to another, he paid due reverence to the hoary heads, saluted the middle aged with kind dignity as their friend and spiritual guide, greeted the young with mingled authority and love, and laid his hands on the little children's heads to bless them. Such was always his custom on the Sabbath day. Strange and bewildered looks repaid him for his courtesy. None, as on former occasions, aspired to the honor of walking by their pastor's side. Old Squire Saunders, doubtless by an accidental lapse of memory, neglected to invite Mr. Hooper to his table, where the good clergyman had been wont to bless the food, almost every Sunday since his settlement. He returned, therefore, to the parsonage, and, at the moment of closing the door, was observed to look back upon the people, all of whom had their eyes fixed upon the minister. A sad smile gleamed faintly from beneath the black veil, and flickered about his mouth, glimmering as he disappeared.

"How strange," said a lady, "that a simple black veil, such as any woman might wear on her bonnet, should become such a terrible thing on Mr. Hooper's face!"

"Something must surely be amiss with Mr. Hooper's intellects," observed her husband, the physician of the village. "But the strangest part of the affair is the effect of this vagary, even on a sober-minded man like myself. The black veil, though it covers only our pastor's face, throws its influence over his whole person, and makes him ghost-like from head to foot. Do you not feel it so?"

"Truly do I," replied the lady; "and I would not be alone with him for the world. I wonder he is not afraid to be alone with himself!"

"Men sometimes are so," said her husband.

The afternoon service was attended with similar circumstances. At its conclusion, the bell tolled for the funeral of a young lady. The relatives and friends were assembled in the house, and the more distant acquaintances stood about the door, speaking of the good qualities of the deceased, when their talk was interrupted by the appearance of Mr. Hooper, still covered with his black veil. It was now an appropriate emblem. The clergyman stepped into the room where the corpse was laid, and bent over the coffin, to take a last farewell of his deceased parishioner. As he stooped, the veil hung straight down from his forehead, so that, if her eyelids had not been closed forever, the dead maiden might have seen his face. Could Mr. Hooper be fearful of her glance, that he so hastily caught back the black veil? A person who watched the interview between the dead and living, scrupled not to affirm, that, at the instant when the clergyman's features were disclosed, the corpse had slightly shuddered, rustling the shroud and muslin cap, though the countenance retained the composure of death. A superstitious old woman was the only witness of this prodigy. From the coffin Mr. Hooper passed into the chamber of the mourners, and thence to the head of the staircase, to make the funeral prayer. It was a tender and heart-dissolving prayer, full of sorrow, yet so imbued with celestial hopes, that the music of a heavenly harp, swept by the fingers of the dead, seemed faintly to be heard among the saddest accents of the minister. The people trembled, though they but darkly understood him when he prayed that they, and himself, and all of mortal race, might be ready, as he trusted this young maiden had been, for the dreadful hour that should snatch the veil from their faces. The bearers went heavily forth, and the mourners followed, saddening all the street, with the dead before them, and Mr. Hooper in his black veil behind.

"Why do you look back?" said one in the procession to his partner.

"I had a fancy," replied she, "that the minister and the maiden's spirit were walking hand in hand."

"And so had I, at the same moment," said the other.

That night, the handsomest couple in Milford village were to be joined in wedlock. Though reckoned a melancholy man, Mr. Hooper had a placid cheerfulness for such occasions, which often excited a sympathetic smile, where livelier merriment would have been thrown away. There was no quality of his disposition which made him more beloved than this. The company at the wedding awaited his arrival with impatience, trusting that the strange awe, which had gathered over him throughout the day, would now be dispelled. But such was not the result. When Mr. Hooper came, the first thing that their eyes rested on was the same horrible black veil, which had added deeper gloom to the funeral, and could portend nothing but evil to the wedding. Such was its immediate effect on the guests that a cloud seemed to have rolled duskily from beneath the black crape, and dimmed the light of the candles. The bridal pair stood up before the minister. But the bride's cold fingers quivered in the tremulous hand of the bridegroom, and her deathlike paleness caused a whisper that the maiden who had been buried a few hours before was come from her grave to be married. If ever another wedding were so dismal, it was that famous one where they tolled the wedding-knell[6]. After performing the ceremony, Mr. Hooper raised a glass of wine to his lips, wishing happiness to the new-married couple, in a strain of mild pleasantry that ought to have brightened the features of the guests, like a cheerful gleam from the hearth. At that instant, catching a glimpse of his figure in the looking-glass, the black veil involved his own spirit in the horror with which it overwhelmed all others. His frame shuddered, his lips grew white, he spilt the untasted wine upon the carpet, and rushed forth into the darkness. For the Earth, too, had on her Black Veil.

The next day, the whole village of Milford talked of little else than Parson Hooper's black veil. That, and the mystery concealed behind it, supplied a topic for discussion between acquaintances meeting in the street, and good women gossiping at their open windows. It was the first item of news that the tavern-keeper told to his guests. The children babbled of it on their way to school. One imitative little imp covered his face with an old black handkerchief, thereby so affrighting his playmates, that the panic seized himself, and he well-nigh lost his wits by his own waggery.

It was remarkable, that, of all the busybodies and impertinent people in the parish, not one ventured to put the plain question to Mr. Hooper, wherefore he did this thing. Hitherto, whenever there appeared the slightest call for such interference, he had never lacked advisers, nor shown himself adverse to be guided by their judgment. If he erred at all, it was by so painful a degree of self-distrust, that even the mildest censure would lead him to consider an indifferent action as a crime. Yet, though so well acquainted with this amiable weakness, no individual among his parishioners chose to take the black veil a subject of friendly remonstrance. There was a feeling of dread, neither plainly confessed nor carefully concealed, which caused each to shift the responsibility upon another, till at length it was found expedient to send a deputation of the church, in order to deal with Mr. Hooper about the mystery, before it should grow into a scandal. Never did an embassy so ill discharge its duties. The minister received them with friendly courtesy, but became silent, after they were seated, leaving to his visitors the whole burden of introducing their important business. The topic, it might be supposed, was obvious enough. There was the black veil swathed round Mr. Hooper's forehead, and concealing every feature above his placid mouth, on which, at times, they could perceive the glimmering of a melancholy smile. But that piece of crape, to their imagination, seemed to hang down before his heart, the symbol of a fearful secret between him and them. Were the veil but cast aside, they might speak freely of it, but not till then. Thus they sat a considerable time, speechless, confused, and shrinking uneasily from Mr. Hooper's eye, which they felt to be fixed upon them with an invisible glance. Finally, the deputies returned abashed to their constituents, pronouncing the matter too weighty to be handled, except by a council of the churches, if, indeed, it might not require a general synod[7].

But there was one person in the village, unappalled by the awe with which the black veil had impressed all beside herself. When the deputies returned without an explanation, or even venturing to demand one, she, with the calm energy of her character, determined to chase away the strange cloud that appeared to be settling round Mr. Hooper, every moment more darkly than before. As his plighted wife[8], it should be her privilege to know what the black veil concealed. At the minister's first visit, therefore, she entered upon the subject with a direct simplicity, which made the task easier both for him and her. After he had seated himself, she fixed her eyes steadfastly upon the veil, but could discern nothing of the dreadful gloom that had so overawed the multitude: it was but a double fold of crape, hanging down from his forehead to his mouth, and slightly stirring with his breath.

"No," said she aloud, and smiling, "there is nothing terrible in this piece of crape, except that it hides a face which I am always glad to look upon. Come, good sir, let the sun shine from behind the cloud. First lay aside your black veil: then tell me why you put it on."

Mr. Hooper's smile glimmered faintly.

"There is an hour to come," said he, "when all of us shall cast aside our veils. Take it not amiss[9], beloved friend, if I wear this piece of crape till then."

"Your words are a mystery, too," returned the young lady. "Take away the veil from them, at least."

"Elizabeth, I will," said he, "so far as my vow may suffer me. Know, then, this veil is a type and a symbol, and I am bound to wear it ever, both in light and darkness, in solitude and before the gaze of multitudes, and as with strangers, so with my familiar friends. No mortal eye will see it withdrawn. This dismal shade must separate me from the world: even you, Elizabeth, can never come behind it!"

"What grievous affliction hath befallen you," she earnestly inquired, "that you should thus darken your eyes forever?"

"If it be a sign of mourning," replied Mr. Hooper, "I, perhaps, like most other mortals, have sorrows dark enough to be typified by a black veil."

"But what if the world will not believe that it is the type of an innocent sorrow?" urged Elizabeth. "Beloved and respected as you are, there may be whispers that you hide your face under the consciousness of secret sin. For the sake of your holy office, do away this scandal!"

The color rose into her cheeks as she intimated the nature of the rumors that were already abroad in the village. But Mr. Hooper's mildness did not forsake him. He even smiled again—that same sad smile, which always appeared like a faint glimmering of light, proceeding from the obscurity beneath the veil.

"If I hide my face for sorrow, there is cause enough," he merely replied; "and if I cover it for secret sin, what mortal might not do the same?"

And with this gentle, but unconquerable obstinacy, did he resist all her entreaties. At length Elizabeth sat silent. For a few moments she appeared lost in thought, considering, probably, what new methods might be tried to withdraw her lover from so dark a fantasy, which, if it had no other meaning, was perhaps a symptom of mental disease. Though of a firmer character than his own, the tears rolled down her cheeks. But, in an instant, as it were, a new feeling took the place of sorrow: her eyes were fixed insensibly on the black veil, when, like a sudden twilight in the air, its terrors fell around her. She arose, and stood trembling before him.

"And do you feel it then, at last?" said he mournfully.

She made no reply, but covered her eyes with her hand, and turned to leave the room. He rushed forward and caught her arm.

"Have patience with me, Elizabeth!" cried he, passionately. "Do not desert me, though this veil must be between us here on earth. Be mine, and hereafter there shall be no veil over my face, no darkness between our souls! It is but a mortal veil—it is not for eternity! O! You know not how lonely I am, and how frightened, to be alone behind my black veil. Do not leave me in this miserable obscurity forever!"

"Lift the veil but once, and look me in the face," said she.

"Never! It cannot be!" replied Mr. Hooper.

"Then farewell!" said Elizabeth.

She withdrew her arm from his grasp, and slowly departed, pausing at the door, to give one long shuddering gaze, that seemed almost to penetrate the mystery of the black veil. But, even amid his grief, Mr. Hooper smiled to think that only a material emblem had separated him from happiness, though the horrors, which it shadowed forth, must be drawn darkly between the fondest of lovers.

From that time no attempts were made to remove Mr. Hooper's black veil, or, by a direct appeal, to discover the secret which it was supposed to hide. By persons who claimed a superiority to popular prejudice, it was reckoned merely an eccentric whim, such as often mingles with the sober actions of men otherwise rational, and tinges them all with its own semblance of insanity. But with the multitude, good Mr. Hooper was irreparably a bugbear. He could not walk the street with any peace of mind, so conscious was he that the gentle and timid would turn aside to avoid him, and that others would make it a point of hardihood to throw themselves in his way. The impertinence of the latter class compelled him to give up his customary walk at sunset to the burial ground; for when he leaned pensively over the gate, there would always be faces behind the gravestones, peeping at his black veil. A fable went the rounds that the stare of the dead people drove him thence. It grieved him, to the very depth of his kind heart, to observe how the children fled from his approach, breaking up their merriest sports, while his melancholy figure was yet afar off. Their instinctive dread caused him to feel more strongly than aught else, that a preternatural horror was interwoven with the threads of the black crape. In truth, his own antipathy to the veil was known to be so great, that he never willingly passed before a mirror, nor stooped to drink at a still fountain, lest, in its peaceful bosom, he should be affrighted by himself. This was what gave plausibility to the whispers, that Mr. Hooper's conscience tortured him for some great crime too horrible to be entirely concealed, or otherwise than so obscurely intimated. Thus, from beneath the black veil, there rolled a cloud into the sunshine, an ambiguity of sin or sorrow, which enveloped the poor minister, so that love or sympathy could never reach him. It was said that ghost and fiend consorted with him there. With self-shudderings and outward terrors, he walked continually in its shadow, groping darkly within his own soul, or gazing through a medium that saddened the whole world. Even the lawless wind, it was believed, respected his dreadful secret, and never blew aside the veil. But still good Mr. Hooper sadly smiled, at the pale visages of the worldly throng as he passed by.

Among all its bad influences, the black veil had the one desirable effect, of making its wearer a very efficient clergyman. By the aid of his mysterious emblem—for there was no other apparent cause—he became a man of awful power, over souls that were in agony for sin. His converts always regarded him with a dread peculiar to themselves, affirming, though but figuratively, that, before he brought them to celestial light, they had been with him behind the black veil. Its gloom, indeed, enabled him to sympathize with all dark affections. Dying sinners cried aloud for Mr. Hooper, and would not yield their breath till he appeared; though ever, as he stooped to whisper consolation, they shuddered at the veiled face so near their own. Such were the terrors of the black veil, even when Death had bared his visage! Strangers came long distances to attend service at his church, with the mere idle purpose of gazing at his figure, because it was forbidden them to behold his face. But many were made to quake ere they departed! Once, during Governor Belcher's[10] administration, Mr. Hooper was appointed to preach the election sermon. Covered with his black veil, he stood before the chief magistrate, the council, and the representatives, and wrought so deep an impression, that the legislative measures of that year, were characterized by all the gloom and piety of our earliest ancestral sway.

In this manner Mr. Hooper spent a long life, irreproachable in outward act, yet shrouded in dismal suspicions; kind and loving, though unloved, and dimly feared; a man apart from men, shunned in their health and joy, but ever summoned to their aid in mortal anguish. As years wore on, shedding their snows above his sable veil, he acquired a name throughout the New England churches, and they called him Father Hooper. Nearly all his parishioners, who were of mature age when he was settled, had been borne away by many a funeral: he had one congregation in the church, and a more crowded one in the churchyard; and having wrought so late into the evening, and done his work so well, it was now good Father Hooper's turn to rest.

Several persons were visible by the shaded candle-light, in the death chamber of the old clergyman. Natural connections[11] he had none. But there was the decorously grave, though unmoved physician, seeking only to mitigate the last pangs of the patient whom he could not save. There were the deacons, and other eminently pious members of his church. There, also, was the Reverend Mr. Clark, of Westbury, a young and zealous divine, who had ridden in haste to pray by the bedside of the expiring minister. There was the nurse, no hired handmaiden of death, but one whose calm affection had endured thus long in secrecy, in solitude, amid the chill of age, and would not perish, even at the dying hour. Who, but Elizabeth! And there lay the hoary head of good Father Hooper upon the death pillow, with the black veil still swathed about his brow, and reaching down over his face, so that each more difficult gasp of his faint breath caused it to stir. All through life that piece of crape had hung between him and the world: it had separated him from cheerful brotherhood and woman's love, and kept him in that saddest of all prisons, his own heart; and still it lay upon his face, as if to deepen the gloom of his darksome chamber, and shade him from the sunshine of eternity.

For some time previous, his mind had been confused, wavering doubtfully between the past and the present, and hovering forward, as it were, at intervals, into the indistinctness of the world to come. There had been feverish turns, which tossed him from side to side, and wore away what little strength he had. But in his most convulsive struggles, and in the wildest vagaries of his intellect, when no other thought retained its sober influence, he still showed an awful solicitude lest the black veil should slip aside. Even if his bewildered soul could have forgotten, there was a faithful woman at his pillow, who, with averted eyes, would have covered that aged face, which she had last beheld in the comeliness of manhood. At length the death-stricken old man lay quietly in the torpor of mental and bodily exhaustion, with an imperceptible pulse, and breath that grew fainter and fainter, except when a long, deep, and irregular inspiration seemed to prelude the flight of his spirit.

The minister of Westbury approached the bedside.

"Venerable Father Hooper," said he, "the moment of your release is at hand. Are you ready for the lifting of the veil that shuts in time from eternity?"

Father Hooper at first replied merely by a feeble motion of his head; then, apprehensive, perhaps, that his meaning might be doubtful, he exerted himself to speak.

"Yea," said he, in faint accents, "my soul hath a patient weariness until that veil be lifted."

"And is it fitting," resumed the Reverend Mr. Clark, "that a man so given to prayer, of such a blameless example, holy in deed and thought, so far as mortal judgment may pronounce; is it fitting that a father in the church should leave a shadow on his memory, that may seem to blacken a life so pure? I pray you, my venerable brother, let not this thing be! Suffer us to[12] be gladdened by your triumphant aspect, as you go to your reward. Before the veil of eternity be lifted, let me cast aside this black veil from your face!"

And thus speaking, the Reverend Mr. Clark bent forward to reveal the mystery of so many years. But, exerting a sudden energy, that made all the beholders stand aghast, Father Hooper snatched both his hands from beneath the bedclothes, and pressed them strongly on the black veil, resolute to struggle, if the minister of Westbury would contend with a dying man.

"Never!" cried the veiled clergyman. "On earth, never!"

"Dark old man!" exclaimed the affrighted minister, "with what horrible crime upon your soul are you now passing to the judgment?"

Father Hooper's breath heaved; it rattled in his throat; but, with a mighty effort, grasping forward with his hands, he caught hold of life, and held it back till he should speak. He even raised himself in bed; and there he sat, shivering with the arms of death around him, while the black veil hung down, awful at that last moment, in the gathered terrors of a lifetime. And yet the faint, sad smile, so often there, now seemed to glimmer from its obscurity, and linger on Father Hooper's lips.

"Why do you tremble at me alone?" cried he, turning his veiled face round the circle of pale spectators. "Tremble also at each other! Have men avoided me, and women shown no pity, and children screamed and fled, only for my black veil? What, but the mystery which it obscurely typifies, has made this piece of crape so awful? When the friend shows his inmost heart to his friend; the lover to his best beloved; when man does not vainly shrink from the eye of his Creator, loathsomely treasuring up the secret of his sin; then deem me a monster, for the symbol beneath which I have lived, and die! I look around me, and, lo! on every visage a Black Veil!"

While his auditors shrank from one another, in mutual affright, Father Hooper fell back upon his pillow, a veiled corpse, with a faint smile lingering on the lips. Still veiled, they laid him in his coffin, and a veiled corpse they bore him to the grave. The grass of many years has sprung up and withered on that grave, the burial stone is moss-grown, and good Mr. Hooper's face is dust; but awful is still the thought, that it mouldered beneath the Black Veil!

【注解】

1. 霍桑原注："Another clergyman in New England, Mr. Joseph Moody, of York, Maine, who died about eighty years since, made himself remarkable by the same eccentricity that is here related of the Reverend Mr. Hooper. In his case, however, the symbol had a different import. In early life he had accidentally killed a beloved friend; and from that day till the hour of his own death, he hid his face from men."
2. Goodman Gray：Goodman 是当时的一种称谓，相当于"先生"。
3. the Scriptures：《圣经》。
4. the dread Being：上帝。后面的 "the Omniscient" 亦指上帝。
5. the Word：上帝的话。
6. the wedding-knell：暗指霍桑的另一篇短篇小说《婚礼上的钟声》("The Wedding Knell")。
7. synod：教会主要成员的集会，用于商讨和决定重大问题。
8. his plighted wife：他的未婚妻。
9. Take it not amiss：相当于 Don't take offence at it, 请不要生气。
10. Governor Belcher：乔纳森·贝尔契尔总督，1730 至 1741 年任马萨诸塞和新罕布什尔殖民地总督。在总督就职仪式上布道是牧师极大的荣幸。
11. Natural connections：亲戚。
12. Suffer us to：相当于 allow us to, 表示允许、同意。

【思考题】

1. What are some of the consequences of hiding oneself from others? What is the effect of the black veil upon the villagers?
2. What happens during the funeral and the wedding? Do you think Mr. Hooper has anything to do with the young maiden's death? What is the minister particularly afraid of when he is alone with himself and sees himself in mirrors?
3. Why does Mr. Hooper change his mind at the death bed and persist in wearing the black veil forever? Then, what does the veil symbolize?
4. Argue for or against the notion that all people are sinners. What do you think is the author's attitude on this matter?

解读举例

1. 胡珀教长戴上黑面纱的原因始终是一团难解的谜，也许像故事中多处所暗示的那样，他曾犯下某种罪孽，为给自己赎罪而戴上黑面纱。而有的批评家指出，他所犯的罪孽和霍桑的长篇小说《红字》中的海丝特一样，都是情欲之罪。在他戴上黑面纱的第二天，就主持了一个年轻女士的葬礼，文本给出了暧昧的暗示，这位女士的死亡或许与教长有关。

2. 胡珀教长戴上黑面纱的原因是为教众赎罪。在临终时他对世人的一番诘问至少给读者提供了一个答案，那就是世间所有的人都带有与生俱来的罪孽，而且每个人都设法隐藏它，因此是不可饶恕的。胡珀教长执意戴着面纱去谒见上帝表现了他的赤诚。他戴面纱本身就等于犯下了上帝所不允许的"隐匿罪孽"的罪孽，他所承受的异化和孤独的煎熬是他应受的惩罚。他也以此警戒世人。

3. 胡珀教长戴上黑面纱并不是因为他自己犯了什么滔天罪行，也不是为了赎罪，而是他的清教主义罪恶观使他的双眼蒙上了一层黑纱。这层黑纱给一切有生命和无生命的东西都蒙上了一层黑影。实际上霍桑对清教主义的"原罪""内在堕落"提出了怀疑。尽管戴着面纱布道产生了神奇效果，但教长不敢看镜中的自己，而且失去了人间温情。

4. 胡珀教长戴上黑面纱直到死也不肯去掉，似乎是以一种自相矛盾的方式抗议人们缺乏坦诚，存有隔阂，缺乏同情与友爱之心。胡珀教长的临终遗言显示出他和作者本人对人类、对上帝悲观失望的情绪。

Edgar Allan Poe
1809—1849

美国 19 世纪文坛怪才埃德加·爱伦·坡的一生是悲剧的一生。他 1809 年出生于波士顿，1 岁时父亲离家出走，3 岁时母亲又因病辞世。里士满商人约翰·爱伦收养了坡，并为他提供了良好的生活环境，让他接受一个南方绅士所应有的教育。但两人关系暗藏危机：爱伦重利务实，坡却生性浪漫，爱好文学。1826 年，坡进入弗吉尼亚大学读书，因赌博欠债，爱伦拒绝帮助偿付学费而辍学。1827 年，爱伦与坡反目，坡愤而出走。1830 年，坡进入西点军校，后因得知爱伦再婚，自己继承无

望，故意违反军纪被开除。其后的十八年间，坡以卖文为生，发表诗作，出版小说，担任文学编辑，辗转于巴尔的摩、里士满、纽约和费城之间，却总摆脱不了穷困潦倒的命运。1835年，他与当时年仅13岁的堂妹弗吉尼亚秘密结婚，两人感情甚笃，弗吉尼亚却于25岁时抱病身亡。在生活一连串的打击下，坡唯有借助酒精麻痹自己。1849年10月，人们发现他倒在巴尔的摩的街头，送入医院几天后不治而亡。

坡的一生命运多舛，辞世时年仅40岁，却为后人留下了一笔丰厚的文学遗产。他的艺术成就跨越诗歌、小说和文论三大领域。坡生活的时代，美国的文学评论还是一片空白，停留在以欣赏为主的印象主义批评层面，坡却视评论为毕生追求的事业，立志建立一个完整的理论体系。在他最富代表性的三篇论文《评霍桑"重述的故事"》("The Review of Hawthorne's Twice-told Tales", 1840)、《创作哲学》("The Philosophy of Composition", 1846) 及《诗歌原理》("The Poetic Principle", 1850) 中，坡指出好的作家应视艺术为生命，创作时丝毫不应有功利之心。当时的社会重视商业利润，推崇道德完善，坡却高扬"唯美"的旗帜：他强调作品所能达到的最高境界不是真实，而是美，因为只有美才能在读者心中激起情感的共鸣。他注重作品形式和内容的和谐，认为一部作品应有一定的长度，能让人一次读完为宜，否则因为阅读的中断，作品的整体效果将被削弱。正因为坡持有"为艺术而艺术"的创作观，他去世后虽在一段相当长的时间里不为美国批评家所承认，却在大西洋彼岸受到夏尔·波德莱尔 (Charles Baudelaire, 1821—1867) 和斯特凡·马拉美 (Stephane Mallarme, 1842—1898) 等法国象征派诗人的热烈推崇。

坡的文学理念，直接影响到了他的创作。他一生共创作了48首诗，其中著名的有《海中之城》("The City in the Sea", 1831)、《致海伦》("To Helen", 1831)、《乌鸦》("The Raven", 1845)、《钟声》("The Bells", 1849) 和《安娜贝尔·李》("Annabel Lee", 1849) 等。坡的诗歌创作受到欧洲古典主义和当时方兴未艾的浪漫主义的双重影响。他的诗作的古典性主要体现在他对诗歌格律的重视：他讲究音韵美、注意锤词炼句，希望借文字刺激人的感官。他的诗作的浪漫性则体现在象征手法的普遍运用、对哥特式氛围的精心营造及对忧郁感伤情调的偏爱上。与布莱恩特和朗费罗等同时期的美国浪漫主义诗人不同，坡的诗歌很少描写自然、歌颂北美洲壮阔的山川景物，而是竭力营造一种梦幻般的环境，渲染充满异国情调的神秘色彩。他的大多数诗歌关注的是"美"与"死亡"这两个超越时空限制的文学永恒主题。

坡小说上的成就主要集中在短篇小说。除了两部中篇小说《亚瑟·戈登·皮姆的故事》(*The Narrative of Arthur Gordon Pym*, 1838) 和《裘力斯·罗德曼的札记》(*The Journal of Julius Rodman*, 1840) 外，他为后人留下了 68 篇短篇小说。他的短篇分为两大类：想象小说和推理小说。想象小说又可推演出怪诞类和恐怖类两种。坡在怪诞小说中采用了滑稽反讽的手法，将情节推至匪夷所思的境地，把恐怖渲染到令人发噱的程度。《困境》("A Predicament") 便是此类小说的代表。

然而，最能体现坡精湛艺术成就的还是他以心理描写为主的恐怖小说。这类作品大力渲染哥特式气氛，把人对死亡的恐惧及由之衍生的病态迷恋描写得淋漓尽致。作品充分运用象征主义手法，直指人物黑暗的灵魂深处，挖掘人的潜在欲望，刻画本我和自我的激烈冲突，揭示人性的两面性，代表作有《一桶白葡萄酒》("The Cask of Amontillado")、《泄密的心》("The Tell-Tale Heart")、《丽姬娅》("Ligeia") 等。

坡不仅是撰写恐怖小说的高手，还发表了一系列推理小说。在《毛格街血案》("Murders in the Rue Morgue")、《失窃的信》("The Purloined Letter") 和《玛丽·罗热疑案》("The Mystery of Marie Rogêt") 中，坡塑造了一个神探——C. 奥古斯特·杜宾 (C. Auguste Dupin)。他既有敏锐的直觉，又有强烈的逻辑判断能力，是阿瑟·柯南·道尔 (Arthur Conan Doyle, 1859—1930) 笔下夏洛克·福尔摩斯的前身。这些作品构建了侦探小说的基本程式：敏锐精明但略显怪僻的大侦探；平庸而稍带笨拙的搭档；情节拓展以比拼智力为主线，而不强调体力；逻辑推理是解决疑难的关键；真相往往隐藏在最明显但最易被人所忽视的地方。

坡所处的时代，美国文学正处在上升期。坡同时代的作家，如爱默生和梭罗，正在为创立属于美国自己的文学而大声疾呼。然而从坡的作品中却看不出多少美国本土的影子。他的想象世界仿佛超越了现实与梦想的边界，游离于物外，他所真正关注的是精神的世界，是人的本性。如果说库珀这样的作家致力于展示勇敢无畏的边疆精神，坡则是在人类灵魂的黑暗领地上拓荒。他和霍桑、麦尔维尔一起为美国文学开创了一片全新的疆土。

The Raven

【题解】

当我们欣赏《乌鸦》一诗时，应将它与坡的《创作哲学》一文结合起来阅读。坡在《创作哲学》中指出，诗歌最应表现的是美，最适合的氛围是忧郁，世上最令人忧怀感伤的莫过于死亡，而一位痛惜爱人辞世的男子的真情流露，无疑是表达这一主题最贴切的方式。《乌鸦》一诗中，主人公一连串急切的追问，传达出他对逝去的爱人真挚的思念；而乌鸦机械地一遍又一遍重复"永不复还"，更让人感受到死亡的力量。整首诗气氛阴森忧郁：暗夜，暴风雨，不速之客的突然造访，代表着霉运的乌鸦，读来无不令人心悸。

The Raven

Once upon a midnight dreary, while I pondered, weak and weary,
Over many a quaint and curious volume of forgotten lore—
While I nodded, nearly napping, suddenly there came a tapping,
As of some one gently rapping, rapping at my chamber door.
"'Tis some visitor," I muttered, "tapping at my chamber door—   5
    Only this and nothing more."

Ah, distinctly I remember it was in the bleak December;
And each separate dying ember wrought its ghost upon the floor.
Eagerly I wished the morrow;—vainly I had sought to borrow
From my books surcease of sorrow—sorrow for the lost Lenore—   10
For the rare and radiant maiden whom the angels name Lenore—
    Nameless *here* for evermore.

And the silken, sad, uncertain rustling of each purple curtain
Thrilled me—filled me with fantastic terrors never felt before;
So that now, to still the beating of my heart, I stood repeating   15
"'Tis some visitor entreating entrance at my chamber door—
Some late visitor entreating entrance at my chamber door;—
    This it is and nothing more."

Presently my soul grew stronger; hesitating then no longer,
"Sir," said I, "or Madam, truly your forgiveness I implore;   20
But the fact is I was napping, and so gently you came tapping,
And so faintly you came tapping, tapping at my chamber door;—
That I scarce was sure I heard you"—here I opened wide the door;—
    Darkness there and nothing more.

Deep into that darkness peering, long I stood there wondering, fearing,   25
Doubting, dreaming dreams no mortals ever dared to dream before;
But the silence was unbroken, and the stillness gave no token,
And the only word there spoken was the whispered word, "Lenore?"
This I whispered, and an echo murmured back the word "Lenore!"
    Merely this and nothing more.   30

Back into the chamber turning, all my soul within me burning,
Soon again I heard a tapping somewhat louder than before.
"Surely," said I, "surely that is something at my window lattice;
Let me see, then, what thereat is, and this mystery explore—
Let my heart be still a moment and this mystery explore;—   35
    "'Tis the wind and nothing more!"

Open here I flung the shutter, when, with many a flirt and flutter,
In there stepped a stately Raven of the saintly days of yore;
Not the least obeisance made he; not a minute stopped or stayed he;
But, with mien of lord or lady, perched above my chamber door—   40
Perched upon a bust of Pallas[1] just above my chamber door—
    Perched, and sat, and nothing more.

Then this ebony bird beguiling my sad fancy into smiling,
By the grave and stern decorum of the countenance it wore,
"'Though thy crest be shorn and shaven, thou," I said, "art sure no craven,   45
Ghastly grim and ancient Raven wandering from the nightly shore—
Tell me what thy lordly name is on the Night's Plutonian[2] shore!
    Quoth the Raven "Nevermore."

Much I marvelled this ungainly fowl to hear discourse so plainly,
Though its answer little meaning—little relevancy bore;   50
For we cannot help agreeing that no living human being
Ever yet was blessed with seeing bird above his chamber door—

Bird or beast upon the sculptured bust above his chamber door,
    With such name as "Nevermore."

But the Raven sitting lonely on the placid bust, spoke only
That one word, as if his soul in that one word he did outpour.
Nothing farther then he uttered—not a feather then he fluttered—
Till I scarcely more than muttered "Other friends have flown before—
On the morrow he will leave me, as my Hopes have flown before.

    "Then the bird said "Nevermore."
Startled at the stillness broken by reply so aptly spoken,
"Doubtless," said I, "what it utters is its only stock and store
Caught from some unhappy master whom unmerciful Disaster
Followed fast and followed faster till his songs one burden bore—
Till the dirges of his Hope that melancholy burden bore
    Of 'Never—nevermore.' "

But the Raven still beguiling all my fancy into smiling,
Straight I wheeled a cushioned seat in front of the bird, the bust and door;
Then, upon the velvet sinking, I betook myself to linking
Fancy unto fancy, thinking what this ominous bird of yore—
What this grim, ungainly, ghastly, gaunt, and ominous bird of yore
    Meant in croaking "Nevermore."

This I sat engaged in guessing, but no syllable expressing
To the fowl whose fiery eyes now burned into my bosom's core;
This and more I sat divining, with my head at ease reclining,
On the cushion's velvet lining that the lamplight gloated o'er
But whose velvet-violet lining that the lamp-light gloating o'er,
    She shall press, ah, nevermore!

Then, methought, the air grew denser, perfumed from an unseen censer
Swung by Seraphim whose foot-falls tinkled on the tufted floor.

"Wretch," I cried, "thy God hath lent thee—by these angels he hath sent thee
Respite—respite and nepenthe³ from thy memories of Lenore;
Quaff, oh quaff this kind nepenthe and forget this lost Lenore!"
    Quoth the Raven "Nevermore."

"Prophet!" said I, "thing of evil!—prophet still, if bird or devil!—   85
Whether Tempter sent, or whether tempest tossed thee here ashore,
Desolate yet all undaunted, on this desert land enchanted—
On this home by Horror haunted—tell me truly, I implore—
Is there—is there balm in Gilead⁴?—tell me-tell me, I implore!"
    Quoth the Raven "Nevermore."   90

"Prophet!" said I, "thing of evil!—prophet still, if bird or devil!
By that Heaven that bends above us—by that God we both adore—
Tell this soul with sorrow laden if, within the distant Aidenn⁵,
It shall clasp a sainted maiden whom the angels name Lenore—
Clasp a rare and radiant maiden whom the angels name Lenore."   95
    Quoth the Raven "Nevermore."

"Be that word our sign of parting, bird or fiend!" I shrieked, upstarting—
"Get thee back into the tempest and the Night's Plutonian shore!
Leave no black plume as a token of that lie thy soul hath spoken!
Leave my loneliness unbroken!—quit the bust above my door!   100
Take thy beak from out my heart, and take thy form from off my door!"
    Quoth the Raven "Nevermore."

And the Raven, never fitting, still is sitting, still is sitting
On the pallid bust of Pallas just above my chamber door;
And his eyes have all the seeming of a demon's that is dreaming,   105
And the lamp-light o'er him streaming throws his shadow on the floor;
And my soul from out that shadow that lies floating on the floor
    Shall be lifted—nevermore!

【注解】

1. Pallas: 帕拉斯，全称为帕拉斯·雅典娜 (Pallas Athena)，古希腊神话中雅典的女保护神。
2. Plutonian：普路托的，即阴间的 (普路托是古罗马神话中的死亡之神和阴间的统治者)。
3. nepenthe: 相传这是一种麻醉剂，古希腊人用来忘忧。
4. Gilead: 基列山，位于约旦河 (the River Jordan) 东边，在加利利海 (the Sea of Galilee) 与死海之间。
5. Aidenn：坡创造的地名，与 Eden 谐音。

【思考题】

1. Does the speaker believe the words he says in lines 16–18 and line 36? How do you know?
2. Who is the "she" in line 78? Who is the "wretch" in line 81? Trace the speaker's thoughts in lines 78–83.
3. What does the raven come to represent for the speaker? What does "Plutonian shore" (in line 98) suggest about the speaker's final evaluation of the raven? Of himself?
4. Evaluate the speaker's emotional state at the beginning of the poem, in the next to the last stanza, and in the last stanza. What does the future probably hold for the speaker?
5. Describe the mood of the poem. Which expressions in stanzas 1–2 help establish the mood?
6. Emerson calls Poe a "Jingle man", meaning he is only good at making pleasant sounds in poems. Whitman also says Poe's verses "belong among the electric lights of imagination literature, brilliant and dazzling, but with no heat." Do you think their criticism is justified?

The Masque of the Red Death

【题解】

　　《红死魔的面具》中，普罗斯佩罗的王国瘟疫肆虐，普罗斯佩罗遂率领人退入一处大寺院。小说对寺院布局的描写极尽铺陈之能事，着重渲染奢靡气氛，烘托人们今朝有酒今朝醉的末世心理。小说大量采用了富有象征意义的意象，无论是房间的颜色，还是屋里的大钟，都具有特定的含义。然而，坡虽然在环境描述上细致入微，却故意忽略了对故事发生的时代背景的介绍，使作品处于梦幻迷离的色彩之中。

The Masque of the Red Death

The "Red Death" had long devastated the country. No pestilence had ever been so fatal, or so hideous. Blood was its Avatar[1] and its seal—the redness and the horror of blood. There were sharp pains, and sudden dizziness, and then profuse bleeding at the pores, with dissolution. The scarlet stains upon the body and especially upon the face of the victim, were the pest ban which shut him out from the aid and from the sympathy of his fellow-men. And the whole seizure, progress and termination of the disease, were the incidents of half an hour.

But the Prince Prospero[2] was happy and dauntless and sagacious. When his dominions were half depopulated, he summoned to his presence a thousand hale and light-hearted friends from among the knights and dames of his court, and with these retired to the deep seclusion of one of his castellated abbeys. This was an extensive and magnificent structure, the creation of the prince's own eccentric yet august taste. A strong and lofty wall girdled it in. This wall had gates of iron. The courtiers, having entered, brought furnaces and massy hammers and welded the bolts. They resolved to leave means neither of ingress or egress to the sudden impulses of despair or of frenzy from within. The abbey was amply provisioned. With such precautions the courtiers might bid defiance to contagion. The external world could take care of itself. In the meantime it was folly to grieve, or to think. The prince had provided all the appliances of pleasure. There were buffoons, there were improvisatori, there were ballet-dancers, there were musicians, there was Beauty, there was wine. All these and security were within. Without was the "Red Death."

It was toward the close of the fifth or sixth month of his seclusion, and while the pestilence raged most furiously abroad, that the Prince Prospero entertained his thousand friends at a masked ball of the most unusual magnificence.

It was a voluptuous scene, that masquerade. But first let me tell of the rooms in which it was held. There were seven—an imperial suite. In many palaces, however, such suites form a long and straight vista, while the folding doors slide back nearly to the walls on either hand, so that the view of the whole extent is scarcely impeded. Here the case was very different; as might have been expected from the duke's love of the bizarre. The apartments were so irregularly disposed that the vision embraced but little more than one at a time. There was a sharp turn at every twenty or thirty yards, and at each turn a novel effect. To the right and left, in the middle of each wall, a tall and narrow Gothic window looked out upon a closed corridor which pursued the windings of the suite. These windows were of stained glass whose color varied in accordance with the prevailing hue of the decorations of the chamber into which it opened. That at the eastern extremity was hung, for example in blue—and vividly blue were its windows. The second chamber was purple in its ornaments and tapestries, and here the panes were purple. The third was green throughout, and so were the casements. The fourth was furnished and lighted with orange—the fifth with white—the sixth with violet. The seventh apartment was closely shrouded in black velvet tapestries that hung all over the ceiling and down the walls, falling in heavy folds upon a carpet of the same material and hue. But in this chamber only, the color of the windows failed to correspond with the decorations. The panes here were scarlet—a deep blood color. Now in no one of the seven apartments was there any lamp or candelabrum, amid the profusion of golden ornaments that lay scattered to and fro or depended from the roof. There was no light of any kind emanating from lamp or candle within the suite of chambers. But in the corridors that followed the suite, there stood, opposite to each window, a heavy tripod, bearing a brazier of fire, that projected its rays through the tinted glass and so glaringly illumined the room. And thus were produced a multitude of gaudy and fantastic appearances. But in the western or black chamber the effect of the fire-light that streamed upon the dark hangings through the blood-tinted panes, was ghastly in the extreme, and produced so wild a look upon the countenances of those who entered, that there were few of the company bold enough to set foot within its precincts at all.

It was in this apartment, also, that there stood against the western wall, a gigantic clock of ebony. Its pendulum swung to and fro with a dull, heavy, monotonous clang; and when the minute-hand made the circuit of the face, and the hour was to be stricken, there came from the brazen lungs of the clock a sound which was clear and loud and deep and exceedingly musical, but of so peculiar a note and emphasis that, at each lapse of an hour, the musicians of the orchestra were constrained to pause, momentarily, in their performance, to harken to the sound; and thus the waltzers perforce ceased their evolutions; and there was a brief disconcert of the whole gay company; and, while the chimes of the clock yet rang, it was observed that the giddiest grew pale, and the more aged and sedate passed their hands over their brows as if in confused revery or meditation. But when the echoes had fully ceased, a light laughter at once pervaded the assembly; the musicians looked at each other and smiled as if at their own nervousness and folly, and made whispering vows, each to the other, that the next chiming of the clock should produce in them no similar emotion; and then, after the lapse of sixty minutes, (which embrace three thousand and six hundred seconds of the Time that flies,) there came yet another chiming of the clock, and then were the same disconcert and tremulousness and meditation as before.

But, in spite of these things, it was a gay and magnificent revel. The tastes of the duke were peculiar. He had a fine eye for colors and effects. He disregarded the decora[3] of mere fashion. His plans were bold and fiery, and his conceptions glowed with barbaric lustre. There are some who would have thought him mad. His followers felt that he was not. It was necessary to hear and see and touch him to be sure that he was not.

He had directed, in great part, the moveable embellishments of the seven chambers, upon occasion of this great fete[4]; and it was his own guiding taste which had given character to the masqueraders. Be sure they were grotesque. There were much glare and glitter and piquancy and phantasm—much of what has been since seen in "Hernani[5]". There were arabesque figures with unsuited limbs and appointments. There were delirious fancies such as the madman fashions. There were much of the beautiful, much of the wanton, much of the bizarre, something of the terrible, and not a little of that which might have excited disgust. To and fro in the seven chambers there stalked, in fact, a multitude of dreams. And these—the dreams—writhed in and about, taking hue from the rooms, and causing the wild music of the orchestra to seem as the echo of their steps. And, anon, there strikes the ebony clock which stands in the hall of the velvet. And then, for a moment, all is still, and all is silent save the voice of the clock. The dreams are stiff-frozen as they stand. But the echoes of the chime die away—they have endured but an instant—and a light, half-subdued laughter floats after them as they depart. And now again the music swells, and the dreams live, and writhe to and fro more merrily than ever, taking hue from the many tinted windows through which stream the rays from the tripods. But to the chamber which lies most westwardly of the seven, there are now none of the maskers who venture; for the night is waning away; and there flows a ruddier light through the blood-colored panes; and the blackness of the sable drapery appals; and to him whose foot falls upon the sable carpet, there comes from the near clock of ebony a muffled peal more solemnly emphatic than any which reaches their ears who indulge in the more remote gaieties of the other apartments.

But these other apartments were densely crowded, and in them beat feverishly the heart of life. And the revel went whirlingly on, until at length there commenced the sounding of midnight upon the clock. And then the music ceased, as I have told; and the evolutions of the waltzers were quieted; and there was an uneasy cessation of all things as before. But now there were twelve strokes to be sounded by the bell of the clock; and thus it happened, perhaps that more of thought crept, with more of time, into the meditations of the thoughtful among those who revelled. And thus too, it happened, perhaps, that before the last echoes of the last chime had utterly sunk into silence, there were many individuals in the crowd who had found leisure to become aware of the presence of a masked figure which had arrested the attention of no single individual before. And the rumor of this new presence having spread itself whisperingly around, there arose at length from the whole company a buzz, or murmur, expressive of disapprobation and surprise—then, finally, of terror, of horror, and of disgust.

In an assembly of phantasms such as I have painted, it may well be supposed that no ordinary appearance could have excited such sensation. In truth the masquerade license of the night was nearly unlimited; but the figure in question had out-Heroded Herod[6], and gone beyond the bounds of even the prince's indefinite decorum. There are chords in the hearts of the most reckless which cannot be touched without emotion. Even with the utterly lost, to whom life and death are equally jests, there are matters of which no jest can be made. The whole company, indeed, seemed now deeply to feel that in the costume and bearing of the stranger neither wit nor propriety existed. The figure was tall and gaunt, and shrouded from head to foot in the habiliments of the grave. The mask which concealed the visage was made so nearly to resemble the countenance of a stiffened corpse that the closest scrutiny must have had difficulty in detecting the cheat. And yet all this might have been endured, if not approved, by the mad revellers around. But the mummer had gone so far as to assume the type of the Red Death. His vesture was dabbled in blood—and his broad brow, with all the features of the face, was besprinkled with the scarlet horror.

When the eyes of Prince Prospero fell upon this spectral image (which with a slow and solemn movement, as if more fully to sustain its role, stalked to and fro among the waltzers) he was seen to be convulsed, in the first moment with a strong shudder either of terror or distaste; but, in the next, his brow reddened with rage.

"Who dares?" he demanded hoarsely of the courtiers who stood near him—"who dares insult us with this blasphemous mockery? Seize him and unmask him—that we may know whom we have to hang at sunrise, from the battlements!"

It was in the eastern or blue chamber in which stood the Prince Prospero as he uttered these words. They rang throughout the seven rooms loudly and clearly—for the prince was a bold and robust man, and the music had become hushed at the waving of his hand.

It was in the blue room where stood the prince, with a group of pale courtiers by his side. At first, as he spoke, there was a slight rushing movement of this group in the direction of the intruder, who, at the moment was also near at hand, and now, with deliberate and stately step, made closer approach to the speaker. But from a certain nameless awe with which the mad assumptions of the mummer had inspired the whole party, there were found none who put forth hand to seize him; so that, unimpeded, he passed within a yard of the prince's person; and, while the vast assembly, as if with one impulse, shrank from the centres of the rooms to the walls, he made his way uninterruptedly, but with the same solemn and measured step which had distinguished him from the first, through the blue chamber to the purple—through the purple to the green—through the green to the orange—through this again to the white—and even thence to the violet, ere a decided movement had been made to arrest him. It was then, however, that the Prince Prospero, maddening with rage and the shame of his own momentary cowardice, rushed hurriedly through the six chambers, while none followed him on account of a deadly terror that had seized upon all. He bore aloft a drawn dagger, and had approached, in rapid impetuosity, to within three or four feet of the retreating figure, when the latter, having attained the extremity of the velvet apartment, turned suddenly and confronted his pursuer. There was a sharp cry—and the dagger dropped gleaming upon the sable carpet, upon which, instantly afterwards, fell prostrate in death the Prince Prospero. Then, summoning the wild courage of despair, a throng of the revellers at once threw themselves into the black apartment, and, seizing the mummer, whose tall figure stood erect and motionless within the shadow of the ebony clock, gasped in unutterable horror at finding the grave cerements and corpse-like mask which they handled with so violent a rudeness, untenanted by any tangible form.

And now was acknowledged the presence of the Red Death. He had come like a thief in the night. And one by one dropped the revellers in the blood-bedewed halls of their revel, and died each in the despairing posture of his fall. And the life of the ebony clock went out with that of the last of the gay. And the flames of the tripods expired. And Darkness and Decay and the Red Death held illimitable dominion over all.

【注解】

1. Avatar: 原指印度神下凡的化身，此处引申为化身、表征。
2. Prospero: 坡将主人公取名为普罗斯佩罗，是借用"繁荣"（prosperous）一词。这个名字与威廉·莎士比亚的名剧《暴风雨》（*The Tempest*, 1611）的主人公名字相同。《暴风雨》中的普罗斯佩罗在荒岛上建立了一个世外桃源，坡笔下的主角也率人遁世于古堡之中。
3. decora: 形式，花样。
4. fete: 宴会。
5. Hernani: 这是维克多·雨果（Victor Hugo, 1802—1885）的一出悲剧的名字，此剧以繁复的布景、精美的服饰著称。
6. out-Heroded Herod: 比希律王还要希律王。该典故出自威廉·莎士比亚的《哈姆雷特》（*Hamlet*, c.1599—1601），此处意指"表演过度"。

【思考题】

1. How does Poe establish the mood of this story?
2. What is the central conflict in this story? Who is the protagonist? The antagonist?
3. Where is the climax of the story? How is the building in which Prince Prospero and his thousand nobles take shelter described? To what extent does the description of this "abbey" help us form an opinion of Prince Prospero?
4. How many rooms are used in the masquerade ball in the story? In what ways might this number be significant?
5. What is the dominant color of each room? How are the rooms arranged? How do these details help create the atmosphere and mood of the story?
6. Poe is deliberately vague about the time and place of the story. How does this affect our reading?

解读举例

1. "红死魔"表现的是任何人都无法摆脱的死亡。小说中放浪奢华的假面舞会，暗示人们在用及时行乐的人生态度与死神抗衡。小说中的七个房间分别涂以蓝、紫、绿、橘红、白、紫罗兰和黑色，象征人生从充满梦幻的童年到暮年。乌檀木大座钟的存在也时刻提醒人们，随着时光的流逝，死亡的阴影日益逼近。普罗斯佩罗在第七间房间，即黑色的房间被"红死魔"追上，随即倒地身亡，象征着死亡的最终胜利。

2. 《红死魔的面具》表现的是瑰丽放荡的梦境，人们沉溺其中，不愿苏醒。"红死魔"

的红与红日的意象相连，是白昼的象征。假面舞会光怪陆离，糅恐怖和想象于一体，是梦魂飘飞的产物。七间色彩各异的房间代表梦的不同阶段。时钟每一次敲响，白昼便逼近一分，角色们都会惊慌失措地暂时停下狂欢。小说结尾普罗斯佩罗与"红死魔"正面遭遇，他的死亡意味着梦境结束，回到现实。

3. 《红死魔的面具》表现的是艺术家、艺术品与客观现实之间的对立冲突，具体表现为普罗斯佩罗与"红死魔"之间的冲突。与莎士比亚《暴风雨》中的同名主角一样，普罗斯佩罗想在游离于时空之外的地方建立了一个自治的世外桃源。这一细节象征着艺术家想摆脱现实世界的控制，建立一个单纯以想象为主的艺术世界。七间房间，象征着人类有限的认知体验。普罗斯佩罗凭借恣肆的想象力所建造的大寺院美轮美奂，却无法摆脱时间的掌控。一个建立在纯粹审美意义上的艺术品，在面临象征现实的"红死魔"的侵袭时，只能土崩瓦解。

Henry David Thoreau
1817—1861

作者简介

亨利·戴维·梭罗是土生土长的康科德人，他除了外出学习、短期旅行外，一生大部分时间都生活在当时美国思想、文化的中心康科德。虽然家中生活并不富裕，但父母仍坚持供他读完哈佛大学。20岁大学毕业后，梭罗没有像当时大部分美国人那样，寻找一份体面的工作养家糊口，而是干各种杂活维生：教书，种豆谷，刷墙壁，造铅笔，当花匠、木匠、砖石匠。当时的人们都不理解他，指责他古怪、闲散、懒惰、不务正业、缺乏责任心。但是，在与爱默生的交往中，在康科德附近的无数次探险、考察和旅游中，在对自然、社会、生活和人的反思中，梭罗摆脱了当时大部分人过着的那种"非生活的生活"，实现了他的人生价值和人生理想。

梭罗一生与长他12岁的爱默生交往甚密。他深受超验主义的影响，也是超验主义俱乐部的成员之一。他帮助爱默生编辑刊物《日晷》，并撰文发表在杂志上。梭罗毕生探求的中心问题是复杂的人如何返璞归真，因而对当时物质至上、金钱万能的美国社会深感厌倦和不满。他提倡人们过"简朴，简朴，再简朴"的物质生活，主张人与自然直接对话，到自然中去寻求"神秘的狂喜"(mystic ecstasy)和"崇高的启示"(sublime illumination)。

有人批评梭罗作为爱默生的弟子，只会在爱默生的果园中捡拾被风吹落的苹果，但在广泛涉猎东西方文化的浩瀚巨帙后，梭罗在继承爱默生思想的同时也逐渐形成了自己的观点。他和爱默生都推崇回归自然，强调人与自然的和谐统一，在自然中寻求心灵的净化和精神的超越。然而，爱默生的自然是被抽象了的自然，在一定程度上沦为了人类获得精神拯救的手段。他强调人对自然的主宰，认为人是宇宙的中心。而梭罗的自然既是超验的自然，服务于人类的精神，同时也是原始的自然，因其自身的美丽而存在。人作为自然的一部分，应该沉浸于自然，体会自然初始之魅力；同时，人类也应该保护自然，爱护自然，创建和谐的生态环境。因观点的抵牾，爱默生与梭罗最终分道扬镳。梭罗对环保的关注也使他成为20世纪90年代生态批评浪潮掀起以来重要的生态作家，被誉为"生态学创立之前的生态学家"。

梭罗常在游记中记录他对大自然的感受。他根据自己在梅里马克河上的漂流经历，写成《在康科德和梅里马克河上的一周》(*A Week on the Concord and Merrimack Rivers*, 1849)。1845年7月至1847年9月他在康科德附近的瓦尔登湖畔筑屋隐居，并根据两年的生活经历写成了经典名著《瓦尔登湖，或林中生活》(*Walden; or, Life in the Woods*, 1854)。

梭罗追求的并非逃避现实、超凡出世，他同样关注着社会的风云变化，抗议现实的不公正，积极支持废除奴隶制。他发表《马萨诸塞州的奴隶制》("Slavery in Massachusetts", 1854)，为黑人领袖汤姆·布朗撰写《为汤姆·布朗队长请愿》("A Plea for Captain Brown", 1857)。他因拒付两美元的战争税被捕关押一夜，据此写出著名的《抵制公民政府》("Resistance to Civil Government", 1849)。他主张非暴力反抗，这也深深影响了印度圣雄甘地和美国的黑人民权运动领袖马丁·路德·金。

梭罗的文笔细腻优美，风格清新流畅，对自然的描写生动形象，有极强的感染力。他的散文在美国文学史上有着独特的地位。尽管他不被同时代人理解与欣赏，但在20世纪后声誉鹊起，受到读者的青睐和评论界的重视。

Walden; or, Life in the Woods

【题解】

《瓦尔登湖，或林中生活》是梭罗的代表作，也是使他享誉世界文坛的经典著作。这是他根据自己1845至1847年间在瓦尔登湖畔结庐隐居的经历写成的。初稿很快完成，经过几年的反复润色修改，于1854年发表。

全书将两年多的经历浓缩为一年，按季节记载了湖边林中幽静迷人的自然风光。

在田园牧歌般的原始生活中，读者不难感受到梭罗对自然的热爱，感受到根植于他心灵深处的本能和追求，感受到他对人生意义的沉思，对理想世界的渴望，以及对自然、简单、独立、大度、自信的生活方式的推崇。

梭罗写作《瓦尔登湖》旨在让读者对他的生活和思考方式进行评价，希望能引导读者对当时美国社会的各项制度、文化和惯例进行反思，从而发掘生活的真谛。从这个意义上说，梭罗这位具有哲学头脑的文学家就像柏拉图洞穴理论里那个挣脱枷锁、逃出洞穴的囚犯。他在亲自领略到真实的生活后，感到有责任告诉自己的同伴，真正的生活是什么样的。他通过《瓦尔登湖》委婉地告诉读者，在现实世界中，人们看到的只是被火光扭曲了的影子。真正的阳光、真正的生活存在于人的心灵和精神体验之中。因此，梭罗在瓦尔登湖畔隐居两年，非但不是在逃避现实、逃避社会，而是站在更高的角度，呼吁人们走出物质化的世界。

近年来，人们认识到《瓦尔登湖》不仅阐释了超验主义哲学，也是对大自然本身的描写。随着20世纪90年代以来生态批评的兴起，《瓦尔登湖》更是受到生态批评者的欢迎。《瓦尔登湖》中不仅有一个超验的自然，还有一个原始本色的自然。梭罗不仅阐释了自然对人的精神生活的启示作用，也表现了大自然本身的美好，以及人与大自然和谐共处的意义。

下文选自该书第二章《我生活的地方；我为何生活》，描述梭罗对于家园的看法，具体介绍他在瓦尔登湖畔建造的家园，以及他与大自然的和谐相处。

From Walden; or, Life in the Woods

Chapter 2　　Where I Lived, and What I Lived for (Excerpt)

AT A CERTAIN season of our life we are accustomed to consider every spot as the possible site of a house. I have thus surveyed the country on every side within a dozen miles of where I live. In imagination I have bought all the farms in succession, for all were to be bought, and I knew their price. I walked over each farmer's premises[1], tasted his wild apples, discoursed on husbandry with him, took his farm at his price, at any price, mortgaging it to him in my mind; even put a higher price on it—took everything but a deed of it—took his word for his deed, for I dearly love to talk—cultivated it, and him too to some extent[2], I trust, and withdrew when I had enjoyed it long enough, leaving him to carry it on. This experience entitled me to be regarded as a sort of real-estate broker by my friends. Wherever I sat, there I might live, and the landscape radiated from me accordingly.

What is a house but a *sedes*, a seat?—better if a country seat. I discovered many a site for a house not likely to be soon improved, which some might have thought too far from the village, but to my eyes the village was too far from it. Well, there I might live, I said; and there I did live, for an hour, a summer and a winter life; saw how I could let the years run off, buffet the winter through, and see the spring come in. The future inhabitants of this region, wherever they may place their houses, may be sure that they have been anticipated. An afternoon sufficed to lay out the land into orchard, wood-lot, and pasture, and to decide what fine oaks or pines should be left to stand before the door, and whence each blasted tree could be seen to the best advantage; and then I let it lie, fallow, perchance, for a man is rich in proportion to the number of things which he can afford to let alone.

My imagination carried me so far that I even had the refusal of several farms—the refusal was all I wanted—but I never got my fingers burned by actual possession. The nearest that I came to actual possession was when I bought the Hollowell place, and had begun to sort my seeds, and collected materials with which to make a wheelbarrow to carry it on or off with; but before the owner gave me a deed of it, his wife—every man has such a wife—changed her mind and wished to keep it, and he offered me ten dollars to release him. Now, to speak the truth, I had but ten cents in the world, and it surpassed my arithmetic to tell, if I was that man who had ten cents, or who had a farm, or ten dollars, or all together. However, I let him keep the ten dollars and the farm too, for I had carried it far enough; or rather, to be generous, I sold him the farm for just what I gave for it, and, as he was not a rich man, made him a present of ten dollars, and still had my ten cents, and seeds, and materials for a wheelbarrow left. I found thus that I had been a rich man without any damage to my poverty. But I retained the landscape, and I have since annually carried off what it yielded without a wheelbarrow. With respect to landscapes,

> "I am monarch of all I *survey*,
> My right there is none to dispute."[3]

I have frequently seen a poet withdraw, having enjoyed the most valuable part of a farm, while the crusty farmer supposed that he had got a few wild apples only. Why, the owner does not know it for many years when a poet has put his farm in rhyme, the most admirable kind of invisible fence, has fairly impounded it, milked it, skimmed it, and got all the cream, and left the farmer only the skimmed milk.

The real attractions of the Hollowell farm, to me, were: its complete retirement, being, about two miles from the village, half a mile from the nearest neighbor, and separated from the highway by a broad field; its bounding on the river, which the owner said protected it by its fogs from frosts in the spring, though that was nothing to me; the gray color and ruinous state of the house and barn, and the dilapidated fences, which put such an interval between me and the last occupant; the hollow and lichen-covered apple trees, nawed by rabbits, showing what kind of neighbors I should have; but above all, the recollection I had of it from my earliest voyages up the river, when the house was concealed behind a dense grove of red maples, through which I heard the house-dog bark. I was in haste to buy it, before the proprietor finished getting out some rocks, cutting down the hollow apple trees, and grubbing up some young birches which had sprung up in the pasture, or, in short, had made any more of his improvements. To enjoy these advantages I was ready to carry it on; like Atlas[4], to take the world on my shoulders—I never heard what compensation he received for that—and do all those things which had no other motive or excuse but that I might pay for it and be unmolested in my possession of it; for I knew all the while that it would yield the most abundant crop of the kind I wanted, if I could only afford to let it alone. But it turned out as I have said.

All that I could say, then, with respect to farming on a large scale—I have always cultivated a garden—was, that I had had my seeds ready. Many think that seeds improve with age. I have no doubt that time discriminates between the good and the bad; and when at last I shall plant, I shall be less likely to be disappointed. But I would say to my fellows, once for all, as long as possible live free and uncommitted. It makes but little difference whether you are committed to a farm or the county jail.

Old Cato, whose "De Re Rusticâ"[5] is my "Cultivator," says—and the only translation I have seen makes sheer nonsense of the passage—"When you think of getting a farm turn it thus in your mind, not to buy greedily; nor spare your pains to look at it, and do not think it enough to go round it once. The oftener you go there the more it will please you, if it is good." I think I shall not buy greedily, but go round and round it as long as I live, and be buried in it first, that it may please me the more at last.

The present was my next experiment of this kind, which I purpose to describe more at length, for convenience putting the experience of two years into one. As I have said, I do not propose to write an ode to dejection, but to brag as lustily as chanticleer in the morning, standing on his roost, if only to wake my neighbors up.

When first I took up my abode in the woods, that is, began to spend my nights as well as days there, which, by accident, was on Independence Day, or the Fourth of July, 1845, my house was not finished for winter, but was merely a defence against the rain, without plastering or chimney, the walls being of rough, weather-stained boards, with wide chinks, which made it cool at night. The upright white hewn studs and freshly planed door and window casings gave it a clean and airy look, especially in the morning, when its timbers were saturated with dew, so that I fancied that by noon some sweet gum would exude from them. To my imagination it retained throughout the day more or less of this auroral character, reminding me of a certain house on a mountain which I had visited a year before. This was an airy and unplastered cabin, fit to entertain a travelling god, and where a goddess might trail her garments. The winds which passed over my dwelling were such as sweep over the ridges of mountains, bearing the broken strains, or celestial parts only, of terrestrial music. The morning wind forever blows, the poem of creation is uninterrupted; but few are the ears that hear it. Olympus[6] is but the outside of the earth everywhere.

The only house I had been the owner of before, if I except a boat, was a tent, which I used occasionally when making excursions in the summer, and this is still rolled up in my garret; but the boat, after passing from hand to hand, has gone down the stream of time. With this more substantial shelter about me, I had made some progress toward settling in the world. This frame, so slightly clad, was a sort of crystallization around me, and reacted on the builder. It was suggestive somewhat as a picture in outlines. I did not need to go outdoors to take the air, for the atmosphere within had lost none of its freshness. It was not so much within doors as behind a door where I sat, even in the rainiest weather. The Harivansa[7] says, "An abode without birds is like a meat without seasoning." Such was not my abode, for I found myself suddenly neighbor to the birds; not by having imprisoned one, but having caged myself near them. I was not only nearer to some of those which commonly frequent the garden and the orchard, but to those smaller and more thrilling songsters of the forest which never, or rarely, serenade a villager—the wood thrush, the veery, the scarlet tanager, the field sparrow, the whip-poor-will, and many others.

I was seated by the shore of a small pond, about a mile and a half south of the village of Concord and somewhat higher than it, in the midst of an extensive wood between that town and Lincoln, and about two miles south of that our only field known to fame, Concord Battle Ground[8]; but I was so low in the woods that the opposite shore, half a mile off, like the rest, covered with wood, was my most distant horizon. For the first week, whenever I looked out on the pond it impressed me like a tarn high up on the side of a mountain, its bottom far above the surface of other lakes, and, as the sun arose, I saw it throwing off its nightly clothing of mist, and here and there, by degrees, its soft ripples or its smooth reflecting surface was revealed, while the mists, like ghosts, were stealthily withdrawing in every direction into the woods, as at the breaking up of some nocturnal conventicle[9]. The very dew seemed to hang upon the trees later into the day than usual, as on the sides of mountains.

This small lake was of most value as a neighbor in the intervals of a gentle rain-storm in August, when, both air and water being perfectly still, but the sky overcast, mid-afternoon had all the serenity of evening, and the wood thrush sang around, and was heard from shore to shore. A lake like this is never smoother than at such a time; and the clear portion of the air above it being, shallow and darkened by clouds, the water, full of light and reflections, becomes a lower heaven itself so much the more important. From a hill-top near by, where the wood had been recently cut off, there was a pleasing vista southward across the pond, through a wide indentation in the hills which form the shore there, where their opposite sides sloping toward each other suggested a stream flowing out in that direction through a wooded valley, but stream there was none. That way I looked between and over the near green hills to some distant and higher ones in the horizon, tinged with blue. Indeed, by standing on tiptoe I could catch a glimpse of some of the peaks of the still bluer and more distant mountain ranges in the northwest, those true-blue coins from heaven's own mint, and also of some portion of the village. But in other directions, even from this point, I could not see over or beyond the woods which surrounded me. It is well to have some water in your neighborhood, to give buoyancy to and float the earth. One value even of the smallest well is, that when you look into it you see that earth is not continent but insular. This is as important as that it keeps butter cool. When I looked across the pond from this peak toward the Sudbury meadows, which in time of flood I distinguished elevated perhaps by a mirage in their seething valley, like a coin in a basin, all the earth beyond the pond appeared like a thin crust insulated and floated even by this small sheet of interverting water, and I was reminded that this on which I dwelt was but dry land.

Though the view from my door was still more contracted, I did not feel crowded or confined in the least. There was pasture enough for my imagination. The low shrub oak plateau to which the opposite shore arose stretched away toward the prairies of the West and the steppes of Tartary, affording ample room for all the roving families of men. "There are none happy in the world but beings who enjoy freely a vast horizon"—said Damodara[10], when his herds required new and larger pastures.

Both place and time were changed, and I dwelt nearer to those parts of the universe and to those eras in history which had most attracted me. Where I lived was as far off as many a region viewed nightly by astronomers. We are wont to imagine rare and delectable places in some remote and more celestial corner of the system, behind the constellation of Cassiopeia's Chair[11], far from noise and disturbance. I discovered that my house actually had its site in such a withdrawn, but forever new and unprofaned, part of the universe. If it were worth the while to settle in those parts near to the Pleiades or the Hyades, to Aldebaran or Altair[12], then I was really there, or at an equal remoteness from the life which I had left behind, dwindled and twinkling with as fine a ray to my nearest neighbor, and to be seen only in moonless nights by him. Such was that part of creation where I had squatted,—

"There was a shepherd that did live,
And held his thoughts as high
As were the mounts whereon his flocks
Did hourly feed him by."[13]

What should we think of the shepherd's life if his flocks always wandered to higher pastures than his thoughts?

【注解】

1. premises: 房屋及其附属的土地。
2. cultivated it, and him too to some extent: 耕耘了那片田地，在某种程度上，也耕耘了他的心田。
3. "I am monarch of all I *survey*, / My right there is none to dispute.": "我勘察一切，像个皇帝，/ 谁也不能否认我的权利。"引自英国诗人威廉·考珀 (William Cowper, 1731—1800) 写的 "Verses Supposed to Be Written by Alexander Selkirk"。塞尔柯克是笛福小说《鲁滨孙漂流记》中主人公鲁滨孙的原型。这里 "survey" 一词斜体，一语双关，暗示梭罗曾做过土地测量员 (surveyor)，也有观看之意。
4. Atlas: 阿特拉斯，希腊神话中的神，提坦巨人伊阿珀托斯和克吕墨涅 (或亚细亚) 之子。据传他曾参加反对众神之首宙斯的战争，为此受到惩罚，让他用头和手将天空高高举起。

5. Old Cato, whose "De Re Rusticâ": 指大加图和他的《农书》。大加图 (Old Cato, 234 BCE—149 BCE), 罗马政治家, 演说家, 著名的拉丁散文作家,《农书》(De Re Rusticâ, 又称 De Agri Cultura) 是他流传至今的唯一著作。
6. Olympus: 奥林匹斯山, 希腊神话中众神居住之地。
7. Harivansa: 印度五世纪的宗教史诗。
8. Concord Battle Ground: 康科德战场, 美国独立战争期间的著名战场。独立战争开始的第一天, 即 1775 年 4 月 19 日, 美英双方军队在此遭遇。
9. nocturnal conventicle: 夜间举行的秘密宗教集会。
10. Damodara: 达摩达拉, 又名讫里什那 (Krishna), 印度神话中象征丰收和幸福的牧牛神。
11. Cassiopeia's Chair: 仙后座。
12. the Pleiades or the Hyades, to Aldebaran or Altair: 昴星团或毕星团, 金牛星座或天鹰星座。Pleiades 为昴星团, 金牛星座中的疏散星团, 其中有六七颗明亮的恒星肉眼可以看到。根据希腊神话, 它们由阿特拉斯 (Atlas) 与布莱娥妮 (Pleione) 所生的七个女儿变成。Hyades 为毕星团, 金牛星座中的星团, 其中毕宿五 (Aldebaran) 是金牛星座中最亮的恒星。Altair 指牵牛星, 天鹰星座中最亮的恒星。
13. "There was a shepherd that did live, /And held his thoughts as high/ As were the mounts whereon his flocks/Did hourly feed him by.": 英国国王詹姆斯一世 (James I, 1603—1625 在位) 时代无名诗人写的诗歌。

【思考题】

1. When Thoreau says, "A man is rich in proportion to the number of things which he can afford to let alone," what does he mean?
2. What kind of life does Thoreau advocate?
3. When Thoreau says, "Olympus is but the outside of the earth everywhere," what does he mean?
4. What is the significance of the paragraph beginning with "The only house I had been the owner of before," and ending with "the wood thrush, the veery, the scarlet tanager, the field sparrow, the whip-poor-will, and many others"?
5. How will you answer the question Thoreau asks at the end of this selection?
6. In *Walden*, Thoreau quotes "the Four Books" of Confucianism ten times. Please make a comment on the similarities and differences between the ideas of Thoreau and Confucianism.

解读举例

1.《瓦尔登湖》强调人的自我修养, 自我完善, 提倡在孤独、简朴的生活中, 以婴孩的纯真，寻找生命的本质，挖掘人性中的潜力，使人的精神境界更完美、自由，与自然更完全地融为一体，达到精神的无限自由。

2. 《瓦尔登湖》是对现代西方物质文明的叛逆和摒斥，批判了当时的拜金主义和物质主义，否定工业文明带来的物质进步，旨在把人类从精神的沉睡中和思想的禁锢中唤醒、解放出来，使他们意识到自己过着"非生活的生活"，呼吁人们开拓真正的生活。

3. 《瓦尔登湖》是超验主义的宣言。自然反映了人的精神，是人物化、异化了的意识。它不仅揭示了物质规律，也蕴含着道德真理。梭罗更将自然看作是人类活动的舞台。

4. 《瓦尔登湖》是生态批评的范本，既有对美丽自然风光的陶醉，也有对人们破坏自然的愤怒，表现了梭罗对大自然本身的热爱，提倡人应与自然和谐共处。

Walt Whitman
1819—1892

沃特·惠特曼是美国19世纪伟大的浪漫主义诗人，他的诗歌从形式到内容都与传统诗歌有所区别，极具开创性。惠特曼的创新精神完全可与英国浪漫主义诗人华兹华斯相媲美。

惠特曼出生于纽约长岛的一个普通农民家庭，1823年随全家迁往布鲁克林。由于出身贫寒，惠特曼11岁时就离开了学校开始工作，由此开启了不平凡的人生：他在公司、医院里打过杂，当过印刷工，做过教师，当过编辑，积极参与各种政治活动，还当过记者、泥瓦匠、木匠、承包商、义工等，并最终在司法部当了一名职员，后由于身体原因被辞退。如此丰富的人生经历给他的诗歌创作带来了不竭的源泉，也使他具有了一种包罗万象的广阔胸襟。在《自我之歌》("Song of Myself") 中，他宣称："沃特·惠特曼，一个宇宙，曼哈顿的儿子……/ 我是一个南方人，也是一个北方人，一个对人冷淡而又好客的阿可尼河边的农民……"。值得注意的是，无论身处何种境遇，诗人都从未放弃对知识的热爱和追求，没有放弃他对诗歌的创作热情。即使在其诗集《草叶集》(Leaves of Grass, 1855) 出版后遭受长达 20 年的冷落，他也从未放弃过诗歌创作，而是在逆境中愈发勤奋，并最终赢得了认可和尊重，《草叶集》更是被公认为美国 19 世纪最伟大的浪漫主义诗作，成为惠特曼的代表作。早在十几岁时，惠特曼就开始了他的诗歌创作，最初以创作传统诗歌为主。其真正具有开创性的诗歌创作则始于 1848 年夏天他回到纽约后的那段时间。在随后的几年里，他结识了一批布鲁克林的艺术家，并受到了深刻的影响。那时，他还经常利用记者的身份去聆听当时著名歌唱家们演唱的歌剧，这对惠特曼的影响也是不容忽视的：惠特曼甚至说过要不是受到歌剧的"情感、狂喜、激励和陶冶"的影响，他就不可能创作出《草叶集》。爱默生在读过《草叶集》后，撰文大加赞扬，说惠特曼正"处于一个伟大生涯的开端，而这样一个开端必定是经过某个阶段的长期准备的"。在《草叶集》的版权页后是一篇洋洋洒洒长达十页的无题文章，段落很长，标点看上去全像省略号，但文章读起来却像演讲般的通畅。在这篇类似宣言的文章里，惠特曼声称美国诗人不应该谴责和背弃过去的信仰，而应积极吸收融合，美国本身就是由不同民族融合而成的；他们不应反对科学及历史的各个分支，而应从中寻找激励和支持；他们所创作的诗歌不应是逃避现实和虚幻的，而应是顺应历史现实，并可以得到证实的知识。他还号召美国诗人对诗歌的形式、语言、内容等各个方面都要进行大胆的革新，并在自己的诗歌创作中身体力行。

总的说来，惠特曼的自由诗有这几个特征：①内在的音乐与节奏 (under-melody and rhythm)，即废除传统格式与韵律，采用更为自由的诗律，体现出一种自然的节拍，较之于听觉上的节奏，惠特曼更为强调"视觉的节奏"(eye rhythm)；②诗行中多用倒装、宕笔 (suspension)、呼语 (apostrophe)、谐音 (assonance)、辅音连缀 (consonantial clusters)、头韵 (alliteration)、拟声 (onomatopoeia) 等手法；③句式与词语重复以产生节奏感；④歌剧吟唱风格 (operatic aria and recitative)；⑤响亮、激昂的情感与鲜明的象征，给人一种预言家般的气魄。惠特曼毫不怀疑英语的表达力，认为它是一种"可以表达那些无法表达的东西的媒介"。

在内容上，惠特曼则认为美国诗歌不应当重复古典派诗人的无病呻吟，也不应当推广朗费罗等人道德说教般的诗歌。无论是风格还是内容方面的夸张都应被"真"所取代，被事物的原貌所取代，诗歌应该具有人民性。惠特曼十分自信地认为他可以把文学阶层扩大到所有的人："诗人的最好证明就是他能够像国家包容他那样热情地去包容国家。"

1861 年，美国爆发内战。1862 年，惠特曼曾到战场看望伤病员，内心受到极大震动，此后开始创作与内战有关的诗歌，并于 1865 年结集出版，题名《桴鼓集》(Drum Taps)，翌年出版《桴鼓集续集》(Sequel to Drum Taps)。其中的名篇有惠特曼为悲悼内战胜利后却遇刺倒下的林肯总统而创作的《最近紫丁香在庭院里开放的时候》("When Lilacs Last in the Dooryard Bloom'd") 和《哦，船长！我的船长！》("O Captain! My Captain")。1871 年，惠特曼发表《民主远景》(*Democratic Vistas*)，以内战后南方重建过程中的种种腐败弊端为例，表明了他对美国民主的极大失望。他认为美国正在成为一个庸俗、追求物质享受的社会。1881 年，第七版《草叶集》问世，其内容形式基本固定。1889 年出版袖珍版《草叶集》，收录了《11 月的枝丫》("November Boughs", 1888) 和《回顾曾经走过的道路》("A Backward Glance o'er Travel'd Roads") 等新诗。惠特曼去世后《草叶集》又出版了第九版，即"临死版"(*Death-Bed Edition*，又曰"作者认可版")《草叶集》。

惠特曼用其一生为世人提供了一个忠于艺术的范例。不论世人对其接受与否，无论作家和评论家对其如何评价，他都始终坚持走自己的道路，终生无悔。他用博大的胸怀、过人的魄力、坚韧的精神、执拗的个性及不拘一格的诗歌创作为后人留下了一笔宝贵的财富。

Song of Myself

【题解】

《自我之歌》是惠特曼历经十几年辛勤创作的成果，是《草叶集》初版的开卷之作，起初并无标题，在第二版 (1856) 时诗人将其命名为《沃特·惠特曼，一个美国人的诗》，第三版 (1860) 时易名为《沃特·惠特曼》，直到第四版 (1881) 时才最后定名为《自我之歌》。全诗内涵深广，情感激越，气势磅礴，颇有雄顾全书之势。

《自我之歌》是《草叶集》中的经典之作，亦是《草叶集》的精神总领，体现了《草叶集》的基本主题。在这首长达 52 节的诗歌中，诗人探讨人生，歌唱自我，以一种博大的胸怀去拥抱全世界，歌颂普通人的崇高和伟大，是一首典型的惠特曼式的浪漫自我之歌。

以下节选第 1、6、16、17、24、42、51、52 诗节。

From Song of Myself

1

I celebrate myself, and sing myself,
And what I assume you shall assume,

For every atom belonging to me as good belongs to you.

I loafe[1] and invite my soul,
I lean and loafe at my ease observing a spear of summer grass.　　　　　　5

My tongue, every atom of my blood, form'd from this soil, this air,
Born here of parents born here from parents the same, and their parents the same,
I, now thirty-seven years old in perfect health begin,
Hoping to cease not till death.

Creeds and schools in abeyance,　　　　　　10
Retiring back a while sufficed at what they are, but never forgotten,
I harbor for good or bad, I permit to speak at every hazard,
Nature without check with original energy.

6

A child said *What is the grass*? fetching it to me with full hands;
How could I answer the child? I do not know what it is any more than he.　　　　　　15

I guess it must be the flag of my disposition[2], out of hopeful green stuff woven.

Or I guess it is the handkerchief of the Lord,
A scented gift and remembrancer[3] designedly dropt,
Bearing the owner's name someway in the corners, that we may see and remark, and say *Whose*?

Or I guess the grass is itself a child, the produced babe of the vegetation.　　　　　　20

Or I guess it is a uniform hieroglyphic,
And it means, Sprouting alike in broad zones and narrow zones,
Growing among black folks as among white,
Kanuck, Tuckahoe, Congressman, Cuff[4], I give them the same, I receive them the same.

. . .

What do you think has become of the young and old men? 25
And what do you think has become of the women and children?
They are alive and well somewhere,
The smallest sprout shows there is really no death,
And if ever there was it led forward life, and does not wait at the end to arrest it,
And ceas'd the moment life appear'd. 30

All goes onward and outward, nothing collapses,
And to die is different from what any one supposed, and luckier.

16

I am of old and young, of the foolish as much as the wise,
Regardless of others, ever regardful of others,
Maternal as well as paternal, a child as well as a man, 35
Stuff'd with the stuff that is coarse and stuff'd with the stuff that is fine,
One of the Nation of many nations, the smallest the same
  and the largest the same,
A Southerner soon as a Northerner, a planter nonchalant
  and hospitable down by the Oconee[5] I live, 40
A Yankee bound my own way ready for trade, my joints the
  limberest joints on earth and the sternest joints on earth,
A Kentuckian walking the vale of the Elkhorn in my deer-skin
  leggings, a Louisianian or Georgian,

. . .

Of every hue and caste am I, of every rank and religion, 45
A farmer, mechanic, artist, gentleman, sailor, quaker,
Prisoner, fancy-man, rowdy, lawyer, physician, priest.
I resist any thing better than my own diversity,
Breathe the air but leave plenty after me,
And am not stuck up, and am in my place. 50
(The moth and the fish-eggs are in their place,
The bright suns I see and the dark suns I cannot see are in

their place,
The palpable is in its place and the impalpable is in its place.)

17

These are really the thoughts of all men in all ages and lands, they are not original
    with me,   55
If they are not yours as much as mine they are nothing, or next to nothing
If they are not the riddle and the untying of the riddle they are nothing,
If they are not just as close as they are distant they are nothing.
This is the grass that grows wherever the land is and the water is,
This the common air that bathes the globe.   60

24

Walt Whitman, a kosmos[6], of Manhattan the son,
Turbulent, fleshy, sensual, eating, drinking and breeding.
No sentimentalist, no stander above men and women or apart from them,
No more modest than immodest.

Unscrew the locks from the doors!   65
Unscrew the doors themselves from their jambs!

Whoever degrades another degrades me,
And whatever is done or said returns at last to me.

Through me the afflatus[7] surging and surging, through me the
    current and index.   70

I speak the pass-word primeval, I give the sign of democracy,
By God! I will accept nothing which all cannot have their counterpart of on the same
    terms.

Through me many long dumb voices,
Voices of the interminable generations of prisoners and slaves,

Voices of the diseas'd and despairing and of thieves and dwarfs, 75
Voices of cycles of preparation and accretion,
And of the threads that connect the stars, and of wombs
      and of the father-stuff,
And of the rights of them the others are down upon,
Of the deform'd, trivial, flat, foolish, despised, 80
Fog in the air, beetles rolling balls of dung.
Through me forbidden voices,
Voices of sexes and lusts, voices veil'd and I remove the veil,
Voices indecent by me clarified and transfigur'd.

I do not press my fingers across my mouth, 85
I keep as delicate around the bowels as around the head and heart,
Copulation is no more rank to me than death is.

I believe in the flesh and the appetites,
Seeing, hearing, feeling, are miracles, and each part and tag of me is a miracle.

Divine am I inside and out, and I make holy whatever I touch 90
      or am touch'd from,
The scent of these arm-pits aroma finer than prayer,
This head more than churches, bibles, and all the creeds.

If I worship one thing more than another it shall be the spread of my own body,
      or any part of it,
Translucent mould of me it shall be you! 95
Shaded ledges and rests it shall be you!
Firm masculine colter[8] it shall be you!
Whatever goes to the tilth[9] of me it shall be you!
You my rich blood! your milky stream pale strippings of my life!
Breast that presses against other breasts it shall be you! 100
My brain it shall be your occult convolutions!
Root of wash'd sweet-flag! timorous pond-snipe! nest of

guarded duplicate eggs! it shall be you!

Mix'd tussled hay of head, beard, brawn, it shall be you!

Trickling sap of maple, fibre of manly wheat, it shall be you! 105

Sun so generous it shall be you!

Vapors lighting and shading my face it shall be you!

You sweaty brooks and dews it shall be you!

Winds whose soft-tickling genitals rub against me it shall be you!

Broad muscular fields, branches of live oak, loving lounger in my winding paths, it shall be you! 110

Hands I have taken, face I have kiss'd, mortal I have ever touch'd, it shall be you.

42

. . .

This is the city and I am one of the citizens,

Whatever interests the rest interests me, politics, wars, markets, newspapers, schools,

The mayor and councils, banks, tariffs, steamships, factories, stocks, stores, real estate and personal estate.

The little plentiful manikins[10] skipping around in collars and taile'd coats, 115

I am aware who they are, (they are positively not worms or fleas.)

I acknowledge the duplicates of myself, the weakest and shallowest is deathless with me,

What I do and say the same waits for them,

Every thought that flounders in me the same flounders in them.

I know perfectly well my own egotism, 120

Know my omnivorous[11] lines and must not write any less,

And would fetch you whoever you are flush with myself.

Not words of routine this song of mine,

But abruptly to question, to leap beyond yet nearer bring; . . .

51

The past and present wilt—I have fill'd them, emptied them, 125
And proceed to fill my next fold of the future.

Listener up there! what have you to confide to me?
Look in my face while I snuff the sidle of evening[12],
(Talk honestly, no one else hears you, and I stay only a minute longer.)
Do I contradict myself? 130
Very well then I contradict myself,
(I am large, I contain multitudes.)

I concentrate toward them that are nigh, I wait on the door-slab.
Who has done his day's work? who will soonest be through with his supper?
Who wishes to walk with me? 135

Will you speak before I am gone? will you prove already too late?

52

The spotted hawk swoops by and accuses me, he complains of my gab and my loitering.

I too am not a bit tamed, I too am untranslatable,
I sound my barbaric yawp over the roofs of the world.

The last scud of day[13] holds back for me, 140
It flings my likeness after the rest and true as any on the shadow'd wilds,
It coaxes me to the vapor and the dusk.

I depart as air, I shake my white locks at the runaway sun,
I effuse my flesh in eddies, and drift it in lacy jags.
I bequeath myself to the dirt to grow from the grass I love, 145
If you want me again look for me under your boot-soles.

You will hardly know who I am or what I mean,
But I shall be good health to you nevertheless,
And filter and fibre your blood.

Failing to fetch me at first keep encouraged, 150
Missing me one place search another,
I stop somewhere waiting for you.

【注解】

1. loafe：相当于 loaf。
2. my disposition：我性格的象征。
3. remembrancer：相当于 reminder。
4. Kanuck, Tuckahoe, Congressman, Cuff：法裔加拿大人、弗吉尼亚人、议会会员、黑人。Cuff 一词源自非洲，原拼为 cuffee。
5. the Oconee：佐治亚中部一河流。
6. kosmos：相当于 cosmos。
7. afflatus：灵感。
8. colter：犁头。
9. tilth：犁地，此处喻指个人发展。
10. manikins：矮子，侏儒。
11. omnivorous：包罗万象的。
12. snuff the sidle of evening：熄灭落日的余晖。
13. last scud of day：被风吹散的云或落日的余晖。

【思考题】

1. According to line 1 of Section 1, whom is the poet celebrating? Whom do lines 2–3 also include in the celebration?
2. What facts about himself does Whitman reveal in lines 6–9 of Section 1?
3. Who fetches the grass in Section 6? What does Whitman guess the grass might be? What does the "smallest sprout" show?
4. According to Section 17, are Whitman's thoughts original? Whose thoughts are they?
5. What does Whitman say he knows "perfectly well" in Section 42? What does he say his song is not? According to this section, what is the purpose of his song?
6. In Section 51, what explanation does the poet give for contradicting himself?
7. To what animal does Whitman compare himself in Section 52? What does he sound "over

the roofs of the world"? Where does he tell us to look for him if we want him again?
8. Consider the image of the grass in Section 6 and Section 52. What does the grass have to do with life and death?
9. By associating himself with the grass, what does the poet suggest about himself? Summarize Whitman's attitude toward nature.

【简评】

　　《自我之歌》中的"自我"既是惠特曼本人，又代表着19世纪普通的美国人。在诗的第一节和最后一节，诗人描写了一个具有象征性的"自我"，他"辽阔广大，包罗万象"，代表着人、自然、宇宙万物和一切美好的东西；而在诗的中间则是一个具体的"自我"。《自我之歌》的第六节体现了《草叶集》的中心象征：草。"草是什么？"孩童捧着草问诗人。这个简单又天真的问题让诗人感到困惑：也许"草本身就是个孩子"，也许草是"上帝的手绢"。于是草这个自然界最普通不过的植物被赋予了神性，而这种神性又与孩子这个普普通通的生命联系到了一起，因此即使"最细小的抽芽也表明其实没有死亡"。生命与死亡只是一种循环，如同四季更迭。更重要的是，草无处不在、普通寻常的属性还象征着广大草根阶层。诗人表明自己不仅热爱他们，还是他们中的一分子。同样，在第17节中，诗人再次表明了自我的广泛性：他的思想即"所有人的思想，不分年龄，无论国度"。第24节中，诗人自称为"宇宙"，再次表明了"自我"的核心内涵，即"自我"与所有人的命运休戚相关、荣辱与共，"自我"热爱所有人。第45节中，诗人除了将"自我"等同于全人类外，还赋予了"自我"预言家的身份，他宣称："最柔弱和最肤浅的人都将与我一起永生"。《自我之歌》的最后两节则是在向读者告别，同时也从读者的角度表明了《自我之歌》的复杂性："我在自相矛盾吗？/那好吧就让我自相矛盾吧,/(我胸怀博大，我包容万千。)"诗人相信自己的诗总会被人理解，因此"一个地方找不到我就另找一个, / 我在某个地方停下脚步等待你们"。如同惠特曼的绝大多数诗作，《自我之歌》用自由诗体写成，其韵律、节奏、诗行长度、标点符号等基本不受传统诗律限制，而是我行我素，恣肆纵横，激情奔放，舒卷自如，充分体现了《自我之歌》自由、开放的思想主题与精神特征。这种来源于意大利古典歌剧和《钦定版圣经》的诗歌韵律被惠特曼成功地移植到美国诗歌中，并极大地影响着美国现代诗歌的发展。埃兹拉·庞德(Ezra Pound,1885—1972)、威廉·卡洛斯·威廉姆斯(William Carlos Williams, 1883—1963)、华莱士·史蒂文斯(Stevens Wallace, 1879—1955)、艾伦·金斯堡(Allen Ginsberg, 1926—1997)等都深受惠特曼影响。

O Captain! My Captain!

【题解】

《哦,船长!我的船长》写于美国第16任总统亚伯拉罕·林肯被刺后不久,是惠特曼最脍炙人口的诗篇之一。在诗中,诗人将美国比作一艘航船,将林肯比作船长,将美国内战比作"可怕的航行"。就在航船越过惊涛骇浪,经过艰难险阻即将到达胜利的彼岸时,船长却倒下了。全诗感情深厚,气势磅礴,将惠特曼及美国人民对林肯的挚爱与怀念表达得淋漓尽致,被美国现代诗人卡尔·桑德堡誉为"最奇幻,最富象征性"的林肯挽歌。

O Captain! My Captain!

O Captain! My Captain! our fearful trip is done,
The ship has weather'd every rack, the prize we sought is won,
The port is near, the bells I hear, the people all exulting,
While follow eyes the steady keel, the vessel grim and daring;
    But O heart! heart! heart!   5
     O the bleeding drops of red,
      Where on the deck my Captain lies,
       Fallen cold and dead.

O Captain! My Captain! rise up and hear the bells;
Rise up—for you the flag is flung—for you the bugle trills,   10
For you bouquets and ribbon'd wreaths—for you the shores
    a-crowding,
For you they call, the swaying mass, their eager faces turning;
    Here Captain! dear father!
     This arm beneath your head!   15
      It is some dream that on the deck,
       You've fallen cold and dead.

My Captain does not answer, his lips are pale and still,
My father does not feel my arm, he has no pulse nor will,
The ship is anchor'd safe and sound, its voyage closed and done,   20
From fearful trip the victor ship comes in with object won;
  Exult O shores, and ring O bells!
   But I with mournful tread,
    Walk the deck my Captain lies,
     Fallen cold and dead.   25

【思考题】

1. Compare this with Whitman's other poems. (See another elegy for Lincoln, "When Lilacs Last in the Dooryard Bloom'd".) In what ways is "O Captain! My Captain!" uncharacteristic of his works?
2. Study the poem's rhythms and comment on the appropriateness of the rhythms to the poem's subjects.
3. Whitman compares Lincoln to a captain and a father. What do you think of his comparison? Would other comparisons be more appropriate and passionate?

Herman Melville
1819—1891

  赫曼·麦尔维尔是个具有传奇色彩的人物。他只有小学文化,却通过自己的努力成为美国最伟大的作家之一。

  麦尔维尔出生于纽约。1832年,麦尔维尔的父亲突然病故,身后留下一大笔债务。几个月后,年仅12岁的麦尔维尔辍学回家,到一家银行当职员,3年后又到兄弟甘瑟福特的帽子店打工。18岁那年,麦尔维尔到离家不远的乡村小学教书,翌年入读奥尔伯尼兰新堡学院。1839年,因找不着工作,麦尔维尔报名到一艘前往利物浦的三桅船上当水手,首次体验到了远洋船上的艰苦生活。1841年新年刚过,他又登上了一条前往南太平洋的捕鲸船。18个月后,麦尔维尔由于种种原因在马克萨斯群岛的努卡希瓦弃船上岸，不慎进入素有"食人生番"之名的泰皮人部落。两周后，麦尔维尔搭上另一条捕鲸船逃离努卡希瓦岛，但又因参与该船水手的哗变而被捕，被囚禁在塔希提岛。候审期间他和朋友逃到埃米奥岛，在一个土豆种植园打工。1842年，麦尔维尔又搭上另一条捕鲸船，并于翌年四月在夏威夷的檀香山上岸。在那里他目睹了号称代表文明的白人对当地土著居民的剥削与欺压，激起了他极大的愤慨。这些经历与见闻在他的第二本小说《奥摩》(*Omoo*, 1847) 中均有描述。4个月后，麦尔维尔又到"美国"号三桅军舰上当了一名普通水手。军队残酷、暴虐、摧残人性的纪律与权威使他受到极大震动。这些经历后来都成为他两部小说《白外套》(*White Jacket*, 1850) 和《比利·巴德》(*Billy Budd*, 1924) 的重要素材。

经过一年多的航行后，麦尔维尔终于在1844年10月抵达波士顿后告别水手生涯，时年25岁。此后不久，他便开始写作，以自己在泰皮岛等地的经历为素材，先后创作出了《泰皮》(*Typee*, 1846) 及续集《奥摩》。作品描写了海上冒险和异域奇闻，在英国发表后大受欢迎，麦尔维尔也一举成名。

成功后，麦尔维尔娶了马萨诸塞州大法官的女儿伊丽莎白为妻。他很快又投入到第三部小说《玛地》(*Mardi*, 1849) 的创作之中，但发表后却因作品冗长、呆板，寓言与思辨内容过多，以及形式上的标新立异等原因受到冷落。出于经济的考虑，麦尔维尔很快又创作出版了他自称"无玄思，只有糕点和啤酒"的《雷德本》(*Redburn*, 1849) 和《白外套》，重新获得了读者的认可。1850年麦尔维尔开始创作《鲸鱼》(*The Whale*)，翌年改名《莫比·狄克》(*Moby Dick*, 1851，又译《白鲸》，以下用此译名）。然而由于在思想主题与表现手法上的超前性，《白鲸》出版后并没有受到欢迎，反而恶评如潮。一位叫亨利·考利的评论家在《伦敦雅典娜神庙》发表文章称《白鲸》"是一部浪漫加现实的拙劣混合物。作者显然了解故事叙述应连贯完整，但却在写作过程中一而再，再而三地忽略这一概念。他故事的风格在许多地方由于其疯狂的（而非蹩脚的）英语而面目全非……对于这样一部荒唐的作品，我们没什么可谴责的，也没什么好推荐的"。麦尔维尔显然也预料到了类似的评论，在给霍桑的一封信中表示："在五个年轮中，不会有一个聪明人会期待《白鲸》得到自己的朋友，或任何一个人的欣赏和承认。"在霍桑的建议下，麦尔维尔重写了《白鲸》，并将作品题献给霍桑。完成后的《白鲸》篇幅更长，手法更新，内容更丰富，思想也变得更加深刻。将所有这些主题串联到一起的是作者麦尔维尔对人类终极真理的不懈探索。

与《白鲸》的命运相仿，此后发表的《皮埃尔》(*Pierre*, 1852)、《以斯里尔·波特》(*Israel Potter*, 1855)、《骗子》(*The Confidence Man*, 1857) 等作品也同样不受好评，甚至有人以"麦尔维尔疯了"为题发表评论，指责《皮埃尔》是一本"不道德"的书。社会评论对他作品的不理解与偏执给了麦尔维尔沉重的打击。失望与愤懑之余，他决定从此搁笔，不再创作长篇小说。除了1856年发表的《比萨故事集》(*The Piazza Tales*) 外，麦尔维尔晚年的创作成果主要是诗歌，包括《战争诗集》(*Battle-Pieces and Aspects of the War*, 1866) 和长达18 000行的《克拉瑞尔》(*Clarel*, 1876)。1885年左右，麦尔维尔开始修改一首表现一名英国水手的诗歌的前言，经过再三扩充，前言演变为一部中篇小说《比利·巴德》。在麦尔维尔生命的最后几年，已有人开始认识到他的超前与伟大。一位叫罗伯特·布宪南的评论家认为麦尔维尔是一位足以与惠特曼比肩的伟大作家。

在他去世后不久，英美两国重新出版了《泰皮》《奥摩》《白外套》《白鲸》四部作品。然而他真正开始被"重新发现"则是在他百年诞辰之际。1917年，美国作家、评论家卡尔·范·多伦 (Carl Van Doren, 1885—1950) 率先发现了麦尔维尔的价值，在其1921年出版的《美国小说》第三章中专辟一节论述麦尔维尔的文学创作与成就，称其为"美国浪漫主义的顶峰"。英国著名小说家D. H. 劳伦斯也撰文称赞麦尔维尔为"伟大的海洋诗人"。1941年，美国评论家F. O. 马蒂桑 (F. O. Matthiessen, 1902—1950) 在《美国文艺复兴：爱默生与惠特曼时代的艺术与表现》(*American Renaissance: Art and Expression in the Age of Emerson and Whitman*) 中将爱默生、惠特曼、梭罗、霍桑和麦尔维尔并称为美国内战后文学的巨擘。如今，麦尔维尔已被认为是美国文学史上最伟大作家之一，《白鲸》也已成为美国文学的经典。

麦尔维尔在20世纪初被"重新发现"有许多原因。一个重要原因是第一次世界大战彻底摧毁了许多人对西方文明及其价值体系所持有的信念，而麦尔维尔在小说创作中思想与艺术的大胆革新正好顺应了人们在战后对新观念、新文学表现方式的强烈要求，并成为美国及西方现代派、后现代派创作的重要参照。从这个意义上说，麦尔维尔已经超越了历史，他的《白鲸》也常被当作后现代文本来阅读和研究。

Moby Dick

【题解】

《白鲸》共135章，是一部结构复杂、意象层叠、寓意丰富的作品。它既是一部史诗般的海上冒险小说，又是一部研究鲸鱼和捕鲸业的百科全书。作者通过对埃哈伯、伊希梅尔等人物的刻画和对捕鲸船与大白鲸莫比·狄克在海上激烈搏斗的描写，展现了人与自然、人与命运之间的冲突，同时也探讨了善与恶、生与死、宏观世界与微观世界等关系人类命运的重大主题，赋予作品深刻的象征性与寓言性。美国著名文学评论家罗伯特·斯皮勒 (Robert E. Spiller) 认为《白鲸》是麦尔维尔为美国文学创造出的"悲剧或普罗米修斯式的史诗"。

  《白鲸》的叙述者伊希梅尔由于厌倦了在曼哈顿的生活，便报名到皮奎德号捕鲸船上当一名水手。船长埃哈伯从事捕鲸业四十余年，在一次出海时被一条名叫莫比·狄克的大白鲸咬掉一条腿。他发誓一定要不惜一切代价捕杀这条鲸鱼。大副斯达巴克企图阻止这种疯狂的行为，但无济于事。他们横贯大西洋，绕过好望角进入印度洋，然后又驶入太平洋，沿途捕杀鲸鱼，炼出大桶大桶的鲸油。一次一名叫作费德拉的神秘船员预言，埃哈伯将在海上看到两只古怪的棺架后被绞死。这两只棺架一只用美国的木材制造，另一只则非人工制造。费德拉还说自己将死在埃哈伯前面，以便当他的"领航人"。对于费德拉的预言，埃哈伯毫不放在心上，海上哪儿来的棺架？于是他继续追踪莫比·狄克。终于有一天，在波涛汹涌的大海中他看见了莫比·狄克。他驾船急追，与大白鲸展开了殊死的搏斗，捕鲸艇受到了接二连三地冲撞，费德拉也落入水中。第三天，当大白鲸再次浮现水面时，埃哈伯看见费德拉的尸体被绳索、鱼叉缠绕在白鲸身上——一个非人工的棺架！接着大白鲸又撞毁了赶来救援的捕鲸船。埃哈伯这才明白这条船原来就是费德拉预言所指的用美国木材制造的棺架。这时白鲸突然拉紧缠结着的绳子，正好把埃哈伯的脖子套了进去，顷刻之间，埃哈伯就被绞死。海面上除了皮奎德号下沉时造成的漩涡外，一切都消失得无影无踪。伊希梅尔在落水后不久被赶来搜寻失踪船员的拉吉号捕鲸船救起。

  下文为第三十六章"后甲板"和第四十二章"白鲸的白色"的片段。在第三十六章中，船长埃哈伯向全体船员宣布了他追杀白鲸的决心。第四十二章则表现了大白鲸白色的各种象征意义。

From Moby Dick

Chapter 36
Quarter-Deck

(Enter Ahab: Then, all.)

It was not a great while after the affair of the pipe[1], that one morning shortly after breakfast, Ahab, as was his wont, ascended the cabin-gangway to the deck. There most sea captains usually walk at that hour, as country gentlemen, after the same meal, take a few turns in the garden.

Soon his steady, ivory stride[2] was heard, as to and fro he paced his old rounds, upon planks so familiar to his tread, that they were all over dented, like geological stones, with the peculiar mark of his walk. Did you fixedly gaze, too, upon that ribbed and dented brow; there also, you would see still stranger foot-prints—the foot-prints of his one unsleeping, ever-pacing thought.

But on the occasion in question, those dents looked deeper, even as his nervous step that morning left a deeper mark. And, so full of his thought was Ahab, that at every uniform turn that he made, now at the main-mast and now at the binnacle, you could almost see that thought turn in him as he turned, and pace in him as he paced; so completely possessing him, indeed, that it all but seemed the inward mould of every outer movement.

"D'ye mark him, Flask?" whispered Stubb; "the chick that's in him pecks the shell". "'Twill soon be out."

The hours wore on;—Ahab now shut up within his cabin; anon, pacing the deck, with the same intense bigotry of purpose in his aspect.

It drew near the close of day. Suddenly he came to a halt by the bulwarks, and inserting his bone into the auger-hole there, and with one hand grasping a shroud, he ordered Starbuck to send everybody aft.

"Sir!" said the mate, astonished at an order seldom or never given on ship-board except in some extraordinary case.

"Send everybody aft," repeated Ahab. "Mast-heads, there! come down!"

When the entire ship's company were assembled, and with curious and not wholly unapprehensive faces, were eyeing him, for he looked not unlike the weather horizon when a storm is coming up, Ahab, after rapidly glancing over the bulwarks, and then darting his eyes among the crew, started from his stand-point; and as though not a soul were nigh him resumed his heavy turns upon the deck. With bent head and half-slouched hat he continued to pace, unmindful of the wondering whispering among the men; till Stubb cautiously whispered to Flask, that Ahab must have summoned them there for the purpose of witnessing a pedestrian feat. But this did not last long. Vehemently pausing, he cried:—

"What do ye do when ye see a whale, men?"

"Sing out for him!" was the impulsive rejoinder from a score of clubbed voices.

"Good!" cried Ahab, with a wild approval in his tones; observing the hearty animation into which his unexpected question had so magnetically thrown them.

"And what do ye next, men?"

"Lower away[3], and after him!"

"And what tune is it ye pull to, men?[4]"

"A dead whale or a stove boat!"

More and more strangely and fiercely glad and approving, grew the countenance of the old man at every shout; while the mariners began to gaze curiously at each other, as if marvelling how it was that they themselves became so excited at such seemingly purposeless questions.

But, they were all eagerness again, as Ahab, now half-revolving in his pivot-hole, with one hand reaching high up a shroud, and tightly, almost convulsively grasping it, addressed them thus:—

"All ye mast-headers have before now heard me give orders about a white whale. Look ye! D'ye see this Spanish ounce of gold?"—holding up a broad bright coin to the sun—"it is a sixteen dollar piece, men,—a doubloon. D'ye see it? Mr. Starbuck, hand me yon top-maul."

While the mate was getting the hammer, Ahab, without peaking, was lowly rubbing the gold piece against the skirts of his jacket, as if to heighten its lustre, and without using any words was meanwhile lowly humming to himself, producing a sound so strangely muffled and inarticulate that it seemed the mechanical humming of the wheels of his vitality in him.

Receiving the top-maul from Starbuck, he advanced towards the main-mast with the hammer uplifted in one band, exhibiting the gold with the other, and with a high raised voice exclaiming: "Whosoever of ye raises me a white-headed whale with a wrinkled brow and a crooked jaw; whosoever of ye raises me that white-headed whale, with three holes punctured in his starboard fluke-look ye, whosoever of ye raises me that same white whale, he shall have this gold ounce, my boys!"

"Huzza! Huzza!" cried the seamen, as with swinging tarpaulins they hailed the act of nailing the gold to the mast.

"It's a white whale, I say," resumed Ahab, as he threw down the top-maul; "a white whale. Skin your eyes for him, men; look sharp for white water; if ye see but a bubble, sing out".

All this while Tashtego, Daggoo, and Queequeg[5] had looked on with even more intense interest and surprise than the rest, and at the mention of the wrinkled brow and crooked jaw they had started as if each was separately touched by some specific recollection.

"Captain Ahab," said Tashtego, "that white whale must be the same that some call Moby Dick."

"Moby Dick?" shouted Ahab. "Do ye know the white whale then, Tash?"

"Does he fan-tail a little curious, sir, before he goes down?" said the Gay-Header deliberately.

"And has he a curious spout, too," said Daggoo "very bushy, even for a parmacetty[6], and mighty quick, Captain Ahab?"

"And he have one, two, tree[7]—oh! good many iron in him hide, too, Captain," cried Queequeg disjointedly, "all twiske-tee betwisk[8], like him—him—" faltering hard for a word, and screwing his hand round and round as though uncorking a bottle—"like him—him—"

"Corkscrew!" cried Ahab, "aye, Queequeg, the harpoons lie all twisted and wrenched in him; aye, Daggoo, his spout is a big one, like a whole shock of wheat, and white as a pile of our Nantucket[9] wool after the great annual sheep-shearing; aye, Tashtego, and he fan-tails like a split jib in a squall. Death and devils! men, it is Moby Dick ye have seen—Moby Dick—Moby Dick!"

"Captain Ahab," said Starbuck, who, with Stubb and Flask, had thus, far been eyeing his superior with increasing surprise, but at last seemed struck with a thought which somewhat explained all the wonder. "Captain Ahab, I have heard of Moby Dick—but it was not Moby Dick that took off thy leg?"

"Who told thee that?" cried Ahab; then pausing, "Aye, Starbuck; aye, my hearties all round; it was Moby Dick that dismasted me; Moby Dick that brought me to this dead stump I stand on now. Aye, aye," he shouted with a terrific, loud, animal sob, like that of a heart-stricken moose; "Aye, aye! It was that accursed white whale that razeed me; made a poor pegging lubber of me for ever and a day!" Then tossing both arms, with measureless imprecations he shouted out: "Aye, aye! and I'll chase him round Good Hope, and round the Horn, and round the Norway Maelstrom[10], and round perdition's flames before I give him up. And this is what ye have shipped for, men? to chase that white whale on both sides of land, and over all sides of earth, till he spouts black blood and rolls fin out. What say ye, men, will ye splice hands on it, now? I think ye do look brave."

"Aye aye!" shouted the harpooneers, and seamen, running closer to the excited old man: "A sharp eye for the White Whale; a sharp lance for Moby Dick!"

"God bless ye," he seemed to half sob and half shout. "God bless ye, men. Steward! go draw the great measure of grog. But what's this long face about, Mr. Starbuck; wilt thou not chase the white whale? art not game for Moby Dick?"

"I am game for his crooked jaw, and for the jaws of Death too, Captain Ahab, if it fairly comes in the way of the business we follow; but I came here to hunt whales, not my commander's vengeance. How many barrels will thy vengeance yield thee even if thou gettest it, Captain Ahab? it will not fetch thee much in our Nantucket market."

"Nantucket market! Hoot! But come closer, Starbuck; thou requirest a little lower layer[11]. If money's to be the measure, man, and the accountants have computed their great counting-house the globe, by girdling it with guineas, one to every three parts of an inch; then, let me tell thee, that my vengeance will fetch a great premium here!"

"He smites his chest," whispered Stubb, "what's that for? me thinks it rings most vast, but hollow."

"Vengeance on a dumb brute!" cried Starbuck, "that simply smote thee from blindest instinct! Madness! To be enraged with a dumb thing, Captain Ahab, seems blasphemous."

"Hark ye yet again,—the little lower layer. All visible objects, man, are but as pasteboard mask. But in each event—in the living act, the undoubted deed—there, some unknown but still reasoning thing puts forth the mouldings of its features from behind the unreasoning mask. If man will strike, strike through the mask! How can the prisoner reach outside except by thrusting through the wall? To me, the white whale is that wall, shoved near to me. Sometimes I think there's naught beyond. But 'tis enough. He tasks me; he heaps me; I see in him outrageous strength, with an inscrutable malice sinewing it. That inscrutable thing is chiefly what I hate; and be the white whale agent, or be the white whale principal[12]. I will wreak that hate upon him. Talk not to me of blasphemy, man; I'd strike the sun if it insulted me. For could the sun do that, then could I do the other; since there is ever a sort of fair play herein, jealousy presiding over all creations. But not my master, man, is even that fair play. Who's over me? Truth hath no confines. Take off thine eye! More intolerable than fiends' glarings is a doltish stare! So, so; thou reddenest and palest; my heart has melted thee to anger-glow. But look ye, Starbuck, what is said in heat, that thing unsays itself. There are men from whom warm words are small indignity. I meant not to incense thee. Let it go. Look! see yonder Turkish cheeks of spotted tawn— living, breathing picture, painted by the sun. The Pagan leopards—the unrecking and unworshipping things, that live; and seek, and give no reasons, for the torrid life they feel! The crew, man, the crew! Are they not one and all with Ahab, in this matter of the whale? See Stubb! he laughs! See yonder Chilean! he snorts to think of it. Stand up amid the general hurricane, thy one tost sapling cannot, Starbuck! And what is it? Reckon it. 'Tis but to help strike a fin; no wondrous feat for Starbuck. What is it more? From this one poor hunt, then, the best lance out of all Nantucket, surely he will not hang back, when every foremast-hand has clutched a whet-stone? Ah! constrainings, seize thee; I see! the billow lifts thee! Speak, but speak!—Aye, aye! thy silence, then, that voices thee. (Aside) Something shot from my dilated nostrils, he has inhaled it in his lungs. Starbuck now is mine; cannot oppose me now, without rebellion."

"God keep me!—keep us all!" murmured Starbuck, lowly. But in his joy at the enchanted, tacit acquiescence of the mate, Ahab did not hear his foreboding invocation; nor yet the low laugh from the hold[13]; nor yet the presaging vibrations of the wind in the cordage; nor yet the hollow flap of the sails against the masts, as for a moment their hearts sank in. For again Starbuck's downcast eyes lighted up with the stubbornness of life; the subterranean laugh died away; the winds blew on; the sails filled out; the ship heaved and rolled as before. Ah, ye admonitions and warnings! why stay ye not when ye come? But rather are ye predictions, than warnings, ye shadows! Yet not so much predictions from without, as verifications of the foregoing things within. For with little external to constrain us, the innermost necessities in our being, thee still drive us on.

"The measure! the measure!"[14] cried Ahab.

Receiving the brimming pewter, and turning to the harpooneers, he ordered them to produce their weapons. Then ranging them before him near the captain, with their harpoons in their hands, while his three mates stood at his side with their lances, and the rest of the ship's company formed a circle round the group; he stood for an instant searchingly eyeing every man of his crew. But those wild eyes met his, as the bloodshot eyes of the prairie wolves meet the eye of their leader, ere he rushes on at their head in the trail of the bison; but, alas! only to fall into the hidden snare of the Indian.

"Drink and pass!" he cried, handing the heavy charged flagon to the nearest seaman. "The crew alone now drink. Round with it, round! Short draughts—long swallows, men; 'tis hot as Satan's hoof[15]. So so; it goes round excellently. It spiralizes in ye; forks out at the serpent-snapping eye. Well done; almost drained. That way it went, this way it comes. Hand it me—here's a hollow! Men, ye seem the years; so brimming life is gulped and gone. Steward, refill!"

"Attend now, my braves. I have mustered ye all round this capstan; and ye mates, flank me with your lances; and ye harpooneers, stand there with your irons; and ye, stout mariners, ring me in, that I may in some sort revive a noble custom of my fisherman fathers before me. O men, you will yet see that—Hat boy, come back? bad pennies come not sooner[16]. Hand it me. Why, now, this pewter had run brimming again, wert not thou St. Vitus' imp[17]—away, thou ague!"

"Advance, ye mates! Cross your lances full before me. Well done! Let me touch the axis." So saying with extended arm, he grasped the three level, radiating lances, at their crossed centre; while so doing, suddenly and nervously twitched them; meanwhile, glancing intently from Starbuck to Stubb; from Stubb to Flask. It seemed as though, by some nameless, interior volition, he would fain have shocked into them the same fiery emotion accumulated within the Leyden jar[18] of his own magnetic life. The three mates quailed before his strong, sustained, and mystic aspect. Stubb and Flask looked sideways from him; the honest eye of Starbuck fell downright.

"In vain!" cried Ahab, "but, maybe,'tis well. For did ye three but once take the full-forced shock, then mine own electric thing, that had perhaps expired from out me. Perchance, too, it would have dropped ye dead. Perchance ye need it not. Down lances! And now, ye mates, I do appoint ye three cup-bearers to my three pagan kinsmen there—yon three most honorable gentlemen and noblemen, my valiant harpooneers. Disdain the task? What, when the great Pope[19] washes the feet of beggars, using his tiara for ewer? Oh, my sweet cardinals! your own condescension, that shall bend ye to it. I do not order ye; ye will it. Cut your seizings and draw the poles, ye harpooneers!"

Silently obeying the order, the three harpooneers now stood with the detached iron part of their harpoons, some three feet long, held, bards up, before him.

"Stab me not with that keen steel! Cant them; cant them over! know ye not the goblet end? Turn up the socket! So, so; now, ye cup-bearers, advance. The irons! take them; hold them while I fill!" Forthwith, slowly going from one officer to the other, he brimmed the harpoon sockets with the fiery waters from the pewter.

"Now, three to three, ye stand. Commend the murderous chalices[20]! Bestow them, ye who are now made parties to this indissoluble league. Ha! Starbuck! but the deed is done! Yon ratifying sun now waits to sit upon it. Drink, ye harpooneers! drink and swear, ye men that man the deathful whaleboat's bow—Death to Moby Dick! God hunt us all, if we do not hunt Moby Dick to his death!" The long, barbed steel goblets were lifted; and to cries and maledictions against the white whale, the spirits were simultaneously quaffed down with a hiss. Starbuck paled, and turned, and shivered. Once more, and finally, the replenished pewter went the rounds among the frantic crew; when, waving his free hand to them, they all dispersed; and Ahab retired within his cabin.

Chapter 42
The Whiteness of the Whale
(Excerpt)

What the white whale was to Ahab, has been hinted; what, at times, he was to me, as yet remains unsaid.

Aside from those more obvious considerations touching Moby Dick, which could not but occasionally awaken in any man's soul some alarm, there was another thought, or rather vague, nameless horror concerning him, which at times by its intensity completely overpowered all the rest; and yet so mystical and well nigh ineffable was it, that I almost despair of putting it in a comprehensible form. It was the whiteness of the whale that above all things appalled me. But how can I hope to explain myself here; and yet, in some dim, random way, explain myself I must, else all these chapters might be naught.

Though in many natural objects, whiteness refiningly enhances beauty, as if imparting some special virtue of its own, as in marbles, japonicas, and pearls; and though various nations have in some way recognised a certain royal pre-eminence in this hue; even the barbaric, grand old kings of Pegu[21] placing the title "Lord of the White Elephants" above all their other magniloquent ascriptions of dominion; and the modern kings of Siam unfurling the same snowy-white quadruped in the royal standard; and the Hanoverian flag bearing the one figure of a snow-white charger; and the great Austrian Empire, Caesarian, heir to overlording Rome, though this pre-eminence in it applies to the human race itself, giving the white man ideal mastership over every dusky tribe; and though, besides all this, whiteness has been even made significant of gladness, for among the Romans a white stone marked a joyful day; and though in other mortal sympathies and symbolizings, this same hue is made the emblem of many touching, noble things—the innocence of brides, the benignity of age; though among the Red Men of America the giving of the white belt of wampum was the deepest pledge of honor; though in many climes, whiteness typifies the majesty of Justice in the ermine of the Judge, and contributes to the daily state of kings and queens drawn by milk-white steeds; though even in the higher mysteries of the most august religions it has been made the symbol of the divine spotlessness and power; by the Persian fire worshippers, the white forked flame being held the holiest on the altar; and in the Greek mythologies, Great Jove himself being made incarnate in a snow-white bull; and though to the noble Iroquois, the midwinter sacrifice of the sacred White Dog[22] was by far the holiest festival of their theology, that spotless, faithful creature being held the purest envoy they could send to the Great Spirit with the annual tidings of their own fidelity; and though directly from the Latin word for white, all Christian priests derive the name of one part of their sacred vesture, the alb or tunic, worn beneath the cassock; and though among the holy pomps of the Romish faith, white is specially employed in the celebration of the Passion of our Lord[23]; though in the Vision of St. John[24], white robes are given to the redeemed, and the four-and-twenty elders stand clothed in white before the great white throne, and the Holy One that sitteth there white like wool; yet for all these accumulated associations, with whatever is sweet, and honorable, and sublime, there yet lurks an elusive something in the innermost idea of this hue, which strikes more of panic to the soul than that redness which affrights in blood.

　　This elusive quality it is, which causes the thought of whiteness, when divorced from more kindly associations, and coupled with any object terrible in itself, to heighten that terror to the furthest bounds. Witness the white bear of the poles, and the white shark of the tropics; what but their smooth, flaky whiteness makes them the transcendent horrors they are? That ghastly whiteness it is which imparts such an abhorrent mildness, even more loathsome than terrific, to the dumb gloating of their aspect. So that not the fierce-fanged tiger in his heraldic coat can so stagger courage as the white-shrouded bear or shark.

　　. . .

【注解】

1. the affair of the pipe：在第三十章中，船长埃哈伯独自在甲板上抽烟斗，因心绪无法平静，便把烟斗扔进大海，表示放弃平静，准备迎战大白鲸。
2. ivory stride：埃哈伯被白鲸咬去一条腿，因此用鲸骨安了一条假腿。
3. lower away：放下追逐鲸鱼的快艇。
4. "And what tune is it ye pull to, men?"："那你们喊什么号子呢，伙计们？"
5. Tashtego, Daggoo, and Queequeg：皮奎德捕鲸船上的三名投叉手。"Tashtego"来自Martha's Vineyard岛上的Grey Head族，故又被称为"Grey-Header"。
6. parmacetty：抹香鲸sperm whale的别称。
7. tree：相当于three。
8. twiske-tee betwisk：相当于twisted between。
9. Nantucket：南塔基特，大西洋上的一座岛屿，位于马萨诸塞州东南，是当时美国捕鲸业的中心。
10. Norway Maelstrom：挪威以西海面的危险漩涡，常有海船在那里遇险。
11. thou requirest a little lower layer：你自己要分得少一点。lay表示从捕获的鲸鱼中分得的一份。
12. be the white whale agent, or...principal：不管白鲸是从犯还是首犯。
13. nor yet the low laugh from the hold：也没有听到从船舱传来的窃笑声。此处的"窃笑"指船员之一的费德拉发出的笑声。他预言了埃哈伯的结局。
14. "The measure! the measure!"："拿酒来！拿酒来！""measure"原指标准量，此处借喻一定量的酒。
15. Satan's hoof：喻指魔鬼的引诱。
16. bad pennies come not sooner：你刚出去就回来啦！
17. St. Vitus' imp：圣维塔的小鬼。圣维塔是一种神经性舞蹈病。埃哈伯接酒杯时，酒洒了出来，他怪递酒人的手抖动，像是患了圣维塔舞蹈病。
18. Leyden jar：莱顿电瓶，一种早期的蓄电瓶。
19. great Pope：此处指教皇格雷高里一世。
20. the murderous chalices：chalices指耶稣与圣徒们最后晚餐时用的圣杯。此处指埃哈伯船长在出发前与水手们举杯共饮，立誓要消灭莫比·狄克。
21. Pegu：勃固，缅甸南部城市，16世纪为缅甸联合王国首都。
22. White Dog：北美印第安人、易洛魁人用于祭神的祭物。
23. in the celebration of...Lord：纪念基督受难日。
24. in the Vision of St. John：《圣经·新约》的《启示录》。

【思考题】

1. According to Ahab, what did Moby Dick do to him? What in Ahab's words is the purpose of their voyage?
2. What is Starbuck's first objection to the hunt for Moby Dick?
3. What two qualities does Ahab say he sees in the whale? What does he say about blasphemy?

4. What "foreboding invocation" does Ahab not hear? What does Ishmael ask of "admonitions and warnings"?
5. What do we learn about Ahab's character from his statement, "I'd strike the sun if it insulted me"?
6. What deeper meaning is suggested by Ahab's desire to "strike through the mask" of things?
7. What distinction does Ahab make when he speaks of the whale as "agent" or "principal"? What does he mean by each of these terms?
8. Chapter 36 reads very much like a scene from a play. Point out places in this chapter that suggest the dramatic atmosphere.
9. Rewrite the passage in Ahab's "soliloquy" that begins with "Take off thine eye!" and ends with ". . . with Ahab, in this matter of the whale?" so that it reads like a piece of Shakespearean blank verse.
10. Put this novel in the cultural context of Chinese philosophy "the unity of man and nature" and try to analyze the destruction of Ahab.

【简评】

　　第三十六章是小说主要冲突的开始。在这一章中，船长埃哈伯首次明确提出此行的最终目的是要追踪并杀死一条被称为"莫比·狄克"的白鲸。为了生动展示埃哈伯动员全体船员积极响应的场景，作者一改小说叙述的传统套路，采用戏剧手法（舞台指导、独白、对白、演讲）来制造一种现场感，让读者亲自感受埃哈伯如何展现他作为领袖的雄辩与风采，以及如何运用他的口才、思辨与激情来打动船员，赢得大多数人的支持。例如，在宣布航行的目的时，埃哈伯像一个在群众集会进行演讲的政治家，对船员（群众）提出了一连串富有煽动性的问题。当群众的情绪被调动到高潮时，埃哈伯适时地拿出一枚西班牙金币钉在桅杆上，作为对第一个发现白鲸者的奖赏。这一煽动群众的场面很容易让读者联想到莎剧《恺撒》中安东尼煽动群众，成功让他们"掉转枪口"追杀布鲁特斯的情节。

解读举例

1. 船长埃哈伯是一个品行高贵的人物，他敢于借用人类自身的力量来挑战与反抗以白鲸为象征的邪恶势力，只是他错误地使用了武力，而不是爱。

2. 船长埃哈伯傲慢、自大，一切以自我为中心，甚至为了报私仇不惜牺牲所有船员的性命，是一个不折不扣的暴君和邪恶的化身。

3. 船长埃哈伯是作者有意制造的一个矛盾体，他是一个既伟岸又邪恶的人物。他敢于挑战秩序、神明、命运，是一个典型的拜伦式英雄。但他在实现自己意志的过程中不顾他人，无视大自然的内在规律，最后自己也变成邪恶的化身。通过对这种矛盾性格的刻画，麦尔维尔表达了他对社会、宗教、哲学的多重性等问题的深刻思考。

Emily Dickinson
1830—1886

艾米莉·迪金森是美国19世纪的伟大诗人。她是与惠特曼齐名的现代诗歌的先行者。批评家指出，"迄今为上在诗歌这个人迹罕至的精神领域里，他们两人代表了19世纪美国心灵拓荒最高的才智。"但是，与惠特曼不同的是，迪金森的才华在她去世后才逐渐为世人所认可。

迪金森出生在美国马萨诸塞州安默斯特镇一个律师家庭。1840至1847年间，迪金森就读于马萨诸塞州安默斯特学校；1847至1848年就读于赫里约克山女子神学院；一年后返回家乡，开始自学古典神话、《圣经》和莎士比亚戏剧。19世纪50年代，迪金森去过费城、波士顿和华盛顿。此后她深居简出专心致志地进行诗歌创作。1862年，女诗人第一次考虑发表自己的诗作。她给身为《大西洋月刊》的撰稿人托马斯·温斯沃·希金森写了一封信，同时附上自己的几篇诗作。此后希金森同迪金森一直有书信来往。在迪金森过世之后，希金森也成为迪金森的诗歌和书信集的最佳编辑者。

迪金森的感情生活也曾经历波折。劳德法官曾经是迪金森父亲的好友。1874年迪金森的父亲去世后，劳德带给了她莫大的安慰，成为知心朋友。1877年，劳德妻子去世，他们也彼此表示过对爱情的向往，但由于迪金森不愿放弃独身与创作的生活，二人与婚姻擦肩而过。1884年，劳德去世，迪金森深感悲痛，她的健康自此每况愈下，于1886年5月15日与世长辞。

迪金森一生共作诗1775首，但生前只匿名发表过其中十余首。她的诗均为短诗，多是四行一节，大多信手写在纸上，有些也细细修改，但无论怎样都清楚地烙印着诗人个人的鲜明特征。在她去世后，她妹妹拉维尼亚和朋友希金森于1890年出版了她的部分作品。1955年，T. H. 约翰逊编辑了三卷本的《艾米莉·迪金森诗集》(*The Poems of Emily Dickinson*)，并把所有这些诗进行编号，终于使读者有机会窥见这位伟大女诗人的创作全貌。

迪金森留下的诗歌，可以分为自然、爱情、死亡和永生三大类。迪金森的自然诗蕴含哲理，其中的一花、一叶、一草、一木既蕴含着生命的真谛，又变化莫测，隐藏着令人敬畏甚至恐惧的力量。她的爱情诗感情浓烈，使用大量形象化的意象表达对爱情的渴望。由于她的感情经历并不圆满，因此她创作的爱情诗中常带有疯狂、绝望与无奈的色彩。除了自然与爱情，死亡也是迪金森诗作中反复出现的主题。迪金森生长在清教气氛浓重的新英格兰，这使她对彼岸世界有一种特殊的关注。她对死亡持有一种超验主义的态度，认为生命轮回，死与生紧紧相连。在她的诗中，我们可以发现死亡有时是灵魂的解脱与超越，有时则被庸常化，成了日常生活的一部分，不再阴森可怖，令人畏惧。

迪金森的诗风独特，多采取迂回式的表述，含义隐秘，有时不易理解，但很多诗作都是发自内心的一种情感宣泄，带有明显的抒情色彩。她的诗作表现手法新颖。比如，她用词十分节省，像是电报文字；她常省略介词、连词和冠词，且不遵守语法规则；在大写和破折号的使用上也蹊径独辟，以加强语气或诗歌的节奏感。她善于通过多变的比喻和新奇的意象将抽象的概念和思想具体化，因此她的诗作有时读来轻快活泼，有时又怪诞不经。她喜欢采用民谣和圣歌的普通韵律，但常有变化，还喜欢用近似韵脚、头韵、半谐音和不和谐的韵脚，以期产生某种感情效果。在语言上，她抛弃传统的诗歌词汇，尽量使诗歌语言口语化。总之，她的诗充满激情，思想与形式自然结合，语法和韵律让位于思想和情感，为现代诗歌的发展做出了许多有益的探索。

Because I Could Not Stop for Death

【题解】

死亡与永生是迪金森诗歌中常出现的主题。但对于迪金森来讲，死亡不仅是一个诗歌话题，也是她在现实生活中时常碰到，并对她的生活观产生重大影响的事情。迪金森家的果园靠近公墓，送葬的人群经常从她家门口经过。一曲曲哀歌都给迪金森留下了难以磨灭的印象。汉弗策和牛顿这两个她年轻时的朋友都先她而去。父母的死也给她的心灵留下了阴影。她最小的侄儿吉尔伯特的夭折给了她沉痛的打击。晚年寄予深情的法官劳德的死也让她心痛不已。亲朋好友的先后离世促使她对死亡进行深刻思索，并将思索的结果在她的诗中反映出来。迪金森一生创作的有关死亡和永生的诗约五六百首，约占其作品总数的三分之一。

Because I Could Not Stop for Death

Because I could not stop for Death—
He kindly stopped for me—
The Carriage held but just Ourselves—
And Immortality.

We slowly drove—He knew no haste   5
And I had put away
My labor and my leisure too,
For His Civility—

We passed the School, where Children strove
At Recess—in the Ring—   10
We passed the Fields of Gazing Grain—
We passed the Setting Sun—

Or rather—He passed Us—
The Dews drew quivering and chill—
For only Gossamer, my Gown¹—   15
My Tippet²—only Tulle—

We paused before a House that seemed
A Swelling of the Ground—
The Roof was scarcely visible—
The Cornice—in the Ground³—
                                                   20
Since then—'tis Centuries—and yet

Feels shorter than the Day
I first surmised the Horse' Heads
Were toward Eternity—

【注解】

1. my Gown：喻指寿衣。
2. Tippet：肩上的披风。
3. in the Ground：在地下，即坟墓中。

【思考题】

1. According to Stanza 1, why did Death stop for the speaker?
2. What metaphor does Dickinson use for Death? How does she maintain it throughout the poem?
3. Heidegger in *Being and Time* mentions his opinion of "being-towards death". In light of this, what is Emily Dickenson's attitude towards the connection of life and death?

【简评】

在这首诗中，诗人运用了拟人手法。开头描写诗人被死神的彬彬有礼打动，因而放弃工作和休息，坐上他的马车，穿越课间休息的小学校，路过长满庄稼的田地，忽然感到衣衫单薄，寒冷彻骨，实际上已经进了坟墓。几个世纪飞逝而去，诗人发现自己正乘着马车驶向永生。诗人用亲切平易、富于动感和意象鲜明的语言描述了对死亡能否达到永生境界的困惑。诗中出人意料的转折、停顿、主宾易位，以及间歇而又反复出现的头韵等都使诗歌读起来波澜起伏，使人生、死亡和永生之路显得曲折漫长。

I Heard a Fly Buzz—When I Died

【题解】

有人认为这首诗是迪金森描写死亡的代表作。诗人将颜色与声音两者巧妙地结合在一起，非常自然地描述了人在弥留之际时而迷惑、时而清醒、时而混沌的状态，以及死亡来临时缓慢而又戛然而止的过程。

I Heard a Fly Buzz—When I Died

I heard a Fly buzz—when I died—
The Stillness in the Room
Was like the Stillness in the Air—
Between the Heaves of Storm—

The Eyes around—had wrung them dry—   5
And Breaths were gathering firm
For the last Onset—when the King
Be witnessed—in the Room—

I willed my Keepsakes—Signed away
What portion of me be   10
Assignable—and then it was
There interposed a Fly—

When Blue—uncertain stumbling Buzz—
Between the light—and me—
And then the Windows failed—and then   15
I could not see to see—

【思考题】

1. What is happening to the speaker? What is unusual about the description of the people in lines 5–6? From whose point of view are they being described?
2. What does "buzz" stand for? Why is the fly's appearance somewhat ironic? What basic message about death is suggested to the poet by the appearance of the fly?

Tell All the Truth But Tell It Slant

【题解】

这首诗是女诗人阐述诗歌创作思想的名篇。迪金森首先主张"要说出所有的真理,但切莫直言"。迪金森对于诗歌创作的手段、技巧有自己独到的见解。她喜欢用比喻、讽刺等手法来表达个人思想。该诗运用凝练而巧妙的笔法表达了迪金森对于诗歌创作的观点。她认为诗歌应该是婉转曲折的,重在暗示与启示。诗中的"真理"可以有多种解释,其中一个解释是指迪金森的创作思想。她认为真理应该缓慢地释放出它耀眼的光芒。她运用了大自然中的闪电作为比喻,指出对真理的领悟是需要时间的,诗人的职责是用微暗的光逐渐照亮人们的心灵。

Tell All the Truth But Tell It Slant

Tell all the Truth but tell it slant—
Success in Circuit lies
Too bright for our infirm Delight
The Truth's superb surprise

As Lightning to the Children eased
With explanation kind[1]
The Truth must dazzle gradually
Or every man be blind—

【注解】

1. explanation kind:相当于 kind explanation。

【思考题】

1. Why is truth a superb surprise?
2. Analyze Emily's use of rhyme in this poem.

American Literature
Between 1865 and 1914

背景介绍

1865 年，美国内战结束。美国为这场"兄弟之战"付出了惨重代价，南北双方的经济实力都受到重创，然而战争也刺激了工业与科技的发展。1869 年，第一条横贯北美大陆的铁路竣工通车，极大地便利了物资的流通，工业产值开始以几何级数递增。战前在政治、经济、社会、文化等方面相对独立，并以农业经济为主的南方此时也被绑在了北方经济发展的车轮上。资本主义开始在美国得到迅速发展。蒸汽机的发明不仅使交通领域发生了革命性的改变，也给生产方式带来了革命性的变化，传统的手工劳动被大机器生产所取代。工业化的迅速发展使大批农村人口涌进城市，加入工人的行列中，城市的规模日益扩大。社会、政治、经济等方面的变化也在文学、艺术等领域产生了巨大影响。

美国内战后，随着新思想、新题材、新形式、新作家、新读者群的涌现，美国文学出现了繁荣的景象。在这一时期率先崛起的是以索斯沃斯夫人 (Mrs Southworth, 1819—1899)、玛丽·简·霍尔姆斯 (Mary Jane Holmes, 1825—1907) 等为代表的女性作家。她们的创作吸引了大批读者，拥有了稳定的读者群。同时，出现了一些价格低廉、专门登载小说的报纸。之后，这种报纸又发展成廉价的书籍。这些发展变化提高了通俗小说的普及率，并使之成为人们日常生活中最普遍的娱乐方式。在这个时期，涌现出一些如瑞贝卡·哈丁·戴维斯 (Rebecca Harding Davis, 1831—1910) 等严肃作家和查理·艾略特·诺顿 (Charles Eliot Norton, 1827—1908) 等推崇高品味文化艺术的上层人士，他们都为美国文学的发展作出了重大的贡献。

内战后出现的第一部重要小说是约翰·德·福雷斯特 (John de Forest, 1826—1906) 反映南北战争的小说《瑞芙纳小姐从分裂到忠诚的转变》(*Miss Ravenal's Conversion from Secession to Loyalty*, 1867)。在后来的几十年中又陆续出现了斯蒂芬·克莱恩 (Stephen Crane, 1871—1900) 的《红色英勇勋章》(*The Red Badge of Courage*, 1895)、安布罗斯·比尔斯 (Ambrose Bierce, 1842—1914) 的《士兵与平民的故事》(*Tales of Soldiers and Civilians*, 1909) 等内战小说，开创了美国战争小说的反战传统。内战后最早产生影响的是一批乡土派作家 (Local colorists)。他们热衷表现小镇风情，着重描写某个地区的人物，表现他们独特的行为、方言和乡土人情，字里行间散发出怀旧的气息。布莱特·哈特 (Bret Harte, 1836—1902) 的短篇小说《咆哮营的幸运儿》("The Luck of Roaring Camp", 1868) 因风趣生动地描写了加州淘金热时期煤矿工人的言行举止和生活细节而大获成功，成为著名的乡土文学作家。萨拉·奥恩·朱厄特 (Sarah Orne Jewett, 1849—1909)、乔治·华盛顿·盖宝 (George Washington Cable, 1844—1925) 等乡土派作家都以辛辣幽默的笔调描写了自己所熟悉的乡土生活。

然而在内战后崛起的文坛新秀中，成就最大的莫过于马克·吐温 (Mark Twain, 1835—1910)、威廉·狄恩·豪威尔斯 (William Dean Howells, 1837—1920)、亨利·詹

姆斯 (Henry James) 等现实主义作家。他们取代霍桑、麦尔维尔、爱默生和坡的地位，开启了美国文学史上的现实主义时代。现实主义文学思潮是对浪漫主义的反拨，强调忠实地反映与再现生活，而不是将生活理想化。吐温既是乡土派文学的优秀传人，又是现实主义创作的杰出代表。吐温的小说生动、细腻地反映了美国密西西比河流域的生活，但又突破了乡土文学的局限。他娴熟地运用美国的俚语和俗语，插科打诨，风趣机智，充分体现了美国式的幽默，而在轻松调侃的同时又融入了他对美国社会与工业文明的深刻思索。他的代表作《哈克贝利·芬历险记》(The Adventures of Huckleberry Finn, 1884) 被欧内斯特·海明威 (Ernest Hemingway, 1899—1961) 誉为所有现代美国文学作品的源泉。吐温在短篇小说方面也取得了巨大成就，其中《卡拉维拉县有名的跳蛙》("The Celebrated Jumping Frog of Calaveras County", 1865)、《百万英镑》("The Million Pound Bank Note", 1893) 等都是美国家喻户晓的名篇。

豪威尔斯是另一位具有影响力的美国现实主义文学家、评论家，也是美国现实主义文学与理论的奠基人。在他六十年的职业生涯中，创作了约100部作品，包括小说、戏剧、散文、游记、文学批评及自传等各种体裁。他反对浪漫主义的创作方式，认为浪漫主义的文学使人们忘记了现实生活，忘记了生活中人们应当关心的事情和承担的责任。他强调小说应当促使人们思考，从而把自己改造成更有用的人。同时他也反对狄更斯式的批判现实主义，认为那是丑化现实生活。他主张美国的小说应当描绘生活中"微笑的一面"(smiling aspects)，因此他的小说基本上都对美国的现实生活进行乐观的处理，作品也往往在妥协、圆满的气氛中结束。由于这个原因，豪威尔斯的现实主义也常常被称为文雅主义 (genteelism) 或文雅现实主义 (genteel realism)。

在19世纪的最后二十多年里，詹姆斯堪称是美国现实主义小说创作的总结性人物，也是19世纪美国文学的最后一位巨匠。他的作品往往深入细致地剖析笔下人物的思想性格与心理特征，其文体优美雅致，但其后期作品则过于繁复晦涩。《黛西·米勒》(Daisy Miller, 1878) 是第一部给他带来国际声誉的作品，表现了美国文化与欧洲文化的矛盾与冲撞。詹姆斯在创作早期的代表作当属《贵妇画像》(The Portrait of a Lady, 1881)。作品继续演绎着他早期创作中开始的国际主题和对美国妇女的关注，在刻画了一伙欧洲利己主义者的同时也巧妙地评价了美国性格。此后创作的《波士顿人》(The Bostonians, 1886) 和《卡萨玛西玛公主》(The Princess Casamassima, 1886) 标志着詹姆斯文学创作中期的开始。这一时期最为人熟知的是他表现儿童题材的中篇小说《螺丝在拧紧》(The Turn of the Screw, 1898)。在他文学生涯的最后阶段，詹姆斯先后创作出版了《鸽翼》(The Wings of the Dove, 1902)、《专使》(The Ambassadors, 1903) 和《金碗》(The Golden Bowl, 1984) 三部作品。在这些作品中，文化冲突的主题让位于融合与沟通，反映了詹姆斯晚期思想的变化与发展。

与吐温和豪威尔斯不同的是，詹姆斯对美国文学的贡献在于他开创了美国心理分析小说的传统，对 20 世纪的意识流运动产生了重要影响。此外，詹姆斯不仅在小说创作领域取得了巨大成就，在小说理论方面也颇有建树。他的《小说的艺术》("The Art of Fiction", 1984) 系统阐述了他关于小说创作的主张，提出真实是小说创作的最高原则，至今仍被认为是美国小说创作理论的重要论述。

19 世纪末，美国工业生产迅速增长，资本主义从自由竞争发展到垄断阶段，美国社会也出现了各种问题。许多中小企业破产或被兼并，大批工人失业，政治腐败，受贿成风，物质主义泛滥，美国社会进入一个"镀金时代"。亨利·亚当斯 (Henry Adams, 1838—1918)、弗朗西斯·克劳福 (Francis Crawford, 1854—1909)、爱德华·贝拉米 (Edward Bellamy, 1850—1898) 等作家纷纷发表政治小说，针砭时事、揭露黑暗。吐温与查尔斯·华纳 (Charles Warner, 1829—1900) 共同创作的《镀金时代》(*The Gilded Age*, 1873) 更是尖锐地揭示了这一时代的社会特征。随着垄断资本主义的进一步发展和社会达尔文主义 (Social Darwinism) 的盛行，"适者生存"成为现代社会的生活法则，这也极大地影响了当时西方国家的文学创作。许多在世纪之交开始创作的美国作家也不例外。他们一反豪威尔斯所倡导的"文雅主义"创作原则，效仿法国作家左拉 (Émile Zola, 1840—1902)，开始用一种自然主义 (Naturalism) 和宿命论 (Fatalism) 的态度对待生活与文学创作。克莱恩是美国第一位重要的自然主义作家。他曾谈到环境对人的命运起着决定性的作用。他的第一部小说《街头女郎麦琪》(*Maggie: A Girl of the Streets*, 1893) 就是这种悲观主义思想的具体体现。《红色英勇勋章》和《海上扁舟及其他》(*The Open Boat and Other Stories*, 1898) 等作品也或多或少地反映出这种自然主义的创作观。在创作技巧上，克莱恩则借鉴法国印象派的绘画技巧，使作品富有象征性，其语言明快、简洁，对海明威等后代作家产生了很大影响。

汉姆林·加兰 (Hamlin Garland, 1860—1940) 是另一位重要的自然主义作家，他在《大路》(*Main-Travelled Roads*, 1891) 和《德切尔家库利的玫瑰》(*Rose of Dutcher's Coolly*, 1895) 中对现实生活采取了更加坦率的态度。他 1894 年出版的论文集《坍塌的偶像》(*Crumbling Idols*, 1894) 则被视为美国自然主义创作方式的宣言。书中，加兰呼吁美国小说摈弃遁世的浪漫主义写作方式，应超越小资产阶级的所谓现实主义，去表现真正的现实，即社会大众的生活与苦难。加兰的观点对福兰克·诺里斯 (Frank Norris, 1870—1902)、杰克·伦敦 (Jack London, 1876—1916)、西奥多·德莱塞 (Theodore Dreiser, 1871—1945) 等 20 世纪初的美国自然主义作家产生了重要影响。诺里斯的《小麦史诗》(*The Epic of the Wheat*) 三部曲通过个人与社会的冲突反映了个人的弱小与无奈。伦敦早期创作发表的《生命法则》(*The Law of Life*)、《荒野的呼唤》(*The Call of the Wild*, 1903)、《海狼》(*The Sea-Wolf*, 1904) 等作品都强烈地反映了他对人生与社会的自然主义态度，即自然法则统治着整个社会，掌管着每个人的命运。德莱塞创作的《嘉丽妹妹》(*Sister Carrie*, 1900)、《珍妮姑娘》(*Jennie Gerhardt*, 1911)、《美国悲剧》(*An American Tragedy*, 1925) 等一系列作品揭露了"美国梦"(American Dream) 的欺骗性和它对人性的巨大腐蚀作用。他作品中对人物、环境等方面的自然主义描述，对美国下层百姓生活状况的表现，对大城市生活的描述和对美国当代社会问题的关注使他的作品拥有广大的普通读者，在美国文学史上占据重要地位。

在 1865 年美国内战结束到 1914 年第一次世界大战爆发这五十年里，美国文学经历了从现实主义向自然主义、从乐观主义向悲观主义的过渡。这不仅仅是文学创作手法或者是文学创作题材的转变，更从深层次反映了美国主流作家哲学观与价值观的变化，以及对"美国梦"，乃至整个美国社会更为清醒深刻的认识。这一转变使得美国文学更贴近现实生活，同时也更具有批判性与社会性。

就诗歌创作而言，1865 年到 1914 年是个贫乏而沉寂的时代。1865 年后，艾米莉·迪金森已很少创作诗歌。庞德、罗伯特·弗罗斯特 (Robert Frost, 1873—1963) 等震撼 20 世纪美国诗坛的巨人要到这一时代的尾声才开始崭露头角。其间的美国诗人多数仍沉浸在英国浪漫主义的诗歌传统中，没有像多数小说家那样正视内战后美国社会的现实。在《美国诗人》(*Poets of America*, 1885) 中，评论家埃德蒙·斯泰曼 (Edmund Stedman, 1833—1908) 不无讥讽地诘问："如果说大家对当代诗歌不感兴趣，那么是否是因为诗歌对大家不感兴趣，未能占据有利地位？"也许只有南方诗人西尼·拉尼尔 (Sidney Lanier, 1842—1881) 真正对人民表示关注。他表现南方农业的诗《玉米》("Corn", 1875) 和表现北方工业的诗《交响乐》("Symphony", 1875) 发表后风靡全国，深受好评，成为 19 世纪末期美国诗歌的一道风景。

1835—1910

作者简介

马克·吐温是美国著名作家塞缪·兰亨·克莱门斯(Samuel Langhorne Clemens)的笔名。吐温出生于密苏里州的佛罗里达，3岁全家迁往密西西比河畔的汉尼拔镇，自由粗犷的河上生活和天真无邪的童年给吐温留下了深刻印象。吐温12岁时，父亲病故，他不得不辍学，13岁便开始自立谋生，在一家印刷厂当学徒。18岁至22岁期间，吐温在密西西比河上当领航员，为他后来创作《哈克贝利·芬历险记》提供了丰富的素材和广阔的背景资料。1861年，吐温随兄赴内华达州，先后做过股票生意，淘过金，当过记者。这些经历进一步丰富了吐温的生活。1863年，他开始以"马克·吐温"为笔名进行文学创作。马克·吐温的英文Mark Twain为水手使用的术语，表明河水的深度恰足以行船。1864年他将在旧金山矿区听到的传说写成幽默短篇《卡拉维拉县有名的跳蛙》，并于翌年11月发表在纽约的《星期六刊》，一举成名。作品讲述了一个外表老实的外地人欺骗了一个有名的赛蛙高手的故事，吐温制造幽默的才能初显。1866年，他来到美国东部，在那里见到了豪威尔斯。1867年，他游历了檀香山、欧洲、中东等地，并以这次出游的经历为素材创作出版了幽默小品集《傻子国外旅行记》(*The Innocents Abroad*, 1869)，向世界展示了一种崭新的美国风格。此后，吐温先后发表了自传性作品《艰苦岁月》(*Roughing It*, 1872)，短篇小说《百万英镑》《竞选州长》("Running for Governor", 1870)等，后又与查尔斯·华纳合作出版了长篇讽刺小说《镀金时代》，揭露了当时美国所谓黄金时代虚伪外表掩盖下的贪腐实质，但在艺术上却不够成功。

三年后吐温因发表儿童小说《汤姆·索亚历险记》(*The Adventures of Tom Sawyer*, 1876)而再获成功，并为他赢得了持久的声誉。小说讲述了两个"坏男孩"童年时代的故事，同时也描写了内战前密西西比河畔小镇宁静的田园生活。在这一时期，吐温还先后创作了讽刺古英国王朝的《王子与贫儿》(*The Prince and Pauper*, 1881)和自传性作品《密西西比河上的生活》(*Life on the Mississippi*, 1883)。后一部作品以怀旧的情绪和风趣幽默的笔调回溯了美国内战前吐温在密西西比河畔度过的童年时代。

1884年，在《汤姆·索亚历险记》问世八年后，吐温又推出了它的姊妹篇《哈克贝利·芬历险记》(The Adventures of Huckleberry Finn)。小说仍以儿童读物的形式出现，却被赋予了《汤姆·索亚历险记》所缺乏的道德层面。《哈克贝利·芬历险记》耗费了作者八年心血，无论就思想内容还是艺术成就而言，都是吐温最成熟、最优秀的作品。如果说惠特曼是美国文学史上第一位打破英国诗歌传统的诗人，那么吐温就是美国文学史上第一位打破英国小说传统的小说家。海明威曾高度评价此书："所有现代的美国文学都来自一本吐温的作品《哈克贝利·芬历险记》……这是我们所有书中最好的。一切美国文学都来自这本书。在它之前或之后都没有一本书能与它媲美。"福克纳也做出了类似的评价，称吐温是美国作家的祖父，所有后来的美国作家都是他的传人。

　　海明威、福克纳等人之所以如此盛赞吐温，其中一个重要原因是吐温是美国文学史上首个运用地道的美国口语(vernacular)讲述故事，并大获成功的作家，而此前的美国作家，无论是库柏、霍桑还是麦尔维尔，都是用书面体进行创作的。然而吐温并非机械地模仿口语，而是对粗糙的口语进行艺术加工，使之既摆脱了书面语的束缚，又有口语的逼真、自然与流畅。比如哈克文化水平低，语言简单，词汇量小，一般来说难以表达丰富的内心与情感，但经过吐温的加工锤炼，哈克简单的语言依然能表达出丰富的情感，而且还大大增加了作品的真实氛围。从这个意义上，豪威尔斯称吐温是"美国文学上的林肯"，因为如同林肯解放黑奴一样，吐温将作家从传统的书面语言中解放了出来。

　　1894年后，吐温旅居欧洲达五年之久，期间除四处讲演外，也创作出版了《傻瓜威尔逊的悲剧》(The Tragedy of Pudd'n-head Wilson, 1894)、《贞德传》(Personal Recollections of Joan of Arc, 1895)、《败坏了哈德莱堡的人》(The Man That Corrupted Hadleyburg, 1900)等作品。在他后期的作品中，吐温对人类与人类社会的批判日益尖锐。在1901年发表的《给在黑暗中的人》("To the Person Sitting in the Darkness")、1905年发表的《利奥波德国王的独白》("King Leopold's Soliloquy")等作品中，吐温对欧洲帝国主义对殖民地国家的扩张、掠夺等行为给予了尖刻的评判。对于美国帝国主义的侵略扩张，吐温也同样进行了辛辣的批判。在《战争祈祷》("War Prayer", 1923)中，吐温表达了他对美国政府用血腥的手段吞并菲律宾的愤怒。吐温不仅反对帝国主义的侵略扩张，也反对美国国内的种族主义制度。他强烈支持林肯解放黑奴的壮举，同时也为所有非白种人在美国遭受的不公对待发出批评。他曾表明自己目睹华人遭到了令人发指的虐待与凌辱，却从没见到任何法庭为华人遭受的屈辱伸张正义。在他去世前发表的《人是什么？》("What Is Man", 1906)、《神秘的陌生人》("The Mysterious Stranger", 1916)等文章中，吐温变得更加直言不讳，笔触凌厉。吐温晚年对人类社会的失望及他对帝国主义和社会弊病的批判更是表明了他始终如一的正义感。

The Adventures of Huckleberry Finn

【题解】

哈克和汤姆意外得到财宝后，哈克失踪一年的酒鬼父亲回到了家。哈克不堪忍受父亲的打骂，逃到一个荒岛上，并在那里巧遇华森小姐家的黑奴吉姆。吉姆因害怕被主人转卖藏身于此。于是两人结伴而行，乘木筏沿密西西比河漂流而下。他们希望来到一个没有黑奴买卖的"自由州"。一开始哈克曾打算告发吉姆，因为他担心帮助黑奴逃跑是犯罪行为，会受到上帝的惩处，但他善良的本性占了上风，在发现追捕逃奴的船时，本能地掩护吉姆。在漂流中，他们收留了自称是"国王"和"公爵"的两个逃犯。这两人一路招摇撞骗，甚至背着哈克卖掉吉姆。之后哈克在汤姆的帮助下冒险救出吉姆。然而这时哈克从汤姆那里得知华森小姐已在遗嘱中声明吉姆为自由人。

以下内容选自小说第十九章，描述哈克和吉姆乘筏顺河而下，一路饱览古老的密西西比河两岸秀丽的风光，自由自在生活的情景。但这种生活很快由于两个骗子的到来而结束。

From The Adventures of Huckleberry Finn

Chapter 19

Two or three days and nights went by; I reckon I might say they swum by, they slid along so quiet and smooth and lovely. Here is the way we put in the time. It was a monstrous big river down there—sometimes a mile and a half wide; we run nights, and laid up and hid daytimes; soon as night was most gone we stopped navigating and tied up—nearly always in the dead water under a towhead; and then cut young cottonwoods and willows, and hid the raft with them. Then we set out the lines[1]. Next we slid into the river and had a swim, so as to freshen up and cool off; then we set down on the sandy bottom wher[2] the water was about knee deep, and watched the daylight come. Not a sound anywheres—perfectly still—just like the whole world was asleep, only sometimes the bullfrogs a-cluttering, maybe. The first thing to see, looking away over the water, was a kind of dull line—that was the woods on t'other side; you couldn't make nothing else out;

then a pale place in the sky; then more paleness spreading around; then the river softened up away off, and warn't black any more, but gray; you could see little dark spots drifting along ever so far away—trading scows, and such things; and long black streaks—rafts; sometimes you could hear a sweep screaking; or jumbled-up voices, it was so still, and sounds come so far; and by and by you could see a streak on the water which you know by the look of the streak that there's a snag there in a swift current which breaks on it and makes that streak look that way; and you see the mist curl up off of the water, and the east reddens up, and the river, and you make out a log cabin in the edge of the woods, away on the bank on t'other side of the river, being a woodyard, likely, and piled by them cheats so you can throw a dog through it anywheres[3]; then the nice breeze springs up, and comes fanning you from over there, so cool and fresh and sweet to smell on account of the woods and the flowers; but sometimes not that way, because they've left dead fish laying around, gars and such, and they do get pretty rank; and next you've got the full day, and everything smiling in the sun, and the songbirds just going it!

    A little smoke couldn't be noticed now, so we would take some fish off of the lines and cook up a hot breakfast. And afterwards we would watch the lonesomeness of the river, and kind of lazy along, and by and by lazy off to sleep. Wake up by and by, and look to see what done it, and maybe see a steamboat coughing along upstream, so far off towards the other side you couldn't tell nothing about her only whether she was a stern-wheel or side-wheel; then for about an hour there wouldn't be nothing to hear nor nothing to see—just solid lonesomeness. Next you'd see a raft sliding by, away off yonder, and maybe a galoot on it chopping, because they're most always doing it on a raft; you'd see the ax flash and come down—you don't hear nothing; you see that ax go up again, and by the time it's above the man's head then you hear the k'chunk!—it had took all that time to come over the water. So we would put in the day, lazying around, listening to the stillness. Once there was a thick fog, and the rafts and things that went by was beating tin pans so the steamboats wouldn't run over them. A scow or a raft went by so close we could hear them talking and cussing and laughing—heard them plain; but we couldn't see no sign of them; it made you feel crawly; it was like spirits carrying on that way in the air. Jim said he believed it was spirits; but I says:

    "No; spirits wouldn't say, 'Dern[4] the dern fog.'"

    Soon as it was night out we shoved; when we got her out to about the middle we let her alone, and let her float wherever the current wanted her to; then we lit the pipes, and dangled our legs in the water, and talked about all kinds of things—we was always naked, day and night, whenever the mosquitoes would let us—the new clothes Buck's[5] folks made for me was too good to be comfortable, and besides I didn't go much on clothes, nohow.

Sometimes we'd have that whole river all to ourselves for the longest time. Yonder was the banks and the islands, across the water; and maybe a spark—which was a candle in a cabin window; and sometimes on the water you could see a spark or two—on a raft or a scow, you know; and maybe you could hear a fiddle or a song coming over from one of them crafts. It's lovely to live on a raft. We had the sky up there, all speckled with stars, and we used to lay on our backs and look up at them, and discuss about whether they was made or only just happened. Jim he allowed they was made, but I allowed they happened; I judged it would have took too long to make so many. Jim said the moon could 'a' laid[6] them; well, that looked kind of reasonable, so I didn't say nothing against it, because I've seen a frog lay most as many, so of course it could be done. We used to watch the stars that fell, too, and see them streak down. Jim allowed they'd got spoiled and was hove out of the nest.

Once or twice of a night we would see a steamboat slipping along in the dark, and now and then she would belch a whole world of sparks up out of her chimbleys[7], and they would rain down in the river and look awful pretty; then she would turn a corner and her lights would wink out and her powwow shut off and leave the river still again; and by and by her waves would get to us, a long time after she was gone, and joggle the raft a bit, and after that you wouldn't hear nothing for you couldn't tell how long, except maybe frogs or something.

After midnight the people on shore went to bed, and then for two or three hours the shores was black—no more sparks in the cabin windows. These sparks was our clock—the first one that showed again meant morning was coming, so we hunted a place to hide and tie up right away.

One morning about daybreak I found a canoe and crossed over a chute to the main shore—it was only two hundred yards—and paddled about a mile up a crick amongst the cypress woods, to see if I couldn't get some berries. Just as I was passing a place where a kind of a cowpath crossed the crick, here comes a couple of men tearing up the path as tight as they could foot it. I thought I was a goner, for whenever anybody was after anybody I judged it was me—or maybe Jim. I was about to dig out from there in a hurry, but they was pretty close to me then, and sung out and begged me to save their lives—said they hadn't been doing nothing, and was being chased for it—said there was men and dogs a-coming. They wanted to jump right in, but I says:

"Don't you do it. I don't hear the dogs and horses yet; you've got time to crowd through the brush and get up the crick a little ways; then you take to the water and wade down to me and get in—that'll throw the dogs off the scent."

They done it, and soon as they was aboard I lit out for our towhead, and in about five or ten minutes we heard the dogs and the men away off, shouting. We heard them come along towards the crick, but couldn't see them; they seemed to stop and fool around awhile; then, as we got further and further away all the time, we couldn't hardly hear them at all; by the time we had left a mile of woods behind us and struck the river, everything was quiet, and we paddled over to the towhead and hid in the cottonwoods and was safe.

One of these fellows was about seventy or upwards, and had a bald head and very gray whiskers. He had an old battered-up slouch hat on, and a greasy blue woolen shirt, and ragged old blue jeans britches stuffed into his boot tops, and home-knit galluses—no, he only had one. He had an old long-tailed blue jeans coat with slick brass buttons flung over his arm, and both of them had big, fat, ratty-looking carpetbags.

The other fellow was about thirty, and dressed about as ornery. After breakfast we all laid off and talked, and the first thing that come out was that these chaps didn't know one another.

"What got you into trouble?" says the baldhead to t' other chap.

"Well, I'd been selling an article to take the tartar off the teeth—and it does take it off, too, and generly[8] the enamel along with it—but I stayed about one night longer than I ought to, and was just in the act of sliding out when I ran across you on the trail this side of town, and you told me they were coming, and begged me to help you to get off. So I told you I was expecting trouble myself, and would scatter out with you. That's the whole yarn—what's yourn[9]?"

"Well, I'd ben[10] a-runnin' a little temperance revival thar[11], 'bout a week, and was the pet of the women folks, big and little, for I was makin' it mighty warm for the rummies, I tell you, and takin' as much as five or six dollars a night—ten cents a head, children and niggers free—and business a-growin' all the time, when somehow or another a little report got around, last night, that I had a way of puttin' in my time with a private jug on the sly. A nigger rousted me out this mornin', and told me the people was gatherin' on the quiet with their dogs and horses, and they'd be along pretty soon and give me 'bout half an hour's start, and then run me down if they could; and if they got me they'd tar and feather me and ride me on a rail, sure. I didn't wait for no breakfast—I warn't hungry."

"Old man," said the young one, "I reckon we might double-team it together; what do you think?"

"I ain't undisposed. What's your line—mainly?"

"Jour printer[12] by trade; do a little in patent medicines; theater actor—tragedy, you know; take a turn to mesmerism and phrenology when there's a chance; teach singing-geography school for a change; sling a lecture sometimes—oh, I do lots of things—most anything that comes handy, so it ain't work. What's your lay?"

"I've done considerable in the doctoring way in my time. Layin' on o' hands is my best holt[13]—for cancer and paralysis, and sich[14] things; and I k'n[15] tell a fortune pretty good when I've got somebody along to find out the facts for me. Preachin's my line, too, and workin' camp meetin's, and missionaryin' around."

Nobody never said anything for a while; then the young man hove a sigh and says:

"Alas!"

"What're you alassin' about?" says the baldhead.

"To think I should have lived to be leading such a life, and be degraded down into such company." And he begun to wipe the corner of his eye with a rag.

"Dern your skin, ain't the company good enough for you?" says the baldhead, pretty pert and uppish.

"Yes, it is good enough for me; it's as good as I deserve; for who fetched me so low when I was so high? I did myself. I don't blame you, gentlemen—far from it; I don't blame anybody. I deserve it all. Let the cold world do its worst; one thing I know—there's a grave somewhere for me. The world may go on just as it's always done, and take everything from me—loved ones, property, everything; but it can't take that. Some day I'll lie down in it and forget it all, and my poor broken heart will be at rest." he went on a-wiping.

"Drot your pore broken heart," says the baldhead; "what are you heaving your pore broken heart at us f'r? We hain't done nothing."

"No, I know you haven't. I ain't blaming you, gentlemen. I brought myself down—yes, I did it myself. It's right I should suffer—perfectly right—I don't make any moan."

"Brought you down from whar? Whar was you brought down from?"

"Ah, you would not believe me; the world never believes—let it pass—'tis no matter. The secret of my birth—"

"The secret of your birth! Do you mean to say—"

"Gentlemen," says the young man, very solemn, "I will reveal it to you, for I feel I may have confidence in you. By rights I am a duke!"

Jim's eyes bugged out when he heard that; and I reckon mine did, too. Then the baldhead says: "No! you can't mean it?"

"Yes. My great-grandfather, eldest son of the Duke of Bridgewater, fled to this country about the end of the last century, to breathe the pure air of freedom; married here, and died, leaving a son, his own father dying about the same time. The second son of the late duke seized the titles and estates—the infant real duke was ignored. I am the lineal descendant of that infant—I am the rightful Duke of Bridgewater; and here am I, forlorn, torn from my high estate, hunted of men, despised by the cold world, ragged, worn, heartbroken, and degraded to the companionship of felons on a raft!"

Jim pitied him ever so much, and so did I. We tried to comfort him, but he said it warn't much use, he couldn't be much comforted; said if we was a mind to acknowledge him, that would do him more good than most anything else; so we said we would, if he would tell us how. He said we ought to bow when we spoke to him, and say "Your Grace," or "My Lord," or "Your Lordship"—and he wouldn't mind it if we called him plain "Bridgewater," which, he said, was a title anyway, and not a name; and one of us ought to wait on him at dinner, and do any little thing for him he wanted done.

Well, that was all easy, so we done it. All through dinner Jim stood around and waited on him, and says, "Will yo' Grace have some o' dis or some o' dat?" and so on, and a body could see it was mighty pleasing to him.

But the old man got pretty silent by and by—didn't have much to say, and didn't look pretty comfortable over all that petting that was going on around that duke. He seemed to have something on his mind. So, along in the afternoon, he says:

"Looky here, Bilgewater," he says, "I'm nation sorry for you, but you ain't the only person that's had troubles like that."

"No?"

"No, you ain't. You ain't the only person that's ben snaked down wrongfully out 'n a high place."

"Alas!"

"No, you ain't the only person that's had a secret of his birth." And, by jings[16], he begins to cry.

"Hold! What do you mean?"

"Bilgewater, kin I trust you?" says the old man, still sort of sobbing.

"To the bitter death!" He took the old man by the hand and squeezed it, and says, "That secret of your being: speak!"

"Bilgewater, I am the late Dauphin[17]!"

You bet you, Jim and me stared this time. Then the duke says:

"You are what?"

"Yes, my friend, it is too true—your eyes is lookin' at this very moment on the pore disappeared Dauphin, Looy[18] the Seventeen, son of Looy the Sixteen and Marry Antonette."

"You! At your age! No! You mean you're the late Charlemagne[19]; you must be six or seven hundred years old, at the very least."

"Trouble has done it, Bilgewater, trouble has done it; trouble has brung these gray hairs and this premature balditude. Yes, gentlemen, you see before you, in blue jeans and misery, the wanderin', exiled, trampled on, and sufferin' rightful King of France."

Well, he cried and took on so that me and Jim didn't know hardly what to do, we was so sorry—and so glad and proud we'd got him with us, too. So we set in, like we done before with the duke, and tried to comfort him. But he said it warn't no use, nothing but to be dead and done with it all could do him any good; though he said it often made him feel easier and better for a while if people treated him according to his rights, and got down on one knee to speak to him, and always called him "Your majesty," and waited on him first at meals, and didn't set down in his presence till he asked them. So Jim and me set to majestying him, and doing this and that and t'other for him, and standing up till he told us we might set down. This done him heaps of good, and so he got cheerful and comfortable. But the duke kind of soured on him, and didn't look a bit satisfied with the way things was going; still, the king acted real friendly towards him, and said the duke's great grandfather and all the other Dukes of Bilgewater was a good deal thought of by his father, and was allowed to come to the palace considerable; but the duke stayed huffy a good while, till by and by the king says:

"Like as not we got to be together a blamed long time on this h-yer[20] raft, Bilgewater, and so what's the use o' your bein' sour? It'll only make things uncomfortable. It ain't my fault I warn't born a duke, it ain't your fault you warn't born a king—so what's the use to worry? Make the best o' things the way you find 'em, says I—that's my motto. This ain't no bad thing that we've struck here—plenty grub and an easy life—come, give us your hand, duke, and le's all be friends."

The duke done it, and Jim and me was pretty glad to see it. It took away all the uncomfortableness and we felt mighty good over it, because it would 'a' been a miserable business to have any unfriendliness on the raft; for what you want, above all things, on a raft, is for everybody to be satisfied, and feel right and kind towards the others.

It didn't take me long to make up my mind that these liars warn't no kings nor dukes at all, but just low-down humbugs and frauds. But I never said nothing, never let on; kept it to myself; it's the best way; then you don't have no quarrels, and don't get into no trouble. If they wanted us to call them kings and dukes, I hadn't no objections, 'long as it would keep peace in the family; and it warn't no use to tell Jim, so I didn't tell him. If I never learnt nothing else out of pap, I learnt that the best way to get along with his kind of people is to let them have their own way.

【注解】

1. lines: 钓线。
2. wher: 美国俚语，相当于 where。
3. and piled by them ... through it anywheres: 由那些骗子堆起来，中间任何地方都大得可扔过去一条狗。
4. Dern：相当于 damn。
5. Buck：书中一个 14 岁小男孩的名字。
6. 'a' laid：相当于 lay。
7. chimbleys：相当于 chimneys，烟囱。
8. generly：相当于 generally。
9. yourn：相当于 yours。
10. ben：相当于 been。
11. thar：相当于 there。
12. Jour printer：相当于 Journeyman printer，按天结算工资的印刷工。
13. holt：相当于 hold。
14. sich：相当于 such。
15. k'n：相当于 can。
16. by jings：相当于 by jinx。
17. the late Dauphin: 已故的道芬。道芬为法国国王路易十六之子，生于 1785 年，后死于狱中。
18. Looy: Louis 的错误发音。
19. Charlemagne：查理曼大帝 (724—814)，查理曼帝国建立者。
20. h-yer：相当于 here。

【思考题】

1. In the first third of the chapter, Twain gives much attention to the details about Huck and Jim's life on the raft. What do you suppose is Twain's intention here? Is there anything symbolic about the rafting on the Mississippi? And the two men who take refuge on the raft?
2. What do you think of the two escapees who claim themselves king and duke?
3. Study the vernacular used by Huck or the two escapees, and point out how close it resembles the language really spoken by people.
4. Study the last two paragraphs carefully, and comment on Huck's attitude towards the king and duke when he finds out they are just "low-down humbugs and frauds".

解读举例

1. 《哈克贝利·芬历险记》的主题是对自由生活的追寻。哈克逃离的是家庭的专制与束缚，吉姆逃离的是南方奴隶制的奴役与压迫，而他们共同追求的则是自由自在、无忧无虑的生活。

2. 《哈克贝利·芬历险记》的主题是对所谓现代文明的批判。小镇的生活及哈克被迫接受的教育代表了现代文明对人的愚弄与束缚。而密西西比河上的自由漂流则代表着哈克或吐温对美国虚假文明的摈弃。大河中和河岸上的不同生活象征着现代文明与传统道德间的冲突。

3. 《哈克贝利·芬历险记》的主题是自我与社会的冲突，并以社会的妥协告终。哈克极力想摆脱社会对他的约束和压制，按照自己的愿望做一个自由的人，最后获得成功。同样，黑奴吉姆虽然和南方奴隶制之间存在着根本矛盾，但也在逃亡的过程中实现了一定程度的自由。作品最后，主人在遗嘱中还吉姆自由，象征着奴隶制度的寿终正寝——吉姆也获得了成功。

American Literature
Between 1865 and 1914

亨利·詹姆斯是美国杰出的小说家和文学评论家。他出生于纽约一个殷实富足的家庭，一生专注于艺术创作和精神生活。他的父亲是当地文化圈内的知名人士，让孩子们从小接触各种思想，养成独立思考和判断的能力。为了开阔孩子们的眼界，选择自己的生活方式，老詹姆斯还带着孩子们去欧洲游历，了解那里古老的文化和传统。詹姆斯和哥哥，即后来成为著名实用主义哲学家和心理学家的威廉·詹姆斯 (William James, 1842—1910)，一起在那里学习绘画，接受教育。在欧洲游历期间，詹姆斯被欧洲的文化深深吸引，于1876年永久定居伦敦，1915年加入英国国籍。

詹姆斯小时候没有接受正规的学校教育，而是在父亲和不断更换的家庭教师的指导下学习，大量阅读美国及世界名著。1862至1864年他就读于哈佛大学法学院。在此期间，他大量阅读了法国作家巴尔扎克 (Honoré de Balzac, 1799—1850) 和乔治·桑 (George Sand, 1804—1876) 等人的作品，同时学习创作，并开始在《大西洋月刊》等杂志上发表作品。1875年旅居巴黎期间，他又结识了著名作家福楼拜 (Gustave Flaubert, 1821—1980)、左拉 (Émile Zola, 1840—1902)、屠格涅夫 (Ivan Sergeyevich Turgenev, 1818—1883)、莫泊桑 (Guy de Maupassant, 1850—1893) 和龚古尔兄弟 (Edmond de and Jules de Goncour, 1822—1896, 1830—1870) 等人，颇受他们影响。

詹姆斯的创作生涯长达五十年之久，著作繁多。他的创作通常分为三个时期。第一个时期 (1875—1881) 的创作集中表现了"国际主题"(international theme)，即美国人来到欧洲后所面临的文化、感情和道德等一系列问题，强调了新大陆和旧大陆之间的文化差异。作品人物性格鲜明，语言流畅，故事发展直接。这一时期的主要作品包括《罗德里克·赫得森》(Roderick Hudson, 1876)、《美国人》(The American, 1877)、《黛西·米勒》(Daisy Miller, 1879) 等。《淑女画像》(The Portrait of a Lady, 1881) 是这一时期的代表作。詹姆斯对女主人公伊莎贝尔的心理描写为他以后的心理现实主义创作奠定了基础。在第二个时期 (1881—1901) 中，詹姆斯对文学形式和主题进行了一系列尝试。他不仅创作长篇和短篇小说，还写剧本，但并不成功。他这一时期的作品涉及社会、政治等领域。他探索艺术家与社会之间的矛盾和关系，描写邪恶对儿童等无辜受害者造成的心理影响。这一时期的主要作品有《波士顿人》《卡萨玛西公主》《悲剧缪斯神》(*The Tragic Muse*, 1890)、《梅西所知道的》(*What Maisie Knew*, 1897) 和《拧螺丝》。进入 20 世纪后，詹姆斯的创作进入第三个时期，也是创作的主要阶段。这时他又回到了自己熟悉的国际主题，但不再强调欧美的文化冲突，而是突出两者之间的相互理解与融合。同时，他十分关注叙事的角度和作品的形式美，语言精雕细凿，矫饰华丽，形成"后期詹姆斯风格"。这一时期詹姆斯创作了几部很有影响力的小说，如《鸽翼》《专使》和《金碗》，其中《专使》被詹姆斯本人认为是他最杰出的作品。

詹姆斯与吐温、豪威尔斯一同被誉为 19 世纪美国三位伟大的现实主义作家。他关心人的状况，展现生活现实，阐释生命价值，认为小说是"直接再现生活的艺术"。在创作中，他更加关注人物的精神生活和人物之间的情感关系，而不是物质的世界和人物的具体行动。詹姆斯的现实主义是心理现实主义，他认为现实只存在于生活给旁观者的印象中，而不存在于未经旁观者意识到的事物中。小说的价值在于个人对生活的直接印象，因而，他注重描写人物的内心世界和心理变化，把小说的发展从外部情节转向精神世界和意识活动。这使他成为现代文学中意识流创作的先驱。詹姆斯还十分关注视角和技巧。他没有采取传统的全知角度或第一人称叙事法，而是运用一种被他称为"意识中心"的叙述方式，即通过作品中某个熟悉他人、观察敏锐的人物来叙述故事。这一人物在情节发展中多是一个旁观者，常常代表了詹姆斯本人的观点。他的小说结构严谨、细致、复杂，极少有纯修饰的部分，人物、情节、背景、对话都相互联系，共同为主题服务。

詹姆斯的国际主题小说揭示了两种生活道德观念和社会风尚的冲突，为消解欧美文化之间的误读作出了贡献。他的人物大都富有教养、举止优雅，出入于上流社会。他笔下的美国人天真、热情，虽然本性善良，但有时过于幼稚、粗俗，对欧洲礼仪和传统缺乏了解或置之不顾，但本质却是好的。欧洲人则是传统文化、教养风度的象征。虽然有时在美国人眼里显得伪善、乏味，但似乎总是正确的。詹姆斯还一改美国文学以男性为中心的特点，创造了一批聪慧美丽、有思想、有见地、纯洁无瑕的女性形象，这些女性角色体现了詹姆斯对爱、道德、忠贞、善良和美的追求。

除了创作文学作品，詹姆斯还写下大量评论文章，1884 年发表的《小说的艺术》("The Art of Fiction") 至今仍被认为是有关小说创作理论的重要作品。他创造的许多术语，如视角 (point of view)、主题 (donnée)、技巧 (execution) 等沿用至今，为小说的发展作出了贡献。

Daisy Miller

【题解】

女主人公黛西·米勒随母亲和弟弟来欧洲旅游,她独立自主、热情纯真、活泼任性,蔑视传统的繁文缛节,坚持自己喜欢的生活方式。在罗马和瑞士旅游时,由于她我行我素,不顾欧洲的礼节,不听在欧洲求学的美国青年温特伯恩的劝说,自由与男子交往,结果受到侨居欧洲的美国人社交圈的非议和排斥,而她的一意孤行也使她最终患病身亡。临终前,她带信给温特伯恩,说她从未与任何人订婚。温特伯恩这才意识到黛西原来是个纯真的女孩。

作品突出体现了新旧两个世界、欧洲文化和美国文化之间的冲突。正如其名Daisy所示,黛西像一朵常见的野菊花,虽不高雅,却充满活力,虽普通,却清纯无瑕。作品通过受欧洲文化熏陶的温特伯恩的眼光,来判断黛西的行为是否合乎道德、合乎规范。詹姆斯很少直接描写欧洲人,而是通过刻画深受欧洲文化影响的美国侨民来反映欧洲人的特点。他们学会了欧洲人的世故、刻板、诡诈和圆滑,以正统和高雅自居,对黛西的行为横加指责。黛西不能入乡随俗,她的天真和勇气既是她的骄傲,也是导致她死亡的直接因素。她的死是美国人在接触、了解当时欧洲繁文缛节和等级观念时付出的代价。欧美文化之间的冲突在詹姆斯以后的作品中得到了缓和,走向和解。

《黛西·米勒》生动地表现了詹姆斯对视角的运用。叙事者温特伯恩是故事的"意识中心",对故事的展开起到了至关重要的作用。

《黛西·米勒》共分四章,以下内容选自第三章。

From Daisy Miller

3

Winterbourne, who had returned to Geneva the day after his excursion to Chillon, went to Rome toward the end of January. His aunt had been established there a considerable time and he had received from her a couple of characteristic letters. "Those people you were so devoted to last summer at Vevey have turned up here, courier and all," she wrote. "They seem to have made several acquaintances, but the courier continues to be the most intime. The young lady, however, is also very intimate with various third-rate Italians, with whom she rackets about in a way that makes much talk. Bring me that pretty novel of Cherbuliez's— 'Paule Méré'—and don't come later than the 23rd."

Our friend would in the natural course of events, on arriving in Rome, have presently ascertained Mrs. Miller's address at the American banker's and gone to pay his compliments to Miss Daisy. "After what happened at Vevey, I certainly think I may call upon them," he said to Mrs. Costello.

"If after what happens—at Vevey and everywhere—you desire to keep up the acquaintance, you are very welcome. Of course you're not squeamish—a man may know everyone. Men are welcome to the privilege!"

"Pray what is it then that 'happens'—here for instance?" Winterbourne asked.

"Well, the girl tears about alone with her unmistakably low foreigners. As to what happens further you must apply elsewhere for information. She has picked up half a dozen of the regular Roman fortune hunters of the inferior sort and she takes them about to such houses as she may put her nose into. When she comes to a party—such a party as she can come to—she brings with her a gentleman with a good deal of manner and a wonderful mustache."

"And where's the mother?"

"I haven't the least idea. They're very dreadful people."

Winterbourne thought them over in these new lights. "They're very ignorant—very innocent only, and utterly uncivilised. Depend on it they're not 'bad'."

"They're hopelessly vulgar," said Mrs. Costello. "Whether or no being hopelessly vulgar is being 'bad' is a question for the metaphysicians. They're bad enough to blush for, at any rate; and for this short life that's quite enough."

The news that his little friend the child of nature of the Swiss lakeside was now surrounded by half a dozen wonderful mustaches checked Winterbourne's impulse to go straightway to see her. He had perhaps not definitely flattered himself that he had made an ineffaceable impression upon her heart, but he was annoyed at hearing of a state of affairs so little in harmony with an image that had lately flitted in and out of his own meditations; the image of a very pretty girl looking out of an old Roman window and asking herself urgently when Mr. Winterbourne would arrive. If, however, he determined to wait a little before reminding this young lady of his claim to her faithful remembrance, he called with more promptitude on two or three other friends. One of these friends was an American lady who had spent several winters at Geneva, where she had placed her children at school. She was a very accomplished woman and she lived in the Via Gregoriana. Winterbourne found her in a little crimson drawing-room on the third floor; the room was filled with southern sunshine. He hadn't been there ten minutes when the servant, appearing in the doorway, announced complacently "Madame Mila!" This announcement was presently followed by the entrance of little Randolph Miller, who stopped in the middle of the room and stood staring at Winterbourne. An instant later his pretty sister crossed the threshold; and then, after a considerable interval, the parent of the pair slowly advanced.

"I guess I know you!" Randolph broke ground without delay.

"I'm sure you know a great many things"—and his old friend clutched him all interestedly by the arm. "how's your education coming on?"

Daisy was engaged in some pretty babble with her hostess, but when she heard Winterbourne's voice she quickly turned her head with a "Well, I declare!" which he met smiling. "I told you I should come, you know."

"Well, I didn't believe it," she answered.

"I'm much obliged to you for that," laughed the young man.

"You might have come to see me then," Daisy went on as if they had parted the week before.

"I arrived only yesterday."

"I don't believe any such thing!" the girl declared afresh.

Winterbourne turned with a protesting smile to her mother, but this lady evaded his glance and, seating herself, fixed her eyes on her son. "We've got a bigger place than this," Randolph hereupon broke out. "It's all gold on the walls."

Mrs. Miller, more of a fatalist apparently than ever, turned uneasily in her chair. "I told you if I was to bring you you'd say something!" she stated as for the benefit of such of the company as might hear it.

"I told you!" Randolph retorted. "I tell you, sir!" he added jocosely, giving Winterbourne a thump on the knee. "It is bigger too!"

As Daisy's conversation with her hostess still occupied her Winterbourne judged it becoming to address a few words to her mother—such as "I hope you've been well since we parted at Vevey," he said.

Mrs. Miller now certainly looked at him—at his chin. "Not very well, sir," she answered.

"She's got the dyspepsia," said Randolph. "I've got it too. Father's got it bad. But I've got it worst!"

This proclamation, instead of embarrassing Mrs. Miller, seemed to soothe her by reconstituting the environment to which she was most accustomed. "I suffer from the liver," she amiably whined to Winterbourne. "I think it's the climate; it's less bracing than Schenectady, especially in the winter season. I don't know whether you know we reside at Schenectady. I was saying to Daisy that I certainly hadn't found any one like Dr. Davis and I didn't believe I would. Oh up in Schenectady, he stands first; they think everything of Dr. Davis. He has so much to do, and yet there was nothing he wouldn't do for me. He said he never saw anything like my dyspepsia, but he was bound to get at it. I'm sure there was nothing he wouldn't try, and I didn't care what he did to me if he only brought me relief. He was just going to try something new, and I just longed for it, when we came right off. Mr. Miller felt as if he wanted Daisy to see Europe for herself. But I couldn't help writing the other day that I supposed it was all right for Daisy, but that I didn't know as I could get on much longer without Dr. Davis. At Schenectady he stands at the very top; and there's a great deal of sickness there too. It affects my sleep."

Winterbourne had a good deal of pathological gossip with Dr. Davis's patient, during which Daisy chattered unremittingly to her companion. The young man asked Mrs. Miller how she was pleased with Rome. "Well, I must say I'm disappointed," she confessed. "We had heard so much about it—I suppose we had heard too much. But we couldn't help that. We had been led to expect something different."

Winterbourne, however, abounded in reassurance. "Ah wait a little, and you'll grow very fond of it."

"I hate it worse and worse every day!" cried Randolph.

"You're like the infant Hannibal[1]," his friend laughed.

"No, I ain't—like any infant!" Randolph declared at a venture.

"Well, that's so—and you never were!" his mother concurred. "But we've seen places," she resumed, "that I'd put a long way ahead of Rome." And in reply to Winterbourne's interrogation, "There's Zurich—up there in the mountains," she instanced, "I think Zurich's real lovely; and we hadn't heard half so much about it."

"The best place we've seen's the City of Richmond!" said Randolph.

"He means the ship," his mother explained. "We crossed in that ship. Randolph had a good time on the City of Richmond."

"It's the best place I've struck," the child repeated. "Only it was turned the wrong way."

"Well, we've got to turn the right way sometime," said Mrs. Miller with strained but weak optimism. Winterbourne expressed the hope that her daughter at least appreciated the so various interest of Rome, and she declared with some spirit that Daisy was quite carried away. "It's on account of the society—the society's splendid. She goes round everywhere; she has made a great number of acquaintances. Of course she goes round more than I do. I must say they've all been very sweet—they've taken her right in. And then she knows a great many gentlemen. Oh she thinks there's nothing like Rome. Of course it's a great deal pleasanter for a young lady if she knows plenty of gentlemen."

By this time Daisy had turned her attention again to Winterbourne, but in quite the same free form. "I've been telling Mrs. Walker how mean you were!"

"And what's the evidence you've offered?" he asked, a trifle disconcerted, for all his superior gallantry, by her inadequate measure of the zeal of an admirer who on his way down to Rome had stopped neither at Bologna nor at Florence, simply because of a certain sweet appeal to his fond fancy, not to say to his finest curiosity. He remembered how a cynical compatriot had once told him that American women—the pretty ones, and this gave a largeness to the axiom—were at once the most exacting in the world and the least endowed with a sense of indebtedness.

"Why you were awfully mean up at Vevey," Daisy said. "You wouldn't do most anything. You wouldn't stay there when I asked you."

"Dearest young lady," cried Winterbourne, with generous passion, "have I come all the way to Rome only to be riddled by your silver shafts?"

"Just hear him say that!"—and she gave an affectionate twist to a bow on her hostess's dress. "Did you ever hear anything so quaint?"

"So 'quaint', my dear?" echoed Mrs. Walker more critically—quite in the tone of a partisan of Winterbourne.

"Well, I don't know"—and the girl continued to finger her ribbons. "Mrs. Walker, I want to tell you something."

"Say, mother-r," broke in Randolph with his rough ends to his words, "I tell you you've got to go. Eugenio'll raise something!"

"I'm not afraid of Eugenio," said Daisy with a toss of her head. "Look here, Mrs. Walker," she went on, "you know I'm coming to your party."

"I am delighted to hear it."

"I've got a lovely dress!"

"I'm very sure of that."

"But I want to ask a favor—permission to bring a friend."

"I shall be happy to see any of your friends," said Mrs. Walker, who turned with a smile to Mrs. Miller.

"Oh they're not my friends," cried that lady, squirming in shy repudiation. "It seems as if they didn't take to me—I never spoke to one of them."

"It's an intimate friend of mine, Mr. Giovanelli[2]," Daisy pursued without a tremor in her young clearness or a shadow on her shining bloom.

Mrs. Walker had a pause and gave a rapid glance at Winterbourne. "I shall be glad to see Mr. Giovanelli," she then returned.

"He's just the finest kind of Italian," Daisy pursued with the prettiest serenity. "He's a great friend of mine and the handsomest man in the world—except Mr. Winterbourne! He knows plenty of Italians, but he wants to know some Americans. It seems as if he was crazy about Americans. He's tremendously bright. He's perfectly lovely!"

It was settled that this paragon should be brought to Mrs. Walker's party, and then Mrs. Miller prepared to take her leave. "I guess we'll go right back to the hotel," she remarked with a confessed failure of the larger imagination.

"You may go back to the hotel, mother," Daisy replied, "but I'm just going to walk round."

"She's going to go it with Mr. Giovanelli," Randolph unscrupulously commented.

"I'm going to go it on the Pincio," Daisy peaceably smiled, while the way that she "condoned" these things almost melted Winterboune's heart.

"Alone, my dear—at this hour?" Mrs. Walker asked. The afternoon was drawing to a close—it was the hour for the throng of carriages and of contemplative pedestrians. "I don't consider it's safe, Daisy," her hostess firmly asserted.

"Neither do I then," Mrs. Miller thus borrowed confidence to add. "You'll catch the fever as sure as you live. Remember what Dr. Davis told you!"

"Give her some of that medicine before she starts in," Randolph suggested.

The company had risen to its feet; Daisy, still showing her pretty teeth, bent over and kissed her hostess. "Mrs. Walker, you're too perfect," she simply said. "I'm not going alone; I'm going to meet a friend."

"Your friend won't keep you from catching the fever even if it is his own second nature," Mrs. Miller observed.

"Is it Mr. Giovanelli that's the dangerous attraction?" Mrs. Walker asked without mercy.

Winterbourne was watching the challenged girl; at this question his attention quickened. She stood there smiling and smoothing her bonnet-ribbons; she glanced at Winterbourne. Then, while she glanced and smiled, she brought out all affirmatively and without a shade of hesitation, "Mr. Giovanelli—the beautiful Giovanelli."

"My dear young friend,"—and, taking her hand, Mrs. Walker turned to pleading—"don't prowl off to the Pincio at this hour to meet a beautiful Italian."

"Well, he speaks first-rate English," Mrs. Miller incoherently mentioned.

"Gracious me!" Daisy piped up, "I don't want to do anything that's going to affect my health—or my character either! There's an easy way to settle it." Her eyes continued to play over Winterbourne. "The Pincio's only a hundred yards off; and if Mr. Winterbourne were as polite as he pretends he'd offer to walk right in with me!"

Winterbourne's politeness hastened to proclaim itself, and the girl gave him gracious leave to accompany her. They passed downstairs before her mother, and at the door Winterbourne saw Mrs. Miller's carriage drawn up, with the ornamental courier whose acquaintance he had made at Vevey seated within. "Goodbye, Eugenio!" cried Daisy; "I'm going to take a walk!" The distance from Via Gregoriana to the beautiful garden at the other end of the Pincian Hill is in fact rapidly traversed. As the day was splendid, however, and the concourse of vehicles, walkers, and loungers numerous, the young Americans found their progress much delayed. This fact was highly agreeable to Winterbourne, in spite of his consciousness of his singular situation. The slow-moving, idly-gazing Roman crowd bestowed much attention on the extremely pretty young woman of English race who was passed through it, with some difficulty, on his arm; and he wondered what on earth had been in Daisy's mind when she proposed to exhibit herself unattended to its appreciation. His own mission, to her sense, was apparently to consign her to the hands of Mr. Giovanelli; but at once annoyed and gratified, he resolved that he would do no such thing.

"Why haven't you been to see me?" she meanwhile asked. "You can't get out of that."

"I've had the honor of telling you that I've only just stepped out of the train."

"You must have stayed in the train a good while after it stopped!" she derisively cried. "I suppose you were asleep. You've had time to go to see Mrs. Walker."

"I knew Mrs. Walker—" Winterbourne began to explain.

"I know where you knew her. You knew her at Geneva. She told me so. Well, you knew me at Vevey. That's just as good. So you ought to have come." She asked him no other question than this; she began to prattle about her own affairs. "We've got splendid rooms at the hotel; Eugenio says they're the best rooms in Rome. We're going to stay all winter—if we don't die of the fever; and I guess we'll stay then! It's a great deal nicer than I thought; I thought it would be fearfully quiet—in fact I was sure it would be deadly poky. I foresaw we should be going round all the time with one of those dreadful old men who explain about the pictures and things. But we only had about a week of that, and now I'm enjoying myself. I know ever so many people, and they're all so charming. The society's extremely select. There are all kinds—English and Germans and Italians. I think I like the English best. I like their style of conversation. But there are some lovely Americans. I never saw anything so hospitable. There's something or other every day. There's not much dancing—but I must say I never thought dancing was everything. I was always fond of conversation. I guess I'll have plenty at Mrs. Walker's—her rooms are so small." When they had passed the gate of the Pincian Gardens, Miss Miller began to wonder where Mr. Giovanelli might be. "We had better go straight to that place in front, where you look at the view."

Winterbourne at this took a stand. "I certainly shan't help you to find him."

"Then I shall find him without you," Daisy said with spirit.

"You certainly won't leave me!" he protested.

She burst into her familiar little laugh. "Are you afraid you'll get lost—or run over? But there's Giovanelli leaning against that tree. He's staring at the women in the carriages; did you ever see anything so cool?"

Winterbourne descried hereupon at some distance a little figure that stood with folded arms and nursing its cane. It had a handsome face, a hat artfully poised, a glass in one eye and a nosegay in its buttonhole. Daisy's friend looked at it a moment and then said: "Do you mean to speak to that thing?"

"Do I mean to speak to him? Why you don't suppose I mean to communicate by signs!"

"Pray understand then," the young man returned, "that I intend to remain with you."

Daisy stopped and looked at him without a sign of troubled consciousness, with nothing in her face but her charming eyes, her charming teeth and her happy dimples. "Well she's a cool one!" he thought.

"I don't like the way you say that," she declared. "It's too imperious."

"I beg your pardon if I say it wrong. The main point's to give you an idea of my meaning."

The girl looked at him more gravely, but with eyes that were prettier than ever. "I've never allowed a gentleman to dictate to me or to interfere with anything I do."

"I think that's just where your mistake has come in," he retorted. "You should sometimes listen to a gentleman—the right one."

At this she began to laugh again. "I do nothing but listen to gentlemen! Tell me if Mr. Giovanelli is the right one?"

The gentleman with the nosegay in his bosom had now made out our two friends, and was approaching Miss Miller with obsequious rapidity. He bowed to Winterbourne as well as to the latter's compatriot; he seemed to shine, in his coxcombical way, with the desire to please and the fact of his own intelligent joy, though Winterbourne thought him not a bad-looking fellow. But he nevertheless said to Daisy, "No, he's not the right one."

She had clearly a natural turn for free introductions; she mentioned with the easiest grace the name of each of her companions to the other. She strolled forward with one of them on either hand; Mr. Giovanelli, who spoke English very clearly—Winterbourne afterward learned that he had practiced the idiom upon a great many American heiresses—addressed her a great deal of very polite nonsense. He had the best possible manners, and the young American, who said nothing, reflected on the depth of Italian subtlety, so strangely opposed to Anglo-Saxon simplicity, which enables people to show a smoother surface in proportion as they're more acutely displeased. Giovanelli of course had counted upon something more intimate—he had not bargained for a party of three; but he kept his temper in a manner that suggested far stretching intentions. Winterbourne flattered himself that he had taken his measure. "He's anything but a gentleman," said the young American; "he isn't even a very plausible imitation of one. He's a music master or a penny-a-liner or a third-rate artist. He's awfully on his good behavior, but damn his fine eyes!" Mr. Giovanelli had indeed great advantages; but it was deeply disgusting to Daisy's other friend that something in her shouldn't have instinctively discriminated against such a type. Giovanelli chattered and jested and made himself agreeable according to his honest Roman lights. It was true that if he was an imitation the imitation was studied. "Nevertheless," Winterbourne said to himself, "a nice girl ought to know!" And then he came back to the dreadful question of whether this was in fact a nice girl. Would a nice girl—even allowing for her being a little American flirt—make a rendezvous with a presumably low-lived foreigner? The rendezvous in this case indeed had been in broad daylight and in the most crowded corner of Rome, but wasn't it impossible to regard the choice of these very circumstances as a proof more of vulgarity than of anything else? Singular though it may seem, Winterbourne was vexed that the girl, in joining her amoroso[3], shouldn't appear more impatient of his own company, and he was vexed precisely because of his inclination. It was impossible to regard her as a wholly unspotted flower—she lacked a certain indispensable fineness; and it would therefore simplify the situation to be able to treat her as the subject of one of the visitations known to romancers as "lawless passions." That she should seem to wish to get rid of him would have helped him to think more lightly of her, just as to be able to think more lightly of her would make her much less perplexing. Daisy at any rate continued on this occasion to present herself as an inscrutable combination of audacity and innocence.

She had been walking some quarter of an hour, attended by her two cavaliers, and responding in a tone of very childish gaiety, as it after all struck one of them, to the pretty speeches of the other, when a carriage that had detached itself from the revolving train drew up beside the path. At the same moment Winterbourne noticed that his friend Mrs. Walker—the lady whose house he had lately left—was seated in the vehicle and was beckoning to him. Leaving Miss Miller's side, he hastened to obey her summons—and all to find her flushed, excited, scandalised. "It's really too dreadful,"—she earnestly appealed to him. "That crazy girl mustn't do this sort of thing. She mustn't walk here with you two men. Fifty people have remarked her."

Winterbourne—suddenly and rather oddly rubbed the wrong way by this—raised his grave eyebrows. "I think it's a pity to make too much fuss about it."

"It's a pity to let the girl ruin herself!"

"She's very innocent," he reasoned in his own troubled interest.

"She's very reckless!" cried Mrs. Walker, "and goodness knows how far—left to itself—it may go. Did you ever," she proceeded to enquire, "see anything so blatantly as the mother? After you had all left me just now I couldn't sit still for thinking of it. It seemed too pitiful not even to attempt to save them. I ordered the carriage and put on my bonnet and came here as quickly as possible. Thank Heaven I've found you!"

"What do you propose to do with us?" Winterbourne uncomfortably smiled.

"To ask her to get in, to drive her about here for half an hour—so that the world may see she's not running absolutely wild—and then to take her safely home."

"I don't think it's a very happy thought," he said after reflexion, "but you're at liberty to try."

Mrs. Walker accordingly tried. The young man went in pursuit of their young lady who had simply nodded and smiled, from her distance, at her recent patroness in the carriage and then had gone her way with her companion. On learning, in the event, that Mrs. Walker had followed her, she retraced her steps, however, with a perfect good grace and with Mr. Giovanelli at her side. She professed herself "enchanted" to have a chance to present this gentleman to her good friend, and immediately achieved the introduction; declaring with it, and as if it were of as little importance, that she had never in her life seen anything so lovely as that lady's carriage rug.

"I'm glad you admire it," said her poor pursuer, smiling sweetly. "Will you get in and let me put it over you?"

"Oh no, thank you!"—Daisy knew her mind. "I'll admire it ever so much more as I see you driving round with it."

"Do get in and drive round with me!" Mrs. Walker pleaded.

"That would be charming, but it's so fascinating just as I am!"—with which the girl radiantly took in the gentlemen on either side of her.

"It may be fascinating, dear child, but it's not the custom here," urged the lady of the victoria[4], leaning forward in this vehicle with her hands devoutly clasped.

"Well, it ought to be then!" Daisy imperturbably laughed. "If I didn't walk I'd expire."

"You should walk with your mother, dear," cried Mrs. Walker with a loss of patience.

"With my mother dear?" the girl amusedly echoed. Winterbourne saw that she scented interference. "My mother never walked ten steps in her life. And then, you know," she blandly added, "I'm more than five years old."

"You're old enough to be more reasonable. You're old enough, dear Miss Miller, to be talked about."

Daisy wondered to extravagance. "Talked about? What do you mean?"

"Come into my carriage and I'll tell you."

Daisy turned shining eyes again from one of the gentlemen beside her to the other. Mr. Giovanelli was bowing to and fro, rubbing down his gloves and laughing irresponsibly;

Winterbourne thought the scene the most unpleasant possible. "I don't think I want to know what you mean," the girl presently said. "I don't think I should like it."

Winterbourne only wished that Mrs. Walker would tuck up her carriage rug and drive away, but this lady, as she afterward told him, didn't feel she could "rest there." "Should you prefer being thought a very reckless girl?" she accordingly asked.

"Gracious me!" exclaimed Daisy. She looked again at Mr. Giovanelli, then she turned to her other companion. There was a small pink flush in her cheek; she was tremendously pretty. "Does Mr. Winterbourne think," she put to him with a wonderful bright intensity of appeal, "that—to save my reputation—I ought to get into the carriage?"

It really embarrassed him; for an instant he cast about—so strange was it to hear her speak that way of her "reputation." But he himself in fact had to speak in accordance with gallantry. The finest gallantry here was surely just to tell her the truth; and the truth, for our young man, as the few indications I have been able to give have made him known to the reader, was that his charming friend should listen to the voice for civilised society. He took in again exquisite prettiness and then said the more distinctly: "I think you should get into the carriage."

Daisy gave the rein to her amusement. "I never heard anything so stiff! If this is improper, Mrs. Walker," she pursued, "then I'm all improper, and you had better give me right up. Goodbye; I hope you'll have a lovely ride!"—and with Mr. Giovanelli, who made a triumphantly obsequious salute, she turned away.

Mrs. Walker sat looking after her, and there were tears in Mrs. Walker's eyes. "Get in here, sir," she said to Winterbourne, indicating the place beside her. The young man answered that he felt bound to accompany Miss Miller; whereupon the lady of the victoria declared that if he refused her this favor she would never speak to him again. She was evidently wound up. He accordingly hastened to overtake Daisy and her more faithful ally, and, offering her his hand, told her that Mrs. Walker had made a stringent claim on his presence. He had expected her to answer with something rather free, something still more significant of the perversity from which the voice of society, through the lips of their distressed friend, had so earnestly endeavored to dissuade her. But she only let her hand slip, as she scarce looked at him, through his slightly awkward grasp; while Mr. Giovanelli, to make it worse, bade him farewell with too emphatic a flourish of the hat.

Winterbourne was not in the best possible humor as he took his seat beside the author of his sacrifice. "That was not clever of you," he said candidly, as the vehicle mingled again with the throng of carriages.

"In such a case," his companion answered, "I don't wish to be clever—I only want to be true!"

"Well, your truth has only offended the strange little creature—it has only put her off."

"It has happened very well"—Mrs. Walker accepted her work. "If she's so perfectly determined to compromise herself the sooner one knows it the better—one can act accordingly."

"I suspect she meant no great harm, you know," Winterbourne maturely opined.

"So I thought a month ago. But she has been going too far."

"What has she been doing?"

"Everything that's not done here. Flirting with any man she could pick up; sitting in corners with mysterious Italians; dancing all the evening with the same partners; receiving visits at eleven o'clock at night. Her mother melts away when visitors come."

"But her brother," laughed Winterbourne, "sits up till two in the morning."

"He must be edified by what he sees. I'm told that at their hotel every one's talking about her and that a smile goes round among all the servants when a gentleman comes and asks for Miss Miller."

"Ah we needn't mind the servants." Winterbourne compassionately signified. "The poor girl's only fault," he presently added, "is her complete lack of education."

"She's naturally indelicate," Mrs. Walker, on her side, reasoned. "Take that example this morning. How long had you known her at Vevey?"

"A couple of days."

"Imagine then the taste of her making it a personal matter that you should have left the place!"

He agreed that taste wasn't the strong point of the Millers—after which he was silent for some moments; but only at last to add: "I suspect, Mrs. Walker, that you and I have lived too long at Geneva!" And he further noted that he should be glad to learn with what particular design she had made him enter her carriage.

"I wanted to enjoin on you the importance of your ceasing your relations with Miss Miller; that of your not appearing to flirt with her; that of your giving her no further opportunity to expose herself; that of your in short letting her alone."

"I'm afraid I can't do anything quite so enlightened as that," he returned. "I like her awfully, you know."

"All the more reason that you shouldn't help her to make a scandal."

"Well, there shall be nothing scandalous in my attentions to her." He was willing to promise.

"There certainly will be in the way she takes them. But I've said what I had on my conscience," Mrs. Walker pursued. "If you wish to rejoin the young lady I'll put you down. Here, by the way, you have a chance."

The carriage was engaged in that part of the Pincian drive which overhangs the wall of Rome and overlooks the beautiful Villa Borghese. It is bordered by a large parapet, near which are several seats. One of these, at a distance, was occupied by a gentleman and a lady, toward whom Mrs. Walker gave a toss of her head. At the same moment these persons rose and walked to the parapet. Winterbourne had asked the coachman to stop; he now descended from the carriage. His companion looked at him a moment in silence and then, while he raised his hat, drove majestically away. He stood where he had alighted; he had turned his eyes toward Daisy and her cavalier. They evidently saw no one; they were too deeply occupied with each other. When they reached the low garden-wall they remained a little looking off at the great flat-topped pine-clusters of the Villa Borghese; then the girl's attendant admirer seated himself familiarly on the broad ledge of the wall. The western sun in the opposite sky sent out a brilliant shaft through a couple of cloud-bars; whereupon the gallant Giovanelle took her parasol out of her hands and opened it. She came a little nearer and he held the parasol over her; then, still holding it, he let it rest on her shoulder, that both of their heads were hidden from Winterbourne. This young man stayed but a moment longer; then he began to walk. But he walked—not toward the couple united beneath the parasol, rather toward the residence of his aunt, Mrs. Costello.

【注解】

1. Hannibal：汉尼拔（公元前247—公元前183），迦太基著名战将，数次发兵攻打罗马，最后被俘，服毒自杀。据说他一出生就发誓与罗马有不共戴天之仇。此处温特伯恩借此暗示伦道夫跟汉尼拔一样，从小就不喜欢罗马。
2. Giovanelli：该名字意为"年轻人"。
3. amoroso：情人。
4. victoria：一种四轮两座马车。

American Literature Between 1865 and 1914

【思考题】

1. What are the contradictory attitudes of Winterbourne towards Daisy? Does he think she is a flirt? Why or why not?
2. What does Winterbourne imply when he says "I suspect, Mrs. Walker, that you and I have lived too long at Geneva!"?
3. How does Mrs. Walker change her attitude towards Daisy? Why does she want to save Daisy? As an American living in Europe, what does she represent? What do Winterbourne, Daisy, Mrs. Miller and Giovanelli represent respectively?
4. What is the conflict between Daisy and Mrs. Walker? What is the theme of the story? Discuss James' "international theme" by citing examples from the text above.
5. In this chapter, how does James reveal the conflict between Mrs. Walker and Daisy through the eyes of Winterbourne? What is the function of Winterbourne as a "central consciousness"? Comment on the technique of the point of view in this story.

解读举例

1. 《黛西·米勒》从根本上说是一个关于美国人的故事，讲述了美国青年，尤其是女性与欧洲人截然不同的思维和生活方式，鼓励人们应该坚决反对那些陈规陋习和偏见。黛西奋起反抗残忍而复杂的旧习俗和人情世故，是新女性的象征。她纯洁、活泼、独立、无畏，具有追求自由和独立的精神。

2. 《黛西·米勒》讽刺了侨居欧洲的美国人。黛西本人就是轻佻的市侩作风的代表。她的母亲代表了暴富后的美国人的浅陋粗俗和缺乏教养。科斯特洛太太和沃克太太则是久居欧洲，深受欧洲保守、世故和圆滑等作风影响的美国人的缩影。

Kate Chopin
1851—1904

凯特·肖邦出生于美国中部密苏里州的圣路易斯。她4岁丧父，由母亲、外祖母和曾外祖母抚养成人。肖邦的曾外祖母是一位纯正的克利奥尔人 (Creole)，她教给肖邦克利奥尔的语言、礼仪、规范，对肖邦的思想影响很大。克利奥尔这个词最早是用来特指出生于美洲新大陆的法国人或者是西班牙人后裔，在肖邦生活的时代，

克利奥尔这个词带有很强的贵族意味。1870年，肖邦嫁给了英俊的克利奥尔人奥斯卡·肖邦，随他来到了克利奥尔人生活的中心——新奥尔良。1882年丈夫去世，肖邦开始了孀居生活。1884年，肖邦回到了圣路易斯，四年后投身文学创作。

肖邦在写作生涯开始之初，曾尝试过长篇小说这一形式，创作了《过错》(*At Fault*, 1890)。这部作品的思想性虽有可取之处，以女性婚姻生活及面临的困惑为主题，但艺术价值不高，结构较零散，情节安排略显牵强。之后她将自己的主要精力放在把握人物瞬间心理片段见长的中、短篇作品上，佳作迭出。

肖邦写作的素材主要来源于路易斯安那州克利奥尔人的生活，她的作品也是19世纪后半叶美国高涨的乡土文学浪潮中的一朵美丽浪花。在短篇小说集《牛轭湖的乡亲》(*Bayou Folk*, 1894) 和《阿卡迪亚之夜》(*A Night at Acadie*, 1897) 中，她用细腻的笔法描绘了路易斯安那州如画的风景，她笔下的克利奥尔人、卡真人和黑人也特色鲜明，形象栩栩如生。

肖邦的作品能够成为美国乡土文学的优秀代表，并不仅仅因为她对一方水土进行了惟妙惟肖的描绘，还在于她能以一种冷静审慎的眼光来看待她所描摹的世界。她虽有克利奥尔背景，但终究是生长在中部，这种既是局内人又是外来者的双重身份，为她的作品赋予了一种细腻质感，使她能够在作品中客观地对克利奥尔的价值观进行评述，也使她的作品拥有了超越乡土文学狭隘地域范畴的深度。混血儿是克利奥尔社会的重要成员，克利奥尔人对种族间通婚的态度比南方其他各州要宽松。即使如此，种族间依然存在矛盾和对立，种族歧视的现象仍较为普遍。凯特·肖邦敏锐地洞察到了这一点，早在她的第一部短篇小说集《牛轭湖的乡亲》中，肖邦就对种族歧视这一违反人性的现象进行了抨击。在《德西雷的儿子》(*Desiree's Baby*) 一篇中，主人公阿曼德不念伉俪情深，仅凭所谓血统将自己的妻子德西雷抛弃，置襁褓中的幼子于不顾，这些都证明了种族歧视的观念对人灵魂的毒害。《德西雷的儿子》中阿曼德的家庭破碎要归咎于种族制度，但德西雷的不幸却有更深层的根源。德西雷不仅是种族歧视的牺牲品，也是夫权社会的牺牲品。她的丈夫丝毫不给她申辩的可能就将她赶出家门，女性在家庭中根本没有发言权，完全是丈夫随时可以丢弃的附属品。尽管小说没有明确交代德西雷的命运如何，但凭"她消失在深深的大湖岸边浓密的芦苇和柳树丛中；她再也没有回来"一句可判断，她很可能选择了死亡。

《德西雷的儿子》表达了肖邦对受压迫女性无限的同情。事实上，肖邦对女性命运的关注贯穿了她的整个创作过程。除了逆来顺受的德西雷，肖邦的作品中还有另一类女性,她们与德西雷完全不同,她们强悍自主,懂得要把握自我命运,出现了女性意识的觉醒。在小说《阿卡迪亚舞会》("At the Cadian Ball")中女主角克拉丽莎对个人幸福的追求使她摆脱了社会礼法的束缚,是恋爱关系中真正的主宰者。时隔六年,肖邦为《阿卡迪亚舞会》写下了续篇《暴风雨》("The Storm"),主题比《阿卡迪亚舞会》更为大胆,对女性在爱情中的需求给予了肯定,直接对19世纪维多利亚式的传统道德价值观念提出了挑战。

感情与肉体的双重觉醒也是肖邦的代表作《觉醒》(*The Awakening*, 1899)的主题。女主人公埃德娜结婚六年,有着安定富裕的生活和一个在外人看来令人羡慕的家庭。但她却渐渐意识到自己在生活中扮演的角色不过是两个孩子的母亲,一位专制的丈夫的妻子和私有财产,毫无自我可言。为此,她毅然决然地离开了禁锢着她身心自由的家,一个人试图靠绘画为生,并有了新的感情归属,与一位敏感的克利奥尔青年相爱。然而,她的叛逆行为注定不能为社会所接受,连她的爱人也不能理解她。最终她选择了自尽,消失在茫茫大海中。

《觉醒》深刻的主题使人们经常将它与法国作家福楼拜的名著《包法利夫人》(*Madam Bovary*, 1857)相提并论。这两部作品有不少相似之处。女主人公都抛家弃子,为追求感情生活付出生命代价。然而,《包法利夫人》中的爱玛是个浅薄的女性,她追求的是浪漫主义的迷梦,至死也没能觉醒。而《觉醒》中的埃德娜却为了摆脱男权社会的束缚,离家出走,主动离开所谓的上流社会,大胆追求真爱。然而在一个由男性主宰的社会里,女性永远不可能获得完全的自由。为此她选择了自杀。这并不是一种懦弱的表示,而是对男权社会有力的控诉。女主人公不惜以生命来捍卫自己的觉醒和自由。从某个角度上说,埃德娜当之无愧是新女性的代表。

觉醒的代价是痛苦的。这句话不仅可以用来形容埃德娜身处的困境,也同样可以用来形容作者肖邦的命运。《觉醒》大胆抨击了男权社会,肯定了女性对肉体和灵魂双重自由的追求,这在19世纪末维多利亚式的美国社会引起轩然大波。人们责备肖邦诲淫诲盗,在小说中描写了一个不守妇道、道德败坏的女性。同她笔下描绘的主人公一样,肖邦也因此被摒弃于社会之外,在舆论的重重围攻下对写作丧失了信心,自此封笔。而肖邦的遭遇,也从一个侧面说明了旧时代女性作家的艰难处境。

The Story of an Hour

【题解】

《一个小时的故事》刻画了女主人公米拉德太太在得知自己的丈夫在车祸中丧

生的消息后的心路历程：从开始的放声恸哭，到后来独自回到房间所体会到的狂喜，到走出房间的兴奋，到看到丈夫归来吃惊地心脏病发作而亡，在短短的一个小时以内，女主人公的心情经历了多次突转，作者传神的描写让读者体会到了一个女性渴望摆脱男性束缚，追求自由的心声。

The Story of an Hour

Knowing that Mrs. Millard was afflicted with a heart trouble, great care was taken to break to her as gently as possible the news of her husband's death.

It was her sister Josephine who told her, in broken sentences; veiled hints that revealed in half concealing. Her husband's friend Richards was there, too, near her. It was he who had been in the newspaper office when intelligence of the railroad disaster was received, with Brently Mallard's name leading the list of "killed." He had only taken the time to assure himself of its truth by a second telegram, and had hastened to forestall any less careful, less tender friend in bearing the sad message.

She did not hear the story as many women have heard the same, with a paralyzed inability to accept its significance[1]. She wept at once, with sudden, wild abandonment, in her sister's arms. When the storm of grief had spent itself she went away to her room alone. She would have no one follow her.

There stood, facing the open window, a comfortable, roomy armchair. Into this she sank, pressed down by a physical exhaustion that haunted her body and seemed to reach into her soul.

She could see in the open square before her house the tops of trees that were all aquiver with the new spring life. The delicious breath of rain was in the air. In the street below a peddler was crying his wares. The notes of a distant song which some one was singing reached her faintly, and countless sparrows were twittering in the eaves.

There were patches of blue sky showing here and there through the clouds that had met and piled one above the other in the west facing her window.

She sat with her head thrown back upon the cushion of the chair, quite motionless, except when a sob came up into her throat and shook her, as a child who has cried itself to sleep continues to sob in its dreams.

She was young, with a fair, calm face, whose lines bespoke repression and even a certain strength. But now there was a dull stare in her eyes, whose gaze was fixed away off yonder on one of those patches of blue sky. It was not a glance of reflection, but rather indicated a suspension of intelligent thought.

There was something coming to her and she was waiting for it, fearfully. What was it? She did not know; it was too subtle and elusive to name. But she felt it, creeping out of the sky, reaching toward her through the sounds, the scents, the color that filled the air.

Now her bosom rose and fell tumultuously. She was beginning to recognize this thing that was approaching to possess her, and she was striving to beat it back with her will—as powerless as her two white slender hands would have been. When she abandoned herself a little whispered word escaped her slightly parted lips. She said it over and over under her breath: "Free, free, free!" The vacant stare and the look of terror that had followed it went from her eyes. They stayed keen and bright. Her pulses beat fast, and the coursing blood warmed and relaxed every inch of her body.

She did not stop to ask if it were or were not a monstrous joy that held her. A clear and exalted perception enabled her to dismiss the suggestion as trivial.

She knew that she would weep again when she saw the kind, tender hands folded in death; the face that had never looked save with love upon her, fixed and gray and dead. But she saw beyond that bitter moment a long procession of years to come that would belong to her absolutely. And she opened and spread her arms out to them in welcome.

There would be no one to live for her during those coming years; she would live for herself. There would be no powerful will bending her in that blind persistence with which men and women believe they have a right to impose a private will upon a fellow creature. A kind intention or a cruel intention made the act seem no less a crime as she looked upon it in that brief moment of illumination. And yet she had loved him—sometimes. Often she had not. What did it matter! What could love, the unsolved mystery, count for in face of this possession of self-assertion which she suddenly recognized as the strongest impulse of her being! "Free! Body and soul free!" she kept whispering.

Josephine was kneeling before the closed door with her lips to the keyhole, imploring for admission. "Louise, open the door! I beg, open the door—you will make yourself ill. What are you doing Louise? For heaven's sake open the door."

"Go away. I am not making myself ill." No; she was drinking in a very elixir[2] of life through that open window.

Her fancy was running riot along those days ahead of her. Spring days, and summer days, and all sorts of days that would be her own. She breathed a quick prayer that life might be long. It was only yesterday she had thought with a shudder that life might be long.

She arose at length and opened the door to her sister's importunities. There was a feverish triumph in her eyes, and she carried herself unwittingly like a goddess of Victory. She clasped her sister's waist, and together they descended the stairs. Richards stood waiting for them at the bottom.

Some one was opening the front door with a latchkey. It was Brently Mallard who entered, a little travel-stained, composedly carrying his grip-sack[3] and umbrella. He had been far from the scene of accident, and did not even know there had been one. He stood amazed at Josephine's piercing cry; at Richards' quick motion to screen him from the view of his wife. But Richards was too late. When the doctors came they said she had died of heart disease—of joy that kills.

【注解】

1. a paralyzed inability to accept its significance：反应麻木迟钝，一时间无法理解它的含义。
2. elixir：相当于 elixir of life，意思是长生不老药。
3. grip-sack：手提包，旅行袋。

【思考题】

1. When Mrs. Millard retreats into her own room, what does she see through the open window? How does she feel about what she has seen? Does it carry any symbolic significance?
2. When locked in her own room, Mrs. Millard feels a "monstrous joy" and says to herself over and over: "free, free, free!" Are you surprised by her private reaction towards her husband's death? How does it differ from her "public" reaction?
3. How do you think about the relationship between Mr. and Mrs. Millard? Does Mr. Millard treat Mrs. Millard cruelly? Does Mrs. Millard love her husband?
4. Irony occurs in literature when there is a contrast between what is said and what is meant. In what way is this last paragraph of "The Story of an Hour" ironic?
5. Discuss how women can achieve liberation in a patriarchal society.

【简评】

《一个小时的故事》中大量运用了反讽的手法。比如在小说开篇的时候，米拉德太太的亲戚和朋友等都不敢将她丈夫的死讯告诉她,他们担心她会因伤心过度,引发心脏病。事实上,我们所看到的是米拉德太太得知丈夫死讯后,感到一身轻松,她体会到了从来没有过的解放,对未来充满了憧憬和希望。不幸的是她丈夫很快又活生生地出现在她面前。所有有关美好生活的构想随着丈夫的"复活"化成了泡影,米拉德太太伤心地死去,周围的人却都以为她是因为欣喜过度而病发身亡,这不能不说是一种莫大的讽刺。更具有讽刺意味的是,米拉德太太被平庸无聊的感情生活所困,对生命并没有太多的眷恋,当她得知丈夫的死讯,想到终于可以为自己而活的时候,才开始祈盼自己可以活得长久,以便好好享受获得的新生。没有想到她的生命在她刚刚对之有了渴望后不到一个小时就结束了。丈夫的"死",换来了她对"生"的渴望,而丈夫的"生"为她带来的却是"死亡"。

小说中反讽手法的运用不仅达到了强烈的戏剧性效果,使短短千余字的小说充满了戏剧性张力,更重要的是,这种反讽也揭示出男权社会对女性的压制,以及对女性的程式化认识的荒谬。对周围人来说,他们谁也没有料想到米拉德太太会为自己丈夫的死而高兴,为丈夫的活而悲伤。在他们看来,丈夫就是妻子的一切,这是毋庸置疑的真理。事实上,没有人能够真正了解女主人公的内心世界。在这样一个男权社会中,米拉德太太对自由的渴望最后也只能以死亡的形式悲剧性地终结。

Stephen Crane
1871—1900

斯蒂芬·克莱恩生于新泽西州纽瓦克市,曾先后就读于军事预备学校、拉法耶特学院和西拉库斯大学,但都没有毕业。20岁那年(1891年),他辍学来到纽约,当了一名自由记者,经常出没于纽约的贫民窟,目睹了生活在社会底层的人们悲惨的境遇,自己也常常忍饥挨饿,贫困潦倒。然而这段生活也为他后来的文学创作提供了真实、丰富的第一手资料。1893年,他根据自己当记者这几年的耳闻目睹和亲身经历创作出版了表现纽约贫民窟悲惨生活状况的小说《街头女郎麦琪》(*Maggie: A Girl of the Streets*, 1893),讲述了一位年轻的爱尔兰裔美国女孩在纽约贫民窟被遗弃,沦为街头妓女,最后投河自尽的悲惨故事。作品尽管没有为主人公的生活困境提供出路,却表达了作者对社会黑暗的愤怒与对穷苦人民的巨大同情。《街头女郎麦琪》是美国第一部以自然主义手法创作的小说,是美国文学史上的一个里程碑。文学史家 R.E. 斯皮勒声称，随着《街头女郎麦琪》的出版，"现代美国小说诞生了"。

1895 年，时年 24 岁的克莱恩创作出版了美国内战题材的小说《红色英勇勋章》。作品描写了美国内战时期一位年轻士兵在战争中从无知、狂热到恐惧、愤怒、成熟的成长过程。作品描写了主人公亨利·弗莱明所在部队经历的战斗。所有人都在为自己能活下来而拼命杀戮。杀人或被杀——这就是战场上的逻辑，也是贯穿作品的基本主题。从更大意义上说，资本主义"适者生存"的社会就是一个战场，所有生命都在这个战场上进行着你死我活的战斗。作品没有表明这是美国内战中的哪一场战役，也没有表明作者的政治立场，甚至有名有姓的人物都很少。通过这一手法，克莱恩将具体的战斗扩展为一个社会隐喻。

《红色英勇勋章》的题目取自莎士比亚的历史剧《亨利六世》(*Henry VI*) 第三部中的一句台词"谋杀的猩红勋章"，也指小说中科尼将军 (General Stephen Watts Kearny) 所属部队军装上的红色徽章。因此，《红色英勇勋章》中的红色暗指鲜血与死亡，而"红色英勇勋章"则暗示只有通过流血牺牲才能获得勋章。但讽刺的是，弗莱明得到的"红色英勇勋章"却是被自己人用枪托打在额头上的伤口，是他当逃兵的标志。作品结束时，弗莱明侥幸活了下来，然而战争已将他改造成了一头野兽。他终于醒悟过来，自己原来想象的战争和渴望的荣誉是多么荒唐可笑。从这个意义上说，《红色英勇勋章》开创了美国战争小说的反战传统，奠定了反战小说的基本思想与主题：战争的残酷、毁灭与荒谬、生命在战争中的微不足道、军队中的专制与压迫、传统战争观与价值观的幻灭等。

《红色英勇勋章》是一部自然主义作品，但却融入了印象派绘画的创作手法。作品大量运用各种颜色和动物意象。这些颜色和意象看似无任何关联，但汇聚一体，却会使读者产生一个整体印象，如红色与动物相关联则暗指战争本身（作品有两次把战争形容为"红色的兽"，隐喻战争就是一头吃人肉、喝人血的野兽）。

《红色英勇勋章》的出版奠定了克莱恩在美国文坛的坚实地位。他在这部作品中运用的写作方法与语言风格也对海明威、约翰·多斯·帕索斯 (John Dos Passos, 1896—1970) 和雷蒙·卡弗 (Raymond Carver, 1938—1988) 等产生了很大影响。

1896 年，克莱恩出版了《乔治的母亲》(*George's Mother*)，描写社会堕落所带来的恐惧。1897 年，克莱恩在古巴进行战地采访时，搭乘的战船在佛罗里达附近海面被击沉，后靠一艘小船得以逃生。根据这一经历，克莱恩创作了著名短篇小说《海上扁舟》("The Open Boat", 1897)，细腻描写了新闻记者亨利·弗莱明等四人在大海肆虐、死亡逼近时的恐惧、无奈与绝望的心情，以及他们在遇难时相互帮助，与自然、环境、大海搏斗的情景。小说发表后深受好评，被认为是表现同类题材作品中最优秀的一篇。克莱恩后来发表的一些短篇小说，如《蓝色的旅店》("The Blue Hotel", 1898)、《新娘来到黄天镇》("The Bride Comes to Yellow Sky", 1898) 等也都成为美国短篇小说中的精品。1897 年克莱恩和妻子旅居希腊，在那里担任战地记者，报道希土战争 (Greco-Turkish Wars)，后以这段经历创作了小说《服现役》(*Active Service*, 1899)，不久又移居英国，在那里结识了康拉德、詹姆斯等著名作家。1898 年，美西战争 (Spanish-American War) 爆发，克莱恩随即赴古巴采访，但由于健康状况恶化，不得不提前回到英国。1900 年，克莱恩终因肺结核不治而英年早逝，时年 28 岁。

除小说外，克莱恩还创作了许多诗歌，主要收集在《黑骑手及其他》(*The Black Rider*, 1895) 和《战争是仁慈的》(*War Is Kind*, 1900) 两部诗集中。此外还著有短篇小说集《海上扁舟及其他》(*The Open Boat and Other Stories*, 1898) 和《怪物》(*The Monster*, 1898) 等。

The Red Badge of Courage

【题解】

在《红色英勇勋章》这部小说里，克莱恩通过主人公亨利·弗莱明在战争中的经历与成长，探究了人在极端环境中的心理活动和本能反应，同时也揭露了战争的残酷与荒谬。弗莱明在美国内战时加入北方军队，梦想在战争中获得荷马时代那种英雄的荣耀，但战斗一开始，便被枪炮声吓破了胆，当了一名逃兵。由于没有负伤，弗莱明觉得脸上无光，渴望能在身上什么部位落一个伤疤，碰巧被一位急于赶路的北方军队的士兵用枪托碰伤了脑袋，于是这个伤疤便成了他的"红色英勇勋章"。回到部队后，他编造谎言，吹嘘自己英勇负伤，并因此受到赞扬。同时他暗下决心一定要在今后的战斗中有所表现。在后来的战斗中，他果然像一头野兽那样猛打猛冲，获得了胜利。然而在战斗过后，弗莱明冷静思考，终于认识到战争并非如他原来想象得那样富有浪漫主义色彩，被荷马式英雄主义假象所掩盖的是血与火、生与死。战争就是一股无情的力量，而士兵则像棋盘上被随意摆弄的棋子。

以下内容选自小说第九章与最后一章，表现了战争的残酷性与弗莱明对战争的反思。

From The Red Badge of Courage

Chapter 9

The youth fell back in the procession until the tattered soldier was not in sight. Then he started to walk on with the others.

But he was amid wounds. The mob of men was bleeding. Because of the tattered soldier's question he now felt that his shame could be viewed. He was continually casting sidelong glances to see if the men were contemplating the letters of guilt he felt burned into his brow.

At times he regarded the wounded soldiers in an envious way. He conceived persons with torn bodies to be peculiarly happy. He wished that he, too, had a wound, a red badge of courage.

The spectral soldier was at his side like a stalking reproach. The man's eyes were still fixed in a stare into the unknown. His gray, appalling face had attracted attention in the crowd, and men, slowing to his dreary pace, were walking with him. They were discussing his plight, questioning him and giving him advice. In a dogged way he repelled them, signing to them to go on and leave him alone. The shadows of his face were deepening and his tight lips seemed holding in check the moan of great despair. There could be seen a certain stiffness in the movements of his body, as if he were taking infinite care not to arouse the passion of his wounds. As he went on, he seemed always looking for a place, like one who goes to choose a grave.

Something in the gesture of the man as he waved the bloody and pitying soldiers away made the youth start as if bitten. He yelled in horror. Tottering forward he laid a quivering hand upon the man's arm. As the latter slowly turned his waxlike features toward him, the youth screamed:

"Gawd! Jim Conklin!"

The tall soldier made a little commonplace smile. "Hello, Henry," he said.

The youth swayed on his legs and glared strangely. He stuttered and stammered. "Oh, Jim—oh, Jim—oh, Jim—"

The tall soldier held out his gory hand. There was a curious red and black combination of new blood and old blood upon it. "Where yeh been, Henry?" he asked. He continued in a monotonous voice, "I thought maybe yeh got keeled over. There's been thunder t' pay t'-day. I was worryin' about it a good deal."

The youth still lamented. "Oh, Jim—oh, Jim—oh, Jim—"

"Yeh know," said the tall soldier, "I was out there." He made a careful gesture. "An', Lord, what a circus! An', b'jiminey[1], I got shot—I got shot. Yes, b'jiminey, I got shot." He reiterated this fact in a bewildered way, as if he did not know how it came about.

The youth put forth anxious arms to assist him, but the tall soldier went firmly on as if propelled. Since the youth's arrival as a guardian for his friend[2], the other wounded men had ceased to display much interest. They occupied themselves again in dragging their own tragedies toward the rear.

Suddenly, as the two friends marched on, the tall soldier seemed to be overcome by a terror. His face turned to a semblance of gray paste. He clutched the youth's arm and looked all about him, as if dreading to be overheard. Then he began to speak in a shaking whisper:

"I tell yeh what I'm 'fraid of, Henry—I'll tell yeh what I'm 'fraid of. I'm 'fraid I'll fall down—an' then yeh know—them damned artillery wagons—they like as not 'll run over me. That's what I'm 'fraid of—"

The youth cried out to him hysterically: "I'll take care of yeh, Jim! I'll take care of yeh! I swear t' Gawd I will!"

"Sure—will yeh, Henry?" the tall soldier beseeched.

"Yes—yes—I tell yeh—I'll take care of yeh, Jim!" protested the youth. He could not speak accurately because of the gulpings in his throat.

But the tall soldier continued to beg in a lowly way. He now hung babelike to the youth's arm. His eyes rolled in the wildness of his terror. "I was allus a good friend t' yeh, wa'n't I, Henry? I've allus been a pretty good feller, ain't I? An' it ain't much t'ask, is it? Jest t' pull me along outer th' road? I'd do it for you, wouldn't I, Henry?"

He paused in piteous anxiety to await his friend's reply.

The youth had reached an anguish where the sobs scorched him. He strove to express his loyalty, but he could only make fantastic gestures.

However, the tall soldier seemed suddenly to forget all those fears. He became again the grim, stalking specter of a soldier. He went stonily forward. The youth wished his friend to lean upon him, but the other always shook his head and strangely protested. "No—no—no—leave me be—leave me be—"

His look was fixed again upon the unknown. He moved with mysterious purpose, and all of the youth's offers he brushed aside. "No—no—leave me be—leave me be—"

The youth had to follow.

Presently the latter heard a voice talking softly near his shoulders. Turning he saw that it belonged to the tattered soldier. "Ye'd better take 'im outa th' road, pardner. There's a batt'ry comin' helityhoop down th' road an' he'll git runned over. He's a goner anyhow in about five minutes yeh kin see that. Ye'd better take 'im outa th' road. Where th' blazes does he git his tren'th from?"

"Lord knows!" cried the youth. He was shaking his hands helplessly.

He ran forward presently and grasped the tall soldier by the arm. "Jim! Jim!" he coaxed, "come with me."

The tall soldier weakly tried to wrench himself free. "Huh," he said vacantly. He stared at the youth for a moment. At last he spoke as if dimly comprehending.

"Oh! In the th' fields? Oh!"

He started blindly through the grass.

The youth turned once to look at the lashing riders and jouncing guns of the battery. He was startled from this view by a shrill outcry from the tattered man.

"Gawd! He's runnin'!"

Turning his head swiftly, the youth saw his friend running in a staggering and stumbling way toward a little clump of bushes. His heart seemed to wrench itself almost free from his body at this sight. He made a noise of pain. He and the tattered man began a pursuit. There was a singular race.

When he overtook the tall soldier he began to plead with all the words he could find. "Jim—Jim—what are you doing—what makes you do this way—you'll hurt yerself."

The same purpose was in the tall soldier's face. He protested in a dulled way, keeping his eyes fastened on the mystic place of his intentions. "no—no—don't tech me—leave me be—leave me be—"

The youth, aghast and filled with wonder at the tall soldier, began quaveringly to question him. "Where yeh goin', Jim? What you thinking about? Where you going? Tell me, won't you, Jim?"

The tall soldier faced about as upon relentless pursuers. In his eyes there was a great appeal. "leave me be, can't yeh? Leave me be for a minute."

The youth recoiled. "Why, Jim," he said, in a dazed way, "what's the matter with you?"

The tall soldier turned and, lurching dangerously, went on. The youth and the tattered soldier followed, sneaking as if whipped, feeling unable to face the stricken man if he should again confront them. They began to have thoughts of a solemn ceremony. There was something ritelike in these movements of the doomed soldier. And there was a resemblance in him to a devotee of a mad religion, blood-sucking, muscle-wrenching, bone-crushing. They were awed and afraid. They hung back lest he have at command a dreadful weapon.

At last, they saw him stop and stand motionless. Hastening up, they perceived that his face wore an expression telling that he had at last found the place for which he had struggled. His spare figure was erect; his bloody hands were quietly at his side. He was waiting with patience for something that he had come to meet. He was at the rendezvous. They paused and stood, expectant.

There was a silence.

Finally, the chest of the doomed soldier began to heave with a strained motion. It increased in violence until it was as if an animal was within and was kicking and tumbling furiously to be free.

This spectacle of gradual strangulation made the youth writhe, and once as his friend rolled his eyes, he saw something in them that made him sink waling to the ground. He raised his voice in a last supreme call.

"Jim—Jim—Jim—"

The tall soldier opened his lips and spoke. He made a gesture. "Leave me be—don't tech me—leave me be—"

There was another silence while he waited.

Suddenly, his form stiffened and straightened. Then it was shaken by a prolonged ague. He stared into space. To the two watchers there was a curious and profound dignity in the firm lines of his awful face.

He was invaded by a creeping strangeness that slowly enveloped him. For a moment the tremor of his legs caused him to dance a sort of hideous hornpipe. His arms beat wildly about his head in expression of implike enthusiasm.

His tall figure stretched itself to its full height. There was a slight rending sound. Then it began to swing forward, slow and straight, in the manner of a falling tree. A swift muscular contortion made the left shoulder strike the ground first.

The body seemed to bounce a little way from the earth. "God!" said the tattered soldier.

The youth had watched, spellbound, this ceremony at the place of meeting. His face had been twisted into an expression of every agony he had imagined for his friend.

He now sprang to his feet and, going closer, gazed upon the pastelike face. The mouth was opened and the teeth showed in a laugh.

As the flap of the blue jacket fell away from the body, he could see that the side looked as if it had been chewed by wolves.

The youth turned, with sudden, livid rage, toward the battlefield. He shook his fist. He seemed about to deliver a philippic.

"Hell—"

The red sun was pasted in the sky like a wafer.

Chapter 24

The roarings that had stretched in a long line of sound across the face of the forest began to grow intermittent and weaker. The stentorian speeches of the artillery continued in some distant encounter, but the crashes of the musketry had almost ceased. The youth and his friend[2] of a sudden looked up, feeling a deadened form of distress at the waning of these noises, which had become a part of life. They could see changes going on among the troops. There were marchings this way and that way. A battery wheeled leisurely. On the crest of a small hill was the thick gleam of many departing muskets.

The youth arose. "Well, what now, I wonder?" he said. By his tone he seemed to be preparing to resent some new monstrosity in the way of dins and smashes. He shaded his eyes with his grimy hand and gazed over the field.

His friend also arose and stared. "I bet we're goin' t' git along out of this an' back over th' river," said he.

"Well, I swan!" said the youth. They waited, watching. Within a little while the regiment received orders to retrace its way. The men got up grunting from the grass, regretting the soft repose. They jerked their stiffened legs, and stretched their arms over their heads. One man swore as he rubbed his eyes. They all groaned "O Lord!" They had as many objections to this change as they would have had to a proposal for a new battle.

They trampled slowly back over the field across which they had run in a mad scamper.

The regiment marched until it had joined its fellows. The reformed brigade, in column, aimed through a wood at the road. Directly they were in a mass of dust-covered troops, and were trudging along in a way parallel to the enemy's lines as these had been defined by the previous turmoil.

They passed within view of a stolid white house, and saw in front of it groups of their comrades lying in wait behind a neat breastwork. A row of guns were booming at a distant enemy. Shells thrown in reply were raising clouds of dust and splinters. Horsemen dashed along the line of intrenchments.

At this point of its march the division curved away from the field and went winding off in the direction of the river. When the significance of this movement had impressed itself upon the youth he turned his head and looked over his shoulder toward the trampled and debris-strewed[3] ground. He breathed a breath of new satisfaction. He finally nudged his friend. "Well, it's all over," he said to him.

His friend gazed backward. "B'Gawd, it is," he assented. They mused.

For a time the youth was obliged to reflect in a puzzled and uncertain way. His mind was undergoing a subtle change. It took moments for it to cast off its ottful ways and resume its accustomed course of thought. Gradually his brain emerged from the clogged clouds, and at last he was enabled to more closely comprehend himself and circumstance.

He understood then that the existence of shot and countershot was in the past. He had dwelt in a land of strange, squalling upheavals and had come forth. He had been where there was red of blood and black of passion, and he was escaped. His first thoughts were given to rejoicings at this fact.

Later he began to study his deeds, his failures, and his achievements. Thus, fresh from scenes where many of his usual machines of reflection had been idle, from where he had proceeded sheeplike, he struggled to marshal all his acts.

At last they marched before him clearly. From this present viewpoint he was enabled to look upon them in spectator fashion and to criticize them with some correctness, for his new condition had already defeated certain sympathies.

Regarding his procession of memory he felt gleeful and unregretting, for in it his public deeds were paraded in great and shining prominence. Those performances which had been witnessed by his fellows marched now in wide purple and gold, having various deflections. They went gayly with music. It was pleasure to watch these things. He spent delightful minutes viewing the gilded images of memory.

He saw that he was good. He recalled with a thrill of joy the respectful comments of his fellows upon his conduct.

Nevertheless, the ghost of his flight from the first engagement appeared to him and danced. There were small shoutings in his brain about these matters. For a moment he blushed, and the light of his soul flickered with shame.

A specter of reproach came to him. There loomed the dogging memory of the tattered soldier—he who, gored by bullets and faint for blood, had fretted concerning an imagined wound in another; he who had loaned his last of strength and intellect for the tall soldier; he who, blind with weariness and pain, had been deserted in the field. For an instant a wretched chill of sweat was upon him at the thought that he might be detected in the thing. As he stood persistently before his vision, he gave vent to a cry of sharp irritation and agony.

His friend turned. "What's the matter, Henry?" he demanded. The youth's reply was an outburst of crimson oaths.

As he marched along the little branch-hung roadway among his prattling companions this vision of cruelty brooded over him. It clung near him always and darkened his view of these deeds in purple and gold. Whichever way his thoughts turned they were followed by the somber phantom of the desertion in the fields. He looked stealthily at his companions, feeling sure that they must discern in his face evidences of this pursuit. But they were plodding in ragged array, discussing with quick tongues the accomplishments of the late battle.

"Oh, if a man should come up an' ask me, I'd say we got a dum good lickin'[4]."

"Lickin'—in yer eye! We ain't licked, sonny. We're going down here away, swing aroun', an' come in behint 'em.

"Oh, hush, with your comin' in behint 'em. I've seen all 'a that I wanta. Don't tell me about comin' in behint—"

"Bill Smithers, he ses he'd rather been in ten hundred battles than been in that heluva[5] hospital. He ses they got shootin' in th' nighttime, an' shells dropped plum[6] among 'em in th' hospital. He ses sech hollerin' he never see."

"Hasbrouck? He's th' best off'cer in this here reg'ment. He's a whale."

"Didn't I tell yeh we'd come aroun' in behint 'em? Didn't I tell yeh so? We—"

"Oh, shet yer mouth!"

For a time this pursuing recollection of the tattered man took all elation from the youth's veins. He saw his vivid error, and he was afraid that it would stand before him all his life. He took no share in the chatter of his comrades, nor did he look at them or know them, save when he felt sudden suspicion that they were seeing his thoughts and scrutinizing each detail of the scene with the tattered soldier.

Yet gradually he mustered force to put the sin at a distance. And at last his eyes seemed to open to some new ways. He found that he could look back upon the brass and bombast of his earlier gospels and see them truly. He was gleeful when he discovered that he now despised them.

With this conviction came a store of assurance. He felt a quiet manhood, non-assertive but of sturdy and strong blood. He knew that he would no more quail before his guides wherever they should point. He had been to touch the great death, and found that, after all, it was but the great death. He was a man.

So it came to pass that as he trudged from the place of blood and wrath his soul changed. He came from hot plowshares to prospects of clover tranquilly, and it was as if hot plowshares were not. Scars faded as flowers.

It rained. The procession of weary soldiers became a bedraggled train, despondent and muttering, marching with churning effort in a trough of liquid brown mud under a low, wretched sky. Yet the youth smiled, for he saw that the world was a world for him, though many discovered it to be made of oaths and walking sticks[7]. He had rid himself of the red sickness of battle. The sultry nightmare was in the past. He had been an animal blistered and sweating in the heat and pain of war. He turned now with a lover's thirst to images of tranquil skies, fresh meadows, cool brooks—an existence of soft and eternal peace. Over the river a golden ray of sun came through the hosts of leaden rain clouds.

【注解】

1. b'jiminey：“天哪”，口语中表示惊讶、敬畏等。
2. his friend：指另一位北军士兵 Wilson。
3. debris-strewed：被碎石覆盖的。
4. a dum good lickin'：相当于 a damned good licking，一场彻底的败仗。
5. heluva：相当于 hell of a。
6. plum：相当于 plumb，垂直地。
7. walking sticks：此处指军官们使用的剑。

【思考题】

1. At the beginning of Chapter 9, Crane describes the wounded and then says Henry "was envious" of the wounded soldiers, and "conceived persons with torn bodies to be

peculiarly happy." Why was Henry envious of the wounded soldiers? In what sense did he think "persons with torn bodies to be peculiarly happy"?

2. The tall soldier was seriously wounded and obviously afraid. What was he afraid of? What was Henry's reaction to his plea of help? Why did he insist on being left alone when Henry did offer to help?

3. Crane describes the last moment of the tall soldier with meticulous details and compares it to a religious ceremony. Why is a "ritelike" feeling important in describing the dying moment of the tall soldier?

4. How would you describe Henry Fleming's feeling towards the war and himself in Chapter 24? He says "he was a man". Do you agree he has become a man? Cite examples from the story to illustrate your view.

5. Study Crane's use of language in Chapter 9. What words does he particularly choose to create an atmosphere of cruelty and bloodiness of war? What is the symbolic meaning of "red" in "the red badge of courage"?

6. At the end of Chapter 24, Crane again uses the image of the sun to describe scenery. How does the image of the sun here differ from that at the end of Chapter 9?

解读举例

1. 《红色英勇勋章》表现了成长的主题。作品主人公亨利·弗莱明在战争中经历了从幼稚到成熟，从恐惧到勇敢，从懦夫到英雄的成长过程。在故事的结尾，弗莱明告诉自己"他已经触摸到了强大的死亡，发现这不过是个强大的死亡而已。他是一条汉子。"

2. 《红色英勇勋章》表现了成长的主题，但这种"成长"并非"从懦夫到英雄的成长"，而是从对战争的浪漫理想主义到悲观自然主义的觉醒。最后弗莱明成为"一条汉子"是因为战争的残酷与生命的渺小彻底粉碎了他心目中传统浪漫的战争观，让他清醒地认识到战争并不浪漫，也不光荣，而是毁灭、死亡、丑恶。

3. 《红色英勇勋章》表现了战争的残酷性和恐怖性。在作品中，战争被形容成一头"红色的动物"。它把年轻人推向战场，自相残杀，彻底粉碎了他们对美好生活的憧憬。克莱恩在作品中运用自然主义手法和与鲜血、死亡等相关的各种意象就是要渲染战争的恐怖和残酷，其目的正是要揭露战争摧残人性、毁灭生命的本质，从这个意义上说弗莱明和其他士兵临阵脱逃是完全正义的行动，是对战争本身的反叛。

4. 《红色英勇勋章》表现了救赎的主题。作品主人公弗莱明在战争中的变化实际体现了他精神上的成长。只有经历了艰难困苦、流血牺牲,人类才能学会自制,才会在性格、良心与灵魂上得到发展。因此作品中描写的战争实际是一个象征,象征着一种极端的生活状态,只有在这种状态下,人类才最有可能发生变化,得到救赎。

American Literature
Between the Two Wars: 1914–1945

背景介绍

尽管美国直到1917年才正式加入第一次世界大战，但战争给美国社会生活带来的影响难以估量。在纷繁复杂的现代社会面前，人们感到越来越无助和无所适从。一方面，因刚经历了战争，困惑、恐惧、绝望的情绪笼罩着每个人；另一方面，因为与传统的思维、生活方式决裂，人们的情绪中又夹杂着一种获得释放、获得自由的轻松。汽车的普及、电影的诞生、工业的发展、都市的延伸及科技的更新给人们生活注入了新的生机和内容。这些都强烈地冲击着美国的社会结构，对当时的美国文学有着深远的影响。这一时期的主要文艺运动是现代主义(Modernism)，涉及文学、绘画、雕塑、建筑、哲学、心理学等众多领域。各种流派也应运而生，如意象派、立体派、漩涡派、达达主义等。庞德曾呼吁让文学"新起来"(Make it new)。现代主义的确创建了新的传统，它有意识地排斥旧的思维习惯和传统的文学技巧，努力反映这一时代社会、政治的风云变化，以及人们的孤独、焦虑、惶惑和异化感。与现实主义不同，现代主义作家更注重表现人物的内心世界，而非外部世界，更关注主观意愿，而非客观现实的表达。他们努力呈现人与自然之间、人与社会之间、人与人之间、人与自我之间的各种扭曲、异化或病态的关系。现代心理学，尤其是弗洛伊德的精神分析与詹姆斯的意识流理论，对这一时期的文学有着深远的影响。很多作家意识到人在思考时，逻辑往往具有跳跃性，并不连贯。他们开始关注人的思维活动，更注意人物的意识活动和心理时间。因此，现代主义作品常常由片段、碎块拼凑而成，过去、现在与将来同时混乱地存在于人物的意识中。现代主义作品常常省略很多传统文学中必不可少的组成部分，诸如解释说明、因果关系、高潮结局等使文本连续、统一的成分。一个典型的现代主义作品往往会让人感觉突兀：故事发展时没有说明，结束时缺少答案；观点不再明确地陈述，而是运用象征等手法含蓄地予以暗示。因而，读者在阅读现代主义的诗歌和小说时，往往需要参与创作，和作者一起完成作品的全部意义，并得出自己的结论。现代主义描述经验时，常采用具体的感觉意象或细节，作者也常从个人经验、梦境、流行文化中寻找灵感。

英美文学中的现代主义源于法国象征主义诗歌，并得益于对中国唐诗与日本俳句的学习与模仿。现代主义诗人抛弃19世纪传统的节奏、韵律，多用自由诗体进行创作，强调诗歌语言的凝练与意象的鲜明。庞德在1913年美国《诗刊》(*Poetry: A Magazine of Verse*) 发表的意象派宣言中提出诗歌创作的三条主要原则：①无论主观、客观，都要直接描摹事物；②诗中的每一个字都要与表现紧密相关；③按照音乐乐章的特点创作诗歌，而不是按照节拍器的节奏。视觉性是现代主义诗歌创作的另一重要特征。E. E. 卡明斯 (E. E. Cummings, 1894—1962) 在作品中大量使用小写字母，并对词汇进行奇特的排列，获得一种独特的审美效果。另外，诗人也从日常生活中选择极普通的事物作为诗歌创作的题材，如威廉·卡洛斯·威廉姆斯 (William

Carlos Williams, 1883—1963) 就以冰箱、李子、红色的手推车等为题，写出了很多脍炙人口的诗歌。T. S. 艾略特的长诗《荒原》(*The Waste Land*) 奠定了现代文学的基调。诗歌描述了西方社会普遍存在的精神枯竭和生存危机，指出现代社会犹如一片缺乏信仰、丧失道德的荒原。

现代主义作品需要读者的积极参与，这对读者的素养也提出了要求。因而，作品往往并不畅销，总是先在一些文人内部流行的杂志上刊登。《诗刊》(*Poetry: A Magazine of Verse*)、《小评论》(*The Little Review*)、《七艺》(*The Seven Arts*)、《边疆》(*The Frontier*)、《逃亡者》(*Fugitive*) 等刊物为现代派作家相当实验性的作品提供了发表的园地。

这一时期的旅外作家对现代主义在美国的发展起了至关重要的作用。他们离开美国，到古老的欧洲寻找有更丰富内涵的文化。庞德、海明威、舍伍德·安德森 (Sherwood Anderson, 1876—1941)、弗·司各特·菲茨杰拉德 (F. Scott Fitzgerald, 1896—1940)、尤金·奥尼尔 (Eugene O'Neill, 1888—1953)、韦拉·凯瑟 (Willa Cather, 1873—1947)、凯瑟琳·安·波特 (Katherine Anne Porter, 1890—1980)、弗罗斯特等人都在欧洲侨居过一段时间。他们回到美国后，努力把现代主义的理论同美国本土的主题结合起来，与从未离开过美国的本土作家一道，创造出新世纪的美国文学。卡尔·桑德堡 (Carl Sandburg, 1878—1967)、安德森、凯瑟叙述中西部生活；约翰·斯坦贝克 (John Steinbeck, 1902—1968) 描写加州的农业工人；埃德温·阿灵顿·鲁滨孙 (Edwin Arlington Robinson, 1869—1935)、弗罗斯特从新英格兰寻找灵感；波特向读者展示得克萨斯州的风貌；福克纳则反映南方在种种矛盾和工业文明的冲击之下走向衰败、没落的过程。

菲茨杰拉德为"喧嚣的 20 年代"(Roaring Twenties) 创造了"爵士时代"(the Jazz Age) 这一名称。他在作品中表现了包括他自己在内的一代人在一战结束后的经历和心路历程，描写了这一时代表面繁荣下的衰败和人们在"美国梦"破灭时的灰暗心情。这一代人也是"迷惘的一代"，海明威和福克纳是这一代人的代言人。他们的作品拓展了艾略特在战后开始的荒原主题，反映了人们在失去信仰和传统价值观后的颓废沮丧心理。海明威在他的第一部长篇小说《太阳照样升起》(*The Sun Also Rises*, 1926) 中，用简白凝练的语言道出了战后的青年一代对战争及战后荒原的看法，以及他们因理想破灭、信仰丧失而感到的莫大空虚与失落，引起了读者的巨大共鸣。在战争小说《永别了，武器》(*A Farewell to Arms*, 1929) 中，他更是以自己的一战经历为背景，毫不隐讳地表达了对战争、战争机器及所有与战争相关的传统价值的厌恶和不屑。

1929 年，西方爆发长达十年之久的经济危机，将整个西方世界拖到了崩溃的边缘。"爵士时代"的虚假繁荣此时一扫而空，人们堕入了绝望的深渊。20世纪20年代的人们尚处于悲伤之中，舔着战争在他们心灵留下的伤口，而此时许多侨居巴黎、出入沙龙的美国作家则抛弃伤感，纷纷回国。面对经济萧条、民不聊生、社会矛盾激化的严酷现实，他们感到自己有责任为国家做点什么。因此，20世纪30年代的多数作品都显示了美国作家对社会问题的关注。参与社会成为这一时期文学的显著特征。很多作家受到马克思、列宁思想的影响，对社会主义和共产主义产生了浓厚的兴趣。他们以手中的笔作为改革社会、消除弊端的锐利武器，揭露与表现美国社会中的阶级矛盾。帕索斯的"《美国》三部曲"(U. S. A., 1930—1936) 是这一文学思潮的代表，他本人也是左翼文学的积极倡导者和实践者。斯坦贝克的《愤怒的葡萄》(The Grapes of Wrath, 1939) 反映了20世纪30年代经济危机中农民、工人颠沛流离、到加利福尼亚寻找生机的经历，描述了他们被歧视、被剥削的命运。詹姆斯·托马斯·法雷尔 (James Thomas Farrell, 1904—1979)、厄斯金·考德威尔 (Erskine Caldwell, 1903—1987)、约翰·奥哈拉 (John O'Hara, 1905—1970) 等年轻作家也写出了大量揭露社会黑暗的优秀作品。

与此同时，20世纪20年代已崭露头角的海明威、福克纳等在20世纪30年代也坚持创作，写出了他们更具人道主义精神的作品。海明威在《丧钟为谁而鸣》(For Whom the Bell Tolls, 1940) 中第一次尝试从正面描写战争。一批南方女作家，如尤多拉·韦尔蒂 (Eudora Welty, 1909—2001)、卡森·麦卡勒斯 (Carson McCullers, 1917—1967)、波特等也开始登上美国文坛，描述她们所熟悉的人群和生活。

从一战结束到20世纪30年代末，黑人作家也活跃在文学艺术领域，出现了哈莱姆文艺复兴 (Harlem Renaissance)。康提·库伦 (Countee Cullen, 1903—1946)、兰斯顿·休斯 (Langston Hughes, 1902—1967)、佐拉·尼尔·赫斯顿 (Zora Neale Hurston, 1891—1960) 是其中的佼佼者。他们虽然道出了处于社会底层和边缘的黑人对白人至上社会的抗议和不满，但作品基调总体而言较为温和、向上。从20世纪30年代中期到20世纪40年代末，芝加哥取代哈莱姆，成为黑人文学的中心。理查德·赖特 (Richard Wright, 1908—1960) 发表了《土生子》(Native Son, 1940)，用愤怒的笔触深刻地表现了黑人在白人社会中惶惑、恐惧和仇恨的复杂感情，揭露了美国的种族歧视现象和种族隔离政策，开启美国黑人"抗议"文学之先河。

戏剧在这一时期也得到了很大发展。被誉为"美国戏剧之父"的尤金·奥尼尔 (Eugene O'Neil, 1888—1953) 开创了美国严肃戏剧的传统，对戏剧进行了一系列实验、革新。他擅长写作悲剧题材，表现现代人在冷酷、残暴的社会中的无助、迷惘、困惑和绝望。他的作品被诺贝尔文学奖委员会誉为"富于活力，感情真挚，带有独创的悲剧色彩"。奥尼尔对语言并不十分关注，但对戏剧结构、表现技巧进行了很多尝试。他借用现代科技中灯光、音响等发明，以及德国表现主义的一些手法，给戏剧注入了新的活力。田纳西·威廉斯 (Tennessee Williams, 1911—1983) 同样热衷于戏剧表现技巧的尝试，同样擅长运用背景、音乐、灯光等表现主义手法烘托主题。另外，他还利用听觉、视觉上的象征主义手法帮助观众更深刻地理解作品的含义。他比奥尼尔更注重语言的效果，在作品中运用南方方言，生动地塑造人物形象。威廉斯擅长描绘暴力社会中柔弱女子的遭遇。他塑造的畸人形象及对他们内心世界的描绘反映了他对严酷社会现实的憎恨和对美好情感的向往。他将很多场景设在南方，表达他对那块古老而堕落的土地复杂的情感。1931年成立的团体戏剧 (Group Theatre) 从俄国戏剧中学习深层心理自然主义，对美国戏剧也有很大影响。此外，埃尔默·莱斯 (Elmer Rice, 1892—1967) 和克利福德·奥德 (Clifford Odets, 1906—1963) 也是十分杰出的戏剧家。

　　随着第二次世界大战的爆发，美国国内的危机得到了缓解。许多作家开始以二战为题材，真实地再现在战争特定的环境下人的思想和感受，有力地揭露了所谓正义战争的残酷性和虚伪性，批判了美国极权主义的倾向。这些作品在战争结束后陆续得以出版，如埃文·肖 (Irwin Shaw, 1913—1984) 的《幼狮》(*The Young Lions*, 1948)、诺曼·梅勒 (Norman Mailer, 1923—2007) 的《裸者与死者》(*The Naked and the Dead*, 1948)，以及詹姆斯·琼斯 (James Jones, 1921—1977) 的《从这里到永恒》(*From Here to Eternity*, 1951) 等。

作者简介

罗伯特·弗罗斯特虽然以描绘新英格兰乡村的风土人情而著称，但他并非出生于新英格兰，而是西海岸的旧金山。在父亲死于肺结核后，母亲带着 11 岁的弗罗斯特和他的妹妹回到了丈夫在新英格兰的老家。母亲开始在一所小学教书，弗罗斯特便在母亲的班上听课，两年半之后考入当地的中学。中学阶段的学习对他产生了巨大影响，古典语言、文学、浪漫的抒情诗歌深深地吸引了他。弗罗斯特开始尝试诗歌写作，并于 1890 年 4 月在校刊上发表叙事诗《悲惨之夜》("La Noche Triste")。1892 年，弗罗斯特中学毕业，随后进入达特茅斯学院学习，但连第一学期都没有学完便不辞而别，回家协助母亲教书，他还当过纺织工人、记者等。1894 年，他第一首具有职业水平的诗篇《我的蝴蝶》("My Butterfly") 被纽约一家全国性刊物《独立者》(Independent) 刊用。1897 年，他进入哈佛大学学习古典文学、哲学等，两年后辍学。1900 年，他与妻子艾莉诺的第一个孩子夭折，给他们的夫妻关系蒙上了一层阴影。《波士顿以北》(North of Boston, 1914) 中的名篇之一《家葬》("Home Burial") 记叙了丧子后夫妻二人的痛苦和矛盾。1912 年以前他在美国国内只发表了十来首诗，并未获得当时保守的编辑们的青睐。因此，弗罗斯特决定携家人去英国碰碰运气。不到一个月，弗罗斯特的第一部诗集《男儿的志向》(A Boy's Will, 1913) 便被当地出版社接受。当时，现代派诗歌的领袖庞德、T. E. 休姆 (T. E. Hulme, 1883—1917)、W. B. 叶芝 (W. B. Yeats, 1865—1939) 等都被弗罗斯特清新独特的风格所吸引，对其诗作给予了高度评价。翌年，《波士顿以北》出版，得到了更高的评价。1915 年弗罗斯特回国时，已被评论界公认为美国新诗的领袖。

诗集《男儿的志向》中大部分是弗罗斯特写给妻子的浪漫情诗，艺术价值不算高，其中也有少量吸引人的作品，如用口语化的语言写成的优美的十四行诗《割草》("Mowing")。《波士顿以北》被公认为弗罗斯特最好的诗集，里面的诗作大多是人物素描，逼真地再现了新英格兰农民的心理。其中的优秀诗作除了《补墙》("Mending Wall") 外，还有描写夫妻对话的无韵诗《帮工之死》("The Death of the Hired Man")，没有严格押韵格式的押韵诗《采苹果后》("After Apple Picking")，用女仆唠家常的口吻写成的独白诗《伺候仆人的仆人》("A Servant to Servants") 等。

第三本诗集《山间》(*Mountain Interval*, 1916) 包括了一些脍炙人口的名篇，如《未选择的路》("The Road Not Taken")。弗罗斯特的诗歌容易使人们联想到健康乐观的农家生活，但他其实并不是一个总是乐观的诗人。他的许多诗篇表现了大自然对人类的冷漠及人类的孤独与恐惧等主题。《一位老人的冬夜》("An Old Man's Winter Night") 和《山里妻子》("The Hill Wife") 即属于这一类。1924 年发表的诗集《新罕布什尔》(*New Hampshire*) 为弗罗斯特第一次赢得了普利策奖 (此后他又三次获得此项奖励，分别为 1931 年、1937 年和 1943 年)。该诗集包含了他最有名的诗篇《雪夜停林边》("Stopping by Woods on a Snowy Evening") 和《火与冰》("Fire and Ice")。五年后出版的《西去的溪流》(*West-Running Brook*, 1928) 包括许多诸如《春潭》("Spring Pools")、《悄悄地走》("On Going Unnoticed")、《孤寂》("Bereft")、《熟悉黑夜》("Acquainted with the Night") 等短小的抒情诗，继续表现外部世界对人类命运漠不关心的主题。1936 年发表的《又一片牧场》(*A Further Range*) 也是一部较优秀的诗集，包括《荒凉之地》("Desert Places")、《踏叶人》("A Leaf Treader")，以及耐人寻味的短诗《不远也不深》("*Neither out Far nor in Deep*") 和十四行诗《计划》("Design") 等。

《见证树》(*A Witness Tree*, 1942) 是弗罗斯特最后一部艺术成就较高的诗集，其中包括 1961 年诗人在肯尼迪总统就职典礼上朗诵的爱国主义诗篇《一无保留的奉献》("The Gift Outright")，以及《十一月》("November")、《山毛榉》("Beech")、《猎兔者》("The Rabbit Hunter") 等。此后他又创作了两首无韵体叙事诗《理智的假面具》(*A Masque of Reason*, 1945)、《慈悲的假面具》(*A Masque of Mercy*, 1947)，发表了诗集《绣线菊》(*Steeple Bush*, 1947) 和《林中空地》(*In the Clearing*, 1962)。

弗罗斯特的许多优秀诗篇描写的都是自然景色或田园生活，包括树林、雪、冰、果园、鸟、花、池塘、星辰、苹果，以及人与这些自然景物的关系。但这些诗歌并不都是传统意义上的田园牧歌，它们所展现的并不总是恬静而美好的生活画面。弗罗斯特最深刻的诗歌往往是用朴实无华的诗句描写人生的悲剧、人类沟通的困难、人类在不可捉摸的大自然面前的渺小与孤独。

弗罗斯特始终采用传统的诗歌形式。他认为写自由诗犹如打网球而没有球网一样。尽管如此他还是被奉为 1910 年以后美国新诗的领袖，其原因在于他在诗歌创作中始终能够将新英格兰口语的节奏与传统的格律相结合，并将深邃的思想与清新淳朴的风格完美地结合在一起。用他自己的话说，"所有的诗歌都是对实际话语语调的再现"，而所谓完整的诗，就是"情感找到了能够表达它的思想，而思想则找到了能够表达它的字词"的诗。他是位罕见的雅俗共赏的诗人，获得了除诺贝尔奖之外的所有文学大奖。虽然大学没有毕业，他却获得了 44 所大学和学院授予的荣誉名衔。他的诗歌朴实无华，大多以新英格兰的乡村为背景，但却充满人生哲理，所揭示的主题往往具有普遍意义。在长达近七十年的创作生涯中，他始终以一位新英格兰农民自居，并用清新、淳朴、平易而又富于哲理的诗句描绘了新英格兰乡村的风土人情。庞德曾经这样评价弗罗斯特的诗："在读过他的诗后，我对农场生活的了解比没读之前多了许多。这意味着我对'生活'的理解也深入了许多"。这一评论无疑揭示了弗罗斯特诗歌的深刻含义。也正因为如此，弗罗斯特被公认为20世纪的美国民族诗人之一。

Mending Wall

【题解】

关于这首诗的讨论有很多。一方面，诗歌似乎说明人与人之间应存在必要和有意义的距离，邻里间每年春天按照惯例要修补的田间围墙，阻碍了彼此之间的交流，因此可以看作是现代人之间不必要的障碍；另一方面，诗歌也多次提及"有好篱笆才有好邻居"这一谚语，仿佛又对"篱笆"所带来的个体独立和社会和谐持赞许态度。

Mending Wall

(1914)

Something there is that doesn't love a wall,
That sends the frozen-ground-swell[1] under it,
And spills the upper boulders in the sun;
And makes gaps even two can pass abreast.
The work of hunters is another thing:　　　　　　　　　　5
I have come after them and made repair
Where they have left not one stone on a stone,
But they would have the rabbit out of hiding,
To please the yelping dogs. The gaps I mean,
No one has seen them made or heard them made,　　　　　10
But at spring mending-time we find them there.
I let my neighbor know beyond the hill;
And on a day we meet to walk the line
And set the wall between us once again.

We keep the wall between us as we go. 15
To each the boulders that have fallen to each[2].
And some are loaves and some so nearly balls[3]
We have to use a spell[4] to make them balance:
"Stay where you are until our backs are turned!"
We wear our fingers rough with handling them. 20
Oh, just another kind of outdoor game,
One on a side. It comes to little more:
There where it is we do not need the wall:
He is all pine and I am apple orchard.
My apple trees will never get across 25
And eat the cones under his pines, I tell him.
He only says, "Good fences make good neighbors."
Spring is the mischief in me, and I wonder
If I could put a notion in his head;
"Why do they make good neighbors? Isn't it 30
Where there are cows? But here there are no cows.
Before I built a wall I'd ask to know
What I was walling in or walling out,
And to whom I was like[5] to give offense.
Something there is that doesn't love a wall, 35
That wants it down." I could say "Elves" to him,
But it's not elves exactly, and I'd rather
He said it for himself. I see him there
Bringing a stone grasped firmly by the top
In each hand, like an old-stone savage armed. 40
He moves in darkness as it seems to me,
Not of woods only and the shade of trees.
He will not go behind[6] his father's saying,
And he likes having thought of it so well
He says again, "Good fences make good neighbors."

【注解】

1. frozen-ground-swell：潮湿的土地受冻后便会因膨胀而隆起，从而使上面的围墙坍塌。
2. To each the boulders . . . each：第一个"each"指两位邻居，第二个"each"指围墙的两边。
3. some are loaves . . . balls："loaves"和"balls"指的是用于垒墙的石头有片状的，也有球状的。
4. spell：此处有一种调侃的意味，指球形的石头不容易垒上，所以要通过"魔力"或念咒语才行。
5. like：此处作 likely 解。
6. go behind：对……进行探究。

【思考题】

1. In what form is the poem written?
2. What is the speaker's attitude toward the wall, and what is his neighbor's? Pressed in an interview to say where he stood on the issue of fences, Frost once said: "Maybe I was both fellows in the poem." What do you think he meant?
3. Describe the character of the neighbor as seen by the speaker. In what sense does he move in darkness?
4. Describe the tone of the poem and how it is achieved.

解读举例

1. 《补墙》的主题是人与人之间应当坦诚相待、互相关心、团结友爱，并不需要在中间竖起一堵冷冰冰的墙。作品的 5 至 11 行暗示，每当墙被建起或补好之后都会有一股神秘的力量(Elves)将它破坏。在作品的 38 至 42 行中，通过对坚持要补墙的邻居的描写，诗人进一步阐发了他对补墙的看法，即这是一种石器时代野蛮人的行为方式。笼罩在这位邻居身边的灰暗并不是林中自然的灰暗，而是蛰伏在人心中的灰暗。"有好篱笆才有好邻居"这句谚语也反映了传统思维方式的灰暗。

2. 《补墙》的主题是人与人之间虽然需要坦诚相待、互相关心，但也需要竖起一堵墙，以保持一定的距离，因为只有这样人才能够拥有属于自己的隐私与独立，才会懂得尊重对方的人格和保持社会的和谐。只有在这个基础上，人与人之间才可能出现真正的互相关心和团结友爱。因此尽管那位邻居不善言辞，却象征着诗人对如何处理人与人的关系深刻而独特的理解。叙述者虽然提议不再补墙，甚至认为应该拆掉这堵墙，但他每年主动约他的邻居一起前去补墙，这一事实本身说明他也同意邻居的看法，即"有好篱笆才有好邻居"。

The Road Not Taken

【题解】

诗人在作品中用质朴的语言，以日常生活中随处可见的岔路口比喻人生面临的一些选择。这些选择一旦作出便再也没有回头的余地。诗中主人公选择了一条别人走得较少的路，表现了其冒险精神。

The Road Not Taken

Two roads diverged in a yellow wood,
And sorry I could not travel both.
And be one traveler, long I stood
And looked down one as far as I could
To where it bent in the undergrowth;   5

Then took the other, as just as fair[1],
And having perhaps the better claim,
Because it was grassy and wanted wear[2];
Though as for that the passing there
Had worn them really about the same.   10

And both[3] that morning equally lay
In leaves no step had trodden black.
Oh, I kept the first for another day!
Yet knowing how way leads on to way,
I doubted if I should ever come back.   15

I shall be telling this with a sigh
Somewhere ages and ages hence:
Two roads diverged in a wood, and I—
I took the one less traveled by,
And that has made all the difference.

新编美国文学选读（第5版）
Selected Readings of American Literature (The 5th Edition)

【注解】

1. as just as fair：既合适也平坦。
2. wanted wear：踩踏较少的，want 在这里作 lack 解。
3. both：指上文所指的两条路。

【思考题】

1. In which season is the poem set? Does the road have any symbolic meaning here? If yes, how do you think Frost prods us into reading it symbolically? Especially, how does the last stanza change the significance of this simple incident?
2. The speaker, after much deliberation, has finally made a decision on which way to choose in a wood, and in one's life symbolically. How do you comment on his decision?
3. The speaker says that "I shall be telling this with a sigh / Somewhere ages and ages hence". Why would you think he should tell this with a "sigh"?
4. Laurence Perrine sees the poem as "an expression of regret that one's ability to explore different life possibilities is so limited. It comes from a man who loves life and thirsts after more of it." What details in the poem support such an interpretation?

解读举例

1. 《未选择的路》揭示出人生总是会面对艰难抉择的事实。人不能同时选择两条道路，而选择任何一条都可能会有完全不同的人生结局，但是人必须进行选择。"我"不愿随波逐流，而是选择做开拓者，走了一条很少有人走的路，人生因此而更有意义。

2. 《未选择的路》似乎告诉我们，在人生的岔路口，不论我们选择哪一条道路，都会对没有选的那条路感到好奇，甚至感到遗憾，想要知道如果选择另一条道路，人生又会变成什么样子。但人不能总是回头看，因为过去是无法改变的，而应当沿着已经选择的道路坚定地走下去。

Stopping by Woods on a Snowy Evening

【题解】

这是首韵脚为 a a b a 的四步抑扬格短诗，其韵律之美使它经常入选各种诗集。

作者本人也对该诗感到非常满意,称之为"自己最喜欢的诗歌"。诗中描写的是夜晚林中醉人的雪景令诗中人流连忘返的情景。其含义看似一目了然,但是最后的叠句"还要赶好几里路才能安睡"却可以有不同的解释。

Stopping by Woods on a Snowy Evening

Whose woods these are I think I know.
His house is in the village, though;
He will not see me stopping here
To watch his woods fill up with snow.

My little horse must think it queer   5
To stop without a farmhouse near,
Between the woods and frozen lake
The darkest evening of the year.

He gave the harness bells a shake
To ask if there is some mistake.   10
The only other sound's the sweep
Of easy wind and downy flake.

The woods are lovely, dark and deep,
But I have promises to keep,
And miles to go before I sleep,   15
And miles to go before I sleep.

【思考题】

1. What causes the speaker to stop by the woods?
2. What do the owner and the horse have in common? How do they differ from the speaker?
3. Why does the speaker leave the woods? Does he drive on with reluctance? What does this implied reluctance tell us about the motive for stopping?
4. What is the speaker's inner conflict? What kind of mood is he in?

5. What attitude toward nature is implied in this poem? What is the speaker's attitude toward himself? Comment on the relationship between nature and the speaker.

解读举例

1. 《雪夜停林边》描写了"我"在冬日傍晚路过一片寂静的树林，被那里的美丽雪景所吸引，不由停留观赏。"我"想要多停留一会儿，但"我"有责任在身，还要赶很远的路才能休息，因此不得不怅然离去。

2. 《雪夜停林边》表现了文明和自然的冲突，批评了现代社会人们的生活方式。过快的生活节奏使人们不再有时间静下来仔细地观赏身边的世界，从而错过了许多美丽、珍贵的东西。诗中的"我"虽然被树林的自然美景所吸引，但又无法抗拒文明社会的召唤，只有怅然离去。

3. 《雪夜停林边》中幽深、静谧的树林象征着死亡，对疲惫的路人"我"发出召唤，引诱"我"放弃人世的生存斗争，悄然"安睡"。但是马儿的铃铛声将"我"惊醒，把"我"带回现实世界。"我"意识到，如果长久地在林边停留，大雪将会覆盖道路，"我"也会被冻死。因此"我"又挣扎着前行。

Ezra Pound
1885—1972

埃兹拉·庞德是美国现代诗歌的领袖之一，意象派(Imagism)运动的发起者。他出生于偏僻的爱达荷州，但不久便随父母来到宾夕法尼亚州。他15岁时进入宾夕法尼亚大学，学习美国历史、古典文学，以及法语、意大利语、西班牙语等。16岁时他开始自学比较文学。他不喜欢常规的大学课程，便转成特殊身份的学生，只学自己感兴趣的课程。后来他又转至汉密尔顿学院，获该校学士学位。1906年，庞德获宾夕法尼亚大学罗曼斯语硕士学位。

庞德博学多才，不仅能自如地运用大多数欧洲国家的语言，而且熟谙从古至今的文学史，熟悉盎格鲁·撒克逊、普罗旺斯、中世纪意大利及中国的诗歌格律，可谓文学奇才。他曾于1898年和1902年赴欧洲游历。对欧洲文化的亲身体验使他决定献身于诗歌。为了表示自己对美国学术界狭隘的地方主义的藐视，他在服饰上刻意模仿19世纪欧洲放荡不羁的文人，而且终生保持这种风格。在印第安纳州的一所学院教了一学期罗曼斯语之后，他于1908年定居欧洲。在威尼斯，他自费出版了第一本诗集《灯火熄灭之时》(A Lume Spento)，其风格主要是模仿以前的一些名家。1909年，他又出版了诗集《面具》(Personae)和《狂喜》(Exultations)，受到好评，在先锋派圈子里的名声也与日俱增。文集《罗曼斯精神》(The Spirit of Romance)于1910年在英国和美国同时出版。它汇集了庞德早期的学术研究成果。虽然多年旅居国外，但庞德的诗作和大量文论对当时的美国诗歌产生了重大影响。他善于发掘并热心扶持新锐作者，乔伊斯、艾略特和海明威等都曾得到他无私的帮助。

庞德早期的诗歌喜欢堆砌古雅的辞藻。这一问题于1911年被英国作家福特·马多克斯·福特(Ford Madox Ford, 1873—1939)修正后，他的诗歌创作转向反映现代生活的题材。他开始接近英国现代派诗人托马斯·厄内斯特·休姆(Thomas Ernest Hulme, 1883—1917)，并密切关注法国的文学动态，尤其是法国诗人对自由诗和日本俳句的吸收利用。富有创新意识的庞德开始酝酿一种新的诗歌，这种诗歌融合当时法国诗歌界的实验性文学和19世纪末的象征主义，并且更加简洁。他于1911年底开始试用这种新的诗歌形式，1912年将它定名为意象派诗歌。此后他又更明确地提出了这种新诗的宗旨：以鲜明、准确、高度凝练的意象直接表达外界事物或诗人的感受，反对任何多余的辞藻，反对僵硬的格律，并把这些主张发表在芝加哥的《诗刊》(1913)上。庞德认为，"诗歌的基本色素是意象"，诗人应该避免抽象，要使用鲜明的意象，养成清晰凝练的诗风，甚至"一生只呈现一个意象，胜于写出无数作品"。不过当意象派的诗集《意象主义者》(Des Imagistes, 1914)几经周折终于出版时，庞德已开始脱离这一流派，而转向更为激进的旋涡派(Vorticism)，其代表刊物为《风暴》(Blast, A Review of the Great English Vortex, 1914—1915)。他试图向诗歌意象中注入动能，因为意象并不是观点，而是"一个辐射的节点或束丛，……一个旋涡，观点从这个旋涡中不断生成，通过它，并且朝着它不断地涌流而去"。1918年以后，庞德或称自己的风格为旋涡派，或称之为表意，后者也体现出中国诗歌和汉字对他的影响。

庞德最早的也是最出色的意象诗为《在地铁站内》("In a Station of the Metro", 1913)。《姑娘》("A Girl")是他早期另一首较优美的意象诗。它将一位姑娘比作一棵树，但同时又巧妙地把树比作姑娘的情人。1910至1920年间，他出版了3部重要的作品：首先是1915年他根据东方诗歌研究者厄内斯特·芬诺洛莎(Ernest Fenollosa, 1853—1908)的遗稿译成的一批中国古诗《华夏集》(Cathay)，其中包括李白的《长干行》(他译为 "The River-Merchant's Wife: A Letter") 等。虽然他不懂中文，却基本上译出了原诗的精神风貌。另一部重要作品，《向塞克斯图斯·普罗佩提乌斯致敬》(*Homage to Sextus Propertius*, 1934) 将这位古罗马诗人的作品大胆地用现代都市人的口吻进行了重译。这一时期他最重要的作品是他自己创作的《休·赛尔温·毛伯利》(*Hugh Selwyn Mauberley*, 1920)。这首由 12 个部分组成的长诗体现了诗人成熟的诗风与他对诗歌的态度。整首诗评判了一战前的英国文坛，表达了诗人对现实的不满。

庞德最重要的作品是他倾注毕生精力创作的鸿篇巨制——《诗章》(*The Cantos*)。这首始于 1915 年的长诗原计划由 100 个诗章组成，最后成诗为 109 章，第 110 至 117 章为未完成的草稿，1970 年被全部收集在一起。诗章的内容包罗万象，涉及美学、政治、经济、文化各个领域，从古到今，从美洲、欧洲至东方，无所不谈。其中第 52 至 61 章谈论中国各个朝代取得的成就及儒家哲学。通过对历史上各种文化的比较，庞德告诫人们要抛弃资本主义的道德原则，尊崇孔子提倡的修身养性。他提倡国家控制信贷和货币，反对在他看来是万恶之源的高利贷。有些评论家认为其结构与但丁的《神曲》(*Divine Comedy*) 有某些相似之处。受乔伊斯的名著《尤利西斯》(*Ulysses*, 1922) 的启发，庞德将他在此之前写成的《诗章》片段全部重写。《比萨诗章》(*The Pisan Cantos*, 1948) 是其中一组相对独立的诗篇，是诗人根据他被捕后在比萨的一个战俘营中的经历写成，获得了 1949 年的博林根诗歌奖 (Bollingen Award for Poetry)。

庞德学识渊博。他不仅在语言、历史、文学等方面造诣很深，对音乐、绘画也很有研究。他对 20 世纪初美国现代派诗歌所作出的巨大贡献是不可磨灭的。

In a Station of the Metro

【题解】

《在地铁站内》是意象派诗歌的代表作之一。庞德称该诗为"意象派形成前出现的一首意象派诗歌"。据诗人自己说，创作这首短诗花了他一年多的时间。诗人在巴黎一处地铁站见到许多美丽的面孔，当天回去后，一张张美丽的脸仍在他的脑海中闪现。它们逐渐变成了美丽的色块。诗人最初用一首三十多行的诗表达这种意象，觉得不满意，半年后又写了一首十几行的诗，仍不满意，一年多后才写成这首两行短诗。"Petals on a wet" 所提供的朦胧重叠的美贴切地表现了诗人想要传达的信息。这首经过高度提炼的短诗也体现出中国诗歌和日本俳句对庞德的深刻影响。

In a Station of the Metro[1]

The apparition of these faces in the crowd;
Petals on a wet, black bough.

【注解】

1. Metro：巴黎地铁站。

【思考题】

1. What images are used here? Can you have a clear idea of what the poet is trying to convey through this poem? Do you think the comparison effective?
2. Why does the poet choose the word apparition instead of appearance?
3. In what sense is the poem different from most of the traditional poems you have read?

解读举例

1. 诗人站在地铁站的出口，望着涌出的人群，脑海中闪现的是大自然中的一根黑色树枝和依附在树枝上的花朵。扑面而来的无数张面孔如同被雨水打败了的花朵，麻木而毫无灵性。

2. 诗人站在地下铁道的出口，望着涌出的人群，被一张张面孔打动，觉得它们就像一根黑色树枝上依附的湿漉漉的花朵，虽不鲜艳，却真实、美丽。

L'Art, 1910

【题解】

　　这首诗也是意象派诗歌的经典作品，描写了作者对一幅现代派画作的印象，从中可以看出庞德对绘画及所有艺术作品中创新精神的赞赏。它可能创作于1910年英国举办后印象主义派(Post-Impressionism)画展之后。与其他意象派诗歌类似，诗人没有直接告诉读者他对这幅画的感受，只是描写了一些具体的色彩，让读者自己去品味。

L'Art, 1910

Green arsenic[1] smeared on an egg-white cloth,
Crushed strawberries! Come, let us feast our eyes.

【注解】

1. arsenic：含砷的涂料。

【思考题】

1. Can you guess what the content of the poem is from the title?
2. What are the colors mentioned here? Why does the speaker invite the reader to "feast our eyes"?
3. Why does the poet use the word "smeared" here?
4. Does the speaker seem to enjoy the painting?

解读举例

1. 这幅印象派绘画把绿色的涂料看似随意地涂抹在雪白的画布上，就像挤碎了的草莓，这种触目惊心的色彩反衬对观赏者来说是一场视觉盛宴。

2. 这幅印象派绘画只是把绿色的涂料随意地涂抹在雪白的画布上，试图真实地记录光和色彩转瞬即逝的视觉效果，结果却是失败的，整幅画就像挤碎了的草莓，汁水四溅。

The River-Merchant's Wife: A Letter

【题解】

庞德根据东方诗歌研究者芬诺洛莎的遗稿翻译了一批中国古诗，李白的《长干行》便是其中之一。由于庞德不懂汉语，其翻译多有不准确之处，但却很富有诗意，因此这篇译作可以说是根据原诗精神进行的一种再创作。虽然这篇译作的准确性有待商榷，但庞德对传播中国文化所作的贡献是不可否认的。

The River-Merchant's Wife: A Letter

While my hair was still cut straight across my forehead
I played about the front gate, pulling flowers
You came by on bamboo stilts, playing horse,
You walked about my seat, playing with blue plums[1].
And we went on living in the village of Chokan[2]: 5
Two small people, without dislike or suspicion.

At fourteen I married My Lord you.
I never laughed, being bashful.
Lowering my head, I looked at the wall,
Called to, a thousand times, I never looked back. 10

At fifteen I stopped scowling,
I desired my dust to be mingled with yours
Forever and forever and forever
Why should I climb the look out?

At sixteen you departed, 15
You went into far Ku-to-yen[3], by the river of swirling eddies,
And you have been gone five months.
The monkeys make sorrowful noise overhead.

You dragged your feet when you went out.
By the gate now, the moss is grown, the different mosses, 20
Too deep to clear them away!
The leaves fall early this autumn, in wind.
The paired butterflies are already yellow with August
over the grass in the West garden;
They hurt me. I grow older. 25
If you are coming down through the narrows of the river Kiang[4],
Please let me know beforehand,

and I will come out to meet you

as far as Cho-fu-sa[5].

By Rihaku[6] (Li T'aipo)

【注解】

1. You walked...blue plums：这两句诗指两个孩子从小青梅竹马。
2. Chokan：长干或长干里，地名，在南京附近。
3. Ku-to-yen：瞿塘滟滪堆，为长江著名的险处之一。
4. river Kiang：下三巴，三巴指巴郡、巴东、巴西，均在四川省内。
5. Cho-fu-sa：长风沙，今安徽省安庆市东。
6. Rihaku："李白"的日语音译。

【思考题】

1. Did the speaker's attitude toward her husband undergo any change? What was their relationship before marriage, immediately after it, and one year later?
2. After the husband's departure, what was the speaker's mood? Through what means was the mood conveyed?
3. Can you find any similarities between the use of images in this poem and in imagist poems? Can you say something about the Chinese poetic tradition?
4. What is the tone of the poem, sentimental or matter-of-fact? Cite lines to support your view.
5. Make a comparison between this poem and its Chinese original. If you are to translate it, what changes would you make?

解读举例

1. 这首诗描写了一位年轻的妻子同外出经商的丈夫分离后的哀伤与思念之情。妻子回忆了自己同丈夫青梅竹马的美好时光，以及成婚后的幸福生活，反衬出两人分别后的孤独与寂寞，歌颂了坚贞的爱情。

2. 这首诗表达了人面对离别时感到的痛苦与孤独，歌颂了男女之间真挚的爱情，这些本是各个文化所共通的情感，但是西方文化进入20世纪已经逐渐没落，丧失了最基本的价值追求，因此有必要借助东方文化质朴、简练的诗歌传统，帮助西方人找回失落的灵魂。

American Literature
Between the Two Wars:1914–1945

F. Scott Fitzgerald
1896—1940

F. 司各特·菲茨杰拉德是20世纪美国最杰出的小说家之一，"迷惘的一代"的代言人。他出生于明尼苏达州圣保罗市一个商人之家。祖父辈十分富有，但到父亲这代却家道中落。菲茨杰拉德是在亲戚的资助下才得以进入东部贵族预科学校，是一位典型的贵族学校里的穷孩子。菲茨杰拉德也因此感到自卑，对金钱既爱又恨，这些在他后来的主要作品中都有反映。

早在中学时，菲茨杰拉德就展示出极高的文学天赋，曾写过两部戏剧，并自编自导在当地上演。与此同时，他也在学校杂志上发表了几篇小说。1913年秋，菲茨杰拉德进入普林斯顿大学读书，真正开始了他的文学创作生涯。在此期间，他完成了首部长篇小说《人间天堂》(*This Side of Paradise*, 1920)的初稿，并梦想成为"歌德、拜伦、萧伯纳那样传统的完人"。1917年，菲茨杰拉德由于身体原因离校参军。军训期间，菲茨杰拉德结识了当地法官之女姗尔达·塞亚，对她一见钟情。1920年，菲茨杰拉德修改、发表了《人间天堂》而一举成名，随后与姗尔达结婚。同年，菲茨杰拉德出版了短篇小说集《新潮女郎与哲学家》(*Flappers and Philosophers*, 1920)。两年后他又创作出版了《爵士时代的故事》(*Tales of the Jazz Age*, 1922)。这些作品充分表现了在战后"喧闹的20年代"(the Roaring Twenties)中美国青年崇尚新潮、追逐时髦、破除禁忌、纸醉金迷的生活状态。该书题名中的"爵士时代"后来也成为这个时代的代名词，作者本人也因此获得了"爵士时代歌手"的称号。

《人间天堂》被评论家艾尔弗莱德·卡赞称为"宣告了迷惘一代成立"的作品。和菲茨杰拉德的多数作品一样，《人间天堂》中也处处闪现着作者本人的身影。和菲茨杰拉德一样，作品主人公艾莫里·布莱恩也曾在普林斯顿大学就读。他自称为"亮发一族"(slicker)，整日沉溺于寻欢作乐，参加一个又一个宴会、酒会、舞会，追求漂亮女生。对布莱恩一代的战后青年而言，传统的理想、价值都已破灭："众神都已死光，战争全部打完，信念全部消失"，剩下的就只有物质与感官的享受。作品人物的潇洒、浪漫、时髦、新潮，所有这些都极大吸引了战后一代青年，成为他们模仿的对象。

1922年，菲茨杰拉德发表了第二部长篇小说《漂亮冤家》(*The Beautiful and*

Damned)，以自己与妻子珊尔达的情感生活为原型，表现了主人公安索尼和歌乐娅不思进取、贪图享受、追逐金钱，最后梦幻破灭的故事，体现了虚幻梦想与冷酷现实的对立冲突。

《人间天堂》与《漂亮冤家》中的人物形象和故事情节在菲茨杰拉德1925年出版的《了不起的盖茨比》(*The Great Gatsby*) 中得到了延续、发展与提升。虽然主题不再新颖，但作家却把自己对那个时代的深刻体验近乎完美地融入了主人公的生活，使其"美国梦"的破灭演变成一曲"迷惘一代"的悲歌。在创作中，菲茨杰拉德借鉴了康拉德的创作手法，通过尼克·卡洛威这位叙述者兼亲历者的讲述展开小说情节。在作品中，作者娴熟应用了诸如"西卵"与"东卵"(West Egg and East Egg)、"灰谷"(valley of ahes)、艾克尔伯格的眼镜、黛茜家码头的绿色灯光等象征，有效增强了小说的感染力和悲剧色彩，显示出菲茨杰拉德小说创作的高超艺术。诗人艾略特在给菲茨杰拉德的信中称此书"是自亨利·詹姆斯以来美国小说向前迈出的第一步"。

菲茨杰拉德的第四部长篇小说《夜色温柔》(*Tender Is the Night*，1934) 取材于作者自己在欧洲的一段生活经历。作品虽然讲述的是夫妻间从相爱到背弃的故事，却反映了当时社会整体风貌，突出了金钱对人精神上的腐蚀和毒害。作品弥漫着浓重的哀伤情调，也是作者创作后期心态的有力写照。这一时期，菲茨杰拉德已负债累累，珊尔达早已进入精神病院，但病情毫无好转。菲茨杰拉德心灰意冷，借酒浇愁，曾两度自杀未遂。从他去世后发表的书信文集《崩溃》(*The Crack Up*, 1945) 中可以看出，1935年左右，他就已经"过早地崩溃"了。在其人生最后的日子里，他一直尝试着为好莱坞电影当编剧，虽未有大成果，却为其最后一部未竟之作《最后的大亨》(*The Last Tycoon*, 1941) 准备了充足的素材。然而未等完成这部作品，菲茨杰拉德便在穷困潦倒之中离世。

作为20世纪初"迷惘的一代"的代言人、社会观察家和小说家，菲茨杰拉德在不到二十年的创作生涯中为后人留下了许多经典作品。除了几部长篇著作外，菲茨杰拉德在短篇小说的创作中也颇有成就。菲茨杰拉德共出版了4部短篇小说集，除了《新潮女郎与哲学家》《爵士时代的故事》外，还有《所有痛苦的年轻人》(*All the Sad Young Men*, 1926) 和《雷维尔的节拍声》(*Taps at Reveille*, 1935)，《富家子弟》("The Rich Boy")、《冬梦》("Winter Dreams") 等都是其中的精品。菲茨杰拉德的短篇小说集趣味性、文学性、哲理性和艺术性于一体，或朴实生动、言近而旨远，或情趣盎然、妙趣横生，或荒诞奇诡、影射现实，或含蓄深沉、委婉动人，无论是艺术性还是思想性都体现出一种大家风范，可与他的长篇小说相媲美。

The Great Gatsby

【题解】

《了不起的盖茨比》是菲茨杰拉德的代表作。小说通过卡洛威的叙述展开。卡洛威生于美国中西部,后到纽约经营股票,并想以此致富。他与主人公盖茨比为邻而,住在长岛。盖茨比原名盖茨,也来自美国中西部,后因贩卖私酒而暴富。他经常在家大宴宾客,以显豪阔,真正目的却是想以此引起邻居的黛西的注意,从而赢回这位昔日恋人的芳心。五年前,黛西因嫌贫爱富嫁给了纨绔子弟汤姆。当盖茨比与黛西重逢时,盖茨比以为可以旧梦重圆,但久而久之,他发现黛西远不像他梦想中的人。黛西后来酒后驾驶盖茨比的车轧死了汤姆的情妇,却与汤姆一道嫁祸于痴情不悟的盖茨比,导致死者的丈夫持枪闯入盖茨比家中将其枪杀,后自杀身亡。只有卡洛威与少数几位朋友参加了盖茨比的葬礼,卡洛威而后决定回到中西部,远离人心不古、世风日下的东部大都市。

下文为小说的最后一章,记述了卡洛威参加主人公盖茨比葬礼的经过和后来在海滩夜色中的冥思。

From The Great Gatsby

Chapter 9

After two years I[1] remember the rest of that day, and that night and the next day, only as an endless drill of police and photographers and newspaper men in and out of Gatsby's front door. A rope stretched across the main gate and a policeman by it kept out the curious, but little boys soon discovered that they could enter through my yard, and there were always a few of them clustered open-mouthed about the pool. Some one with a positive manner, perhaps a detective, used the expression "madman" as he bent over Wilson's[2] body that afternoon, and the adventitious authority of his voice set the key for the newspaper reports next morning.

Most of those reports were a nightmare—grotesque, circumstantial, eager and untrue. When Michaelis's[3] testimony at the inquest brought to light Wilson's suspicions of his wife I thought the whole tale would shortly be served up in racy pasquinade—but Catherine[4], who might have said anything, didn't say a word. She showed a surprising amount of character about it too—looked at the coroner with determined eyes under that corrected brow of hers, and swore that her sister had never seen Gatsby, that her sister was completely happy with her husband, that her sister had been into no mischief whatever. She convinced herself of it, and cried into her handkerchief, as if the very suggestion was more than she could endure. So Wilson was reduced to a man "deranged by grief" in order that the case might remain in its simplest form. And it rested there.

But all this part of it seemed remote and unessential. I found myself on Gatsby's side, and alone. From the moment I telephoned news of the catastrophe to West Egg village[5], every surmise about him, and every practical question, was referred to me. At first I was surprised and confused; then, as he lay in his house and didn't move or breathe or speak, hour upon hour, it grew upon me that I was responsible, because no one else was interested—interested, I mean, with that intense personal interest to which every one has some vague right at the end.

I called up Daisy[6] half an hour after we found him, called her instinctively and without hesitation. But she and Tom had gone away early that afternoon, and taken baggage with them.

"Left no address?"

"No."

"Say when they'd be back?"

"No."

"Any idea where they are? How I could reach them?"

"I don't know. Can't say."

I wanted to get somebody for him. I wanted to go into the room where he lay and reassure him: "I'll get somebody for you, Gatsby. Don't worry. Just trust me and I'll get somebody for you—"

Meyer Wolfsheim's[7] name wasn't in the phone book. The butler gave me his once address on Broadway, and I called Information, but by the time I had the number it was long after five, and no one answered the phone.

"Will you ring again?"

"I've rung them three times."

"It's very important."

"Sorry. I'm afraid no one's there."

I went back to the drawing-room and thought for an instant that they were chance visitors, all these official people who suddenly filled it. But, though they drew back the sheet and looked at Gatsby with shocked eyes, his protest continued in my brain:

"Look here, old sport, you've got to get somebody for me. You've got to try hard. I can't go through this alone."

Some one started to ask me questions, but I broke away and going upstairs looked hastily through the unlocked parts of his desk—he'd never told me definitely that his parents were dead. But there was nothing—only the picture of Dan Cody[8], a token of forgotten violence, staring down from the wall.

Next morning I sent the butler to New York with a letter to Wolfsheim, which asked for information and urged him to come out on the next train. That request seemed superfluous when I wrote it. I was sure he'd start when he saw the newspapers, just as I was sure there'd be a wire from Daisy before noon—but neither a wire nor Mr. Wolfsheim arrived; no one arrived except more police and photographers and newspaper men. When the butler brought back Wolfsheim's answer I began to have a feeling of defiance, of scornful solidarity between Gatsby and me against them all.

  Dear Mr. Carraway,

  This has been one of the most terrible shocks of my life to me I hardly can believe it that it is true at all. Such a mad act as that man did should make us all think. I cannot come down now as I am tied up in some very important business and cannot get mixed up in this thing now. If there is anything I can do a little later let me know in a letter by Edgar. I hardly know where I am when I hear about a thing like this and am completely knocked down and out.

  Yours truly

                  Meyer Wolfsheim

and then hasty addenda beneath:

Let me know about the funeral etc do not know his family at all.

When the phone rang that afternoon and Long Distance said Chicago was calling I thought this would be Daisy at last. But the connection came through as a man's voice, very thin and far away.

"This is Slagle[9] speaking . . ."

"Yes?" The name was unfamiliar.

"Hell of a note, isn't it? Get my wire?"

"There haven't been any wires."

"Young Parke's in trouble," he said rapidly. "They picked him up when he handed the bonds over the counter. They got a circular from New York giving 'em the numbers just five minutes before. What d'you know about that, hey? You never can tell in these hick towns—"

"Hello!" I interrupted breathlessly. "Look here—this isn't Mr. Gatsby. Mr. Gatsby's dead."

There was a long silence on the other end of the wire, followed by an exclamation . . . then a quick squawk as the connection was broken.

I think it was on the third day that a telegram signed Henry C. Gatz arrived from a town in Minnesota. It said only that the sender was leaving immediately and to postpone the funeral until he came.

It was Gatsby's father, a solemn old man, very helpless and dismayed, bundled up in a long cheap ulster against the warm September day. His eyes leaked continuously with excitement, and when I took the bag and umbrella from his hands he began to pull so incessantly at his sparse grey beard that I had difficulty in getting off his coat. He was on the point of collapse, so I took him into the music-room and made him sit down while I sent for something to eat. But he wouldn't eat, and the glass of milk spilled from his trembling hand.

"I saw it in the Chicago newspaper," he said. "It was all in the Chicago newspaper. I started right away."

"I didn't know how to reach you."

His eyes, seeing nothing, moved ceaselessly about the room.

"It was a madman," he said. 'He must have been mad."

"Wouldn't you like some coffee?" I urged him.

"I don't want anything. I'm all right now, Mr.—"

"Carraway."

"Well, I'm all right now. Where have they got Jimmy?"

I took him into the drawing-room, where his son lay, and left him there. Some little boys had come up on the steps and were looking into the hall; when I told them who had arrived, they went reluctantly away.

After a little while Mr. Gatz opened the door and came out, his mouth ajar, his face flushed slightly, his eyes leaking isolated and unpunctual tears. He had reached an age where death no longer has the quality of ghastly surprise, and when he looked around him now for the first time and saw the height and splendour of the hall and the great rooms opening out from it into other rooms, his grief began to be mixed with an awed pride. I helped him to a bedroom upstairs; while he took off his coat and vest I told him that all arrangements had been deferred until he came.

"I didn't know what you'd want, Mr. Gatsby—"

"Gatz is my name."

"—Mr. Gatz. I thought you might want to take the body West."

He shook his head.

"Jimmy always liked it better down East. He rose up to his position in the East. Were you a friend of my boy's, Mr.—?"

"We were close friends."

"He had a big future before him, you know. He was only a young man, but he had a lot of brain power here."

He touched his head impressively, and I nodded.

"If he'd of lived, he'd of been a great man[10]. A man like James J. Hill[11]. He'd of helped build up the country."

"That's true," I said, uncomfortably.

He fumbled at the embroidered coverlet, trying to take it from the bed, and lay down stiffly—and was instantly asleep.

That night an obviously frightened person called up, and demanded to know who I was before he would give his name.

"This is Mr. Carraway," I said.

"Oh!" He sounded relieved. "This is Klipspringer[12]."

I was relieved too, for that seemed to promise another friend at Gatsby's grave. I didn't want it to be in the papers and draw a sightseeing crowd, so I'd been calling up a few people myself. They were hard to find.

"The funeral's tomorrow," I said. "Three o'clock, here at the house. I wish you'd tell anybody who'd be interested."

"Oh, I will," he broke out hastily. "Of course I'm not likely to see anybody, but if I do."

His tone made me suspicious.

"Of course you'll be there yourself."

"Well, I'll certainly try. What I called up about is—"

"Wait a minute,' I interrupted. 'How about saying you'll come?"

"Well, the fact is—the truth of the matter is that I'm staying with some people up here in Greenwich[13], and they rather expect me to be with them tomorrow. In fact, there's a sort of picnic or something. Of course I'll do my very best to get away."

I ejaculated an unrestrained "Huh!" and he must have heard me, for he went on nervously:

"What I called up about was a pair of shoes I left there. I wonder if it'd be too much trouble to have the butler send them on. You see, they're tennis shoes, and I'm sort of helpless without them. My address is care of B. F.—"

I didn't hear the rest of the name, because I hung up the receiver.

After that I felt a certain shame for Gatsby—one gentleman to whom I telephoned implied that he had got what he deserved. However, that was my fault, for he was one of those who used to sneer most bitterly at Gatsby on the courage of Gatsby's liquor, and I should have known better than to call him.

The morning of the funeral I went up to New York to see Meyer Wolfsheim; I couldn't seem to reach him any other way. The door that I pushed open, on the advice of an elevator boy, was marked "The Swastika Holding Company," and at first there didn't seem to be any one inside. But when I'd shouted "hello" several times in vain, an argument broke out behind a partition, and presently a lovely Jewess appeared at an interior door and scrutinized me with black hostile eyes.

"Nobody's in," she said. "Mr. Wolfsheim's gone to Chicago."

The first part of this was obviously untrue, for some one had begun to whistle "The Rosary," tunelessly, inside.

"Please say that Mr. Carraway wants to see him."

"I can't get him back from Chicago, can I?"

At this moment a voice, unmistakably Wolfsheim's, called "Stella!" from the other side of the door.

"Leave your name on the desk," she said quickly. "I'll give it to him when he gets back."

"But I know he's there."

She took a step toward me and began to slide her hands indignantly up and down her hips.

"You young men think you can force your way in here any time," she scolded. "We're getting sickantired[14] of it. When I say he's in Chicago, he's in Chicago."

I mentioned Gatsby.

"Oh-h!" She looked at me over again. "Will you just—What was your name?"

She vanished. In a moment Meyer Wolfsheim stood solemnly in the doorway, holding out both hands. He drew me into his office, remarking in a reverent voice that it was a sad time for all of us, and offered me a cigar.

"My memory goes back to when first I met him," he said. "A young major just out of the army and covered over with medals he got in the war. He was so hard up he had to keep on wearing his uniform because he couldn't buy some regular clothes. First time I saw him was when he come into Winebrenner's poolroom at Forty-third Street[15] and asked for a job. He hadn't eat[16] anything for a couple of days. "Come on have some lunch with me," I said. He ate more than four dollars' worth of food in half an hour."

"Did you start him in business?" I inquired.

"Start him! I made him."

"Oh."

"I raised him up out of nothing, right out of the gutter. I saw right away he was a fine-appearing, gentlemanly young man, and when he told me he was an Oggsford[17] I knew I could use him good. I got him to join up in the American Legion[18] and he used to stand high there. Right off he did some work for a client of mine up to Albany. We were so thick like that in everything"—he held up two bulbous fingers—"always together."

I wondered if this partnership had included the World's Series transaction[19] in 1919.

"Now he's dead," I said after a moment. "You were his closest friend, so I know you'll want to come to his funeral this afternoon."

"I'd like to come."

"Well, come then."

The hair in his nostrils quivered slightly, and as he shook his head his eyes filled with tears.

"I can't do it—I can't get mixed up in it," he said.

"There's nothing to get mixed up in. It's all over now."

"When a man gets killed I never like to get mixed up in it any way. I keep out. When

I was a young man it was different—if a friend of mine died, no matter how, I stuck with them to the end. You may think that's sentimental, but I mean it—to the bitter end."

I saw that for some reason of his own he was determined not to come, so I stood up.

"Are you a college man?" he inquired suddenly.

For a moment I thought he was going to suggest a "gonnegtion[20]," but he only nodded and shook my hand.

"Let us learn to show our friendship for a man when he is alive and not after he is dead," he suggested. "After that, my own rule is to let everything alone."

When I left his office the sky had turned dark and I got back to West Egg in a drizzle. After changing my clothes I went next door and found Mr. Gatz walking up and down excitedly in the hall. His pride in his son and in his son's possessions was continually increasing and now he had something to show me.

"Jimmy sent me this picture." He took out his wallet with trembling fingers. "Look there."

It was a photograph of the house, cracked in the corners and dirty with many hands. He pointed out every detail to me eagerly. "Look there!" and then sought admiration from my eyes. He had shown it so often that I think it was more real to him now than the house itself.

"Jimmy sent it to me. I think it's a very pretty picture. It shows up well."

"Very well. Had you seen him lately?"

"He come[21] out to see me two years ago and bought me the house I live in now. Of course we was broke up when he run off from home, but I see now there was a reason for it. He knew he had a big future in front of him. And ever since he made a success he was very generous with me."

He seemed reluctant to put away the picture, held it for another minute, lingeringly, before my eyes. Then he returned the wallet and pulled from his pocket a ragged old copy of a book called *Hopalong Cassidy*[22].

"Look here, this is a book he had when he was a boy. It just shows you."

He opened it at the back cover and turned it around for me to see. On the last fly-leaf was printed the word SCHEDULE[23], and the date September 12, 1906. And underneath:

Rise from bed . . .	6.00 A.M.
Dumbbell exercise and wall-scaling	6.15–6.30 A.M.

Study electricity, etc. . . .	7.15–8.15 A.M.
Work . . .	8.30 A.M.–4.30 P.M.
Baseball and sports . . .	4.30–5.00 P.M.
Practice elocution, poise and how to attain it	5.00–6.00 P.M.
Study needed inventions . . .	7.00–9.00 P.M.

GENERAL RESOLVES

No wasting time at shafters or [a name, indecipherable]

No more smokeing[24] or chewing

Bath every other day

Read one improving book or magazine per week

Save $5.00 [crossed out] $3.00 per week

Be better to parents

"I come across this book by accident," said the old man. "It just shows you, don't it?"

"Jimmy was bound to get ahead. He always had some resolves like this or something. Do you notice what he's got about improving his mind? He was always great for that. He told me I et[25] like a hog once, and I beat him for it."

He was reluctant to close the book, reading each item aloud and then looking eagerly at me. I think he rather expected me to copy down the list for my own use.

A little before three the Lutheran[26] minister arrived from Flushing, and I began to look involuntarily out the windows for other cars. So did Gatsby's father. And as the time passed and the servants came in and stood waiting in the hall, his eyes began to blink anxiously, and he spoke of the rain in a worried, uncertain way. The minister glanced several times at his watch, so I took him aside and asked him to wait for half an hour. But it wasn't any use. Nobody came.

About five o'clock our procession of three cars reached the cemetery and stopped in a thick drizzle beside the gate—first a motor hearse, horribly black and wet, then Mr. Gatz and the minister and I in the limousine, and a little later four or five servants and the postman from West Egg, in Gatsby's station-wagon, all wet to the skin. As we started through the gate into the cemetery I heard a car stop and then the sound of someone splashing after us over the soggy ground. I looked around. It was the man with owl-eyed glasses[27] whom I had found marvelling over Gatsby's books in the library one night three months before.

I'd never seen him since then. I don't know how he knew about the funeral, or even his name. The rain poured down his thick glasses, and he took them off and wiped them to see the protecting canvas unrolled from Gatsby's grave.

I tried to think about Gatsby then for a moment, but he was already too far away, and I could only remember, without resentment, that Daisy hadn't sent a message or a flower. Dimly I heard someone murmur "Blessed are the dead that the rain falls on," and then the owl-eyed man said "Amen to that," in a brave voice.

We straggled down quickly through the rain to the cars. Owl-eyes spoke to me by the gate.

"I couldn't get to the house," he remarked.

"Neither could anybody else."

"Go on!" He started. "Why, my God! they used to go there by the hundreds."

He took off his glasses and wiped them again, outside and in.

"The poor son-of-a-bitch," he said.

One of my most vivid memories is of coming back West from prep school and later from college at Christmastime. Those who went farther than Chicago would gather in the old dim Union Station at six o'clock of a December evening, with a few Chicago friends, already caught up into their own holiday gayeties, to bid them a hasty goodbye. I remember the fur coats of the girls returning from Miss This-or-That's and the chatter of frozen breath and the hands waving overhead as we caught sight of old acquaintances, and the matchings of invitations: "Are you going to the Ordways'? the Herseys'? the Schultzes'?" and the long green tickets clasped tight in our gloved hands. And last the murky yellow cars of the Chicago, Milwaukee & St. Paul Railroad looking cheerful as Christmas itself on the tracks beside the gate.

When we pulled out into the winter night and the real snow, our snow, began to stretch out beside us and twinkle against the windows, and the dim lights of small Wisconsin stations moved by, a sharp wild brace came suddenly into the air. We drew in deep breaths of it as we walked back from dinner through the cold vestibules, unutterably aware of our identity with this country for one strange hour, before we melted indistinguishably into it again.

That's my Middle West—not the wheat or the prairies or the lost Swede towns, but the thrilling returning trains of my youth, and the street lamps and sleigh bells in the frosty dark and the shadows of holly wreaths thrown by lighted windows on the snow. I am part of that, a little solemn with the feel of those long winters, a little complacent from growing up in the Carraway house in a city where dwellings are still called through decades by a family's name. I see now that this has been a story of the West, after all—Tom and Gatsby, Daisy and Jordan and I, were all Westerners, and perhaps we possessed some deficiency in common which made us subtly unadaptable to Eastern life.

Even when the East excited me most, even when I was most keenly aware of its superiority to the bored, sprawling, swollen towns beyond the Ohio[28], with their interminable inquisitions which spared only the children and the very old—even then it had always for me a quality of distortion. West Egg, especially, still figures in my more fantastic dreams. I see it as a night scene by El Greco[29]: a hundred houses, at once conventional and grotesque, crouching under a sullen, overhanging sky and a lustreless moon. In the foreground four solemn men in dress suits are walking along the sidewalk with a stretcher on which lies a drunken woman in a white evening dress. Her hand, which dangles over the side, sparkles cold with jewels. Gravely the men turn in at a house—the wrong house. But no one knows the woman's name, and no one cares.

After Gatsby's death the East was haunted for me like that, distorted beyond my eyes' power of correction. So when the blue smoke of brittle leaves was in the air and the wind blew the wet laundry stiff on the line I decided to come back home.

There was one thing to be done before I left, an awkward, unpleasant thing that perhaps had better have been let alone. But I wanted to leave things in order and not just trust that obliging and indifferent sea to sweep my refuse away. I saw Jordan Baker[30] and talked over and around what had happened to us together, and what had happened afterward to me, and she lay perfectly still, listening, in a big chair.

She was dressed to play golf, and I remember thinking she looked like a good illustration, her chin raised a little jauntily, her hair the color of an autumn leaf, her face the same brown tint as the fingerless glove on her knee. When I had finished she told me without comment that she was engaged to another man. I doubted that, though there were several she could have married at a nod of her head, but I pretended to be surprised. For just a minute I wondered if I wasn't making a mistake, then I thought it all over again quickly and got up to say goodbye.

"Nevertheless you did throw me over," said Jordan suddenly. "You threw me over on the telephone. I don't give a damn about you now, but it was a new experience for me, and I felt a little dizzy for a while."

We shook hands.

"Oh, and do you remember"—she added—"a conversation we had once about driving a car?"

"Why—not exactly."

"You said a bad driver was only safe until she met another bad driver? Well, I met another bad driver, didn't I? I mean it was careless of me to make such a wrong guess. I thought you were rather an honest, straightforward person. I thought it was your secret pride."

"I'm thirty," I said. "I'm five years too old to lie to myself and call it honor."

She didn't answer. Angry, and half in love with her, and tremendously sorry, I turned away.

One afternoon late in October I saw Tom Buchanan. He was walking ahead of me along Fifth Avenue[31] in his alert, aggressive way, his hands out a little from his body as if to fight off interference, his head moving sharply here and there, adapting itself to his restless eyes. Just as I slowed up to avoid overtaking him he stopped and began frowning into the windows of a jewellery store. Suddenly he saw me and walked back, holding out his hand.

"What's the matter, Nick? Do you object to shaking hands with me?"

"Yes. You know what I think of you."

"You're crazy, Nick," he said quickly. "Crazy as hell. I don't know what's the matter with you."

"Tom," I inquired, "what did you say to Wilson that afternoon?"

He stared at me without a word, and I knew I had guessed right about those missing hours. I started to turn away, but he took a step after me and grabbed my arm.

"I told him the truth," he said. "He came to the door while we were getting ready to leave, and when I sent down word that we weren't in he tried to force his way upstairs. He was crazy enough to kill me if I hadn't told him who owned the car. His hand was on a revolver in his pocket every minute he was in the house—" He broke off defiantly. "What if I did tell him? That fellow had it coming to him. He threw dust into your eyes[32] just like he did in Daisy's, but he was a tough one. He ran over Myrtle like you'd run over a dog and never even stopped his car."

There was nothing I could say, except the one unutterable fact that it wasn't true.

"And if you think I didn't have my share of suffering—look here, when I went to give up that flat and saw that damn box of dog biscuits sitting there on the sideboard, I sat down and cried like a baby. By God, it was awful—"

I couldn't forgive him or like him, but I saw that what he had done was, to him, entirely justified. It was all very careless and confused. They were careless people, Tom and Daisy—they smashed up things and creatures and then retreated back into their money or their vast carelessness, or whatever it was that kept them together, and let other people clean up the mess they had made . . . .

I shook hands with him; it seemed silly not to, for I felt suddenly as though I were talking to a child. Then he went into the jewellery store to buy a pearl necklace—or perhaps only a pair of cuff buttons—rid of my provincial squeamishness forever.

Gatsby's house was still empty when I left—the grass on his lawn had grown as long as mine. One of the taxi drivers in the village never took a fare past the entrance gate without stopping for a minute and pointing inside; perhaps it was he who drove Daisy and Gatsby over to East Egg[33] the night of the accident, and perhaps he had made a story about it all his own. I didn't want to hear it and I avoided him when I got off the train.

I spent my Saturday nights in New York, because those gleaming, dazzling parties of his were with me so vividly that I could still hear the music and the laughter, faint and incessant, from his garden, and the cars going up and down his drive. One night I did hear a material car[34] there, and saw its lights stop at his front steps. But I didn't investigate. Probably it was some final guest who had been away at the ends of the earth and didn't know that the party was over.

On the last night, with my trunk packed and my car sold to the grocer, I went over and looked at that huge incoherent failure of a house once more. On the white steps an obscene word, scrawled by some boy with a piece of brick, stood out clearly in the moonlight, and I erased it, drawing my shoe raspingly along the stone. Then I wandered down to the beach and sprawled out on the sand.

Most of the big shore places were closed now and there were hardly any lights except the shadowy, moving glow of a ferryboat across the Sound[35]. And as the moon rose higher the inessential houses began to melt away until gradually I became aware of the old island here that flowered once for Dutch sailors' eyes—a fresh, green breast of the new world.

Its vanished trees, the trees that had made way for Gatsby's house, had once pandered in whispers to the last and greatest of all human dreams; for a transitory enchanted moment man must have held his breath in the presence of this continent, compelled into an aesthetic contemplation he neither understood nor desired, face to face for the last time in history with something commensurate to his capacity for wonder.

And as I sat there brooding on the old, unknown world, I thought of Gatsby's wonder when he first picked out the green light at the end of Daisy's dock[36]. He had come a long way to this blue lawn, and his dream must have seemed so close that he could hardly fail to grasp it. He did not know that it was already behind him, somewhere back in that vast obscurity beyond the city, where the dark fields of the republic rolled on under the night.

Gatsby believed in the green light, the orgiastic future that year by year recedes before us. It eluded us then, but that's no matter—tomorrow we will run faster, stretch out our arms farther . . . . And one fine morning—

So we beat on, boats against the current, borne back ceaselessly into the past.

【注解】

1. I：故事的叙述者尼克·卡洛威。
2. Wilson：威尔逊，汤姆的情妇 Myrtle 的丈夫，经营一家汽车修理铺，因听信汤姆的谎言杀死盖茨比，后自杀身亡。
3. Michaelis：威尔逊的邻居，目睹了威尔逊的妻子被汽车轧死的场面。
4. Catherine：Myrtle 的妹妹。
5. West Egg village：西卵村，虚构地名，为小说主人公盖茨比和叙述者尼克·卡洛威居住的地方。
6. Daisy：黛西，即下文提到的汤姆的妻子，以前曾是盖茨比的恋人。
7. Meyer Wolfsheim：梅耶·沃夫希姆，一个与盖茨比合伙做非法生意的人。
8. Dan Cody：丹·科迪，一个书中从未露面，靠挖金矿起家的人物。盖茨比年轻时曾替他干活，将他视作成功的象征。Dan Cody 的名字也可能是西部著名的拓荒者 Daniel Boone 和 Buffalo Bill Cody 两人名字的组合。
9. Slagle：斯莱格，与下文提到的 Parke 都是与盖茨比做非法生意的伙伴。
10. If he'd of lived . . . great man：这一句为教育程度不高的人使用的语言，相当于 If he'd lived, he'd have been a great man。
11. James J. Hill：詹姆斯·希尔 (1838—1916)，美国铁路大王。
12. Klipspringer：盖茨比生前常住在此人家中。
13. Greenwich：此处指美国康涅狄格州的格林尼治市。
14. sickantired：相当于 sick and tired。
15. Forty-third Street：纽约市的 43 街，与百老汇大街交叉，是曼哈顿最繁华的地方。
16. He hadn't eat：应为 eaten。沃夫希姆为欧洲移民，讲英语时有语法及语音错误。

17. Oggsford：应为 Oxford。沃夫希姆不能正确地发 x 的音。
18. American Legion：美国退伍军人协会。
19. World's Series transaction：世界棒球赛的那项交易。在小说第四章中，盖茨比告诉卡洛威，沃夫希姆曾操纵过 1919 年的世界棒球赛。
20. gonnegtion：应为 connection，这里卡洛威故意模仿沃夫希姆的蹩脚语音，以表示他对后者的轻蔑。
21. He come：应为 He came，此处为盖茨比犯的语法错误。
22. *Hopalong Cassidy*：《瘸子卡西迪》。
23. SCHEDULE：这里盖茨比在模仿本杰明·富兰克林在他的《自传》中制定的作息时间表，以表示他对富兰克林提出的"美国梦"的憧憬，并希望像富兰克林那样通过自己刻苦不懈的努力从一个穷孩子成长为一个伟大人物。
24. smokeing：应为 smoking。
25. et：应为 ate。
26. Lutheran：路德教派的。
27. man with owl-eyed glasses：盖茨比生前曾多次不请自来的食客。
28. the Ohio：指 the Ohio River，俄亥俄河。
29. El Greco：艾尔·格列柯 (1541—1614)，西班牙画家，画作色彩偏冷。
30. Jordan Baker：乔丹·贝克，黛西的女友，和卡洛威有一种若即若离的爱情关系。
31. Fifth Avenue：纽约市的第五大道，以气派、时髦著称。
32. He threw dust into your eyes：他蒙骗了你。
33. East Egg：东卵村，汤姆和黛西居住的地方。
34. a material car：真真切切有一辆车。
35. the Sound：指 Long Island Sound，长岛海峡。
36. the green light at the end of Daisy's dock：指东卵村海岸边的码头，那里整夜点着一盏灯，盖茨比常常在夜里独自一人从西卵村向黛西居住的东卵村眺望，但看到的只是一盏闪着绿光的灯。因此"green light"象征着盖茨比的梦想。

【思考题】

1. When Nick Carraway learns about Gatsby's murder, he calls up Daisy "instinctively and without hesitation". What is the point of Fitzgerald's emphasizing the immediacy of Nick's calling up Daisy?
2. What is Nick's attitude toward Gatsby, Tom and Daisy, and all his former party-goers?
3. How would you comment on the protagonist of the novel, the great Gatsby?
4. How many people does Nick call and what are some of their reasons for not being able to show up at Gatzby's funeral?
5. El Greco's painting features a "drunken woman in white evening dress" and on a stretcher. What symbolic meaning does this painting possibly have in relation to Daisy

who loves to be dressed in white?
6. Nick says that before he leaves for the Mid-West, he "wanted to leave things in order". Why? What does that imply about people like Tom and Daisy?
7. The last few paragraphs are written in a poetic language. Study them carefully and explain what symbolic meaning, if there is any, is implied there.

【简评】

  第九章是全书的结局。这时一切该发生的都已发生，剩下的只是处理盖茨比的善后事宜。这里没有先前的那种神秘与悬念，也没有什么戏剧性的冲突场面，主要人物也基本退居后台。全章由以下三部分组成：①葬礼的前后经过；②尼克对小时候中西部生活的回忆片段及与乔丹、汤姆的简短会面；③尼克在海滩凝望盖茨比沉浸在夜色中的房子所抒发的感慨。然而这看似简单的第九章不仅表现了菲茨杰拉德对人性的深刻洞察，也蕴含着作者对美国社会腐蚀人性、道德败坏、世风日下这一状况的愤懑与批判。更重要的是，通过盖茨比的父亲对盖茨比少年时代仿效富兰克林的回忆和尼克在海滩上的睹物伤情，作者表达了他对盖茨比所体现的"美国梦"和浪漫情结的矛盾心态："美国梦"和英雄精神在20世纪的爵士时代和社会中已成为一个神话，然而这一神话所体现的理想、浪漫、向上和求索的精神却是作者所心驰神往的。因此，作者虽然对盖茨比所代表的一切表示鄙夷，却倍加推崇他始终对生活前景充满美好希望的乐观性格。在作品的末尾，菲茨杰拉德通过诗一般的语言向读者暗示，尽管"green light"所象征的那种仪式般的未来正在一天一天地消退，"但没有关系，明天我们将跑得更快，我们的臂膀也将伸展得更远……"

Eugene O'Neill
1888—1953

  尤金·奥尼尔是美国戏剧史上一位重要的剧作家。19世纪的美国剧坛几乎是一片荒原。当时美国舞台上出现的不是欧洲的戏剧就是它们的翻版，奥尼尔使美国有了自己的戏剧，并使它成为20世纪世界戏剧舞台的一个重要组成部分。除了4次获得普利策奖和其他戏剧界大奖之外，他还以独特的悲剧风格赢得了1936年的诺贝尔文学奖。

  奥尼尔出生在纽约。父亲是一位很有才华的演员。由于父亲要随剧团巡回演出，奥尼尔7岁以前的大部分时光是在旅馆和火车里度过的。他曾在天主教学校上过几

American Literature
Between the Two Wars:1914–1945

年学，在普林斯顿大学读了一年书之后因违反校规被开除。此后，奥尼尔在各地流浪，淘过金，当过水手、小职员、歌舞剧演员，还担任过一份小报的记者。1912 年，他因肺结核在一家疗养院治疗了 6 个月。死亡的迫近使奥尼尔开始清醒地思考自己的人生之路，也使他决心成为一名严肃的剧作家。他读过许多名剧，斯特林堡的作品对他的影响尤其深刻。1914 年，奥尼尔进入哈佛大学跟乔治·贝克教授学习戏剧技巧，为时一年。此后他不断在实践中积累创作经验。他对父亲所代表的那种做作、脱离生活的戏剧深感不满，决心抛开一切戏剧传统的约束，向世人展示他所感受到的生活。

奥尼尔早期的剧作 (1913—1920) 主要是基于自己航海经历的独幕剧，虽然有一些自然主义和象征主义的特点，但主要是用现实主义手法描写一些生活片断。《东航卡迪夫》(*Bound East for Cardiff*, 1916) 是奥尼尔第一部被搬上舞台的戏剧。它细微地体现了水手扬克临死前的心理活动和他周围的环境。从这出戏可以看出奥尼尔不想使他的人物成为社会问题或者道德说教的传声筒。那些具有鲜明个性的人物反映了人类的普遍感情。其他较好的早期剧作包括《加勒比斯之月》(*The Moon of the Caribbees*, 1918)，《漫长的归途》(*The Long Voyage Home*, 1917) 和《画十字的地方》(*Where the Cross Is Made*, 1918) 等。

奥尼尔第二阶段的创作 (1920—1924) 不仅题材广泛，还对不同类型的戏剧手法进行了探索。他的成名作《天边外》(*Beyond the Horizon*, 1920) 和以海上生活为题材的《安娜·克利斯蒂》(*Anna Christie*, 1921) 沿袭了前期的写实风格。为了使自己的作品能淋漓尽致地表达深刻的哲学思想和人物的心理深度，奥尼尔在《琼斯皇帝》(*The Emperor Jones*, 1920) 和《毛猿》(*The Hairy Ape*, 1922) 中出色地运用了表现主义手法。他力图表现的不是真实的外部世界，而是心理意义上的真实。奥尼尔的目的是超越生活的表层去研究"人生背后的各种力量"，要揭示"内在的、心理上的命运"。《上帝的儿女都有翅膀》(*All God's Chillun Got Wings*, 1924) 描写了黑人和白人结婚的悲剧结果。在这部写实作品中，作者也运用了一些表现主义的手法。《榆树下的欲望》(*Desire Under the Elms*, 1924) 通过影射希腊神话中的一些悲剧，如俄狄浦斯、菲德拉和美狄亚的故事，加深了其悲剧的普遍意义。

奥尼尔在第三阶段 (1925—1933) 的戏剧中对各种表现手法进行了更为大胆的实验。《大神布朗》(*The Great God Brown*, 1926) 通过面具的使用，表现了人们的公众形象与真实自我之间的距离。在场面宏大的《拉扎勒斯笑了》(*Lazarus Laughed*, 1928) 一剧中，除了主人公以外的所有人物都戴着面具。《财主马可》(*Marco

Millions, 1928) 同样有着史诗般的规模，暗讽了美国的物质至上主义。《奇异的插曲》(*Strange Interlude*, 1928) 是他这一时期较成功的作品。它不仅表现了尼娜作为女儿、妻子、情妇和母亲的各种心理，还通过大量的旁白和内心独白展现了人物被压抑的感情、对他人的真实看法等。《悲悼》(*Mourning Becomes Electra*, 1931) 三部曲描写的是发生在美国南方的现代家庭悲剧，也是对古希腊悲剧作家埃斯库罗斯的"俄瑞斯忒斯"三部曲的改造。

在创作了唯一的喜剧《啊，荒野》(*Ah, Wilderness!* 1933) 和用面具来表现人物内心矛盾的《无尽的日子》(*Days Without End*, 1933) 之后，奥尼尔在剧坛沉寂了十二年之久。此时奥尼尔已疾病缠身，但他并没有停止创作。他最伟大的戏剧恰恰创作于这段时间。《送冰的人来了》(*The Iceman Cometh*, 1939, 1946) 强调人们需要用虚假的幻想来承受平淡或痛苦的现实生活。《进入黑夜的漫长旅程》(*Long Day's Journey into Night*, 1941, 1956) 常被认为是奥尼尔乃至所有美国戏剧中的最佳作品。奥尼尔创作的最后一部戏剧《月照不幸人》(*A Moon for the Misbegotten*, 1943, 1947) 使人们认识到，玩世不恭有时只是掩饰内心痛苦的面具而已。在最后阶段，奥尼尔创作上的主要特点是放弃了技巧上的实验，回到了传统的写实手法。宽恕的主题和笔调是奥尼尔晚期几部戏剧的共同特点。

在漫长的创作生涯中，奥尼尔力图将他对生活的思考、对人性的探索用最恰当的形式表现出来。为此，他对不同类型的戏剧形式进行了探索。奥尼尔早期作品具有写实和自然主义风格，中期为表现主义、象征主义，后期为雄浑的现实主义。他着墨最多的主题是人类的痛苦，并由此写出了许多伟大的悲剧。正如诺贝尔文学奖授辞所言，他创作了大量"富有生命力的、诚挚的、感情强烈的、烙有原始悲剧概念印记的戏剧作品。"

Long Day's Journey into Night

【题解】

这是一部由血和泪写成的带有强烈自传性质的戏剧。泰龙一家四口与奥尼尔的家庭完全吻合：吝啬的当演员的父亲，很有教养却因治疗产后剧痛而染上毒瘾的母亲，生活放纵的哥哥，和身患肺结核的敏感的弟弟。

这个剧展现的是泰龙一家从清早到深夜一整天的生活。剧情非常简单：戒掉毒瘾不久的玛丽不愿面对她所钟爱的小儿子埃德蒙有可能患上肺结核这一悲惨现实，重新开始用毒品麻醉自己。父子三人紧张不安，甚至满怀恐惧地看着她越陷越深，却又无可奈何,除了互相谴责、推卸责任外,唯有借酒浇愁。赋予这出戏高度感染力的是它对人物内心矛盾和痛苦的逼真反映。深刻的关怀和爱与同样深刻的猜疑、怨恨交织在一起,内疚自责与互相伤害交织在一起,形成了一个分不清因果的怪圈。戒毒后清醒的玛丽使全家人都沐浴在幸福的阳光下,但当她不堪生活压力再次吸毒后,一家人又陷入漫漫长夜中,看不到生活的出路。

以下段落选自《进入黑夜的漫长旅程》(第三幕)。这一幕描写了玛丽重新吸毒后的心理状态,以及泰龙父子复杂而矛盾的心情。

From Long Day's Journey into Night

Act 3

SCENE—It's around half past six in the evening. Dusk is gathering in the living room, an early dusk due to the fog which has rolled in from the Sound[1] and is like a white curtain drawn down outside the windows. From a lighthouse beyond the harbor's mouth, a foghorn is heard at regular intervals, moaning like a mournful whale in labor, and from the harbor itself, intermittently, comes the warning ringing of bells on yachts at anchor. The tray with the bottle of whisky, glass, and pitcher of ice water is on the table, as it was in the pre-luncheon scene of the previous act. Mary and the second girl[2], Cathleen, are discovered. The latter is standing at left of table. She holds an empty whisky glass in her hand as if she'd forgotten she had it. She shows the effects of drink. Her stupid, good-humored face wears a pleased and flattered simper.

Mary is paler than before and her eyes shine with unnatural brilliance. The strange detachment in her manner has intensified. She has hidden deeper within herself and found refuge and release in a dream where present reality is but an appearance to be accepted and dismissed unfeelingly—even with a hard cynicism—or entirely ignored. There is at times an uncanny gay, free youthfulness in her manner, as if in spirit she were released to become again, simply and without self-consciousness, the naive, happy, chattering schoolgirl of her convent days.

She wears the dress into which she had changed for her drive to town, a simple, fairly expensive affair, which would be extremely becoming if it were not for the careless, almost slovenly way she wears it. Her hair is no longer fastidiously in place. It has a slightly disheveled, lopsided look. She talks to Cathleen with a confiding familiarity, as if the second girl were an old, intimate friend. As the curtain rises, she is standing by the screen door looking out. A moan of the foghorn is heard.

MARY: *Amused—girlishly.* That foghorn! Isn't it awful, Cathleen?

CATHLEEN: *Talks more familiarly than usual but never with intentional impertinence because she sincerely likes her mistress.* It is indeed, Ma'am. It's like a banshee[3].

MARY: *Goes on as if she hadn't heard. In nearly all the following dialogue there is the feeling that she has Cathleen with her merely as an excuse to keep talking.* I don't mind it tonight. Last night it drove me crazy. I lay awake worrying until I couldn't stand it any more.

CATHLEEN: Bad cess[4] to it. I was scared out of my wits riding back from town. I thought that ugly monkey, Smythe[5], would drive us in a ditch or against a tree. You couldn't see your hand in front of you. I'm glad you had me sit in back with you, Ma'am. If I'd been in front with that monkey—he can't keep his dirty hands to himself. Give him half a chance and he's pinching me on the leg or you-know-where—asking your pardon, Ma'am, but it's true.

MARY: *Dreamily.* It wasn't the fog I minded, Cathleen. I really love fog.

CATHLEEN: They say it's good for the complexion.

MARY: It hides you from the world and the world from you. You feel that everything has changed, and nothing is what it seemed to be. No one can find or touch you any more.

CATHLEEN: I wouldn't care so much if Smythe was a fine, handsome man like some chauffeurs I've seen—I mean, if it was all in fun, for I'm a decent girl. But for a shriveled runt like Smythe—! I've told him, you must think I'm hard up that I'd notice a monkey like you. I've warned him, one day I'll give a clout that'll knock him into next week. And so I will!

MARY: It's the foghorn I hate. It won't let you alone. It keeps reminding you, and warning you, and calling you back. *She smiles strangely.* But it can't tonight. It's just an ugly sound. It doesn't remind me of anything. *She gives a teasing, girlish laugh.*

. . .

CATHLEEN: You ought to eat something, Ma'am. It's queer medicine if it takes away your appetite.

MARY: *Has begun to drift into dreams again—reacts mechanically.* What medicine? I don't know what you mean. *In dismissal.* You better take the drink to Bridget[6].

CATHLEEN: Yes, Ma'am.

She disappears through the back parlor. Mary waits until she hears the pantry door close behind her. Then she settles back in relaxed dreaminess, staring fixedly at nothing. Her arms rest limply along the arms of the chair, her hands with long, warped, swollen-knuckled, sensitive fingers drooping in complete calm. It is growing dark in the room. There is a pause of dead quite. Then from the world outside comes the melancholy moan of the foghorn, followed by a chorus of bells, muffled by the fog, from the anchored craft in the harbor. Mary's face gives no sign she has heard, but her hands jerk and the fingers automatically play for a moment on the air. She frowns and shakes her head mechanically as if a fly had walked across her mind. She suddenly loses all the girlish quality and is an aging, cynically sad, embittered woman.

MARY: *Bitterly*. You're a sentimental fool. What is so wonderful about that first meeting between a silly romantic schoolgirl and a matinee idol? You were much happier before you knew he existed, in the Convent when you used to pray to the Blessed Virgin. *Longingly.* If I could only find the faith I lost, so I could pray again! *She pauses—then begins to recite the Hail Mary in a flat, empty tone.* "Hail, Mary, full of grace! The Lord is with Thee; blessed art Thou among women." *Sneeringly.* You expect the Blessed Virgin to be fooled by a lying dope fiend reciting words! You can't hide from her! *She springs to her feet. Her hands fly up to pat her hair distractedly.* I must go upstairs. I haven't taken enough. When you start again you never know exactly how much you need. *She goes toward the front parlor—then stops in the doorway as she hears the sound of voices from the front path. She starts guiltily.* That must be them—*She hurries back to sit down. Her face sets in stubborn defensiveness—resentfully.* Why are they coming back? They don't want to. And I'd much rather be alone. *Suddenly her whole manner changes. She becomes pathetically relieved and eager.* Oh, I'm so glad they've come! I've been so horribly lonely!

The front door is heard closing and Tyrone calls uneasily from the hall.

TYRONE: Are you there, Mary?

The light in the hall is turned on and shines through the front parlor to fall on Mary.

MARY: *Rises from her chair, her face lighting up lovingly—with excited eagerness.* I'm here, dear. In the living room. I've been waiting for you. *Tyrone comes in through the front parlor. Edmund is behind him. Tyrone has had a lot to drink but beyond a slightly glazed look in his eyes and a trace of blur in his speech, he does not show it. Edmund has also had more than a few drinks without much apparent effect, except that his sunken cheeks are flushed and his eyes look bright and feverish. They stop in the doorway to stare appraisingly at her. What they see fulfills their worst expectations. But for the moment Mary is unconscious of their condemning eyes. She kisses her husband and then Edmund. Her manner is unnaturally effusive. They submit shrinkingly. She talks excitedly.* I'm so happy you've come. I had given up hope. I was afraid you wouldn't come home. It's such a dismal, foggy evening. It must be much more cheerful in the barrooms uptown, where there are people you can talk and joke with. No, don't deny it. I know how you feel. I don't blame you a bit. I'm all the more grateful to you for coming home. I was sitting here so lonely and blue. Come and sit down. *She sits at left rear of table, Edmund at left of table, and Tyrone in the rocker at right of it.* Dinner won't be ready for a minute. You're actually a little early. Will wonders never cease[7]. Here's the whisky, dear. Shall I pour a drink for you? *Without waiting for a reply she does so.* And you, Edmund? I don't want to encourage you, but one before dinner, as an appetizer, can't do harm. *She pours a drink for him. They make no move to take the drinks. She talks on as if unaware of their silence.* Where's Jamie? But, of course, he'll never come home so long as he has the price of drink left. *She reaches out and clasps her husband's hand—sadly.* I'm afraid Jamie has been lost to us for a long time, dear. *Her face hardens.* But we mustn't allow him to drag Edmund down with him, as he's like to do. He's jealous because Edmund has always been the baby—just as he used to be of Eugene[8]. He'll never be content until he makes Edmund as hopeless a failure as he is.

EDMUND: *Miserably.* Stop talking, Mama.

TYRONE: *Dully.* Yes, Mary, the less you say now—*Then to Edmund, a bit tipsily.* All the same there's truth in your mother's warning. Beware of that brother of yours, or he'll poison life for you with his damned sneering serpent's tongue!

EDMUND: *As before.* Oh, cut it out, Papa.

MARY: *Goes on as if nothing had been said.* It's hard to believe, seeing Jamie as he is now, that he was ever my baby. Do you remember what a healthy, happy baby he was, James? The one-night stands and filthy trains and cheap hotels and bad food never made him cross or sick. He was always smiling or laughing. He hardly ever cried. Eugene was the same, too, happy and healthy, during the two years he lived before I let him die through my neglect.

TYRONE: Oh, for the love of God! I'm a fool for coming home!

EDMUND: Papa! Shut up!

MARY: *Smiles with detached tenderness at Edmund.* It was Edmund who was the crosspatch when he was little, always getting upset and frightened about nothing at all. *She pats his hand—teasingly.* Everyone used to say, dear, you'd cry at the drop of a hat.

EDMUND: *Cannot control his bitterness.* Maybe I guessed there was a good reason not to laugh.

TYRONE: *Reproving and pitying.* Now, now, lad. You know better than to pay attention—

MARY: *As if she hadn't heard—sadly again.* Who would have thought Jamie would grow up to disgrace us. You remember, James, for years after he went to boarding school, we received such glowing reports. Everyone liked him. All his teachers told us what a fine brain he had, and how easily he learned his lessons. Even after he began to drink and they had to expel him, they wrote us how sorry they were, because he was so likable and such a brilliant student. They predicted a wonderful future for him if he would only learn to take life seriously. *She pauses—then adds with a strange, sad detachment.* It's such a pity. Poor Jamie! It's hard to understand—*Abruptly a change comes over her. Her face hardens and she stares at her husband with accusing hostility.* No, it isn't at all. You brought him up to be a boozer. Since he first opened his eyes, he's seen you drinking. Always a bottle on the bureau in the cheap hotel rooms! And if he had a nightmare when he was little, or a stomach-ache, your remedy was to give him a teaspoonful of whiskey to quiet him.

TYRONE: *Stung.* So I'm to blame because that lazy hulk has made a drunken loafer of himself? Is that what I came home to listen to? I might have known! When you have the poison in you, you want to blame everyone but yourself!

EDMUND: Papa! You told me not to pay attention. *Then, resentfully.* Anyway it's true. You did the same thing with me. I can remember that teaspoonful of booze every time I woke up with a nightmare.

MARY: *In a detached reminiscent tone.* Yes, you were continually having nightmares as a child. You were born afraid. Because I was so afraid to bring you into the world. *She pauses—then goes on with the same detachment.* Please don't think I blame your father, Edmund. He didn't know any better. He never went to school after he was ten. His people were the most ignorant kind of poverty-stricken Irish. I'm sure they honestly believed whiskey is the healthiest medicine for a child who is sick or frightened.

Tyrone is about to burst out in angry defense of his family but Edmund intervenes.

EDMUND: *Sharply.* Papa! *Changing the subject.* Are we going to have this drink, or aren't we?

TYRONE: *Controlling himself—dully.* You're right. I'm a fool to take notice. *He picks up his glass listlessly.* Drink hearty, lad.

Edmund drinks but Tyrone remains staring at the glass in his hand. Edmund at once realizes how much the whiskey has been watered. He frowns, glancing from the bottle to his mother—starts to say something but stops.

MARY: *In a detached tone—repentantly.* I'm sorry if I sounded bitter, James. I'm not. It's all so far away. But I did feel a little hurt when you wished you hadn't come home. I was so relieved and happy when you came, and grateful to you. It's very dreary and sad to be here alone in the fog with night falling.

TYRONE: *Moved.* I'm glad I came, Mary, when you act like your real self.

MARY: I was so lonesome I kept Cathleen with me just to have someone to talk to. *Her manner and quality drift back to the shy convent girl again.* Do you know what I was telling her, dear? About the night my father took me to your dressing room and I first fell in love with you. Do you remember?

TYRONE: *Deeply moved—his voice husky.* Can you think I'd ever forget, Mary?

Edmund looks away from them, sad and embarrassed.

MARY: *Tenderly.* No. I know you still love me, James, in spite of everything.

TYRONE: *His face works and he blinks back tears—with quiet intensity.* Yes! As God is my judge! Always and forever, Mary!

MARY: And I love you, dear, in spite of everything. *There is a pause in which Edmund moves embarrassedly. The strange detachment comes over her manner again as if she were speaking impersonally of people seen from a distance.* But I must confess, James, although I couldn't help loving you, I would never have married you if I'd known you drank so much. I remember the first night your barroom friends had to help you up to the door of our hotel room, and knocked and then ran away before I came to the door. We were still on our honeymoon, do you remember?

TYRONE: *With guilty vehemence.* I don't remember! It wasn't on our honeymoon! And I never in my life had to be helped to bed, or missed a performance!

MARY: *As though he hadn't spoken.* I had waited in that ugly hotel room hour after hour. I kept making excuses for you. I told myself it must be about the theater. Then I became terrified. I imagined all sorts of horrible accidents. I got on my knees and prayed that nothing had happened to you—and then they brought you up and left you outside the door. *She gives a little, sad sigh.* I didn't know how often that was to happen in the years to come, how many times I was to wait in ugly hotel rooms. I became quite used to it.

EDMUND: *Bursts out with a look of accusing hate at his father.* Christ! No wonder—! *He controls himself—gruffly.* When is dinner, Mama? It must be time.

TYRONE: *Overwhelmed by shame which he tries to hide, fumbles with his watch.* Yes. It must be. Let's see. *He stares at his watch without seeing it. Pleadingly.* Mary! Can't you forget—?

MARY: *With detached pity.* No, dear. But I forgive. I always forgive you. So don't look so guilty. I'm sorry I remembered out loud. I don't want to be sad, or to make you sad. I want to remember only the happy part of the past. *Her manner drifts back to the shy, gay convent girl.* Do you remember our wedding, dear? I'm sure you've completely forgotten what my wedding gown looked like. Men don't notice such things. They don't think they are important. But it was important to me, I can tell you! How I fussed and worried! I was so excited and happy! My father told me to buy anything I wanted and never mind what it cost. The best is none too good, he said. I'm afraid he spoiled me dreadfully. My mother didn't. She was pious and strict. I think she was a little jealous. She didn't approve of my marrying—especially an actor. I think she hoped I would become a nun. She used to scold my father. She'd grumble, "You never tell me, never mind what it costs, when I buy anything! You've spoiled that girl so, I pity her husband if she ever marries. She'll expect him to give her the moon. She'll never make a good wife." *She laughs affectionately.* Poor mother! *She smiles at Tyrone with a strange, incongruous coquetry.* But she was mistaken, wasn't she, James? I haven't been such a bad wife, have I?

TYRONE: *Huskily, trying to force a smile.* I'm not complaining, Mary.

MARY: *A shadow of vague guilt crosses her face.* At least, I've loved you dearly, and done the best I could—under the circumstances. *The shadow vanishes and her shy, girlish expression returns.* That wedding gown was nearly the death of me and the dressmaker, too! *She laughs.* I was so particular. It was never quite good enough.

At last she said she refused to touch it any more or she might spoil it, and I made her leave so I could be alone to examine myself in the mirror. I was so pleased and vain. I thought to myself, "Even if your nose and mouth and ears are a trifle too large, your eyes and hair and figure, and your hands, make up for it. You're just as pretty as any actress he's ever met, and you don't have to use paint." *She pauses, wrinkling her brow in an effort of memory.* Where is my wedding gown now, I wonder? I kept it wrapped up in tissue paper in my trunk. I used to hope I would have a daughter and when it came time for her to marry—She couldn't have bought a lovelier gown, and I knew, James, you'd never tell her, never mind the cost. You'd want her to pick up something at a bargain. It was made of soft, shimmering satin, trimmed with wonderful old duchess lace, in tiny ruffles around the neck and sleeves, and worked in with the folds that were draped round in a bustle effect at the back. The basque was boned and very tight. I remember I held my breath when it was fitted, so my waist would be as small as possible. My father even let me have duchess lace on my white satin slippers, and lace with the orange blossoms in my veil. Oh, how I loved that gown! It was so beautiful! Where is it now, I wonder? I used to take it out from time to time when I was lonely, but it always made me cry, so finally a long while ago— *She wrinkles her forehead again.* I wonder where I hid it? Probably in one of the old trunks in the attic. Some day I'll have to look.

She stops, staring before her. Tyrone sighs, shaking his head hopelessly, and attempts to catch his son's eye, looking for sympathy, but Edmund is staring at the floor.

TYRONE: *Forces a casual tone.* Isn't it dinner time, dear? *With a feeble attempt at teasing.* You're forever scolding me for being late, but now I'm on time foe once, it's dinner that's late. *She doesn't appear to hear him. He adds, still pleasantly.* Well, if I can't eat yet, I can drink. I'd forgotten I had this. *He drinks his drink. Edmund watches him. Tyrone scowls and looks at his wife with sharp suspicion—roughly.* Who's been tampering with my whiskey? The damned stuff is half water! Jamie's been away and he wouldn't overdo his trick like this, anyway. Any fool could tell— Mary, answer me! *With angry disgust.* I hope to God you haven't taken to drink on top of—

EDMUND: Shut up, Papa! *To his mother, without looking at her.* You treated Cathleen and Bridget, isn't it, Mama?

MARY: *With indifferent casualness.* Yes, of course. They work hard for poor wages. And

I'm the housekeeper, I have to keep them from leaving. Besides, I wanted to treat Cathleen because I had her drive uptown with me, and sent her to get my prescription filled.

EDMUND: For God's sake, Mama! You can't trust her! Do you want everyone on earth to know?

MARY: *Her face hardening stubbornly.* Know what? That I suffer from rheumatism in my hands and have to take medicine to kill the pain? Why should I be ashamed of that? *Turns on Edmund with a hard, accusing antagonism—almost a revengeful enmity.* I never knew what rheumatism was before you were born! Ask your father!
Edmund looks away, shrinking into himself.

TYRONE: Don't mind her, lad. It doesn't mean anything. When she gets to the stage where she gives the old crazy excuse about her hands she's gone far away from us.

MARY: *Turns on him—with a strangely triumphant, taunting smile.* I'm glad you realize that, James! Now perhaps you'll give up trying to remind me, you and Edmund! *Abruptly, in a detached, matter-of-fact tone.* Why don't you light the light, James? It's getting dark. I know you hate to, but Edmund had proved to you that one bulb burning doesn't cost much. There's no sense letting your fear of the poorhouse make you too stingy.

TYRONE: *Reacts mechanically.* I never claimed one bulb cost much! It's having them on, one here and one there, that makes the Electric Light Company rich. *He gets up and turns on the reading lamp—roughly.* But I'm a fool to talk reason to you. *To Edmund.* I'll get a fresh bottle of whiskey, lad, and we'll have a real drink. *He goes through the back parlor.*

MARY: *With detached amusement.* He'll sneak around to the outside cellar door so the servants won't see him. He's really ashamed of keeping his whiskey padlocked in the cellar. Your father is a strange man, Edmund. It took many years before I understood him. You must try to understand and forgive him, too, and not feel contempt because he's close-fisted. His father deserted his mother and their six children a year or so after they came to America. He told them he had a premonition he would die soon, and he was homesick for Ireland, and wanted to go back there to die. So he went and he did die. He must have been a peculiar man, too. Your father had to go to work in a machine shop when he was only ten years old.

EDMUND: *Protests dully.* Oh, for Pete's sake, Mama. I've heard Papa tell that machine shop story ten thousand times.

MARY: Yes, dear, you've had to listen, but I don't think you've ever tried to understand.

EDMUND: *Ignoring this—miserably.* Listen, Mama! You're not so far gone yet you've forgotten everything. You haven't asked me what I found out this afternoon. Don't you care a damn?

MARY: *Shakenly.* Don't say that! You hurt me, dear!

EDMUND: What I've got is serious, Mama. Doc Hardy knows for sure now.

MARY: *Stiffens into scornful, defensive stubbornness.* That lying old quack! I warned you he'd invent—!

EDMUND: *Miserably dogged.* He called in a specialist to examine me, so he'd be absolutely sure.

MARY: *Ignoring this.* Don't tell me about Hardy! If you heard what the doctor at the sanatorium, who really knows something, said about how he'd treated me! He said he ought to be locked up! He said it was a wonder I hadn't gone mad! I told him I had once, that time I ran down in my nightdress to throw myself off the dock. You remember that, don't you? And yet you want me to pay attention to what Doctor Hardy says. Oh, no!

EDMUND: *Bitterly.* I remember, all right. It was right after that Papa and Jamie decided they couldn't hide it from me any more. Jamie told me. I called him a liar! I tried to punch him in the nose. But I knew he wasn't lying. *His voice trembles, his eyes begin to fill with tears.* God, it made everything in life seem rotten!

MARY: *Pitiably.* Oh, don't. My baby! You hurt me so dreadfully!

EDMUND: *Dully.* I'm sorry, Mama. It was you who brought it up. *Then with a bitter, stubborn persistence.* Listen, Mama. I'm going to tell you whether you want to hear or not. I've got to go to a sanatorium.

MARY: *Dazedly, as if this was something that had never occurred to her.* Go away? *Violently.* No! I won't have it! How dare Doctor Hardy advise such a thing without consulting me! How dare your father allow him! What right has he? You are my baby! Let him attend to Jamie! *More and more excited and bitter.* I know why he wants you sent to a sanatorium. To take you from me! He's always tried to do that. He's been jealous of every one of my babies! He kept finding ways to make me leave them. That's what caused Eugene's death. He's been jealous of you most of all. He knew I loved you most because—

EDMUND: *Miserably.* Oh, stop talking crazy, can't you, Mama! Stop trying to blame him. And why are you so against my going away now? I've been away a lot, and I've never noticed it broke your heart!

MARY: *Bitterly.* I'm afraid you're not very sensitive, after all. *Sadly.* You might have guessed, dear, that after I knew you knew—about me—I had to be glad whenever you were where you couldn't see me.

EDMUND: *Brokenly.* Mama! Don't! *He reaches out blindly and takes her hand—but he drops it immediately, overcome by bitterness again.* All this talk about loving me—and you won't even listen when I try to tell you how sick—

MARY: *With an abrupt transformation into a detached bullying motherliness.* Now, now. That's enough! I don't care to hear because I know it's nothing but Hardy's ignorant lies. *He shrinks back into himself. She keeps on in a forced, teasing tone but with an increasing undercurrent of resentment.* You're so like your father, dear. You love to make a scene out of nothing so you can be dramatic and tragic. *With a belittling laugh.* If I gave you the slightest encouragement, you'd tell me next you were going to die—

EDMUND: People do die of it. Your own father—

MARY: *Sharply.* Why do you mention him? There's no comparison at all with you. He had consumption. *Angrily.* I hate you when you become gloomy and morbid! I forbid you to remind me of my father's death, do you hear me?

EDMUND: *His face hard—grimly.* Yes, I hear you, Mama. I wish to God I didn't. *He gets up from his chair and stands staring condemningly at her—bitterly.* It's pretty hard to take at times, having a dope fiend for a mother! *She winces—all life seeming to drain from her face, leaving it with the appearance of a plaster cast. Instantly Edmund wishes he could take back what he has said. He stammers miserably.* Forgive me, Mama. I was angry. You hurt me. *There is a pause in which the foghorn and the ship's bells are heard.*

MARY: *Goes slowly to the windows at right like an automaton—looking out, a blank, far-off quality in her voice.* Just listen to that awful foghorn. And the bells. Why is it fog makes everything sound so sad and lost, I wonder?

EDMUND: *Brokenly.* I—I can't stay here. I don't want any dinner.

He hurries away through the front parlor. She keeps staring out the window until she hears the front door close behind him. Then she comes back and sits in her chair, the same blank look on her face.

MARY: *Vaguely.* I must go upstairs. I haven't taken enough. *She pauses—then longingly.* I hope, sometimes, without meaning it, I will take an overdose. I never could do it deliberately. The Blessed Virgin would never forgive me, then. *She hears Tyrone returning and turns as he comes in, through the back parlor, with a bottle of whiskey he has just unlocked. He is fuming.*

TYRONE: *Wrathfully.* The padlock is all scratched. That drunken loafer has tried to pick the lock with a piece of wire, the way he's done before. *With satisfaction, as if this was a perpetual battle of wits with his elder son.* But I've fooled him this time. It's a special padlock a professional burglar couldn't pick. *He puts the bottle on the tray and suddenly is aware of Edmund's absence.* Where's Edmund?

MARY: *With a vague far-away air.* He went out. Perhaps he's going to find Jamie. He still has some money left, I suppose, and it's burning a hole in his pocket. He said he didn't want any dinner. He doesn't seem to have any appetite these days. *Then stubbornly.* But it's just a summer cold. *Tyrone stares at her and shakes his head helplessly and pours himself a big drink and drinks it. Suddenly it is too much for her and she breaks out and sobs.* Oh, James, I'm so frightened! *She gets up and throws her arms around him and hides her face on his shoulder—sobbingly.* I know he's going to die!

TYRONE: Don't say that! It's not true! They promised me in six months he'd be cured.

MARY: You don't believe that! I can tell when you're acting! And it will be my fault. I should never have born him. It would have been better for his sake. I could never hurt him then. He wouldn't have had to know his mother was a dope fiend—and hate her!

TYRONE: *His voice quivering.* Hush, Mary, for the love of God! He loves you. He knows it was a curse put upon you without your knowing or willing it. He's proud you're his mother! *Abruptly as he hears the pantry door opening.* Hush, now! Here comes Cathleen. You don't want her to see you crying.

She turns quickly away from him to the windows at right, hastily wiping her eyes. A moment later Cathleen appears in the back-parlor doorway. She is uncertain in her walk and grinning woozily.

CATHLEEN: *Starts guiltily when she sees Tyrone—with dignity.* Dinner is served, Sir. *Raising her voice unnecessarily.* Dinner is served, Ma'am. *She forgets her dignity and addresses Tyrone with good-natured familiarity.* So you're here, are you? Well,

well. Won't Bridget be in a rage! I told her the Madame said you wouldn't be home. *Then reading accusation in his eye.* Don't be looking at me that way. If I've a drop taken, I didn't steal it. I was invited. *She turns with huffy dignity and disappears through the back parlor.*

TYRONE: *Sighs—then summoning his actor's heartiness.* Come along, dear. Let's have our dinner. I'm hungry as a hunter.

MARY: *Comes to him—her face is composed in plaster again and her tone is remote.* I'm afraid you'll have to excuse me, James. I couldn't possibly eat anything. My hands pain me dreadfully. I think the best thing for me is to go to bed and rest. Good night, dear. *She kisses him mechanically and turns toward the front parlor.*

TYRONE: *Harshly.* Up to take more of that God-damned poison, is that it? You'll be like a mad ghost before the night's over!

MARY: *Starts to walk away—blankly.* I don't know what you're talking about, James. You say such mean, bitter things when you've drunk too much. You're as bad as Jamie or Edmund.

She moves off through the front parlor. He stands a second as if not knowing what to do. He is a sad, bewildered, broken old man. He walks wearily off through the back parlor toward the dining room.

Curtain

【注解】

1. Sound: 当地的海湾。
2. the second girl: maid，女仆。
3. banshee: (爱尔兰和苏格兰民间传说中的) 女鬼，女妖精。
4. cess: (爱尔兰方言) 运气，一般仅用于短语 bad cess to sb 中。
5. Smythe: 泰龙家的司机。
6. Bridget: 泰龙家的厨娘。
7. Will wonders never cease: 泰龙平时难得能准时回来吃饭，今天他回来得比预料的早，所以玛丽称之为"奇迹"。
8. Eugene: 玛丽和泰龙的第二个儿子，两岁时夭折。

【思考题】

1. Is there any symbolic meaning in the fog and the foghorn?
2. Mary says that the foghorn drove her crazy last night. Do you believe it is the truth?

3. Why does Mary take drug again?
4. Why does Mary behave so strangely toward Edmund? Does Mary really believe that Dr. Hardy was incorrect in his diagnosis for Edmund?
5. Mary says, "I hope, sometimes, without meaning it, I will take an overdose." What kind of intention is expressed here? Why won't the Blessed Virgin forgive her if she does so?

【简评】

《进入黑夜的漫长旅程》被众多评论家认为是所有美国戏剧中最伟大的作品。它充分体现了奥尼尔精湛的戏剧表现力，是一部现实主义的杰作。在这里奥尼尔关注的不再是戏剧技巧的实验，而是人生背后那些神秘、不可捉摸的力量。他细腻地描写了生活环境、个人性格与人们的责任感之间微妙的互相作用，揭示了亲人之间爱与恨交织在一起的复杂感情。这部戏剧的自传性非常明显。奥尼尔后期的作品之所以有着强烈的自传性，或许是因为他发现人生许多问题的答案必须从自己的生活经历中去寻找。

Thomas Stearns Eliot
1888—1965

托马斯·斯泰恩·艾略特出生在美国密苏里州圣路易斯市，1906年进入哈佛大学攻读哲学，师从著名文学批评家欧文·白比特 (Irving Babbit, 1865—1933)、哲学家乔治·桑塔雅那 (George Santayana, 1863—1952) 等人，并深受他们的影响，后又赴巴黎、伦敦等地求学。1914年第一次世界大战爆发，艾略特滞留英国，翌年六月与薇薇安·海伍德 (Vivien Haigh-Wood, 1888—1947) 结婚并在《诗歌》刊物上发表了第一首表现荒原主题的重要诗作《阿尔弗雷德·普鲁弗洛克的情歌》("The Love Song of J. Alfred Prufrock")。1917年，艾略特在劳埃德银行 (Lloyds Bank) 谋得一个职位，同时担任《利己者》(The Egotist) 杂志的助理编辑。此后三年间，艾略特先后发表了《普鲁弗洛克及其他思考》(Prufrock and Other Observations, 1917)、《诗集》(Poems, 1919) 等作品。1922年艾略特创办了季刊《准则》(The Criterion)，并在创刊号上发表了长诗《荒原》(The Waste Land)，此诗奠定了艾略特在现代诗坛的重要地位，使他成为当时所谓"幻灭的一代"(the disillusioned Generation) 的代表诗人。1925 年，艾略特辞去了在劳埃德银行的职位，开始担任费伯·费伯 (Faber and Faber) 出版社的主编，1927 年成为英国公民并加入英国国教。在此后的诗歌创作中，艾略特把注意力转向了宗教方面，先后创作发表了《空心人》(*The Hollow Men*, 1925)、《三王的旅程》(*The Journey of the Magi*, 1927)、《灰色星期三》(*The Ash-Wednesday*, 1930) 和获 1948 年诺贝尔文学奖的《四个四重奏》(*Four Quartets*, 1935—1942)。

从 20 世纪 30 年代中期开始，艾略特以振兴英国戏剧为目的，把主要精力投向戏剧创作，先后创作发表了《岩石》(*The Rock*, 1934)、《大教堂的谋杀》(*Murder in the Cathedral*, 1935)、《一家团圆》(*The Family Reunion*, 1939)。这些剧作保持了艾略特后期诗歌创作的思想特色，通过文学的形式表达了自己的宗教观。20 世纪 50 年代创作的三部现代社会喜剧《鸡尾酒会》(*The Cocktail Party*, 1950)、《心腹职员》(*The Confidential Clerk*, 1954) 和《政界元老》(*The Elder Statesman*, 1959) 也体现了严肃的宗教主题。在《给朗斯洛特·安德鲁斯》(*For Lancelot Andrewes*, 1928) 一书的前言中，他声称自己在政治上是个保皇党，在宗教上是英国天主教徒，在文学上是个古典主义者。艾略特这些传统倾向的核心就是要以宗教和教会为政治和文化中心，力图通过宗教复兴来挽救西方的没落。

在诗歌创作方面，艾略特深受意大利诗人但丁、英国玄学派诗人邓恩、法国象征主义诗人波德莱尔、美国意象派诗人休姆和庞德等人的影响，创作出一种干硬 (hard dry)、反讽、机智，以及寓意、联想丰富的诗体，开创了一代诗风。同时，由于艾略特作诗基本不用连词或转承语句，而仅仅依靠各种意象的排列与堆砌来构架全诗，因此他的许多作品都十分晦涩难懂。

艾略特不仅以其诗歌创作影响了一代英美诗风，还以其深刻独到的文学评论影响着现代英美的文学批评理论。总体而言，艾略特影响较广的文学主张有 4 点：①针对 17 世纪末以来英国文坛逐渐出现的"情感脱节"(disassociation of sensibility) 现象，艾略特提出要将机智与情感重新统一，如同邓恩作品表现的那样；②针对浪漫主义"自我主义"(egotism) 的创作方法，提出诗歌创作必须非人格化，诗人应牺牲自我，退出作品；③诗人必须找到并通过某个"客观对应物"(objective correlative) 来表达自己的情感，即以"一套事物，一串事件"来进行暗示与象征；④由于诗人不能直接入诗，而需要通过各种"客观对应物"来表达情绪，因此诗歌形式必定会是复杂破碎的。不难看出，艾略特的这些文学主张都深深地打上了英国玄学派诗歌的烙印。

1948 年，艾略特被英王乔治六世授予功绩勋章 (Order of Merit)，并荣获该年度诺贝尔文学奖。

The Waste Land

【题解】

《荒原》借寻找圣杯的传说，表现了第一次世界大战前后的欧洲因失去宗教信仰而出现的精神枯竭和生存危机。《荒原》是一部博学难读的长诗，涉及五种语言和五十六部前人的作品，意象丰富、结构复杂。作者的思想在历史和现实、远古神话和现实故事等不同的时空跳跃闪烁，构造出一幅多侧面的立体画，成为西方现代诗歌的一块里程碑。

全诗共分五章，本文节选了《荒原》第一诗章，表现在"荒原"的现代人虽生犹死、不愿从麻木中解脱的状态。由于艾略特本人为该诗作的注解已成为诗的一部分，因此编者在作注时保留了艾略特的英语原注，以及其他一些引文的原文或英译文。

From The Waste Land

I. The Burial of the Dead[1]

April is the cruelest month, breeding
Lilacs out of the dead land, mixing
Memory and desire, stirring
Dull roots with spring rain.
Winter kept us warm, covering
Earth in forgetful snow, feeding
A little life with dried tubers.
Summer surprised us, coming over the Starnbergersee[2]
With a shower of rain; we stopped in the colonnade,
And went on in sunlight, into the Hofgarten[3],   10
And drank coffee, and talked for an hour.
Bin gar keine Russin, stamm' aus Litauen, echt deutsch[4].
And when we were children, staying at the archduke's,
My cousin's, he took me out on a sled,
And I was frightened. He said, Marie,

Marie, hold on tight. And down we went.
In the mountains, there you feel free.
I read, much of the night, and go south in the winter.

What are the roots that clutch, what branches grow
Out of this stony rubbish? Son of man[5], 20

You cannot say, or guess, for you know only
A heap of broken images, where the sun beats[6],
And the dead tree gives no shelter, the cricket no relief[7],
And the dry stone no sound of water. Only
There is shadow under this red rock[8],

(Come in under the shadow of this red rock),
And I will show you something different from either
Your shadow at morning striding behind you
Or your shadow at evening rising to meet you;
I will show you fear in a handful of dust. 30

Frisch weht der Wind
Der Heimat zu
Mein Irisch Kind,
Wo weilest du[9]?
'You gave me hyacinths first a year ago;
They called me the hyacinth[10] girl.'
—Yet when we came back, late, from the Hyacinth garden,
Yours arms full, and your hair wet, I could not
Speak, and my eyes failed, I was neither
Living nor dead, and I knew nothing, 40

Looking into the heart of light, the silence.
Oed' und leer das Meer[11].

Madame Sosostris[12], famous clairvoyante,
Had a bad cold, neverhteless
Is known to be the wisest woman in Europe,

With a wicked pack of cards[13]. Here, said she,
Is your card, the drowned Phoenician Sailor[14],
(Those are pearls that were his eyes. Look![15])
Here is Belladonna, the Lady of the Rocks[16],
The lady of situations.   50

Here is the man with three staves, and here the Wheel[17],
And here is the one-eyed merchant[18], and this card,
Which is blank, is something he carries on his back,
Which I am forbidden to see. I do not find
The Hanged Man[19]. Fear death by water.

I see crowds of people, walking round in a ring.
Thank you. If you see dear Mrs. Equitone,
Tell her I bring the horoscope myself:
One must be so careful these days.

Unreal City[20],   60

Under the brown fog of a winter dawn,
A crowd flowed over London Bridge, so many[21],
I had not thought death had undone so many.
Sighs, short and infrequent, were exhaled[22].
And each man fixed his eyes before his feet.

Flowed up the hill and down King William Street,
To where Saint Mary Woolnoth[23] kept the hours
With a dead sound on the final stroke of nine[24].
There I saw one I knew, and stopped him, crying "Stetson![25]"

You who were with me in the ships at Mylae²⁶!　　　　　　　　　　　　　70

That corpse you planted last year in your garden,

Has it begun to sprout? Will it bloom this year?

Or has the sudden frost disturbed its bed?

Oh keep the Dog far hence, that's friend to men,

Or with his nails he'll dig it up again!²⁷　　　　　　　　　　　　　　　75

You! hypocrite lecteur!—mon semblable,—mon frère²⁸!

【注解】

1. The Burial of the Dead: 该诗章的标题出自英国国教的葬仪。
2. Starnbergersee: 慕尼黑附近的一片湖。这一行及以下八行所描写的情节似乎出自玛丽·拉里希伯爵夫人于1913年出版的自传《我的过去》，反映了第一次世界大战前欧洲上流社会空虚无聊的生活。
3. Hofgarten: 慕尼黑一处公园。
4. Bin gar...deutsch: 德语，意为"我根本不是俄国人，我来自立陶宛，是地道的德国人。"
5. Son of man: 据《旧约·以西结书》记载，上帝曾对以西结说: "Stand upon thy feet, and I will speak unto thee."。原注为"Cf. Ezekiel II, i"。
6. A heap...sun beats: 《旧约·以西结书》第六章第六节中这样说道: "In all your dwelling places the cities shall be laid waste, and the high places shall be desolate; that your altars may be laid waste and made desolate, and your idols may be broken and cease, and your images may be cut down, and your works may be abolished."。
7. And the dead...relief: 《旧约·传道书》的这段话描述了古代的毁灭: "when they shall be afraid of that which is high and fears shall be in the way, and the almond tree shall flourish, and the grasshopper shall be a burden, and desire shall fail..."。原注为"Cf. Ecclesiastes XII, v"。
8. There is...red rock: 参见《旧约·以赛亚书》第三十二章第二节 (*Isaiah*, xxxii.2): the "righteous king" shall be "...as rivers of water in a dry place, as the shadow of a great rock in a weary land."。
9. Frisch...weilest du: 出自 *Tristan und Isolde*，德国作曲家瓦格纳创作的歌剧。艾略特引的这几行德语诗表现了一位水手回忆起岸上的心上人的情景，意思是"Fresh blows the wind to the homeland: my Irish child, where are you waiting?"。原注为"V. Tristan und Isolde, I, verses 5–8"。
10. hyachinth: 艾略特用风信子来象征春天。
11. Oed' und...Meer: 在 *Tristan und Isolde* 第三幕中，Tristan临死前盼望着Isolde能从Cornwall归来，未果，因此代他守望的牧羊人只能告诉他"Oed' und leer das Meer"，意思是"Waste and empty is the sea."。原注为"Id. III, verse 24"。
12. Madame Sosostris: Sosostris名字系艾略特模仿 Aldous Huxley 小说 *Chrome Yellow*(1921) 中一位女相士的名字"Sesostris"。小说中，女相士装扮成一位吉卜赛人，到集市上为人算命。但艾略特诗中说她"Had a bad cold"，表明这个现代女相士只不过个冒牌货而已。

13. Wicked pack of cards: 指中世纪的 "the Tarot deck of cards",即塔罗纸牌。这套纸牌原为吉卜赛人用来占卦算命的工具,后传入欧洲。艾略特原注中提到的渔王传说出自杰西·韦斯顿女士 (Miss Jessie L. Weston) 所著的《从祭仪到神话》(*From Ritual to Romance*) 一书。根据此书,渔王为某地国王,因其患病、衰老(也有说受伤),国中原来肥沃的良田变为荒原。因此需要一位少年英雄手提利剑去寻找圣杯。此间他必须经历种种艰险,才能找到圣杯,只有找到圣杯才能医治渔王,使大地复苏。此外在古代,鱼是一种象征生命力的符记,因此渔王与之有关。原注为 "I am not familiar with the exact constitution of the Tarot pack of cards, from which I have obviously departed to suit my own convenience. The Hanged Man, a member of the traditional pack, fits my purpose in two ways: because he is associated in my mind with the Hanged God of Frazer, and because I associate him with the hooded figure in the passage of the disciples to Emmaus in Part V. The Phoenician Sailor and the Merchant appear later; also the 'crowds of people,' and Death by Water is executed in Part IV. The Man with Three staves (an authentic member of the Tarot pack) I associate, quite arbitrarily with the Fisher King himself."

14. the drowned . . . Sailor: 在《荒原》中,水或海的象征意义主要有两种:一指情欲,如腓尼基水手、费迪南多王子 (Prince Ferdinand, 见莎士比亚的 *The Tempest*) 及后面提到的斯麦那 (Smyrna) 商人(或"独眼商人")等都淹没其中;二指净化、洗礼、焕发青春等,如费迪南多王子及其父亲阿隆佐亲王的故事。

15. Those are pearls . . . Look!: 此行出自莎士比亚《暴风雨》中精灵爱丽尔对费迪南多王子唱的歌:

    Full fadom five thy father lies,
    Of his bones are coral made:
    Those are pearls that were his eyes:
    Nothing of him that doth fade,
    But doth suffer a sea-change
    Into something rich and strange.
    Sea-nymphs hourly ring his knell:
    Ding-dong.
    Hark now I hear them—ding-dong bell.

16. Here is . . . of the Rock: Belladonna 为意大利语,意为"美丽的女人"。该词亦暗指 Madonna(圣母玛利亚),因此 "Lady of the Rocks" 即为 Madonna of the Rocks。(在《圣经》中,rocks 代表教堂。)Belladonna 是一种含毒的花,在下行中,"the Lady of the Rocks" 蜕变为一个现代的女士,即 "the lady of situations",预示第二章那位神经衰弱的女人的登场。

17. the man . . . the Wheel: the man 是生命力的象征,艾略特用来暗指渔王。Wheel 意为"命运之轮"。

18. one-eyed merchant:《火诫》中提到的斯麦那商人 Mr. Eugenides。独眼是因为在纸牌上我们只能看到头像的一侧,另外独眼也有邪恶与狡诈的含义。

19. Hanged Man: 在塔罗纸牌上,此人吊死在十字架上。根据弗雷泽的《金枝》,the hanged man 象征繁殖神自我牺牲,以换取国家和人民的繁荣兴旺。此处也寓指耶稣。

20. Unreal City: 原注为 "Cf. Baudelaire: 'Fourmillante cité, cité pleine de reves, /Où le spectre en plein jour raccroche le passant.'"。原注中这几行法语诗出自波德莱尔《恶之花》中《七位老人》一章,意思是 "Swarming city, city full of dreams, /Where the specter in broad daylight accosts the

passerby."。

21. so many: 参见但丁《神曲·地狱篇》第三节第 55 至第 57 行："So long a train of people,/that I should never have believed/That death had undone so many."。[原注为 "Cf. Inferno III, 55–57 . . ."。]

22. Sighs . . . exhaled: 参见但丁《神曲·地狱篇》第四节 25 至 27 行。艾略特在原注中引文的英译文为："Here, so far as I could tell by listening,/there was no lamentation except sighs,/which caused the eternal air to tremble."。原注为 "Cf. Inferno IV, 25–27 . . ."。

23. Saint Mary Woolnoth: 伦敦威廉王大街上的一座教堂。

24. stroke of nine: 钟敲九下表示到了上班时间。通常人们需要穿过伦敦桥到市区的商业中心上班。原注为 "A phenomenon which I have often noticed"。

25. Stetson: 原指一种宽边呢帽的商标，这里用作人名，泛指所有带这种帽子的商人。

26. Mylae: 古代西西里东北部的海港，即现在的 Millazzo。第一次迦太基战争爆发于此，以罗马人获胜告终。

27. Or with . . . again: 原注为 "Cf. the Dirge in Webster's White Devil"。John Webster，英国文艺复兴后期剧作家，其挽歌中有几行如下：

> But keep the wolf far thence, that's foe to men,
>
> For with his nails he'll dig them up again.

艾略特把上句中的 wolf 和 foe 改成了 Dog 和 friend，暗示神话中垂死的繁殖神在被埋葬后被狗重新挖出来。Dog 也寓指天狼星 (Sirius)。据传，天狼星是使尼罗河两岸肥沃的星宿。

28. You! . . . mon frère: 这行诗出自波德莱尔《恶之花》开场诗 "Au Lecteur" 的最后一行，英文译文为 "Hypocrite reader!—my likeness—my brother!"。艾略特认为读者也和自己一样，百无聊赖，因此需要让读者猛醒过来。原注为 "V. Baudelaire, Preface to Fleurs du Mal"。

【思考题】

1. Ordinarily, April is thought to be the month of gaiety when spring comes and everything grows. But in Eliot's poem, April is a "cruelest month." Why?

2. Eliot says in line 30, "I will show you fear in a handful of dust." What fear is there in a handful of dust?

3. "Unreal City", exclaims the speaker in the last section of "the Burial of the Dead." What is so "unreal" about the city?

4. *The Waste Land* is said to have established its own symbolism. What, for example, do you take to be the meaning of water in the poem? And Rock?

解读举例

1. 《荒原》是对现代西方文明的批判。诗中描写的荒原是一个没有信仰、道德沦丧、希望渺茫、充满行尸走肉的世界，是现代西方社会与文明走向崩溃的缩影。

2. 《荒原》并不是对现代社会的批评，而只是表达了"一连串思想的乐章"(a music of ideas)。思想有抽象、有具体、有一般、有个别，其组合排列并非要表达艾略特对当今西方社会的悲叹或嘲讽，而是要制造出一种连贯的情感和态度，以达到意志的解放。

3. 在《荒原》中，艾略特通过繁殖的祭仪和神话，表达了拯救与复活的主题，正如最后的滚滚春雷所表明的那样，其根本目的是企图恢复一个正在被世人抛弃的信仰体系。

4. 《荒原》表达了一个艾略特内心的"荒原"。创作此诗前，诗人经历了离婚、痛失挚友，精神几乎崩溃。在这种情形下，艾略特提笔创作了《荒原》，以表达对失去挚友的悲哀。

5. 《荒原》只不过表达了个人对生活的怨言而已，充其量是一通"带韵律的牢骚"(rhythmical grumbling)，与政治、宗教等问题无关，也没有表达一代人的幻灭。

William Faulkner
1897—1962

作者简介

威廉·福克纳是 20 世纪美国文学史上一位举足轻重的人物，号称南方文艺复兴的旗手和南方文学的精神领袖。他所创作的 19 部长篇小说和几十篇优秀的短篇小说组成了一部现代美国南方的编年史。

威廉·福克纳 1897 年出生于密西西比州的新奥尔巴尼是当地一个名门望族的长房长子。他的曾祖父是一个传奇的人物，曾经在美国南北战争时期的南军服役，并得过勋章。在福克纳的心目中，曾祖父就是旧南方荣誉和历史的见证。1902 年，福克纳一家迁居拉法耶特郡的奥克斯福镇 (Oxford, Lafayette)。福克纳在这个小镇上度过了童年和青年时光。以奥克斯福小镇为原型，福克纳虚构了"约克纳帕塔法"县的杰斐逊镇 (Jefferson, Yoknapatawpha)，创作出了描写美国南方社会生活长卷的"约克纳帕塔法"世系小说，完全可以媲美巴尔扎克的《人间喜剧》。

青少年时代，福克纳对学业并不感兴趣。高中未毕业就辍学进入银行工作。受喜爱文艺的母亲的影响，他从10岁开始，就非常喜爱阅读莎士比亚、菲尔丁、伏尔泰、雨果等世界文豪的作品。1914年福克纳结识了耶鲁大学毕业的菲尔·斯通。在他的影响下，福克纳广泛涉猎了现代主义作家的作品。1918年，福克纳加入英国皇家空军，在多伦多受训。退役后他作为特殊身份学生在密西西比大学就读一年，后去纽约和新奥尔良，还乘船赴欧洲游历了半年。1929年，他与埃丝特拉结婚，居住在奥克斯福镇的一所老房子里，过起了离群索居、潜心写作的生活，创作了一部又一部优秀的作品。

1925年在新奥尔良居住期间，福克纳创作出了第一部长篇小说《士兵的报酬》(*Soldiers' Pay*, 1926)，并在新奥尔良杂志上发表散文和杂记。在那里，他认识了一大批富有创新意识的文学家和艺术家，开始接触弗洛伊德的心理分析和乔伊斯高度实验性的意识流写作手法，并且和著名作家舍伍德·安德森结为莫逆之交。他们一起谈天喝酒，发表对文学的见解。在安德森的热情鼓励下，福克纳走上了发掘南方精神文化的道路，逐步形成了自己的创作风格。

福克纳的创作生涯包括三个主要阶段：第一个阶段是人们通常所说的习作阶段(1924—1929)。作品有诗集《大理石牧神》(*The Marble Faun*, 1924)，小说《士兵的报酬》《群蚊》(*Mosquitoes*, 1927)等。他的诗歌受英国后期浪漫主义诗人和法国象征派诗人的影响，拘泥于形式，成就不大。两部小说则被作者自嘲是"为写作而写作"、缺乏"独立精神"的产物，不过它们也反映了福克纳在题材和风格上所做的探索，比如在《士兵的报酬》中，他就形象地描绘了主人公退伍回乡后的失落感，可以归入"迷惘的一代"小说文本的行列。

第二个阶段是福克纳创作的鼎盛时期(1929—1936)。以《尘土中的旗帜》(*Flags in the Dust*)修改加工成的《沙多里斯》(*Sartoris*, 1929)是这一阶段的重要作品。小说反映了南方的没落。老一代有光荣的传统，但是墨守成规，阻碍着新一代的成长，而新的一代在当今变幻莫测的世界中则感觉无所适从。这一主题在福克纳以后的作品中一再出现并得到深化。1929年，福克纳发表了《喧哗与骚动》(*The Sound and the Fury*)。这部多叙述角度的作品讲述了杰斐逊镇没落贵族康普生家族的衰败史，描写了在现代文明冲击下，一个没落的南方望族各家庭成员的遭遇和精神状态，成为美国文学史上里程碑式的作品。此后，福克纳又连续发表了《我弥留之际》(*As I Lay Dying*, 1930)、《圣殿》(*Sanctuary*, 1931)和《八月之光》(*Light in August*, 1932)，1936年又出版了《押沙龙，押沙龙》(*Absalom, Absalom!*)。这六部小说共同构成了"约克纳帕塔法"世系小说的核心，代表着福克纳小说艺术的最高成就。

福克纳创作生涯中的第三个重要阶段，即巩固和确认阶段，始于 1940 年。在这个阶段，他进一步充实和丰富了以约克纳帕塔法县为背景的世系小说，同时又力图超越世系小说的界限，阐述关于人类文明的普遍真理。这一时期的主要作品有短篇小说集《去吧，摩西》(*Go Down, Moses*, 1942)，以及"斯诺普斯三部曲"《村子》(*The Hamlet*, 1940)、《小镇》(*The Town*, 1957) 和《大宅》(*The Mansion*, 1959)。"斯诺普斯三部曲"讲述了出身贫苦白人阶级的斯诺普斯家族的发家史。对金钱和名望的追求，驱使斯诺普斯家族的人为了目的不择手段。福克纳将他们形容成一群没有信仰的蛆虫。南方文明的衰落，不仅是北方工业文明冲击的结果，也是这些没有道德操守的南方人丢弃了昔日光荣传统的结果。

福克纳具有超凡的叙事能力。他的小说创作融汇了现实主义、象征主义、意识流和多角度叙述等写作手法，以及哥特式小说和侦探小说的风格。他的文体风格扎根于南方的文学传统，通过巧妙地运用南方方言，真实地再现南方各阶层人士的句法及用词特点，使人物形象栩栩如生。他采用口语体写作，不大注重书面语要求的严谨规则，因此他的语言也被称为演说散文体。福克纳坚信自己最熟悉的家乡奥克斯福镇是他想象与创作的最可靠源泉。他的创作突出反映了美国内战后南方人在旧南方向工业化社会转型时的矛盾心态，对同代及后来的美国南方作家产生了巨大的影响。

A Rose for Emily

【题解】

《献给艾米莉的玫瑰》发表于 1930 年。故事发生在福克纳虚构的约克纳帕塔法县的杰弗逊镇。主人公艾米莉出身于南方贵族世家，性情孤傲。其父自视甚高，赶跑了女儿一个又一个的追求者，使艾米莉错过了适婚的年龄。父亲去世后，艾米莉邂逅了一位来此修路的北方工头，两人关系不断发展，遭到镇上人们的非议。正当人们试图阻止艾米莉下嫁给这个"北方佬"时，后者却踪影全无。艾米莉自此深居简出，断绝了与任何人的交往。四十年弹指一挥间，终身未嫁的艾米莉也走完了自己的一生。镇上人给她举行了隆重的葬礼，人们这才有机会进入她封闭数十年的神秘院落，"北方佬"的神秘失踪随之真相大白。小说的结局出人意料，颇有哥特式小说的恐怖意蕴。

A Rose for Emily

I

WHEN Miss Emily Grierson died, our whole town went to her funeral: the men through a sort of respectful affection for a fallen monument, the women mostly out of curiosity to see the inside of her house, which no one save an old man-servant—a combined gardener and cook—had seen in at least ten years.

It was a big, squarish frame house that had once been white, decorated with cupolas and spires and scrolled balconies in the heavily lightsome style of the seventies, set on what had once been our most select street. But garages and cotton gins had encroached and obliterated even the august names of that neighborhood; only Miss Emily's house was left, lifting its stubborn and coquettish decay above the cotton wagons and the gasoline pumps-an eyesore among eyesores. And now Miss Emily had gone to join the representatives of those august names where they lay in the cedar-bemused cemetery among the ranked and anonymous graves of Union and Confederate soldiers who fell at the battle of Jefferson[1].

Alive, Miss Emily had been a tradition, a duty, and a care; a sort of hereditary obligation upon the town, dating from the day in 1894 when Colonel Sartoris[2], the mayor—he who fathered the edict that no Negro woman should appear on the streets without an apron-remitted her taxes, the dispensation dating from the death of her father on into perpetuity. Not that Miss Emily would have accepted charity. Colonel Sartoris invented an involved tale to the effect that Miss Emily's father had loaned money to the town, which the town, as a matter of business, preferred this way of repaying. Only a man of Colonel Sartoris' generation and thought could have invented it, and only a woman could have believed it.

When the next generation, with its more modern ideas, became mayors and aldermen[3], this arrangement created some little dissatisfaction. On the first of the year they mailed her a tax notice. February came, and there was no reply. They wrote her a formal letter, asking her to call at the sheriff's office at her convenience. A week later the mayor wrote her himself, offering to call or to send his car for her, and received in reply a note on paper of an archaic shape, in a thin flowing calligraphy in faded ink, to the effect that she no longer went out at all. The tax notice was also enclosed, without comment.

They called a special meeting of the Board of Aldermen. A deputation waited upon her, knocked at the door through which no visitor had passed since she ceased giving china-painting lessons eight or ten years earlier. They were admitted by the old Negro into a dim hall from which a stairway mounted into still more shadow. It smelled of dust and disuse—a close, dank smell. The Negro led them into the parlor. It was furnished in heavy, leather-covered furniture. When the Negro opened the blinds of one window, they could see that the leather was cracked; and when they sat down, a faint dust rose sluggishly about their thighs, spinning with slow motes in the single sun-ray. On a tarnished gilt easel before the fireplace stood a crayon portrait of Miss Emily's father.

They rose when she entered—a small, fat woman in black, with a thin gold chain descending to her waist and vanishing into her belt, leaning on an ebony cane with a tarnished gold head. Her skeleton was small and spare; perhaps that was why what would have been merely plumpness in another was obesity in her. She looked bloated, like a body long submerged in motionless water, and of that pallid hue. Her eyes, lost in the fatty ridges of her face, looked like two small pieces of coal pressed into a lump of dough as they moved from one face to another while the visitors stated their errand.

She did not ask them to sit. She just stood in the door and listened quietly until the spokesman came to a stumbling halt. Then they could hear the invisible watch ticking at the end of the gold chain.

Her voice was dry and cold. "I have no taxes in Jefferson. Colonel Sartoris explained it to me. Perhaps one of you can gain access to the city records and satisfy yourselves."

"But we have. We are the city authorities, Miss Emily. Didn't you get a notice from the sheriff, signed by him?"

"I received a paper, yes," Miss Emily said. "Perhaps he considers himself the sheriff . . . I have no taxes in Jefferson."

"But there is nothing on the books to show that, you see We must go by the—"

"See Colonel Sartoris. I have no taxes in Jefferson."

"But, Miss Emily—"

"See Colonel Sartoris." (Colonel Sartoris had been dead almost ten years.) "I have no taxes in Jefferson. Tobe!" The Negro appeared. "Show these gentlemen out."

II

So she vanquished them, horse and foot, just as she had vanquished their fathers thirty years before about the smell. That was two years after her father's death and a short time after her sweetheart—the one we believed would marry her—had deserted her. After her father's death she went out very little; after her sweetheart went away, people hardly saw her at all. A few of the ladies had the temerity to call, but were not received, and the only sign of life about the place was the Negro man—a young man then—going in and out with a market basket.

"Just as if a man—any man—could keep a kitchen properly," the ladies said; so they were not surprised when the smell developed. It was another link between the gross, teeming world and the high and mighty Griersons.

A neighbor, a woman, complained to the mayor, Judge Stevens, eighty years old.

"But what will you have me do about it, madam?" he said.

"Why, send her word to stop it," the woman said. "Isn't there a law?"

"I'm sure that won't be necessary," Judge Stevens said. "It's probably just a snake or a rat that nigger of hers killed in the yard. I'll speak to him about it."

The next day he received two more complaints, one from a man who came in diffident deprecation. "We really must do something about it, Judge. I'd be the last one in the world to bother Miss Emily, but we've got to do something." That night the Board of Aldermen met—three graybeards and one younger man, a member of the rising generation.

"It's simple enough," he said. "Send her word to have her place cleaned up. Give her a certain time to do it, and if she don't . . . "

"Dammit, sir," Judge Stevens said, "will you accuse a lady to her face of smelling bad?"

So the next night, after midnight, four men crossed Miss Emily's lawn and slunk about the house like burglars, sniffing along the base of the brickwork and at the cellar openings while one of them performed a regular sowing motion with his hand out of a sack slung from his shoulder. They broke open the cellar door and sprinkled lime there, and in all the outbuildings. As they recrossed the lawn, a window that had been dark was lighted and Miss Emily sat in it, the light behind her, and her upright torso motionless as that of an idol. They crept quietly across the lawn and into the shadow of the locusts that lined the street. After a week or two the smell went away.

That was when people had begun to feel really sorry for her. People in our town, remembering how old lady Wyatt, her great-aunt, had gone completely crazy at last, believed that the Griersons held themselves a little too high for what they really were. None of the young men were quite good enough for Miss Emily and such. We had long thought of them as a tableau, Miss Emily a slender figure in white in the background, her father a spraddled silhouette in the foreground, his back to her and clutching a horsewhip, the two of them framed by the back-flung front door. So when she got to be thirty and was still single, we were not pleased exactly, but vindicated; even with insanity in the family she wouldn't have turned down all of her chances if they had really materialized.

When her father died, it got about that the house was all that was left to her; and in a way, people were glad. At last they could pity Miss Emily. Being left alone, and a pauper, she had become humanized. Now she too would know the old thrill and the old despair of a penny more or less.

The day after his death all the ladies prepared to call at the house and offer condolence and aid, as is our custom. Miss Emily met them at the door, dressed as usual and with no trace of grief on her face. She told them that her father was not dead. She did that for three days, with the ministers calling on her, and the doctors, trying to persuade her to let them dispose of the body. Just as they were about to resort to law and force, she broke down, and they buried her father quickly.

We did not say she was crazy then. We believed she had to do that. We remembered all the young men her father had driven away, and we knew that with nothing left, she would have to cling to that which had robbed her, as people will.

III

She was sick for a long time. When we saw her again, her hair was cut short, making her look like a girl, with a vague resemblance to those angels in colored church windows—sort of tragic and serene.

The town had just let the contracts for paving the sidewalks, and in the summer after her father's death they began the work. The construction company came with riggers and mules and machinery, and a foreman named Homer Barron, a Yankee—a big, dark, ready man, with a big voice and eyes lighter than his face. The little boys would follow in groups to hear him cuss the riggers, and the riggers singing in time to the rise and fall of picks. Pretty soon he knew everybody in town. Whenever you heard a lot of laughing anywhere about the square, Homer Barron would be in the center of the group. Presently we began to see him and Miss Emily on Sunday afternoons driving in the yellow-wheeled buggy and the matched team of bays from the livery stable.

At first we were glad that Miss Emily would have an interest, because the ladies all said, "Of course a Grierson would not think seriously of a Northerner, a day laborer." But there were still others, older people, who said that even grief could not cause a real lady to forget noblesse oblige—without calling it noblesse oblige. They just said, "Poor Emily.

Her kinsfolk should come to her." She had some kin in Alabama; but years ago her father had fallen out with them over the estate of old lady Wyatt, the crazy woman, and there was no communication between the two families. They had not even been represented at the funeral.

And as soon as the old people said, "Poor Emily," the whispering began. "Do you suppose it's really so?" they said to one another. "Of course it is. What else could . . . " This behind their hands rustling of craned silk and satin behind jalousies closed upon the sun of Sunday afternoon as the thin, swift clop-clop-clop of the matched team passed: "Poor Emily."

She carried her head high enough—even when we believed that she was fallen. It was as if she demanded more than ever the recognition of her dignity as the last Grierson; as if it had wanted that touch of earthiness to reaffirm her imperviousness. Like when she bought the rat poison, the arsenic. That was over a year after they had begun to say "Poor Emily," and while the two female cousins were visiting her.

"I want some poison," she said to the druggist. She was over thirty then, still a slight woman, though thinner than usual, with cold, haughty black eyes in a face the flesh of which was strained across the temples and about the eye sockets as you imagine a lighthouse-keeper's face ought to look. "I want some poison," she said.

"Yes, Miss Emily. What kind? For rats and such? I'd recom—"

"I want the best you have. I don't care what kind."

The druggist named several. "They'll kill anything up to an elephant. But what you want is—"

"Arsenic," Miss Emily said. "Is that a good one?"

"Is . . . arsenic? Yes, ma'am. But what you want—"

"I want arsenic."

The druggist looked down at her. She looked back at him, erect, her face like a strained flag. "Why, of course," the druggist said. "If that's what you want. But the law requires you to tell what you are going to use it for."

Miss Emily just stared at him, her head tilted back in order to look him eye for eye, until he looked away and went and got the arsenic and wrapped it up. The Negro delivery boy brought her the package; the druggist didn't come back. When she opened the package at home there was written on the box, under the skull and bones: "For rats."

IV

So the next day we all said, "She will kill herself"; and we said it would be the best thing. When she had first begun to be seen with Homer Barron, we had said, "She will marry him." Then we said, "She will persuade him yet," because Homer himself had remarked—he liked men, and it was known that he drank with the younger men in the Elks' Club—that he was not a marrying man. Later we said, "Poor Emily" behind the jalousies as they passed on Sunday afternoon in the glittering buggy, Miss Emily with her head high and Homer Barron with his hat cocked and a cigar in his teeth, reins and whip in a yellow glove.

Then some of the ladies began to say that it was a disgrace to the town and a bad example to the young people. The men did not want to interfere, but at last the ladies forced the Baptist minister—Miss Emily's people were Episcopal—to call upon her. He would never divulge what happened during that interview, but he refused to go back again. The next Sunday they again drove about the streets, and the following day the minister's wife wrote to Miss Emily's relations in Alabama.

So she had blood-kin under her roof again and we sat back to watch developments. At first nothing happened. Then we were sure that they were to be married. We learned that Miss Emily had been to the jeweler's and ordered a man's toilet set in silver, with the letters H. B. on each piece. Two days later we learned that she had bought a complete outfit of men's clothing, including a nightshirt, and we said, "They are married." We were really glad. We were glad because the two female cousins were even more Grierson than Miss Emily had ever been.

So we were not surprised when Homer Barron—the streets had been finished some time since—was gone. We were a little disappointed that there was not a public blowing-off, but we believed that he had gone on to prepare for Miss Emily's coming, or to give her a chance to get rid of the cousins. (By that time it was a cabal, and we were all Miss Emily's allies to help circumvent the cousins.) Sure enough, after another week they departed. And, as we had expected all along, within three days Homer Barron was back in town. A neighbor saw the Negro man admit him at the kitchen door at dusk one evening.

And that was the last we saw of Homer Barron. And of Miss Emily for some time. The Negro man went in and out with the market basket, but the front door remained closed. Now and then we would see her at a window for a moment, as the men did that night when they sprinkled the lime, but for almost six months she did not appear on the streets.

Then we knew that this was to be expected too; as if that quality of her father which had thwarted her woman's life so many times had been too virulent and too furious to die.

When we next saw Miss Emily, she had grown fat and her hair was turning gray. During the next few years it grew grayer and grayer until it attained an even pepper-and-salt iron-gray, when it ceased turning. Up to the day of her death at seventy-four it was still that vigorous iron-gray, like the hair of an active man.

From that time on her front door remained closed, save for a period of six or seven years, when she was about forty, during which she gave lessons in china-painting. She fitted up a studio in one of the downstairs rooms, where the daughters and granddaughters of Colonel Sartoris' contemporaries were sent to her with the same regularity and in the same spirit that they were sent to church on Sundays with a twenty-five-cent piece for the collection plate. Meanwhile her taxes had been remitted.

Then the newer generation became the backbone and the spirit of the town, and the painting pupils grew up and fell away and did not send their children to her with boxes of color and tedious brushes and pictures cut from the ladies' magazines. The front door closed upon the last one and remained closed for good. When the town got free postal delivery, Miss Emily alone refused to let them fasten the metal numbers above her door and attach a mailbox to it. She would not listen to them.

Daily, monthly, yearly we watched the Negro grow grayer and more stooped, going in and out with the market basket. Each December we sent her a tax notice, which would be returned by the post office a week later, unclaimed. Now and then we would see her in one of the downstairs windows—she had evidently shut up the top floor of the house—like the carven torso of an idol in a niche, looking or not looking at us, we could never tell which. Thus she passed from generation to generation—dear, inescapable, impervious, tranquil, and perverse.

And so she died. Fell ill in the house filled with dust and shadows, with only a doddering Negro man to wait on her. We did not even know she was sick; we had long since given up trying to get any information from the Negro. He talked to no one, probably not even to her, for his voice had grown harsh and rusty, as if from disuse.

She died in one of the downstairs rooms, in a heavy walnut bed with a curtain, her gray head propped on a pillow yellow and moldy with age and lack of sunlight.

V

THE NEGRO met the first of the ladies at the front door and let them in, with their hushed, sibilant voices and their quick, curious glances, and then he disappeared. He walked right through the house and out the back and was not seen again.

The two female cousins came at once. They held the funeral on the second day, with the town coming to look at Miss Emily beneath a mass of bought flowers, with the crayon face of her father musing profoundly above the bier and the ladies sibilant and macabre; and the very old men—some in their brushed Confederate uniforms—on the porch and the lawn, talking of Miss Emily as if she had been a contemporary of theirs, believing that they had danced with her and courted her perhaps, confusing time with its mathematical progression, as the old do, to whom all the past is not a diminishing road but, instead, a huge meadow which no winter ever quite touches, divided from them now by the narrow bottle-neck of the most recent decade of years.

Already we knew that there was one room in that region above stairs which no one had seen in forty years, and which would have to be forced. They waited until Miss Emily was decently in the ground before they opened it.

The violence of breaking down the door seemed to fill this room with pervading dust. A thin, acrid pall as of the tomb seemed to lie everywhere upon this room decked and furnished as for a bridal: upon the valance curtains of faded rose color, upon the rose-shaded lights, upon the dressing table, upon the delicate array of crystal and the man's toilet things backed with tarnished silver, silver so tarnished that the monogram was obscured. Among them lay a collar and tie, as if they had just been removed, which, lifted, left upon the surface a pale crescent in the dust. Upon a chair hung the suit, carefully folded; beneath it the two mute shoes and the discarded socks.

The man himself lay in the bed.

For a long while we just stood there, looking down at the profound and fleshless grin. The body had apparently once lain in the attitude of an embrace, but now the long sleep that outlasts love, that conquers even the grimace of love, had cuckolded him. What was left of him, rotted beneath what was left of the nightshirt, had become inextricable from the bed in which he lay; and upon him and upon the pillow beside him lay that even coating of the patient and biding dust.

Then we noticed that in the second pillow was the indentation of a head. One of us lifted something from it, and leaning forward, that faint and invisible dust dry and acrid in the nostrils, we saw a long strand of iron-gray hair.

【注解】

1. Jefferson：杰弗逊镇，福克纳小说中虚构的约克纳帕塔法县的中心。
2. Colonel Sartoris：本故事中杰弗逊镇的镇长 Bayard Sartoris 继承了父亲老沙多利斯的头衔，后者是福克纳小说《沙多利斯》中的主要人物。
3. aldermen：市政会的成员。

【思考题】

1. What is the significance of the title of the story?
2. What is the point of view? What difficulties would be raised if one should try to tell the story from the point of view of the third person?
3. Why is it significant that Miss Emily chooses for her lover a man who is scornfully regarded by the community as a "Northerner, a day laborer"?
4. What role does Emily's father play in the story? Are there any relationships between Emily's father and Homer Barron?
5. What do the townspeople feel about Emily before they know the truth? After?

解读举例

1. 在《献给艾米莉的玫瑰》中，艾米莉的孤傲和倔强无疑是南方贵族身份给她打下的深深烙印。她不顾舆论的压力，勇于追求爱情，当她发现出身寒微的北方情人即将抛弃她，离她而去的时候，她杀死了他，把他永远留在身边。正像她所代表的旧南方一样，她是不会轻易认输、被人抛弃的。这桩荒诞的凶杀案象征南北方之间的激烈冲突，表达了深刻的社会意义。约克纳帕塔法县的杰弗逊镇实际上是美国旧南方的象征，艾米莉和她的父亲象征着没落的南方势力，而她的未婚夫则是北方的象征。艾米莉的婚嫁透射出传统与现实、南方与北方之间的尖锐矛盾。

2. 在《献给艾米莉的玫瑰》中，艾米莉看似平静却丧失了理智，这是人性的悲剧。她把自己封闭起来，在凝固的时间中生活，不承认过去与现在的区别，模糊了现实与幻想、生与死的界线，企图挽留逝去的爱情与自尊。她的扭曲心理和行为实际上是她自傲与自卑、独立与依赖、倔强与软弱的极端体现。福克纳不仅描写了旧南方的衰落，也描写了人性的复杂和矛盾。在谈及此短篇小说时，他曾说过，他"只是在写人，写一个真实而可悲的故事，因为这个故事发自内心……"

3. 在《献给艾米莉的玫瑰》中，艾米莉是一个悲剧英雄。她拥有一个完整的自我，以自己的方式对待他人的世界，从不作任何妥协。她的"疯狂"是相对的。她丧失理智的行为实际表明她完全生活在她所处社会的行为准则之外，不接受怜悯，也不接受指责。她蔑视社会等级和道德观念。她一定要嫁给比自己地位低、也许并不执意要娶她的那位北方人，并以自己的方式留住了情人，也以自己的方式得到了小镇的接纳和认可。

Ernest Hemingway
1899—1961

作者简介

欧内斯特·海明威出生于美国伊利诺伊州芝加哥附近的奥克帕克村。1917年中学毕业后，海明威拒绝上大学，告别父母来到堪萨斯城，在该市的《明星报》当记者。这一期间，海明威不仅加深了对社会的了解，还学会了怎样写简洁有力的短句和段落。这段经历对海明威今后的写作风格产生了重要的影响。1918年，海明威加入美国红十字会战地救护队，随救护队奔赴欧洲战场。期间，海明威与女护士安尼丝陷入热恋，后来这位女护士成为他的第二部长篇小说《永别了，武器》(*A Farewell to Arms*, 1929) 的原型。海明威很快就亲历了战争的残酷。战争的血腥杀戮和残酷毁灭、战争中人的渺小与生命的脆弱、战争宣传的欺骗与虚伪，所有这些都在他心中造成了巨大而难以治愈的创伤，从根本上改变了他的战争观和世界观，也成为他后来文学创作中着重表现的一个主题。

回美国后，海明威重操旧业，成为加拿大《多伦多明星报》的记者。1921年，海明威和哈德利·理查逊结婚后一同赴巴黎，并在舍伍德·安德森 (Sherwood Anderson) 的建议下，担任该报驻法特派记者，报道希土战争 (Greco-Turkish Wars)。在此期间，安德森介绍海明威前去拜访旅居巴黎的美国女作家格特鲁德·斯坦因 (Gertrude Stein, 1874—1946)。在斯坦因开办的文学沙龙内，海明威又结识了侨居巴黎的许多美国艺术家和知识分子，如菲茨杰拉德、庞德、埃德蒙·威尔逊 (Edmund Wilson, 1895—1972) 等。他们都或多或少地受过第一次世界大战的伤害，对欧洲传统价值观和思想体系产生巨大怀疑，被斯坦因称为"迷惘的一代"。这一称呼也出现在海明威第一部长篇小说《太阳照样升起》(*The Sun Also Rises*, 1926) 的扉页献辞中，并因此为许多人所熟知。

在斯坦因、庞德等人的鼓励与指点下，海明威修改完善了自己的处女作《三个故事和十首诗》(Three Stories & Ten Poems)，并于 1923 年在巴黎发表。两年后，他的第二个短篇小说集《在我们的时代》(In Our Time, 1925) 在美国出版。该短篇小说集第一次出现了以尼克·亚当斯 (Nick Adams) 为中心人物的各种故事，初步显示了海明威凝练、独特的叙事艺术和写作风格，引起了评论界的注意。但真正奠定海明威在现代美国文坛地位的是他于 1926 年在美国发表的第一部长篇小说《太阳照样升起》，表现了亲历战争后的英美青年对西方传统价值体系幻想的破灭。他们表面热闹快活，实际却悲观失望、颓废无奈。然而作品并非完全灰暗，主人公巴恩斯努力走出战争的阴影，学会如何在战后这样一个"荒原"中勇敢地生活下去，成了海明威笔下的第一个"可以被毁灭但不能被打败"(A man can be destroyed but not defeated.) 的硬汉 (code hero) 形象。尽管当时海明威年仅 27 岁，他的作品却表现出了思想和艺术上的高度成熟，体现了海明威小说创作中的主要技巧、手段和语言风格。

1927 年，海明威辞去报社的工作，潜心写作，同年发表了第二个短篇小说集《没有女人的男人》(Men Without Women)。两年后出版了反战小说《永别了，武器》。这部作品以第一次世界大战的意大利战场为背景，以海明威的许多亲身经历为素材，讲述了主人公弗雷德里克·亨利中尉在战场上负伤、叛逃，以及和英国护士凯瑟琳·巴克利的悲剧爱情故事，深刻揭露了战争毁灭生命、摧残人性的本质。许多评论家认为这部作品是美国最优秀的反战小说。

20 世纪 30 年代，海明威常到西班牙看斗牛，到非洲猎狮子，拥有了许多传奇般的经历，也为后来的许多作品提供了珍贵的素材，如描写西班牙斗牛场上悲剧与仪式的《死在午后》(Death in the Afternoon, 1932) 和描写非洲经历的《非洲的青山》(Green Hills of Africa, 1935)、《乞力马扎罗的雪》("The Snows of Kilimanjaro", 1936) 等。此间还发表了短篇小说集《胜者无所得》(Winner Take Nothing, 1933)。1936 年，西班牙内战爆发，海明威奔赴战争前线，成为战争的亲历者。1940 年，他以真人真事为原型，创作发表了表现西班牙人民反抗佛朗哥法西斯政权的战争小说《丧钟为谁而鸣》(For Whom the Bell Tolls)。该作品大受欢迎，被誉为"20 世纪美国文学中一部真正的英雄史诗"。1937 年，受美国左翼运动的影响，海明威发表了他的第三部长篇小说《有钱的和没钱的》(To Have and Have Not)。这是他第一部表现社会问题的政治小说。

这以后的数十年里，海明威再没有写出什么优秀作品，颇有江郎才尽之嫌。1952 年，海明威发表了中篇小说《老人与海》(The Old Man and the Sea)。这部作品带有他早期作品中优雅、纯净、凝练、深邃的写作风格，将他的叙事艺术推向新的高峰，出版的第二年即获普利策小说奖，并于 1954 年因"精通现代叙事艺术"荣获诺贝尔文学奖。此后的几年中，海明威身体每况愈下，还患上了严重的忧郁症。1961 年 7 月，海明威用枪结束了自己的生命。

1999 年，在海明威 100 周年诞辰之际，海明威的儿子帕特里克·海明威编辑出版了海明威生前创作但未发表的小说《黎明时的真实》(True at First Light)。2005 年，帕特里克又编辑出版了其父的另一部作品《乞力马扎罗山下》(Under Kilimanjaro)。两部作品都以虚构形式表现了海明威 1953 至 1954 年间在非洲狩猎旅行的经历。

海明威是继马克·吐温后对美国文学语言影响最大的作家。他的独特文风不仅影响了杰克·凯鲁亚克 (Jack Kerouac, 1922—1969)、J. D. 赛林格 (J. D. Salinger, 1919—2010)、雷蒙德·卡弗 (Raymond Carver, 1938—1988) 等美国作家，也影响到加夫列尔·加西亚·马尔克斯 (Gabriel García Márquez, 1927—2014) 等许多国外作家。

海明威创作的最大特点就是凝练含蓄 (economy and understatement)，作品中一切修辞比喻、解释议论都被删得一干二净，剩下的只是精髓，人物对话也多是电报式的短句，充分体现了海明威关于小说创作的"冰山理论"。[1]

以下选自海明威的短篇小说《杀手》。

The Killers

【题解】

《杀手》为短篇小说集《没有女人的男人》中的 14 个短篇故事之一，描写了芝加哥两名杀手在一家小餐馆伺机暗杀奥尔·安德森的故事。尽管暗杀并没有发生，但通过作者匠心独具的构思与生动细致的描述，读者仍然可以感受到小餐馆内的紧张气氛。故事的结尾也颇令人回味。

The Killers

The door of Henry's lunchroom opened and two men came in. They sat down at the counter.

---

[1] 海明威曾说："如果你知道自己省略了哪些内容，而且知道省略了这些内容可以强化故事情节，并让读者感受到的东西比他们理解的还要多，那么你就完全可以省略这些内容……在冰山露出的每一个尖顶之下都有八分之七隐于水下。"

"What's yours?"[1] George asked them.

"I don't know," one of the men said. "what do you want to eat, Al?"

"I don't know," said Al. "I don't know what I want to eat."

Outside it was getting dark. The streetlight came on outside the window. The two men at the counter read the menu. From the other end of the counter Nick Adams watched them. He had been talking to George when they came in.

"I'll have a roast pork tenderloin with apple sauce and mashed potatoes," the first man said.

"It isn't ready yet."

"What the hell do you put it on the card for?"

"That's the dinner," George explained. "You can get that at six o'clock."

George looked at the clock on the wall behind the counter.

"It's five o'clock."

"The clock says twenty minutes past five," the second man said.

"It's twenty minutes fast."

"Oh, to hell with the clock," the first man said. "What have you got to eat?"

"I can give you any kind of sandwiches," George said. "You can have ham and eggs, bacon and eggs, liver and bacon, or a steak."

"Give me chicken croquette with green peas and cream sauce and mashed potatoes."

"That's the dinner."

"Everything we want's the dinner, eh? That's the way you work it."

"I can give you ham and eggs, bacon and eggs, liver—"

"I'll take ham and eggs," the man called Al said. He wore a derby hat and a black overcoat buttoned across the chest. His face was small and white and he had tight lips. He wore a silk muffler and gloves.

"Give me bacon and eggs," said the other man. He was about the same size as Al. Their faces were different, but they were dressed like twins. Both wore overcoats too tight for them. They sat leaning forward, their elbows on the counter.

"Got anything to drink?" Al asked.

"Silver beer, bevo, ginger-ale," George said.

"I mean you got anything to drink?"

"Just those I said."

"This is a hot town," said the other. "What do they call it?"

"Summit."

"Ever hear of it?" Al asked his friend.

"No," said the friend.

"What do you do here nights?" Al asked.

"They eat the dinner," his friend said. "They all come here and eat the big dinner."

"That's right," George said.

"So you think that's right?" Al asked George.

"Sure."

"You're a pretty bright boy, aren't you?"

"Sure," said George.

"Well, you're not," said the other little man. "Is he, Al?"

"He's a dumb," said Al. He turned to Nick. "What's your name?"

"Adams."

"Another bright boy," Al said. "Ain't he a bright boy, Max?"

"The town's full of bright boys," Max said.

George put the two platters, one of ham and eggs, the other of bacon and eggs, on the counter. He set down two sidedishes of fried potatoes and closed the wicket into the kitchen.

"Which is yours?" he asked Al.

"Don't you remember?"

"Ham and eggs."

"Just a bright boy," Max said. He leaned forward and took the ham and eggs. Both men ate with their gloves on. George watched them eat.

"What are you looking at?" Max looked at George.

"Nothing."

"The hell you were. You were looking at me."

"Maybe the boy meant it for a joke, Max," Al said.

George laughed.

"You don't have to laugh," Max said to him. "You don't have to laugh at all, see?"

"All right," said George.

"So he thinks it's all right." Max turned to Al. "He thinks it's all right. That's a good one."

"Oh, he's a thinker," Al said. They went on eating.

"What's the bright boy's name down the counter?" Al asked Max.

"Hey, bright boy," Max said to Nick. "You go around on the other side of the counter with your boy friend."

"What's the idea?" Nick asked.

"There isn't any idea."

"You better go around, bright boy," Al said. Nick went around behind the counter.

"What's the idea?" George asked.

"None of your damn business," Al said. "Who is out in the kitchen?"

"The nigger."

"What do you mean the nigger?"

"The nigger that cooks."

"Tell him to come in."

"What's the idea?"

"Tell him to come in."

"Where do you think you are?"

"We know damn well where we are," the man called Max said. "Do we look silly?"

"You talk silly," Al said to him. "What the hell do you argue with this kid for? Listen," he said to George, "tell the nigger to come out here."

"What are you going to do to him?"

"Nothing. Use your head, bright boy. What would we do to a nigger?"

George opened the slit that opened back into the kitchen. "Sam," he called. "Come in here a minute."

The door to the kitchen opened and the nigger came in. "What was it?" he asked. The two men at the counter took a look at him.

"All right, nigger. You stand right there," Al said;

Sam, the nigger, standing in his apron, looked at the two men sitting at the counter. "Yes, sir," he said. Al got down from his stool.

"I'm going back to the kitchen with the nigger and bright boy," he said. "Go on back to the kitchen, nigger. You go with him, bright boy." The little man walked after Nick and Sam, the cook, back into the kitchen. The door shut after them. The man called Max sat at the counter opposite George. He didn't look at George but looked in the mirror that ran along back of the counter. Henry's had been made over from a saloon into a lunch-counter.

"Well, bright boy," Max said, looking into the mirror, "why don't you say something?"

"What's it all about?"

"Hey, Al," Max called, "bright boy wants to know what it's all about."

"Why don't you tell him?" Al's voice came from the kitchen.

"What do you think it's all about?"

"I don't know."

"What do you think?"

Max looked into the mirror all the time he was talking.

"I wouldn't say."

"Hey, Al, bright boy says he wouldn't say what he thinks it's all about."

"I can hear you, all right," Al said from the kitchen. He had propped open the slit that dishes passed through into the kitchen with a catsup bottle. "Listen, bright boy," he said from the kitchen to George. "Stand a little further along the bar. You move a little to the left, Max." He was like a photographer arranging for a group picture.

"Talk to me, bright boy," Max said. "What do you think's going to happen?"

"I don't know," one of the men said, "what do you want to eat, Al?"

George did not say anything.

"I'll tell you," Max said. "We're going to kill a Swede. Do you know a big Swede named Ole Andreson?"

"Yes."

"He comes here to eat every night, don't he?"

"Sometimes he comes here."

"He comes here at six o'clock, don't he?"

"If he comes."

"We know all that, bright boy," Max said. "Talk about something else. Ever go to the movies?"

"Once in a while."

"You ought to go to the movies more. The movies are fine for a bright boy like you."

"What are you going to kill Ole Andreson for? What did he ever do to you?"

"He never had a chance to do anything to us. He never even seen us."

"And he's only going to see us once," Al said from the kitchen.

"What are you going to kill him for, then?" George asked.

"We're killing him for a friend. Just to oblige a friend, bright boy."

"Shut up," said Al from the kitchen. "You talk too goddamn much."

"Well, I got to keep bright boy amused. Don't I, bright boy?"

"You talk too damn much," Al said. "The nigger and my bright boy are amused by themselves. I got them tied up like a couple of girl friends in the convent."

"I suppose you were in a convent."

"You never know."

"You were in a kosher covent[2]. That's where you were."

George looked up at the clock.

"If anybody comes in you tell them the cook is off, and if they keep after it, you tell them you'll go back and cook yourself. Do you get that, bright boy?"

"All right," George said. "What you going to do with us afterward?"

"That'll depend," Max said. "That's one of those things you never know at the time."

George looked up at the clock. It was a quarter past six. The door from the street opened. A streetcar motorman came in.

"Hello, George," he said. "Can I get supper?"

"Sam's gone out," George said. "He'll be back in about half an hour."

"I'd better go up the street," the motorman said. George looked at the clock. It was twenty minutes, past six. "That was nice, bright boy," Max said. "You're a regular little gentleman."

"He knew I'd blow his head off," Al said from the kitchen.

"No," said Max. "It ain't that. Bright boy is nice. He's a nice boy. I like him."

At six-fifty-five George said: "He's not coming."

Two other people had been in the lunch-room. Once George had gone out to the kitchen and made a ham-and-egg sandwich "to go[3]" that a man wanted to take with him. Inside the kitchen he saw Al, his derby hat tipped back, sitting on a stool beside the wicket with the muzzle of a sawed-off shot-gun resting on the ledge. Nick and the cook were back to back in the corner, a towel tied in each of their mouths. George had cooked the sandwich, wrapped it up in oiled paper, put it in a bag, brought it in, and the man had paid for it and gone out.

"Bright boy can do everything," Max said. "He can cook and everything. You'd make some girl a nice wife, bright boy."

"Yes?" George said. "Your friend, Ole Andreson, isn't going to come."

"We'll give him ten minutes," Max said.

Max watched the mirror and the clock. The hands of the clock marked seven o'clock, and then five minutes past seven.

"Come on, Al," said Max. "We better go. He's not coming."

"Better give him five minutes," Al said from the kitchen.

In the five minutes a man came in, and George explained that the cook was sick.

"Why the hell don't you get another cook?" the man asked. "Aren't you running a lunch-counter?" He went out.

"Come on, Al," Max said.

"What about the two bright boys and the nigger?"

"They're all right."

"You think so?"

"Sure. We're through with it."

"I don't like it," said Al. "It's sloppy. You talk too much."

"What's the idea?" George asked.

"Oh, what the hell," said Max. "We got to keep amused, haven't we."

"You talk too much, all the same," Al said. He came out from the kitchen. The cut-off barrels of the shotgun made a light bulge under the waist of his too tight-fitting overcoat. He straightened his coat with his gloved hands.

"So long, bright boy," he said to George. "You got a lot of luck."

"That's the truth," Max said. "You ought to play the races[4], bright boy."

The two of them went out the door. George watched them, through the window, pass under the arc-light and cross the street. In their tight overcoats and derby hats they looked like a vaudeville team. George went back through the swinging-door into the kitchen and untied Nick and the cook.

"I don't want any more of that," said Sam, the cook. "I don't want any more of that."

Nick stood up. He had never had a towel in his mouth before.

"Say," he said. "What the hell?" He was trying to swagger it off[5].

"They were going to kill Ole Andreson," George said. "They were going to shoot him when he came in to eat."

"Ole Andreson?"

"Sure." The cook felt the corners of his mouth with his thumbs.

"They all gone?" he asked.

"Yeah," said George. "They're gone now."

"I don't like it," said the cook. "I don't like any of it at all."

"Listen," George said to Nick. "You better go see Ole Andreson."

"All right."

"You better not have anything to do with it at all," Sam, the cook, said. "You better stay out of it."

"Don't go if you don't want to," George said.

"Mixing up in this ain't going to get you anywhere," the cook said. "You stay out of it."

"I'll go see him," Nick said to George. "Where does he live?" The cook turned away.

"Little boys always know what they want to do," he said.

"He lives up at Hirsch's rooming-house," George said to Nick.

"I'll go up there."

Outside the arc-light shone through the bare branches of a tree. Nick walked up the street beside the car-tracks and turned at the next arc-light down a side-street. Three houses up the street was Hirsch's rooming-house. Nick walked up the two steps and pushed the bell. A woman came to the door.

"Is Ole Andreson here?"

"Do you want to see him?"

"Yes, if he's in."

Nick followed the woman up a flight of stairs and back to the end of a corridor. She knocked on the door.

"Who is it?"

"Its's somebody to see you, Mr. Andreson," the woman said.

"It's Nick Adams."

"Come in."

Nick opened the door and went into the room. Ole Andreson was lying on the bed with all his clothes on. He bad been a prizefighter and he was too long for the bed. He lay with his head on two pillows. He did not look at Nick.

"What was it?" he asked.

"I was up at Henry's," Nick said, "and two fellows came in and tied up me and the cook, and they said they were going to kill you."

It sounded silly when he said it. Ole Andreson said nothing.

"They put us out in the kitchen," Nick went on. "They were going to shoot you when you came in to supper."

Old Andreson looked at the wall and did not say anything.

"George thought I better come and tell you about it."

"There isn't anything I can do about it," Ole Andreson said.

"I'll tell you what they were like."

"I don't want to know what they were like," Ole Andreson said. He looked at the wall.

"Thanks for coming to tell me about it."

"That's all right."

Nick looked at the big man lying on the bed.

"Don't you want me to go and see the police?"

"No," Ole Andreson said. "That wouldn't do any good."

"Isn't there something I could do?"

"No. There ain't anything to do."

"Maybe it was just a bluff."

"No. It ain't just a bluff."

Ole Andreson rolled over toward the wall.

"The only thing is," he said, talking toward the wall, "I just can't make up my mind to go out. I been in here all day."

"Couldn't you get out of town?"

"No," Ole Andreson said. "I'm through with all that running around."

He looked at the wall.

"There ain't anything to do now."

"Couldn't you fix it up some way?"

"No, I got in wrong." He talked in the same flat voice. "There ain't anything to do. After a while I'll make up my mind to go out."

"I better go back and see George," Nick said.

"So long," said Ole Andreson. He did not look toward Nick. "Thanks for coming around."

Nick went out. As he shut the door he saw Old Andreson with all his clothes on, lying on the bed looking at the wall.

"He's been in his room all day," the landlady said downstairs. "I guess he don't feel well. I said to him: 'Mr. Andreson, you ought to go out and take a walk on a nice fall day like this,' but he didn't feel like it."

"He doesn't want to go out."

"I'm sorry he don't feel well," the woman said. "He's an awfully nice man. He was in the ring[6], you know."

"I know it."

"You'd never know it except from the way his face is," the woman said.

They stood talking just inside the street door. "He's just as gentle."

"Well, good night, Mrs. Hirsch," Nick said.

"I'm not Mrs. Hirsch," the woman said. "She owns the place. I just look after it for her. I'm Mrs. Bell."

"Well, good night, Mrs. Bell," Nick said.

"Good night," the woman said.

Nick walked up the dark street to the corner under the arc-light, and then along the car-tracks to Henny's eating-house. George was inside, back of the counter. "Did you see Ole?"

"Yes," said Nick. "He's in his room and he won't go out."

The cook opened the door from the kitchen when he heard Nick's voice.

"I don't even listen to it," he said and shut the door.

"Did you tell him about it?" George asked.

"Sure. I told him but he knows what it's all about."

"What's he going to do?"

"Nothing."

"They'll kill him."

"I guess they will."

"He must have got mixed up in something in Chicago."

"It's a hell of a thing."

"I guess so," said Nick.

"It's an awful thing," Nick said.

They did not say anything. George reached down for a towel and wiped the counter.

"I wonder what he did?" Nick said.

"Double-crossed somebody. That's what they kill them for."

"I'm going to get out of this town," Nick said.

"Yes," said George. "That's a good thing to do."

"I can't stand to think about him waiting in the room and knowing he's going to get it. It's too damned awful."

"Well," said George, "you better not think about it."

【注解】

1. What's yours：您点些什么？
2. kosher covent：提供犹太人食物的修道院。
3. to go：外卖的。
4. play the races：赌马。
5. swagger it off：说大话，虚张声势（以表示无所谓）。
6. He was in the ring：他上过拳击台。意思是他曾是个拳击手。

【思考题】

1. The story is said to be made of one long scene, which breaks up into three short scenes. How would you divide the three short scenes? What are the major details of each of these three scenes that are significant to the revelation of the two killers?
2. Study the dialogue of the two gangsters, and explain how they are characterized in the story. How does that characterization together with the boring and banal quality of their dialogue reinforce the underlying horror of the story?
3. Somewhere in the middle of the story, one of the gangsters suggests that Nick should go to the movies more. Why does he make such a suggestion? What movies does he possibly have in mind when he makes such a suggestion?
4. What is the function of Mrs. Bell? What does the dialogue with Mrs. Bell following that with Ole Andreson suggest about Ole Andreson?
5. What hints does the story offer that might provide a possible explanation for Ole Andreson's murder? Why doesn't Hemingway choose to be more specific?
6. Why does Ole Andreson refuse to attempt to escape? What is significant in the fact that he lies with his face to the wall?
7. How do George, Sam and Nick differ in their attitudes toward the incident? What does Nick appear to learn? Why does he say at the end "I'm going to get out of this town"?
8. Who is the story's focal character? Why?
9. The chief characteristic of the style of "The Killers" is simplicity—simple even to the point of monotony, with many simple or compound sentences, and very few complex and involved ones. What does the simplicity of the style suggest about Hemingway's

basic fictional concerns in the story?

解读举例

1. 《杀手》是讲述匪徒阿尔和迈克斯的故事。题目《杀手》即清楚地说明了这一点。故事中，作者细腻生动地描写了他们杀人前若无其事的言行举止，例如他们相互挑逗，戴手套吃饭，不断地望着钟表和镜子，熟练地将尼克和黑人厨子绑起来，毫不讳言他们到亨利餐馆的目的和暗杀对象等，所有这些都表明他们是一对冷酷老练的职业杀手，只是由于安德森没有在预定的时候出现才取消行动，但读者可以预料到安德森最终难逃厄运。

2. 《杀手》是讲述奥尔·安德森的故事。尽管安德森只占故事情节的很少部分，但却是故事发展的中心人物。没有他就没有整个故事。由于某些未点明的原因，他被雇佣的杀手追杀，最后心力交瘁，宁可被枪杀也不愿继续东奔西藏下去 (I'm through with all that running around.)。故事的结尾给读者留下许多悬念，如他到底为什么要被追杀，他最终是否会被害等。

3. 《杀手》是讲述亨利餐馆三位伙计的故事。山姆、乔治和尼克对待杀手及可能发生的凶杀案的不同态度是故事隐含的主题。山姆虽然被绑，但在获释后却抱着"离这事远远的"的态度。乔治虽主张向老安德森报信，但在听说安德森甘愿被杀后也无可奈何，听之任之。而尼克是作品中唯一有正义感和责任感的人物。在劝说安德森躲藏及报警未果后，他决定离开这个邪恶的小镇。在他身上体现了海明威本人对待邪恶的态度与价值观。从这个角度看，《杀手》也可以被认为是尼克的故事。

Contemporary American Literature
1945–

背景介绍

第二次世界大战之后,欧洲许多参战国家都遭受重创,一战后崭露头角的美国非但没有受到削弱,反而在战后迎来了史无前例的繁荣景象。然而这些并没有彻底消除战争留在美国人心头的阴影,很快他们又开始面临冷战、朝鲜战争与核战的威胁。与此同时,美国国内的各种矛盾日益加剧,学生运动、非裔运动、民权运动等风起云涌。美国统治机构则变得越来越专制与恐怖。20世纪50年代麦卡锡主义(McCarthyism)盛行,许多进步人士遭到迫害,在全国造成一种人人自危的政治气氛,个人权利遭到无情践踏。约瑟夫·海勒(Joseph Heller, 1923—1999)在他的《第22条军规》(Catch-22, 1961)中对此进行了嘲讽。20世纪60年代美国对越南战争的大规模介入,肯尼迪总统与民权领袖马丁·路德·金(Martin Luther King, 1929—1968)遇刺,以及20世纪70年代初的水门事件(The Watergate Scandal)等都引起了美国民众愤怒、茫然与怀疑的复杂情绪。20世纪80年代后,美国大众媒体与信息产业高速发展,在传播信息、娱乐生活的同时,也在"不露声色"地改变、操纵与控制民众的思维及行为方式。所有这些都在美国战后文学中得到了深刻的反映。

战后的美国文学呈现出流派纷呈的繁荣局面。它们或以历史事件划分,或以社会思潮划分,或以民族划分,或以肤色划分,其作品思想也集中反映了各流派对战争、哲学、宗教、社会、民族、种族、区域、性别等问题的探讨。战争小说是战后初年涌现的第一股文学浪潮。诺曼·梅勒(Norman Mailer, 1923—2007)、詹姆斯·琼斯(James Jones, 1921—1977)、赫曼·沃克(Herman Wouk, 1915—2019)、詹姆斯·戈德·科曾斯(James Gould Cozzens, 1903—1978)等都是这一时期最有影响的战争小说家。他们经受过二战炮火的洗礼,因此对战争场面的描写与对军人心理的刻画真实生动,细致入微。梅勒的《裸者与死者》(The Naked and the Dead, 1948)与琼斯的《从这里到永恒》(From Here to Eternity, 1951)、《细细的红线》(The Thin Red Line, 1962)等表面描写战争,实则暗示了美军内部的暴虐冷酷,影射了美国社会扼杀人性、践踏人格的法西斯倾向。沃克的《该隐号兵变》(The Caine Mutiny, 1951)和科曾斯的《仪仗队》(Guard of Honor, 1948)则表达了一种正统的、反映官方观点的战争观与军人价值观。

垮掉派(the Beat Generation)文学是20世纪50年代继战争文学后掀起的第一个反叛性文学运动。垮掉派作家在经历了第二次世界大战和麦卡锡主义的高压政治后,对美国社会的专制倾向、物质至上、墨守成规等社会现实深感厌恶。他们强调完全的个人自由,反对社会与各种体系对他们的束缚与控制。垮掉派的领袖人物凯鲁亚克在作品《在路上》(On the Road, 1957)中描写了自由的波希米亚式(Bohemian)生活,表达了对美国物质文明的不屑。金斯堡的长诗《嚎叫》(Howl, 1956)则用一种近似疯狂的愤怒语调抨击了美国社会的专制、压迫与腐朽,引起了社会的巨大反响。

20世纪50年代另一部引起社会反响的反叛性作品是J. D. 塞林格(J. D. Salinger,

1919—2010) 的《麦田里的守望者》(*The Catcher in the Rye*, 1951)。作者通过主人公少年霍尔顿的叙述表达了对美国充满欺诈与虚伪的成人社会的批判。霍尔顿也被称为 20 世纪的哈克贝利·芬。

进入 20 世纪 60 年代后，美国文学发生了重大转变。科学技术的发展 (相对论、不确定原则、熵定律)、现代语言学理论 (解构主义) 的兴起，以及肯尼迪总统遇刺等历史事件极大地改变了人们对事物的看法。许多严肃作家开始认识到 "客观现实" 或 "真实" 实际上是不存在的，因为一切事物都必须通过语言来认识，而人类的语言只是一套人为建构的、武断的、不可靠的文字符号系统，可以被人任意操纵与歪曲。人们凭借语言这个媒介认识的 "客观现实" 实际是一个由语言建构起来的现实，而不是现实本身。在这种革命性的语言理论的启迪下，许多作家纷纷与传统的创作原则和创作方式决裂。他们不再企图 "再现" 客观现实，而是一头钻进语言的 "快乐宫"(the funhouse of language)，开始创作自省小说或元小说 (metafiction)，希望以此来揭露语言及所有建立在语言基础上的意识形态的虚构性。美国小说创作也由此进入了一个后现代 (postmodernism) 阶段。

美国后现代派小说大致经历了两个发展时期：第一个时期是从 20 世纪 60 年代初到 60 年代末；第二个时期是从 20 世纪 70 年代初到 80 年代初。第一时期的后现代小说也被称为 "黑色幽默"(black humor) 小说。"黑色幽默" 以喜剧的形式表现悲剧的内容，以揭露荒诞的社会对人的压迫为目的，其主人公多为反英雄式人物，创作手段主要有各种讽刺性模仿、反讽、荒诞描写、悖论、自我消解等。海勒的《第 22 条军规》、弗拉迪米尔·纳博科夫 (Vladimir Nabokov, 1899—1977) 的《洛莉塔》(*Lolita*, 1963)、托马斯·品钦 (Thomas Pynchon, 1937—) 的《V.》、(*V.*,1963)、库特·冯尼格 (Kurt Vonnegut, 1922—2007) 的《第五号屠场》(*Slaughterhouse-Five*, 1969)、约翰·巴思 (John Barth, 1930—) 的《山羊小子贾尔斯》(*Giles Goat-Boy*, 1966) 等都是 "黑色幽默" 的代表作品。

1967 年，巴思在《大西洋月刊》上发表了《枯竭的文学》("The Literature of Exhaustion")，认为传统文学的叙事形式已经枯竭，只有利用传统文学形式大胆创新才有出路。该文在美国文学界引起强烈反响，将后现代主义小说创作推向第二时期。这一时期的后现代小说也被称为元小说，即关于小说的小说，其基本策略是建立框架，并打破框架 (frame and frame-breaking)。除第一时期的部分作家外，这一时期的代表作家还有威廉·盖迪斯 (William Gaddis, 1922—1998)、罗伯特·库弗 (Robert Coover, 1932—)、雷蒙·费德曼 (Raymond Federman, 1928—2009)、瓦特·埃比什 (Walter Abish, 1931—2022)、罗纳德·苏克尼克 (Ronald Sukenick, 1932—2004) 等人。他们的创作较第一时期的后现代主义作品更为大胆与激进，以达到最大限度地打破框架，揭示文本及意识形态的虚构性之目的。

然而，由于后现代小说的先锋性和无视读者的创作方法，到了20世纪70年代末，美国的后现代主义文学已出现了枯竭。尽管文学家和学者们推崇的是非线性的叙述、意象主义小说、互文性和其他种种叙事革新形式，但美国大众读者仍喜欢真实可信的人物、有意思的故事情节，其中不乏有血有肉、活灵活现的现实主义描写。于是，符合大众喜好的现实主义创作方法开始回归美国文坛。然而，回归后的现实主义已不再是19世纪或20世纪上半叶的现实主义，而是一种更高层次上的新现实主义(New Realism)，代表着美国后现代之后的文学发展趋势。主要作家有托尼·莫里森(Toni Morrison，1931—2019)，美籍华裔女作家马克辛·洪·金斯顿(Maxine Hong Kingston, 1940—，即汤亭亭)，新现实主义小说家乔伊斯·卡洛尔·奥茨(Joyce Carol Oates, 1938—)，简约派(Minimalist)小说家雷蒙·卡弗(Raymond Carver, 1938—1988)等。

在上述各种文学思潮占主导地位的年代中，犹太裔、非裔、印第安裔、西班牙裔、亚裔等少数族裔与流派的创作也得到了蓬勃的发展。以索尔·贝娄(Saul Bellow, 1915—2005)、伯纳德·马拉默德(Bernard Malamud, 1914—1986)、艾萨克·巴什维斯·辛格(Isaac Bashevis Singer, 1904—1991)、菲利普·罗斯(Philip Roth, 1933—)为代表的犹太裔作家脱颖而出。他们继承了犹太传统中对人的思考和对精神世界的探索，专注于再现美国社会中犹太人的生活，创造出"边缘人""受害者""傻瓜倒霉者"等新人物形象。索尔·贝娄的《摇来晃去的人》(*Dangling Man*, 1944)、《受害者》(*The Victim*, 1947)、《赫索格》(*Herzog*, 1964)，马拉默德的《呆头呆脑的人》(*The Natural*, 1952)、《店员》(*The Assistant*, 1957)、《装配工》(*The Fixer*, 1966)，艾萨克·辛格的《傻瓜吉姆佩尔》(*Gimpel the Fool*, 1957)、《冤家：一个爱情故事》(*Enemies: A Love Story*, 1970)，菲利浦·罗斯的《乳房》(*The Breast*, 1972)等作品都深刻表现了现代社会中犹太人的命运与生存状态。他们创作的侧重点有所不同，但都遵循心理现实主义的文学传统，同时又勇于创新，为战后美国文坛增加了独特的色彩。

战后的美国非裔作家继承了理查德·赖特(Richard Wright, 1908—1960)开创的批判传统，继续探讨美国非裔所面对的种族与社会问题。拉尔夫·埃里森(Ralph Ellison, 1913—1994)的小说《看不见的人》(*Invisible Man*, 1952)通过一位无名无姓的非裔青年表现了在以白人为中心的美国社会中非裔被无视的现实。詹姆斯·鲍德温(James Baldwin, 1924—1987)是战后美国非裔文坛另一位具有影响力的作家。他的小说和杂文充满激情，从宗教、性等角度来探究种族问题，风格细腻、婉转。

20世纪60年代崛起的美国非裔女作家也不容忽视。在白人占主导地位的父权社会中，非裔妇女在种族和性别方面的双重身份使她们对生活有着更加深切的感受。

她们的作品大多展示了非裔妇女追寻自我和尊严的心路历程，具有极强的感染力。托尼·莫里森、艾丽丝·沃克 (Alice Walker, 1944—) 是非裔女作家中的佼佼者。

美国印第安文学 (native American literature)、西语裔文学 (Hispanic American literature) 和亚裔文学 (Asian American literature) 的出现和兴盛是 20 世纪 60 年代以来美国文坛最令人瞩目的现象。广义的少数族裔文学史均可追溯至各族裔在美国领土上定居的伊始，因此美国印第安文学和西语裔文学的历史甚至长过美国白人文学。亚裔来到美国的时间相对较晚，大约始于 19 世纪 20 年代。由于少数族裔在美国历史上属于被压迫、被歧视、被噤声的异族，早期的文学作品很少受到主流社会的注意，甚至很少能够保留至今。随着 20 世纪 60 年代黑人民权运动的兴起，各族裔也加入了反种族歧视，争取本族裔政治、经济和文化权益的运动，他们的文学想象力和创造力迸发出前所未有的能量，形成一波波的"复兴"浪潮。各少数族裔的历史、文化和传统有所不同，使得少数族裔文学呈现出百花争芳的壮观景象，但同为"内部殖民"受害者的历史遭遇和同为少数族裔的相同身份决定了各少数族裔文学存在着诸多的共同点。简单说来，少数族裔作家均扎根于本族裔的历史和文化传统，揭露和控诉受白人欺压的屈辱史，致力于消除种族歧视、性别歧视和白人中心主义等人类社会的痼疾，同时主张在保持本族裔文化传统的前提下，着眼于现在和未来，加强跨文化交流，积极融入美国的多元文化社会。总的说来，各少数族裔文学既是本族裔历史文化的见证和载体，又是推动本族裔和美国社会变革与进步的力量。

1969 年，美国文坛迎来"美国印第安文艺复兴"(Native American Renaissance)，其标志便是基奥瓦人 N. 斯科特·莫马戴 (N.Scott Momaday, 1934—) 以长篇小说《曙光之屋》(*House Made of Dawn*, 1968) 赢得了普利策奖。继他之后，同样具有印第安血统的詹姆斯·威尔奇 (James Welch, 1940—2003)、杰拉尔德·维兹诺 (Gerald Vizenor, 1934—)、路易斯·厄德里奇 (Louise Erdrich, 1954—)、路易斯·欧文斯 (Louis Owens, 1948—2002)、莱斯利·马蒙·西尔科 (Leslie Marmon Silko, 1948—) 和舍曼·阿莱克西 (Sherman Alexie, 1966—) 都出版了可圈可点的作品，获得了主流社会的认可。其中厄德里奇的长篇小说《爱药》(*Love Medicine*, 1984) 荣获当年美国国家书评人协会奖。

西语裔文学和亚裔文学的兴盛出现在 20 世纪七八十年代。墨西哥裔作家鲁道弗·阿纳亚 (Rudolfo Anaya, 1937—2020) 的长篇小说《保佑我吧，乌尔蒂玛》(*Bless Me, Ultima*, 1972) 是第一部具有广泛影响的西语裔文学作品。古巴裔作家奥斯卡·希胡罗斯 (Oscar Hijuelos, 1951—2013) 以长篇小说《曼波舞王演奏情歌》(*The Mambo Kings Play Songs of Love*, 1989) 成为第一位获得普利策奖的西语裔作家。墨西哥裔作家桑德拉·希斯内罗丝 (Sandra Cisneros, 1954—) 的长篇小说《杧果街上的小屋》(*The

House on Mango Street, 1983) 与多米尼加裔作家朱莉娅·阿尔瓦雷斯 (Julia Alvarez, 1950—) 的长篇小说《加西亚家的姑娘们如何失去口音》(How the Garcia Girls Lost Their Accents, 1991)、古巴裔作家克里斯蒂娜·加西亚 (Cristina García, 1958—) 的长篇小说《古巴一梦》(Dreaming in Cuban, 1992) 一同引发了西语裔女作家创作的第一次浪潮。

就美国亚裔文学而言，两位华裔女作家汤亭亭和谭恩美 (Amy Tan, 1952—) 的贡献最大，影响也最广泛。汤亭亭的长篇小说《女勇士》(The Woman Warrior: Memoirs of a Girlhood among Ghosts, 1976) 赢得全国书评家协会奖 (National Book Critics Circle Award)，这部小说和谭恩美的长篇小说《喜福会》(The Joy Luck Club, 1989) 是迄今最为畅销的两部亚裔文学作品。1988 年，印裔作家卜哈拉蒂·穆克基 (Bharati Mukherjee, 1940—2017) 的短篇小说集《中间人和其他故事》(The Middleman and Other Stories) 获得全国书评家协会奖。1991 年，由华裔作家撰写的五部长篇小说——赵健秀 (Frank Chin, 1940—) 的《唐老鸭》(Donald Duck)、任璧莲 (Gish Jen, 1956—) 的《地道美国佬》(Typical American)、谭恩美的《灶神之妻》(The Kitchen God's Wife)、李健孙 (Gus Lee, 1946—) 的《中国小子》(China Boy) 和雷祖威 (David Wong Louie, 1954—2018) 的《爱的阵痛》(Pangs of Love)——几乎同时出版，美国亚裔文学迎来了前所未有的繁荣。2000 年，印裔作家朱姆帕·拉希里 (Jhumpa Lahiri, 1967—) 的短篇小说集《疾病解说者》(Interpreter of Maladies) 摘取了普利策奖。

战后的南方也同样涌现出一批才气十足的作家，如杜鲁门·卡波特 (Truman Capote, 1924—1984)、威廉·斯泰伦 (William Styron, 1925—2006) 等。他们的作品，如卡波特的《草竖琴》(The Grass Harp, 1951)、斯泰伦的《躺在黑暗中》(Lie Down in Darkness, 1951) 等带有浓重的南方色彩，并从南方独特的历史渊源中提取素材，表现了南方特殊的社会结构和精神文化实质。卡波特于 1966 年发表的非虚构性小说《冷血》(In Cold Blood, 1965) 讲述了一桩骇人听闻的犯罪事实，提出了有关美国社会、司法制度、青少年犯罪的重大问题。女作家弗兰纳里·奥康纳 (Flannery O'Connor, 1925—1964) 的《慧血》(Wise Blood, 1952)、《暴力得逞》(The Violent Bear It away, 1960)、短篇小说集《好人难寻及其他》(A Good Man Is Hard to Find and Other Stories, 1955) 等通过描写恶与残暴进一步探讨了暴力在南方的意义。

二战后的美国诗歌纷纭呈彩，不拘一格，出现了垮掉派、黑山派 (the Black Mountain)、深层意象派 (the deep image)、纽约派 (the New York School) 等诗歌流派，总的特点是更简单直接，更富情感，并夹杂着浓厚的政治色彩。罗伯特·洛威尔 (Robert Lowell, 1917—1977) 是战后美国诗人中的代表人物。他的重要诗集《生命研究》(Life Studies, 1959) 被称为洛威尔"家族的相册"，开创了"自白诗体"的先河，影响了包括女诗人西尔维亚·普拉斯(Sylvia Plath, 1932—1963)在内的一代诗人。西奥多·罗特克(Theodore Roethke, 1908—1963)和约翰·贝里曼(John Berryman, 1914—1972)同样是这一时期具有影响的诗人。他们的诗作联想丰富，语言简白，善于发掘内心情感。伊丽莎白·毕肖普(Elizabeth Bishop, 1911—1979)、理查德·威尔伯(Richard Wilbur, 1921—2017)的作品则意象清新，思维严谨，不乏幽默。黑山派诗歌的中心人物，曾任黑山大学校长的查尔斯·奥尔森(Charles Olson, 1910—1970)创作的"投影诗"(Projective Verse)注重时间和空间、人物和概念间的相互渗透，提倡消除主观和客观的区别，对美国诗歌的发展产生了重要影响。深层意象派诗人则摈弃黑山派诗人对技巧的过分崇拜，呼吁要有一种新的联想的自由，认为诗人应走出狭小的地域限制，重新在无意识的深层意象中发现现代诗歌。纽约派诗人受到非写实性、抽象派和印象派画家的启示，主张用幽默或幻想来取代意义、结构与和谐，他们往往采用自由诗行写作，语言简朴，比较口语化。进入20世纪80年代以后，诗歌的形式、内容都更加丰富多彩。2016年，瑞典皇家科学院将当年诺贝尔文学奖颁给了美国诗人、摇滚与民谣歌手鲍勃·迪伦(Bob Dylan, 1941—)，以表彰他"为伟大的美国歌曲传统带来了全新的诗意表达方式"。鲍勃·迪伦是迄今为止唯一荣获诺贝尔文学奖的美国诗人。

二战后的美国戏剧继奥尼尔和田纳西·威廉斯后迎来了第二次高峰。阿瑟·米勒(Arthur Miller, 1915—2005)的《推销员之死》(*Death of a Salesman*, 1949)通过小人物韦利·洛曼的死深刻揭露了"美国梦"的虚幻本质，引起了社会的强烈反响。这一时期另一位引人注目的剧作家是威廉·英奇(William Inge, 1913—1973)。他的剧作大多反映美国中西部普通人的生活和理想，表现出一种伤感、无奈的情绪。洛兰·汉斯贝里(Lorraine Hansberry, 1930—1965)的《日光下的葡萄干》(*A Raisin in the Sun*, 1959)是百老汇上演的第一部由非裔女作家创作的戏剧。作品生动刻画了芝加哥一个自强不息的非裔家庭，以及他们为改变自己的生活环境所做的种种努力。

20世纪50年代，一批年轻有为的导演、演员发起了"外百老汇"(Off-Broadway)运动。他们敢于创新，大胆实验，在改革戏剧形式方面做出了有益的尝试。当20世纪60年代后"外百老汇"趋于商业化时，不甘落伍的剧作家们又推出了更为激进的"外外百老汇"(Off-Off-Broadway)戏剧，把舞台搬到了酒吧、咖啡馆、写字楼，甚至公园或者街道。这些"非百老汇剧院"对五六十年代美国戏剧的复兴起了积极作用。爱德华·阿尔比(Edward Albee, 1928—2016)创作的荒诞派戏剧便是在这些地方上演的。

20世纪七八十年代，美国戏剧界又涌现了一批新人，佼佼者包括戴维·马麦特(David Mamet, 1947—)和非裔剧作家奥古斯特·威尔逊(August Wilson, 1945—

2005)。马麦特的《美国野牛》(*American Buffalo*, 1977) 以一个退伍老兵的视角表现了越南战争给人的心灵上造成的巨大创伤。威尔逊的《乔·特纳来了又走了》(*Joe Turner's Come and Gone*, 1988)、《钢琴课》(*The Piano Lesson*, 1990) 等则成功地表现了 20 世纪各个时期美国非裔的经历。勒鲁瓦·琼斯 (LeRoi Jones, 1934—2014) 是另一位颇具影响力的非裔剧作家。他的《荷兰人》(*Dutchman*, 1964)、《奴隶》(*The Slave Ship*, 1967) 等作品反映了黑人与白人的对立与冲突。后来他改名为阿米里·巴拉卡 (Amiri Baraka)，以示与白人文化的决裂。除非裔戏剧外，其他少数族裔的剧作家也力图反映各自民族在美国的经历。华裔剧作家戴维·亨利·黄 (David Henry Hwang, 1957—) 在《新上岸的人》(*FOB*, 1979) 中描写了第二代移民与新移民之间的冲突 (剧名 "FOB" 是 Fresh off the Boat 的缩写，指新来的移民)，他的另一部作品《蝴蝶君》(*Mr. Butterfly*, 1988) 则揭示了中西方文化的巨大差异。

　　进入 21 世纪后，美国作家也越来越关注影响社会的各种问题，热点话题包括宗教、科技、性别与种族身份、经济发展、家庭暴力、地区主义、生态环境、恐怖主义等。美国世纪初的文学创作呈现出一个较为繁荣的局面，尤其是突出了原先被边缘化、被湮没了的作家和作品的声音。一些美国少数族裔新作家也开始崭露头角，如华裔的哈金 (Ha Jin, 1956—)、古巴裔的克里斯蒂娜·加西亚等，他们用英语写作，讲述自己在文化认同、文化同化中所经历的困难体验。在他们的作品中，美国只是背景，母国或母国的政治气候才是一个重要的叙事成分，如加西亚的《古巴一梦》、哈金的《等待》(*Waiting*, 1999)、《战争垃圾》(*War Trash*, 2004) 等。

　　新世纪的美国饱受所谓 "世纪末疾病" 的困扰——枪支泛滥、言论监视、种族歧视、堕胎权利、艾滋病危机等问题为美国作家的创作提供了丰富的题材。一些作家关注的方面超越了阶级、性别和民族界限，表现贫困与问题人群的体验。如乔纳森·拉森 (Jonathan Larson, 1960—1996) 的剧作《吉屋出租》(*Rent*, 1996)、小说家布莱特·埃利斯 (Bret Easton Ellis, 1964—) 的《美国精神病人》(*American Psycho*, 1991)、艾丽丝·霍弗曼 (Alice Hoffman, 1952—) 的《冒险》(*At Risk*, 1988)、都因涉及较为敏感的社会话题而引发争议。

　　随着人类居住的环境日益恶化，生态问题自然成为许多美国作家关注的重要内容。越来越多的作家开始以生态为主题进行创作，推动了生态文学 (eco-literature) 的发展。蕾切尔·卡森 (Rachel Carson, 1907—1964) 的《寂静的春天》(*Silent Spring*, 1962) 反映了杀虫剂对环境造成的污染，希望以此唤醒公众的环保意识。1975 年的普利策文学奖得主安妮·迪拉德 (Annie Dillard, 1945—) 在她的《汀克河上的朝圣者》(*Pilgrim at Tinker Creek*, 1974) 中启迪人们学会真正欣赏自然。同年获普利策奖的加利·施奈德 (Gary Snyder, 1930—) 的诗集《龟岛》(*Turtle Island*, 1975) 也很好地表现了生态主题。生态文学的蓬勃发展自然引起了许多文学批评家的注意，催生了生态批评 (eco-criticism) 理论。彻丽尔·格洛特菲尔蒂 (Cheryll Gloffelty) 和哈罗德·弗洛姆 (Harold Fromm) 合作出版的《生态批评读本：文学生态学的里程碑》(*The Ecocriticism Reader:Landmarks in Literary Ecology*, 1996) 被看作是了解生态文学评论的启蒙读物。

作者简介

阿瑟·米勒出生于纽约曼哈顿一个中产阶级犹太家庭。他父亲在 1929 年的大萧条中破产，之后举家迁至布鲁克林。和他《两个星期一的回忆》(*A Memory of Two Mondays*, 1955) 中的主人公伯特一样，米勒省吃俭用，在汽车配件仓库打工，在攒够学费后于 1934 年进入密歇根大学读书。大学期间米勒开始了戏剧创作。他受挪威剧作家亨利克·易卜生 (Henrik Ibsen, 1828—1906) 的影响较大，曾于 1950 年改编过后者的《人民公敌》(*An Enemy of the People*, 1882)。在他漫长的戏剧创作生涯中，米勒始终关注个人与社会的关系，注重作品的道德意义。他的戏剧经常涉及社会道德、个人良心、负疚感、责任感等，其主要剧作中反复出现的主题是父子关系与兄弟关系。

米勒第一部在百老汇上演的戏剧是《鸿运高照的人》(*The Man Who Had All the Luck*, 1944)。该剧只上演了四场。《全是我的儿子》(*All My Sons*, 1947) 是米勒第一部影响较大的戏剧，获得了纽约戏剧评论家协会奖。这部戏剧与易卜生的一些社会问题剧很相似：过去某件事的逐步曝光使剧中主要人物不得不重新审视自己的价值观和道德观。父子关系是这部戏剧的主题。它对实用主义与理想主义、自私自利与博爱思想、犯罪与赎罪等问题的探讨具有很强的普遍意义。1949 年，米勒的代表作《推销员之死》的问世奠定了他在美国戏剧史上的地位，它与奥尼尔的《进入黑夜的漫长旅程》和威廉斯的《欲望号街车》(*A Streetcar Named Desire*, 1948) 并称为美国最杰出的三部戏剧，曾获得纽约戏剧评论家协会奖和普利策奖。米勒的另一部重要剧作《严峻的考验》(*The Crucible*, 1953) 在一定程度上利用 1692 年的塞勒姆"逐巫案"讽喻了 20 世纪 50 年代初疯狂、恐怖的麦卡锡主义。独幕剧《两个星期一的回忆》自传性较强。《桥头眺望》(*A View from the Bridge*, 1956) 则带有强烈的古希腊悲剧色彩，主人公埃迪潜意识中对侄女的情欲像不可抗拒的命运一样将他推向毁灭。埃迪强烈的自尊心、复杂的内心斗争使人们意识到米勒不仅关注社会问题，而且也像奥尼尔和威廉斯一样注重人物的精神世界。

1964 年上演的两部戏剧《堕落之后》(*After the Fall*) 和《维希事件》(*Incident at Vichy*) 都侧重于个人的内心经历。《堕落之后》是一出表现主义戏剧。评论家对这出戏提及较多的是它的自传性。《代价》(The Price, 1968) 又回到了米勒一贯关心的父子和兄弟关系。米勒创作的其他戏剧包括《创造世界及其他》(The Creation of the World and Other Business, 1972)、《主教的天花板》(The Archbishop's Ceiling, 1977)、《美国时钟》(The American Clock, 1980)、《给一位夫人的挽歌》(Elegy for a Lady, 1982)、《也算爱情故事》(Some Kind of Love Story, 1982)、《我什么也不记得》(I Can't Remember Anything, 1987) 和《克拉拉》(Clara, 1987)。

米勒影响较大的作品都创作于 20 世纪 40 年代至 50 年代。通过他的作品《推销员之死》和《严峻的考验》等，许多人对美国文化有了更深的了解。

Death of a Salesman

【题解】

《推销员之死》描写了小人物威利·洛曼的渴望和自我毁灭，并由此抨击了重表象不重实质、以金钱为尺度、诱使人们不择手段去出人头地的"美国梦"。

年过六十的威利做了几十年的推销员，已明显力不从心。他想换个轻松点的工作，却被老板解雇了。事业上的不如意、家庭经济的压力、与儿子的矛盾等多种因素使他神志恍惚，精神已处于崩溃的边缘。他经常自言自语，出现幻觉，与哥哥本的亡魂对话。其实威利一生都生活在幻想中。在他看来，一个人如果外表潇洒，颇具魅力，就准会成功，成为一个响当当的人物。他不仅以此为自己的行为准则，而且还把这种思想灌输到两个儿子身上。长子比弗三十多岁还是一事无成，浑浑噩噩。另一个儿子则是威利的翻版，盲目自大。威利意识不到这两个儿子的失败实际上是他的教育方式与价值观的失败，反而认为如果他用自己的生命为他们换得 20 万美元的保险作为启动基金，他们就一定能成功。他的可悲之处在于他至死仍执迷不悟。

父子关系在这出戏中占有很重要的位置。多年来父子之间的冲突与爱矛盾地交织在一起。比弗后来终于摆脱了父亲的部分价值观，发现金钱并非一切，自己爱的是大自然和诚实的劳动。虽然比弗的自我认识和价值观无法唤醒沉醉在"美国梦"里的威利，但让威利认识到儿子是爱他的。可是具有讽刺意味的是，这一认识加速了威利的死亡。

《推销员之死》是一部现实主义与表现主义手法完美结合的作品。音乐、灯光、和周围高大的建筑物烘托了全剧的气氛。不仅如此，当威利沉浸于幻觉中时，人物便不再受固定布景的限制，可以随意穿过透明墙。这种技巧在当时引起很大反响。《推销员之死》是一部小人物的悲剧。在它上演两周之后，米勒在《纽约时报》撰写了《悲剧与普通人》一文，提出普通人与帝王一样，都可以成为悲剧的主角。他提出："当我们看到一个人物为了争取一件东西——人的尊严——而不惜牺牲自己的生命时，悲剧感便在我们心中油然而生。"米勒的这种理论在当时的评论界曾引起激烈争论。以下段落选自《推销员之死》第一幕。

From Death of a Salesman

(Act One)

(*A melody is heard, played upon a flute. It is small and fine, telling of grass and trees and the horizon. The curtain rises.*)

*Before us is the **SALESMAN'S** house. We are aware of towering, angular shapes behind it, surrounding it on all sides. Only the blue light of the sky falls upon the house and forestage; the surrounding area shows an angry[1] glow of orange. As more light appears, we see a solid vault of apartment houses around the small, fragile-seeming home. An air of the dream clings to the place, a dream rising out of reality. The kitchen at center seems actual enough, for there is a kitchen table with three chairs, and a refrigerator. But no other fixtures are seen. At the back of the kitchen there is a draped entrance, which leads to the living-room. To the right of the kitchen, on a level raised two feet, is a bedroom furnished only with a brass bedstead and a straight chair. On a shelf over the bed a silver athletic trophy stands. A window opens onto the apartment house at the side.*

Behind the kitchen, on a level raised six and a half feet, is the boys' bedroom, at present barely visible. Two beds are dimly seen, and at the back of the room a dormer window[2]. (This bedroom is above the unseen living-room.) At the left a stairway curves up to it from the kitchen.

The entire setting is wholly or, in some places, partially transparent. The roof-line of the house is one-dimensional; under and over it we see the apartment buildings. Before the house lies an apron[3], curving beyond the forestage into the orchestra[4]. This forward area serves as the back yard as well as the locale of all Willy's imaginings and of his city scenes. Whenever the action is in the present the actors observe the imaginary wall-lines, entering the house only through its door at the left. But in the scenes of the past these boundaries are broken, and characters enter or leave a room by stepping "through" a wall on to the forestage.

[*From the right, Willy Loman, the Salesman, enters, carrying two large sample cases. The flute plays on. He hears but is not aware of it. He is past sixty years of age, dressed quietly[5]. Even as he crosses the stage to the doorway of the house, his exhaustion is apparent. He unlocks the door, comes into the kitchen, and thankfully lets his burden down, feeling the soreness of his palms. A word-sigh escapes his lips—it might be "Oh, boy, oh, boy." He closes the door, then carries his cases out into the living-room, through the draped kitchen doorway.*

Linda, his wife, has stirred in her bed at the right. She gets out and puts on a robe, listening. Most often jovial, she has developed an iron repression of her exceptions[6] to Willy's behavior—she more than loves him, she admires him, as though his mercurial nature, his temper, his massive dreams and little cruelties, served her only as sharp reminders of the turbulent longings within him, longings which she shares but lacks the temperament to utter and follow to their end.]

LINDA [*hearing Willy outside the bedroom, calls with some trepidation*] : Willy!

WILLY: It's all right. I came back.

LINDA: Why? What happened? [*Slight pause.*] Did something happen, Willy?

WILLY: No, nothing happened.

LINDA: You didn't smash the car, did you?

WILLY [*with casual irritation*] : I said nothing happened. Didn't you hear me?

LINDA: Don't you feel well?

WILLY: I'm tired to the death. [*The flute has faded away. He sits on the bed beside her, a little numb.*] I couldn't make it. I just couldn't make it, Linda.

LINDA [*very carefully, delicately*] : Where were you all day? You look terrible.

WILLY: I got as far as a little above Yonkers. I stopped for a cup of coffee. Maybe it was the coffee.

LINDA: What?

WILLY [*after a pause*] : I suddenly couldn't drive any more. The car kept going off onto the shoulder[7], y'know[8]?

LINDA [*helpfully*] : Oh. Maybe it was the steering again. I don't think Angelo[9] knows the Studebaker[10].

WILLY: No, it's me, it's me. Suddenly I realize I'm goin' sixty miles an hour and I don't remember the last five minutes. I'm—I can't seem to—keep my mind to it.

LINDA: Maybe it's your glasses. You never went for your new glasses.

WILLY: No, I see everything. I came back ten miles an hour. It took me nearly four hours from Yonkers.

LINDA [*resigned*]: Well, you'll just have to take a rest, Willy, you can't continue this way.

WILLY: I just got back from Florida.

LINDA: But you didn't rest your mind. Your mind is overactive, and the mind is what counts, dear.

WILLY: I'll start out in the morning. Maybe I'll feel better in the morning. [*She is taking off his shoes.*] These goddam arch supports are killing me.

LINDA: Take an aspirin. Should I get you an aspirin? It'll soothe you.

WILLY [*with wonder*]: I was driving along, you understand? And I was fine. I was even observing the scenery. You can imagine, me looking at scenery, on the road every week of my life. But it's so beautiful up there, Linda, the trees are so thick, and the sun is warm. I opened the windshield and just let the warm air bathe over me. And then all of a sudden I'm goin' off the road! I'm tellin' ya, I absolutely forgot I was driving. If I'd've gone the other way over the white line I might've killed somebody. So I went on again—and five minutes later I'm dreamin' again, and I nearly—[*He presses two fingers against his eyes.*] I have such thoughts, I have such strange thoughts.

LINDA: Willy, dear. Talk to them again. There's no reason why you can't work in New York.

WILLY: They don't need me in New York. I'm the New England man. I'm vital in New England.

LINDA: But you're sixty years old. They can't expect you to keep traveling every week.

WILLY: I'll have to send a wire to Portland. I'm supposed to see Brown and Morrison tomorrow morning at ten o'clock to show the line[11]. Goddammit, I could sell them! [*He starts putting on his jacket.*]

LINDA [*taking the jacket from him*]: Why don't you go down to the place tomorrow and tell Howard[12] you've simply got to work in New York? You're too accommodating, dear.

WILLY: If old man Wagner was alive I'd a been in charge of New York now! That man was a prince, he was a masterful man. But that boy of his, that Howard, he don't appreciate. When I went north the first time, the Wagner Company didn't know where New England was!

LINDA: Why don't you tell those things to Howard, dear?

WILLY [*encouraged*]: I will, I definitely will. Is there any cheese?

LINDA: I'll make you a sandwich.

WILLY: No, go to sleep. I'll take some milk. I'll be up right away. The boys in?

LINDA: They're sleeping. Happy took Biff on a date tonight.

WILLY [*interested*]: That so?

LINDA: It was so nice to see them shaving together, one behind the other, in the bathroom. And going out together. You notice? The whole house smells of shaving lotion.

WILLY: Figure it out. Work a lifetime to pay off a house. You finally own it, and there's nobody to live in it.

LINDA: Well, dear, life is casting off. It's always that way.

WILLY: No, no, some people—some people accomplish something. Did Biff say anything after I went this morning?

LINDA: You shouldn't have criticized him, Willy, especially after he just got off the train. You mustn't lose your temper with him.

WILLY: When the hell did I lose my temper? I simply asked him if he was making any money. Is that a criticism?

LINDA: But, dear, how could he make any money?

WILLY [*worried and angered*]: There's such an undercurrent in him. He became a moody man. Did he apologize when I left this morning?

LINDA: He was crestfallen, Willy. You know how he admires you. I think if he finds himself[13], then you'll both be happier and not fight any more.

WILLY: How can he find himself on a farm? Is that a life? A farmhand? In the beginning, when he was young, I thought, well, a young man, it's good for him to tramp around, take a lot of different jobs. But it's more than ten years now and he has yet to make thirty-five dollars a week!

LINDA: He's finding himself, Willy.

WILLY: Not finding yourself at the age thirty-four is a disgrace!

LINDA: Shh!

WILLY: The trouble is he's lazy, goddammit!

LINDA: Willy, please!

WILLY: Biff's a lazy bum!

LINDA: They're sleeping. Get something to eat. Go on down.

WILLY: Why did he come home? I would like to know what brought him home.

LINDA: I don't know. I think he's still lost[14], Willy. I think he's very lost.

WILLY: Biff Loman is lost. In the greatest country in the world a young man with such—personal attractiveness, gets lost. And such a hard worker. There's one thing about Biff—he's not lazy.

LINDA: Never.

WILLY [*with pity and resolve*]: I'll see him in the morning; I'll have a nice talk with him. I'll get him a job selling. He could be big[15] in no time. My God! Remember how they used to follow him around in high school? When he smiled at one of them their faces lit up. When he walked down the street . . . [*He loses himself in reminiscence.*]

LINDA [*trying to bring him out of it*]: Willy, dear, I got a new kind of American-type cheese today. It's whipped.

WILLY: Why do you get American when I like Swiss?

LINDA: I just thought you'd like a change—

WILLY: I don't want a change! I want Swiss cheese. Why am I always being contradicted?

LINDA [*with a covering cough*]: I thought it would be a surprise.

WILLY: Why don't you open a window in here, for God's sake?

LINDA [*with indefinite patience*]: They're all open, dear.

WILLY: The way they boxed us in here. Bricks and windows, windows and bricks.

LINDA: We should've bought the land next door.

WILLY: The street is lined with cars. There's not a breath of fresh air in the neighborhood. The grass don't grow any more, you can't raise a carrot in the back yard. They should've had a law against apartment houses. Remember those two beautiful elm trees out there? When I and Biff hung the swing between them?

LINDA: Yeah, like being a million miles from the city.

WILLY: They should've arrested the builder for cutting those down. They massacred the neighborhood. [*Lost.*] More and more I think of those days, Linda. This time of year it was lilac and wisteria. And then the peonies would come out, and the daffodils. What a fragrance in this room!

LINDA: Well, after all, people had to move somewhere.

WILLY: No, there's more people now.

LINDA: I don't think there's more people. I think—

WILLY: There's more people! That's what's ruining this country! Population is getting out of control. The competition is maddening! Smell the stink from that apartment house! And another one on the other side . . . How can they whip cheese?

[*On Willy's last line, Biff and Happy raise themselves up in their beds, listening.*]

LINDA: Go down, try it. And be quiet.

WILLY [*turning to Linda, guiltily*]: You're not worried about me, are you, sweetheart?

BIFF: What's the matter?

HAPPY: Listen!

LINDA: You've got too much on the ball[16] to worry about.

WILLY: You're my foundation and my support, Linda.

LINDA: Just try to relax, dear. You make mountains out of molehills.

WILLY: I won't fight with him any more. If he wants to go back to Texas, let him go.

LINDA: He'll find his way.

WILLY: Sure. Certain men just don't get started till later in life. Like Thomas Edison, I think. Or B. F. Goodrich. One of them was deaf. [*He starts for the bedroom doorway.*] I'll put my money on Biff.

LINDA: And Willy—if it's warm Sunday we'll drive in the country. And we'll open the windshield, and take lunch.

WILLY: No, the windshields don't open on the new cars.

LINDA: But you opened it today.

WILLY: Me? I didn't. [*He stops.*] Now isn't that peculiar! Isn't that a remarkable— [*He breaks off in amazement and fright as the flute is heard distantly.*]

LINDA: What, darling?

WILLY: That is the most remarkable thing.

LINDA: What, dear?

WILLY: I was thinking of the Chevvy[17]. [*Slight pause.*] Nineteen twenty-eight . . . when I had that red Chevvy— [*Breaks off.*] That funny? I coulda sworn I was driving that Chevvy today.

LINDA: Well, that's nothing. Something must've reminded you.

WILLY: Remarkable. Ts. Remember those days? The way Biff used to simonize that car? The dealer refused to believe there was eighty thousand miles on it. [*He shakes his head.*] Heh! [*To Linda.*] Close your eyes, I'll be right up. [*He walks out of the bedroom.*]

HAPPY [*to Biff*]: Jesus, maybe he smashed up the car again!

LINDA [*calling after Willy*]: Be careful on the stairs, dear! The cheese is on the middle shelf! [*She turns, goes over to the bed, takes his jacket, and goes out of the bedroom.*]

[*Light has risen on the boys' room. Unseen, Willy is heard talking to himself, "Eighty thousand miles," and a little laugh. Biff gets out of bed, comes downstage a bit, and stands attentively. Biff is two years older than his brother Happy, well built, but in these days bears a worn air and seems less self-assured. He has succeeded less, and his dreams are stronger and less acceptable than Happy's. Happy is tall, powerfully made. Sexuality is like a visible color on him, or a scent that many women have discovered. He, like his brother, is lost, but in a different way, for he has never allowed himself to turn his face toward defeat and is thus more confused and hard-skinned, although seemingly more content.*]

HAPPY [*getting out of bed*]: He's going to get his license taken away if he keeps that up. I'm getting nervous about him, y'know, Biff?

BIFF: His eyes are going.

HAPPY: No, I've driven with him. He sees all right. He just doesn't keep his mind on it. I drove into the city with him last week. He stops at a green light and then it turns red and he goes. [*He laughs.*]

BIFF: Maybe he's color-blind.

HAPPY: Pop? Why he's got the finest eye for color in the business. You know that.

BIFF [*sitting down on his bed*]: I'm going to sleep.

HAPPY: You're not still sour on Dad, are you, Biff?

BIFF: He's all right, I guess.

WILLY [*underneath them, in the living-room*]: Yes, sir, eighty thousand miles—eighty-two thousand!

BIFF: You smoking?

HAPPY [*holding out a pack of cigarettes*]: Want one?

BIFF [*taking a cigarette*]: I can never sleep when I smell it.

WILLY: What a simonizing job, heh!

HAPPY [*with deep sentiment*]: Funny, Biff, y'know? Us sleeping in here again? The old beds. [*He pats his bed affectionately.*] All the talk that went across those two beds, huh? Our whole lives.

BIFF: Yeah. Lotta dreams and plans.

HAPPY [*with a deep and masculine laugh*] : About five hundred women would like to know what was said in this room.

[*They share a soft laugh.*]

BIFF: Remember that big Betsy something—what the hell was her name—over on Bushwick Avenue?

HAPPY [*combing his hair*] : With the collie dog!

BIFF: That's the one. I got you in there, remember?

HAPPY: Yeah, that was my first time—I think. Boy, there was a pig! [*They laugh, almost crudely.*] You taught me everything I know about women. Don't forget that.

BIFF: I bet you forgot how bashful you used to be. Especially with girls.

HAPPY: Oh, I still am, Biff.

BIFF: Oh, go on.

HAPPY: I just control it, that's all. I think I got less bashful and you got more so. What happened, Biff? Where's the old humor, the old confidence? [*He shakes Biff's knee. Biff gets up and moves restlessly about the room.*] What's the matter?

BIFF: Why does Dad mock me all the time?

HAPPY: He's not mocking you, he—

BIFF: Everything I say there is a twist of mockery on his face. I can't get near him.

HAPPY: He just wants you to make good, that's all. I wanted to talk to you about Dad for a long time, Biff. Something's—happening to him. He—talks to himself.

BIFF: I noticed that this morning. But he always mumbled.

HAPPY: But not so noticeable. It got so embarrassing I sent him to Florida. And you know something? Most of the time he's talking to you.

BIFF: What's he say about me?

HAPPY: I can't make it out.

BIFF: What's he say about me?

HAPPY: I think the fact that you're not settled, that you're still kind of up in the air . . .

BIFF: There's one or two other things depressing him, Happy.

HAPPY: What do you mean?

BIFF: Never mind. Just don't lay it all on me.

HAPPY: But I think if you just got started—I mean—is there any future for you out there?

BIFF: I tell ya, Hap, I don't know what the future is. I don't know—what I'm supposed to want.

HAPPY: What do you mean?

BIFF: Well, I spent six or seven years after high school trying to work myself up. Shipping clerk, salesman, business of one kind or another. And it's a measly manner of existence. To get on that subway on the hot mornings in summer. To devote your whole life to keeping stock, or making phone calls, or selling or buying. To suffer fifty weeks of the year for the sake of a two-week vacation, when all you really desire is to be outdoors, with your shirt off. And always to have to get ahead of the next fella. And still—that's how you build a future.

HAPPY: Well, you really enjoy it on a farm? Are you content out there?

BIFF [*with rising agitation*]: Hap, I've had twenty or thirty different kinds of jobs since I left home before the war, and it always turns out the same. I just realized it lately. In Nebraska when I herded cattle, and the Dakotas, and Arizona, and now in Texas. It's why I came home now, I guess, because I realized it. This farm I work on, it's spring there now, see? And they've got about fifteen new colts. There's nothing more inspiring or—beautiful than the sight of a mare and a new colt. And it's cool there now, see? Texas is cool now, and it's spring. And whenever spring comes to where I am, I suddenly get the feeling, my God, I'm not getting anywhere! What the hell am I doing, playing around with horses, twenty-eight dollars a week! I'm thirty-four years old, I oughta be makin' my future. That's when I come running home. And now, I get here, and I don't know what to do with myself. [*After a pause.*] I've always made a point of not wasting my life, and every time I come back here I know that all I've done is to waste my life.

HAPPY: You're a poet, you know that, Biff? You're a—you're an idealist!

BIFF: No, I'm mixed up very bad. Maybe I oughta get married. Maybe I oughta get stuck into something. Maybe that's my trouble. I'm like a boy. I'm not married, I'm not in business, I just—I'm like a boy. Are you content, Hap? You're a success, aren't you? Are you content?

HAPPY: Hell, no!

BIFF: Why? You're making money, aren't you?

HAPPY [*moving about with energy, expressiveness*]: All I can do now is wait for the merchandise manager to die. And suppose I get to be merchandise manager? He's a good friend of mine, and he just built a terrific estate on Long Island. And he lived there about two months and sold it, and now he's building another one. He can't enjoy it once it's finished. And I know that's just what I would do. I don't know what the hell I'm workin' for. Sometimes I sit in my apartment—all alone. And I think of the rent I'm paying. And it's crazy. But then, it's what I always wanted. My own apartment, a car, and plenty of women. And still, goddammit, I'm lonely.

BIFF [*with enthusiasm*]: Listen, why don't you come out West with me?

HAPPY: You and I, heh?

BIFF: Sure, maybe we could buy a ranch. Raise cattle, use our muscles. Men built like we are should be working out in the open.

HAPPY [*avidly*]: The Loman Brothers, heh?

BIFF [*with vast affection*]: Sure, we'd be known all over the counties!

HAPPY [*enthralled*): That's what I dream about, Biff. Sometimes I want to just rip my clothes off in the middle of the store and outbox that goddam merchandise manager. I mean I can outbox, outrun, and outlift anybody in that store, and I have to take orders from those common, petty sons-of-bitches till I can't stand it any more.

BIFF: I'm tellin' you, kid, if you were with me I'd be happy out there.

HAPPY [*enthused*]: See, Biff, everybody around me is so false that I'm constantly lowering my ideals . . .

BIFF: Baby, together we'd stand up for one another, we'd have someone to trust.

HAPPY: If I were around you—

BIFF: Hap, the trouble is we weren't brought up to grub for money. I don't know how to do it.

HAPPY: Neither can I!

BIFF: Then let's go!

HAPPY: The only thing is—what can you make out there?

BIFF: But look at your friend. Builds an estate and then hasn't the peace of mind to live in it.

HAPPY: Yeah, but when he walks into the store the waves part in front of him. That's fifty-two thousand dollars a year coming through the revolving door, and I got more in my pinky finger than he's got in his head.

BIFF: Yeah, but you just said—

HAPPY: I gotta show some of those pompous, self-important executives over there that Hap Loman can make the grade. I want to walk into the store the way he walks in. Then I'll go with you, Biff. We'll be together yet, I swear. But take those two we had tonight. Now weren't they gorgeous creatures?

BIFF: Yeah, yeah, most gorgeous I've had in years.

HAPPY: I get that any time I want, Biff. Whenever I feel disgusted. The only trouble is, it gets like bowling or something. I just keep knockin' them over and it doesn't mean anything. You still run around a lot?

BIFF: Naa. I'd like to find a girl—steady, somebody with substance.

HAPPY: That's what I long for.

BIFF: Go on! You'd never come home.

HAPPY: I would! Somebody with character, with resistance! Like Mom, y'know? You're gonna call me a bastard when I tell you this. That girl Charlotte I was with tonight is engaged to be married in five weeks. [*He tries on his new hat.*]

BIFF: No kiddin'!

HAPPY: Sure, the guy's in line for the vice-presidency of the store. I don't know what gets into me, maybe I just have an overdeveloped sense of competition or something, but I went and ruined her, and furthermore I can't get rid of her. And he's the third executive I've done that to. Isn't that a crummy characteristic? And to top it all, I go to their weddings! [*Indignantly, but laughing*] Like I'm not supposed to take bribes. Manufacturers offer me a hundred-dollar bill now and then to throw an order their way. You know how honest I am, but it's like this girl, see. I hate myself for it. Because I don't want the girl, and still, I take it and—I love it!

BIFF: Let's go to sleep.

HAPPY: I guess we didn't settle anything, heh?

BIFF: I just got one idea that I think I'm going to try.

HAPPY: What's that?

BIFF: Remember Bill Oliver?

HAPPY: Sure, Oliver is very big now. You want to work for him again?

BIFF: No, but when I quit he said something to me. He put his arm on my shoulder, and he said, "Biff, if you ever need anything, come to me."

HAPPY: I remember that. That sounds good.

BIFF: I think I'll go to see him. If I could get ten thousand or even seven or eight thousand dollars I could buy a beautiful ranch.

HAPPY: I bet he'd back you. 'Cause he thought highly of you, Biff. I mean, they all do. You're well liked, Biff. That's why I say to come back here, and we both have the apartment. And I'm tellin' you, Biff, any babe you want . . .

BIFF: No, with a ranch I could do the work I like and still be something. I just wonder though. I wonder if Oliver still thinks I stole that carton of basketball.

HAPPY: Oh, he probably forgot that long ago. It's almost ten years. You're too sensitive. Anyway, he didn't really fire you.

BIFF: Well, I think he was going to. I think that's why I quit. I was never sure whether he knew or not. I know he thought the world of me, though. I was the only one he'd let lock up the place.

WILLY [below]: You gonna wash the engine, Biff?

HAPPY: Shh!

[Biff looks at Happy, who is gazing down, listening. Willy is mumbling in the parlor.]

HAPPY: You hear that?

[They listen. Willy laughs warmly.]

BIFF [growing angry]: Doesn't he know Mom can hear that?

Willy: Don't get your sweater dirty, Biff!

[A look of pain crosses Biff's face.]

HAPPY: Isn't that terrible? Don't leave again, will you? You'll find a job here. You gotta stick around. I don't know what to do about him, it's getting embarrassing.

WILLY: What a simonizing job!

BIFF: Mom's hearing that!

WILLY: No kiddin', Biff, you got a date? Wonderful!

HAPPY: Go on to sleep. But talk to him in the morning, will you?

BIFF [reluctantly getting into bed]: With her in the house. Brother!

HAPPY [getting into bed]: I wish you'd have a good talk with him.

[The light on their room begins to fade.]

BIFF [to himself in bed]: That selfish, stupid . . .

HAPPY: Sh . . . Sleep, Biff.

【注解】

1. angry: (指颜色) 浓烈的。

2. dormer window: 天窗，老虎窗。

3. apron: 舞台幕布前的部分，台口。

4. orchestra: 乐池。

5. quietly:（衣服）素净的，不张扬的。

6. exceptions: 不满，生气。

7. shoulder: 路肩，(车行道两侧的)紧急停车道。

8. y'know: 为了模仿推销员父子的生活语言，剧中有一些单词的拼写和一些句子的语法并不规范，除了"y'know"外，还有所有动词的进行时等。

9. Angelo: 一位机械修理工。

10. Studebaker: 主人公目前使用的汽车。

11. line:（货物的）类，种。

12. Howard: 推销公司现在的老板，他父亲 Wagner 是公司以前的老板。

13. if he finds himself: 如果他找到自己在生活中合适的位置。

14. lost: 迷茫的。

15. big: 出人头地的，成功的。

16. on the ball: 通常为固定短语，原意为机警的、机灵的，但在这里指脑子里。

17. Chevvy: 主人公以前使用过的汽车。

【思考题】

1. Does the situation of the Salesman's house have any relationship to his state of mind?
2. What kind of mood is suggested by the melody? Does it in any way reveal the aspirations of the characters?
3. What is Willy Loman's present situation? Is he still a very efficient salesman?
4. Describe the relationship among the family members. Do you think they love each other?
5. Do you think that Biff's memory of what happens before he leaves Bill Oliver is very exact? What leads to his departure?
6. How would you comment on Wily Loman's belief that the important thing in life is to be well-liked? What seem to be the answer(s) indicated by the play as to the important thing(s) in life?

解读举例

1. 这是一出普通人的悲剧。普通人与帝王将相一样有权利成为悲剧的主角。在当今时代，人们更应该探索普通人的感情和思想。

2. 这是一出社会问题剧，而不是一出传统意义上的悲剧，因为主人公形象不够高大，而且他始终没有像古典悲剧中的主人公那样对自己的处境和生活意义有一个清醒的认识。

3. 这是一出揭示"美国梦"对普通人的毒害的悲剧。在这出戏剧中，米勒借助象征主义和表现主义的手法，揭示了"美国梦"对洛曼一家的毒害。

4. 这是一出反映资本主义社会中普通工人命运的戏剧。当他们为资本家工作了一辈子后，他们得到的报偿却是无情的解雇。

J. D. Salinger
1919—2010

J. D. 塞林格生于纽约曼哈顿的一个中产阶级家庭。父亲是犹太人，母亲则有着苏格兰和爱尔兰血统。15 岁时，塞林格被父母送到宾夕法尼亚州的福谷学校学习。这里实际上是《麦田里的守望者》(*The Catcher in the Rye*, 1951) 中潘西中学的原型。在此期间，他开始为一家文学杂志撰稿，并萌生了成为作家的愿望。1940 年，塞林格在《故事》杂志上发表处女作《年轻人》(*The Young Folks*)。这个故事已包含了贯穿塞林格作品的一个重要主题，即纯真的年轻人如何面对成人社会中无处不在的虚伪和欺诈。1941 至 1948 年间，塞林格先后发表了近 20 篇短篇小说，初步展露了他的写作才华，受到评论界的广泛好评。其中，在《麦迪逊街边的小叛逆》(*Slight Rebellion off Madison*, 1946) 里首次出现了《麦田里的守望者》主人公的名字"霍尔顿"。此后，塞林格又写过几篇以霍尔顿为主人公的故事。这些故事后来经过改编，都成为《麦田里的守望者》的一部分。

1951 年，塞林格发表了让他一举成名的作品《麦田里的守望者》。小说很快在中学生和大学生群体中流传开来，并在近一年的时间内被《纽约时报书评》评为最畅销的书，但评论界在 1956 年左右才开始对这部作品作严肃的评论。此后的五六年里，大量评论文章如潮涌出，甚至出现被称为"塞林格工业"的现象。

之后，塞林格逐渐对东方宗教产生了浓厚的兴趣，并在 1953 年发表的短篇小说集《九个故事》(*Nine Stories*) 中表现出来。该故事集不再像《麦田里的守望者》

那样反映人类应如何接受现实的问题，而是探索人类对这个世界的超越，具有一定的宗教意义。

1953年初，塞林格离开纽约，到新罕布什尔州的乡下定居。虽然他一直坚持写作，但与外界的接触却越来越少。此后，他又发表了五篇关于格拉斯家庭的故事，1961年以《弗兰妮和卓埃》为名结集出版。1963年，他又发表了另一部故事集《木匠们，升高屋梁；西蒙尔简介》(*Raise High the Roof Beam, Carpenters; and Seymour: An Introduction*)。1965年发表了另一篇短篇小说《海普渥斯16，1924》("Hapworth 16" 1924) 后，塞林格再来创作新的作品。

塞林格作品的主人公多为青少年，他擅长抓住一代人的精神，反映战后青少年对成人社会的怀疑和失望。在塞林格之前，有关青少年的小说大多反映中产阶级的道德观和价值观。《麦田里的守望者》则在挑战传统上达到了一个新的高峰。小说通过主人公霍尔顿的苦闷、彷徨和孤独感，刻画了传统中产社会的伪善道德、尔虞我诈，展现了繁荣社会下蕴藏的精神危机。这一主题与20世纪50年代的垮掉派运动和20世纪60年代的反文化运动的精神相契合，故而得到广大读者，尤其是青少年读者的共鸣。

塞林格经常采用第一人称的叙述和内心独白，敏锐地捕捉方言和富有个性的发音。他在作品中用斜体、重音、缩音、增音等手法将特别的发音准确地模仿出来。同时，他大量使用20世纪50年代青少年的俚语，既生动刻画了青少年语言的特点，也彰显了人物的性格特征，充分展现时代的变迁和对传统价值的挑战。另外，他对流畅、自然的对话也有极强的驾驭能力。塞林格虽然不是一位多产的作家，但一部《麦田里的守望者》足以奠定他在美国文坛乃至在世界文坛上的地位。

The Catcher in the Rye

【题解】

《麦田里的守望者》讲述了16岁的中学生霍尔顿的故事。霍尔顿因成绩太差，第四次被学校开除，他不愿在父母得到通知前贸然回家，只身游荡在纽约街头。小说主要描述了霍尔顿三天的流浪生活及其心理感受。小说自出版以来就引发众多争议，因为它对美国社会的传统文化和道德表示质疑和蔑视，向霍尔顿这样一个被主流社会排斥乃至驱逐的人物表示同情。小说真实地展现了霍尔顿的困惑，他厌倦现代文明的虚伪和堕落，不得不面对现实生活中无数"假里假气"(phony) 的人和事物，内心一片焦灼。他渴望逃往西部，但最后仍只能留在他所处的现实社会，接受并不完美的生活，学着调整自己，逐渐适应。在纽约流浪的三天，他思考着理想和成熟的含义，思考着普通人在社会中的地位。

下文选自小说第二十二章。霍尔顿半夜悄悄溜回家，向妹妹告别，给她描述自己渴望成为"麦田里的守望者"的理想。

From The Catcher in the Rye

Chapter 22

When I came back, she had the pillow of her head all right[1]—I knew she would—but she still wouldn't look at me, even though she was laying on her back and all. When I came around the side of the bed and sat down again, she turned her crazy face the other way. She was ostracizing[2] the hell out of me. Just like the fencing team at Pencey when I left all the goddam foils on the subway[3]. "How's old Hazel Weatherfield?" I said. "You write any new stories about her? I got that one you sent me right in my suitcase. It's down at the station. It's very good."

"Daddy'll kill you."

Boy, she really gets something on her mind when she gets something on her mind. "No, he won't. The worst he'll do, he'll give me hell again, and then he'll send me to that goddam military school. That's all he'll do to me. And in the first place, I won't even be around. I'll be away. I'll be—I'll probably be in Colorado on this ranch."

"Don't make me laugh. You can't even ride a horse."

"Who can't? Sure I can. Certainly I can. They can teach you in about two minutes," I said. "Stop picking at that." She was picking at that adhesive tape on her arm. "Who gave you that haircut?" I asked her. I just noticed what a stupid haircut somebody gave her. It was way too short.

"None of your business," she said. She can be very snotty sometimes. She can be quite snotty. "I suppose you failed in every single subject again," she said—very snotty. It was sort of funny, too, in a way. She sounds like a goddam schoolteacher sometimes, and she's only a little child.

"No, I didn't," I said. "I passed English." Then, just for the hell of it, I gave her a pinch on the behind[4]. It was sticking way out in the breeze, the way she was laying on her side. She has hardly any behind. I didn't do it hard, but she tried to hit my hand anyway, but she missed.

Then all of a sudden, she said, "Oh, why did you do it?" She meant why did I get the ax again. It made me sort of sad, the way she said it.

"Oh, God, Phoebe, don't ask me. I'm sick of everybody asking me that," I said. "A million reasons why. It was one of the worst schools I ever went to. It was full of phonies[5]. And mean guys. You never saw so many mean guys in your life. For instance, if you were having a bull session in somebody's room, and somebody wanted to come in, nobody'd let them in if they were some dopey, pimply guy. Everybody was always locking their door when somebody wanted to come in. And they had this goddam secret fraternity that I was too yellow not to join[6]. There was this one pimply, boring guy, Robert Ackley, that wanted to get in. He kept trying to join, and they wouldn't let him. Just because he was boring and pimply. I don't even feel like talking about it. It was a stinking school. Take my word."

Old Phoebe didn't say anything, but she was listening. I could tell by the back of her neck that she was listening. She always listens when you tell her something. And the funny part is she knows, half the time, what the hell you're talking about. She really does.

I kept talking about old Pencey. I sort of felt like it.

"Even the couple of nice teachers on the faculty, they were phonies, too," I said. "There was this one old guy, Mr. Spencer. His wife was always giving you hot chocolate and all that stuff, and they were really pretty nice. But you should've seen him when the headmaster, Old Thurmer, came in the history class and sat down in the back of the room. He was always coming in and sitting down in the back of the room for about a half an hour. He was supposed to be incognito or something. After a while, he'd be sitting back there and then he'd start interrupting what old Spencer was saying to crack a lot of corny jokes. Old Spencer'd practically kill himself chuckling and smiling and all, like as if Thurmer was a goddam prince or something."

"Don't swear so much."

"It would've made you puke, I swear it would," I said. "Then, on Veterans' Day. They have this day, Veterans' Day, that all the jerks that graduated from Pencey around 1776[7] come back and walk all over the place, with their wives and children and everybody. You should've seen this one old guy that was about fifty. What he did was, he came in our room and knocked on the door and asked us if we'd mind if he used the bathroom. The bathroom was at the end of the corridor—I don't know why the hell he asked us. You know what he said? He said he wanted to see if his initials were still in one of the can doors. What he did, he carved his goddam stupid sad old initials in one of the can doors

Contemporary American Literature
1945–

about ninety years ago, and he wanted to see if they were still there. So my roommate and I walked him down to the bathroom and all, and we had to stand there while he looked for his initials in all the can doors. He kept talking to us the whole time, telling us how when he was at Pencey they were the happiest days of his life, and giving us a lot of advice for the future and all. Boy, did he depress me! I don't mean he was a bad guy—he wasn't. But you don't have to be a bad guy to depress somebody—you can be a good *guy* and do it. All you have to do to depress somebody is give them a lot of phony advice while you're looking for your initials in some can door—that's all you have to do. I don't know. Maybe it wouldn't have been so bad if he hadn't been all out of breath. He was all out of breath from just climbing up the stairs, and the whole time he was looking for his initials he kept breathing hard, with his nostrils all funny and sad, while he kept telling Stradlater and I to get all we could out of Pencey. God, Phoebe! I can't explain. I just didn't like anything that was happening at Pencey. I can't explain."

Old Phoebe said something then, but I couldn't hear her. She had the side of her mouth right smack on the pillow, and I couldn't hear her.

"What?" I said. "Take your mouth away. I can't hear you with your mouth that way."

"You don't like anything that's happening."

It made me even more depressed when she said that.

"Yes I do. Yes I do. *Sure* I do. Don't say that. Why the hell do say that?"

"Because you don't. You don't like any schools. You don't like a million things. You don't ."

"I do! That's where you're wrong—that's exactly where you're wrong! Why the hell do you have to say that?" I said. Boy, was she depressing me.

"Because you don't," she said. "Name one thing."

"One thing? One thing I like?" I said. "Okay."

The trouble was, I couldn't concentrate too hot. Sometimes it's hard to concentrate.

"One thing I like a lot you mean?" I asked her.

She didn't answer me, though. She was in a cockeyed position way the hell over the other side of the bed. She was about a thousand miles away. "C'm on, answer me," I said. "One thing I like a lot, or one thing I just like?"

"You like a lot."

"All right," I said. But the trouble was, I couldn't concentrate. About all I could think of were those two nuns that went around collecting dough in those beat-up old straw baskets. Especially the one with the glasses with those iron rims. And this boy I know at Elkton Hills. There was this one boy at Elkton Hills, named James Castle, that wouldn't take back something he said about this very conceited boy, Phil Stabile. James Castle called him a very conceited guy, and one of Stabile's lousy friends went and squealed on him to Stabile. So Stabile, with about six other dirty bastards, went down to James Castle's room and went in and locked the goddam door and tried to make him take back what he said, but he wouldn't do it. So they started in on him. I won't even tell you what they did to him—it's too repulsive—but he *still* wouldn't take it back, old James Castle. And you should've seen him. He was a skinny little weak-looking guy, with wrists about as big as pencils. Finally, what he did, instead of taking back what he said, he jumped out the window. I was in the shower and all, and even I could hear him land outside. But I just thought something fell out the window, a radio or a desk or something, not a *boy* or anything. Then I heard everybody running through the corridor and down the stairs, so I put on my bathrobe and I ran downstairs too, and there was old James Castle laying right on the stone steps and all. He was dead, and his teeth, and blood, were all over the place, and nobody would even go near him. He had on this turtleneck sweater I'd lent him. All they did with the guys that were in the room with him was expel them. They didn't even go to jail.

That was about all I could think of, though. Those two nuns I saw at breakfast and this boy James Castle I knew at Elkton Hills. The funny part is, I hardly even know James Castle, if you want to know the truth. He was one of these very quiet guys. He was in my math class, but he was way over on the other side of the room, and he hardly ever got up to recite or go to the blackboard or anything. Some guys in school hardly ever get up to recite or go to the blackboard. I think the only time I ever even had a conversation with him was that time he asked me if he could borrow this turtleneck sweater I had. I damn near dropped dead when he asked me, I was so surprised and all. I remember I was brushing my teeth, in the can, when he asked me. He said his cousin was coming in to take him for a drive and all. I didn't even know he knew I *had* a turtleneck sweater. All I knew about him was that his name was always right ahead of me at roll call. Cabel, R., Cabel, W., Castle, Caulfield—I can still remember it. If you want to know the truth, I almost didn't lend him my sweater. Just because I didn't know him too well.

"What?" I said to old Phoebe. She said something to me, but I didn't hear her. "You can't even think of one thing."

"Yes, I can. Yes, I can."

"Well, do it, then."

"I like Allie[8]," I said. "And I like doing what I'm doing right now. Sitting here with you, and talking, and thinking about stuff, and—"

"Allie's dead—You always say that! If somebody's dead and everything, and in Heaven, then it isn't really—"

"I know he's dead! Don't you think I know that? I can still like him, though, can't I? Just because somebody's dead, you don't just stop liking them, for God's sake—especially if they were about a thousand times nicer than the people you know that're alive and all."

Old Phoebe didn't say anything. When she can't think of anything to say, she doesn't say a goddam word.

"Anyway, I like it now," I said. "I mean right now. Sitting here with you and just chewing the fat and horsing—"

"That isn't anything really!"

"It is so something really! Certainly it is! Why the hell isn't it? People never think anything is anything really. I'm getting goddam sick of it."

"Stop swearing. All right, name something else. Name something you'd like to be. Like a scientist. Or a lawyer or something."

"I couldn't be a scientist. I'm no good in science."

"Well, a lawyer—like Daddy and all."

"Lawyers are all right, I guess—but it doesn't appeal to me," I said. "I mean they're all right if they go around saving innocent guys' lives all the time, and like that, but you don't do that kind of stuff if you're a lawyer. All you do is make a lot of dough and play golf and play bridge and buy cars and drink Martinis and look like a hot-shot. And besides. Even if you did go around saving guy's lives and all, how would you know if you did it because you really wanted tosave guys' lives, or because you did it because what you really wanted to do was be a terrific lawyer, with everybody slapping you on the back and congratulating you in court when the goddam trial was over, and reporters and everybody, the way it is in the dirty movies? How would you know you weren't being a phony? The trouble is, you wouldn't."

I'm not too sure old Phoebe knew what the hell I was talking about. I mean she's only a little child and all. But she was listening, at least. If somebody at least listens, it's not too bad.

"Daddy's going to kill you. He's going to kill you," she said.

I wasn't listening, though. I was thinking about something else—something crazy. "You know what I'd like to be? I mean if I had my goddam choice?"

"What? Stop *swearing*."

"You know that song 'If a body catch a body comin' through the rye'? I'd like—"

"It's 'If a body *meet* a body coming through the rye'!" Old Phoebe said. "It's a poem. By Robert Burns."

"I know it's a poem by Robert Burns."

She was right, though. It is "If a body meet a body coming through the rye." I didn't know it then, though.

"I thought it was 'If a body catch a body,'" I said. "Anyway, I keep picturing all these little kids playing some game in this big field of rye and all. Thousands of little kids playing some game in this big field of rye and all. Thousands of little kids, and nobody's around—nobody big, I mean—except me. And I'm standing on the edge of some crazy cliff. What I have to do, I have to catch everybody if they start to go over the cliff—I mean if they're running and they don't look where they're going I have to come out from somewhere and catch them. That's all I'd do all day. I'd just be the catcher in the rye and all. I know it's crazy, but that's the only thing I'd really like to be. I know it's crazy." Old Phoebe didn't say anything for a long time. Then, when she said something, all she said was, "Daddy's going to kill you."

"I don't give a damn if he does," I said. I got up from the bed then, because what I wanted to do, I wanted to phone up this guy that was my English teacher at Elkton Hills, Mr. Antolini. He lived in New York now. He quit Elkton Hills. He took this job teaching English at N.Y.U. "I have to make a phone call," I told Phoebe. "I'll be right back. Don't go to sleep." I didn't want her to go to sleep while I was in the living room. I knew she wouldn't, but I said it anyway, just to make sure.

While I was walking toward the door, old Phoebe said, "Holden!" and I turned around.

She was sitting way up in bed. She looked so pretty. "I'm taking belching lessons from this girl, Phyllis Margulies," she said. "Listen."

I listened, and I heard something, but it wasn't much. "Good." I said. Then I went out in the living room and called up this teacher I had, Mr. Antolini.

Contemporary American Literature 1945–

【注解】

1. When I came back … all right：菲比一害怕，就习惯躺在床上，把枕头压在头上。她听说霍尔顿又被学校开除，心中害怕，故又有此举。霍尔顿劝阻无效，去起居室取烟。
2. ostracizing：不理睬，冷淡对待。
3. just like the fencing team … on the subway：霍尔顿是潘西中学击剑队的队长，一次带队去比赛，把击剑装备全部遗忘在地铁站内，遭到队员的责骂。
4. behind：(口) 屁股。
5. phonies：假里假气的 (人或事)。霍尔顿经常使用该词表示他对成人世界的厌恶。
6. I was too yellow not to join：我太胆小，不敢不参加。
7. around 1776：夸张的说法，指历届毕业生。下文的 "ninety years ago" 亦同。
8. Allie：霍尔顿死去的弟弟。

【思考题】

1. What is Holden's attitude towards the adult world and children?
2. Phoebe says "Holden doesn't like anything that's happening". What is the significance of Holden naming Allie, his dead brother, as the one thing he likes?
3. Why does Holden hope to be a catcher in the rye? What is the significance of the title?

解读举例

1. 《麦田里的守望者》是战后美国青年反抗成人社会的虚伪与腐败的宣言，反映了他们对个性和平等的向往，以及对成人社会的强烈不满，是战后 "失望的一代" 真实的写照。

2. 《麦田里的守望者》反映了追寻真理主题，表现了一个与环境格格不入的史诗般的英雄对真理的探寻。霍尔顿真诚地爱着他的邻居们，尤其是那些物质和精神极度匮乏的人们。他在纽约对真理、永恒和稳定的追求正是古典英雄在探索途中艰辛和努力的写照。

3. 《麦田里的守望者》是20世纪的精神流浪儿小说，霍尔顿则是现代版的哈克贝里·芬。小说记录了霍尔顿艰难、痛苦地步入成人社会的过程。他在纽约三天的生活就是他的入会仪式，他所受的折磨和痛苦是进入成人社会过程中的种种考验。

4. 《麦田里的守望者》平庸、单调，充斥着不堪入耳的污言秽语，只是记录了一位敏感的16岁少年对生活的表面感受，完全不适合年轻人阅读。霍尔顿精神错乱，是个忧郁且神经质的人,他代表了20世纪50年代美国那些不循规蹈矩的人,是一个"没有过去,也缺乏理想的叛逆者"。

Joseph Heller
1923—1999

作者简介

约瑟夫·海勒是美国"黑色幽默"文学的代表人物,出生于纽约市布鲁克林区。由于家境贫寒,海勒中学毕业后便当了一名邮差,二战爆发后应征入伍,被编入美国空军后被派往欧洲战场,执行过多次飞行任务。海勒的战争经历为其代表作《第22条军规》提供了重要的创作素材。

二战结束后,海勒先后就读于加州大学和纽约大学,1948年获得文学学士学位,次年在哥伦比亚大学获得文学硕士学位,并获得奖学金到英国牛津大学继续学习。1955年,他以《第18条军规》为题,在《新世界》杂志上发表了小说第一章。后因与莱昂·尤利斯(Leon Uris,1924—2003)刚发表的《Mila 18》书名雷同而将自己的小说更名为《第22条军规》。1961年《第22条军规》正式出版发行,海勒也因此一举成名。出版至今,小说已销售1000多万册,并被多家机构评为20世纪世界100部最优秀作品之一。"第22条军规"也作为一个特殊词条进入《牛津大词典》,成为英语词汇的组成部分。

《第22条军规》是二战后"黑色幽默"文学的典范之作,也是一部犀利的反战小说。它以其内容和形式上的创新,成功地描绘了一幅现代人身陷困境的荒诞图景,是美国60年代荒诞小说创作的先声。作品表现的是第二次世界大战的场景,但讽刺与批判的不是德军,而是美国的官僚体系、军队的荒诞逻辑和因战争高速发展的军火工业,因为这一切都建立在牺牲生命、扼杀人性、制造毁灭的基础上。作品表明,战争中的官僚体系与荒诞逻辑实际普遍存在于和平时期和日常生活中,战争时期军队生活的恐怖景象实际是人类生存状况的真实写照。在强大的国家机器、军事机器与军火巨头面前,生命毫不足惜,个人微不足道。一个极其荒诞的"第22条军规"便将普通大众玩弄于股掌之中。在这样一个现实面前,普通人或成为体制的牺牲品,或向体制妥协、成为其帮凶,或勇敢地反抗体制,以生命的代价博取道德的完整与意志的自由。作品主人公约瑟林选择的是第三条路,成为20世纪60年代反越战浪潮中的代表。

继《第22条军规》之后，海勒又于1974年创作出版了他的第二部长篇小说《出了毛病》(Something Happened)。作品通过主人公罗伯特·斯洛克姆的自述表现了他所在的公司内部人与人之间的钩心斗角及其恶果。海勒以斯洛克姆所在的公司影射美国社会，暗示"出了毛病"的是当今的美国社会。作品出版后获得好评，也使海勒继续努力创作，五年后他又发表了第三部长篇小说《像戈尔德一样好》(Good as Gold, 1979)。1995年，戈尔德才又出版了他的第四部小说——《第22条军规》的续集《终止时刻》(Closing Time)。

除小说外，海勒还创作过剧本《我们轰炸了纽黑文》(We Bombed New Haven, 1967)。如同《第22条军规》一样，这部剧作也是一部反战作品，一出由"演员扮演员"的悲喜剧。1971年海勒，将《第22条军规》改编为电影剧本，翌年当选美国文学艺术学院院士。海勒的作品用不同寻常的方法反映了美国社会及社会成员的特点。他用犀利的目光捕捉到了每个人身上通常被压抑或被掩盖起来的天性，把它融入20世纪60年代独具特色的"绝望的喜剧"之中，从而成为"黑色幽默"文学的代表人物。

Catch-22

【题解】

《第22条军规》以二战期间驻扎在皮亚诺扎岛上的一支美军飞行大队为背景，表现了军队与战争的荒诞逻辑。

主人公约瑟林由于厌战要求停止飞行，复员回国，但是由于第22条军规的存在，他无法实现自己的愿望。第22条军规规定，空军飞行员必须完成规定的战斗次数才能回国；同时，它又规定，无论何时何地都得执行上司的命令，必须做到令行禁止。这样就产生了一个悖论：飞行员飞行了多少次并不重要，重要的是必须听从上司的指挥。只有上司才有权决定你能否回国。第22条军规还规定，一切精神失常之人都可以不完成规定的任务，立即遣送回国；但同时又规定，要停止飞行必须由本人提出申请，但若在危险关头能提出停飞申请，就证明申请人没有精神失常，也就必须继续执行飞行任务，直至阵亡或战争结束。

第22条军规就像一只无形之手，牢牢地掌握着普通官兵的命运。事实上，第22条军规象征的是一种统治世界的荒谬和疯狂，虽然小说中故事发生的背景是在战争时期，但那荒谬和疯狂的特性却也处处表现在和平时期和日常生活中。因此，作者声称，《第22条军规》并非关于二战的小说，而是一部关于冷战时期美国社会的小说。以下节选自《第22条军规》第五章，通过约瑟林和邓尼卡医生的对话揭示了第 22 条军规的荒诞性，同时也描写了美军飞行员在执行任务时的恐惧心理。

From *Catch-22*

Chapter 5　Chief White Halfoat

...

Chief White Halfoat was a handsome, swarthy Indian from Oklahoma with a heavy, hard-boned face and tousled black hair, a half-blooded Creek[1] from Enid[2] who, for occult reasons of his own, had made up his mind to die of pneumonia. He was a glowering, vengeful, disillusioned Indian who hated foreigners with names like Cathcart, Korn, Black[3] and Havermeyer[4] and wished they'd all go back to where their lousy ancestors had come from.

"You wouldn't believe it, Yossarian[5]," he ruminated, raising his voice deliberately to bait Doc Daneeka[6], "but this used to be a pretty good country to live in before they loused it up with their goddam piety."

Chief White Halfoat was out to revenge himself upon the white man. He could barely read or write and had been assigned to Captain Black as assistant intelligence officer.

"How could I learn to read or write?" Chief White Halfoat demanded with simulated belligerence, raising his voice again so that Doc Daneeka would hear. "Every time we pitched out tent, they sank an oil well. Every time they sank a well, they hit oil. And every time they hit oil, they make us pack up our tent and go someplace else. We were human divining rods. Our whole family had a natural affinity for petroleum deposits, and soon every oil company in the world had technicians chasing us around. We were always on the move. It was one hell of a way to bring a child up, I can tell you. I don't think I ever spent more than a week in one place."

His earliest memory was of a geologist.

"Every time another White Halfoat was born," he continued, "the stock market turned bullish. Soon whole drilling crews were following us around with all their equipment just to get the jump on each other. Companies began to merge just so they could cut down on the number of people they had to assign to us. But the crowd in back of us kept growing. We never got a good night's sleep. When we stopped, they stopped. When we moved, they moved, chuckwagons, bulldozers, derricks, generators. We were a walking business boom, and we began to receive invitations from some of the best hotels just for the amount of business we would drag into town with us. Some of those invitations were mighty generous, but we couldn't accept any because we were Indians and all the best hotels that were inviting us wouldn't accept Indians as guests. Racial prejudice is a terrible thing, Yossarian. It really is. It's a terrible thing to treat a decent, loyal Indian like a nigger, kike, wop or spic." Chief White Halfoat nodded slowly with conviction.

"Then, Yossarian, it finally happened—the beginning of the end. They began to follow us around from in front. They would try to guess where we were going to stop next and would begin drilling before we even got there, so we couldn't even stop. As soon as we'd begin to unroll our blankets, they would kick us off. They had confidence in us. They wouldn't even wait to strike oil before they kicked us off. We were so tired we almost didn't care the day our time ran out. One morning we found ourselves completely surrounded by oilmen waiting for us to come their way so they could kick us off. Everywhere you looked there was an oilman on a ridge, waiting there like Indians getting ready to attack. It was the end. We couldn't stay where we were because we had just been kicked off. And there was no place left for us to go. Only the army saved me. Luckily, the war broke out just in the nick of time, and a draft board picked me right out of the middle and put me down safely in Lowery Field, Colorado. I was the only survivor."

Yossarian knew he was lying, but did not interrupt as Chief White Halfoat went on to claim that he had never heard from his parents again. That didn't bother him too much, though, for he had only their word for it that they were his parents, and since they had lied to him about so many other things, they could just as well have been lying to him about that too. He was much better acquainted with the fate of a tribe of first cousins who had wandered away north in a diversionary movement and pushed inadvertently into Canada. When they tried to return, they were stopped at the border by American immigration authorities who would not let them back into the country. They could not come back in because they were red. It was a horrible joke, but Doc Daneeka didn't laugh until Yossarian came to him one mission later and pleaded again, without any real expectation of success, to be grounded. Doc Daneeka snickered once and was soon immersed in problems of his own, which included Chief White Halfoat, who had been challenging him all that morning to Indian wrestle, and Yossarian, who decided right then and there to go crazy.

"You're wasting your time," Doc Daneeka was forced to tell him.

"Can't you ground someone who's crazy?"

"Oh, sure. I have to. There's a rule saying I have to ground anyone who's crazy."

"Then why don't you ground me? I'm crazy. Ask Clevinger[7]."

"Clevinger? Where is Clevinger? You find Clevinger and I'll ask him."

"Then ask any of the others. They'll tell you how crazy I am."

"They're crazy."

"Then why don't you ground them?"

"Why don't they ask me to ground them?"

"Because they're crazy, that's why."

"Of course they're crazy," Doc Daneeka replied. "I just told you they're crazy, didn't I? And you can't let crazy people decide whether you're crazy or not, can you?"

Yossarian looked at him soberly and tried another approach. "Is Orr[8] crazy?"

"He sure is," Doc Daneeka said.

"Can you ground him?"

"I sure can. But first he has to ask me to. That's part of the rule."

"Then why doesn't he ask you to?"

"Because he's crazy," Doc Daneeka said. "He has to be crazy to keep flying combat missions after all the close calls he's had. Sure, I can ground Orr. But first he has to ask me to."

"That's all he has to do to be grounded?"

"That's all. Let him ask me."

"And then you can ground him?" Yossarian asked.

"No. Then I can't ground him."

"You mean there's a catch?"

"Sure there's a catch," Doc Daneeka replied. "Catch-22. Anyone who wants to get out of combat duty isn't really crazy."

There was only one catch and that was Catch-22, which specified that a concern for one's own safety in the face of dangers that were real and immediate was the process of rational mind. Orr was crazy and could be grounded. All he had to do was ask; and as soon as he did, he would no longer be crazy and would have to fly more missions. Orr would be crazy to fly more missions and sane if he didn't, but if he was sane he had to fly them. If he flew them he was crazy and didn't have to; but if he didn't want to he was sane and had to. Yossarian was moved very deeply by the absolute simplicity of this clause of Catch-22 and let out a respectful whistle.

"That's some catch, that Catch-22," he observed.

"It's the best there is," Doc Daneeka agreed.

Yossarian saw it clearly in all its spinning reasonableness. There was an elliptical precision about its perfect pairs of parts that was graceful and shocking, like good modern art, and at times Yossarian wasn't quite sure that he saw it all, just the way he was never quite sure about good modern art or about the flies Orr saw in Appleby's[9] eyes. He had Orr's word to take for the flies in Appleby's eyes.

"Oh, they're there, all right," Orr has assured him about the flies in Appleby's eyes after Yossarian's fist fight with Appleby in the officers' club, "although he probably doesn't even know it. That's why he can't see things as they really are."

"How come he doesn't know it?" inquired Yossarian.

"Because he's got flies in his eyes," Orr explained with exaggerated patience. "How can he see he's got flies in his eyes if he's got flies in his eyes?"

It made as much sense as anything else, and Yossarian was willing to give Orr the benefit of the doubt because Orr was from the wilderness outside New York City and knew so much more about wild-life than Yossarian did, and because Orr, unlike Yossarian's mother, father, sister, brother, aunt, uncle, in-law, teacher, spiritual leader, legislator, neighbor and newspaper, had never lied to him about anything crucial before. Yossarian had mulled his newfound knowledge about Appleby over in private for a day or two and then decided, as a good deed, to pass the word along to Appleby himself.

"Appleby, you've got flies in your eyes," he whispered helpfully as they passed by each other in the doorway of the parachute tent on the day of the weekly milk run to Parma.

"What?" Appleby responded sharply, thrown into confusion by the fact that Yossarian had spoken to him at all.

"You've got flies in your eyes," Yossarian repeated. "That's probably why you can't see them."

Appleby retreated from Yossarian with a look of loathing bewilderment and walked in silence until he was in the jeep with Havermeyer riding down the long, straight road to the briefing room, where Major Dany, the fidgeting group operations officer, was waiting to conduct the preliminary briefing with all the lead pilots, bombardiers and navigators. Appleby spoke in a soft voice so that he would not be heard by the driver or by Captain Black, who was stretched out with his eyes closed in the front seat of the jeep.

"Havermeyer," he asked hesitantly. "Have I got flies in my eyes?"

Havermeyer blinked quizzically. "Sties?" he asked.

"No, flies," he was told.

Havermeyer blinked again. "Flies?"

"In my eyes."

"You must be crazy," Havermeyer said.

"No, I'm not crazy. Yossarian's crazy. Just tell me if I've got flies in my eyes or not. Go ahead. I can take it."

Havermeyer popped another piece of peanut brittle into his mouth and peered very closely into Appleby's eyes. "I don't see any," he announced.

Appleby heaved an immense sigh of relief. Havermeyer had tiny bits of peanut brittle adhering to his lips, chin and cheeks.

"You've got peanut brittle crumbs on your face," Appleby remarked to him.

"I'd rather have peanut brittle crumbs on my face than flies in my eyes," Havermeyer retorted.

The officers of the other five planes in each flight arrived in trucks for the general briefing that took place thirty minutes later. The three enlisted men in each crew were not briefed at all, but were carried directly out on the airfield to the separate planes in which they were scheduled to fly that day, where they waited around with the ground crew until the officers with whom they had been scheduled to fly swung off the rattling tailgates of the trucks delivering them and it was time to climb aboard and start up. Engines rolled over disgruntledly on lollipop-shaped hardstands, resisting first, then idling smoothly awhile, and then the planes lumbered around and nosed forward lamely over the pebbled ground like sightless, stupid, crippled things until they taxied into the line at the foot of the landing strip and took off swiftly, one behind the other, in a zooming, rising roar, banking slowly into formation over mottled treetops, and circling the field at even speed until all the flights of six had been formed and then setting course over cerulean water on the first leg[10] of the journey to the target in northern Italy or France. The planes gained altitude steadily and were above nine thousand feet by the time they crossed into enemy territory. One of the surprising things always was the sense of calm and utter silence, broken only by the test rounds fired from the machine guns, by an occasional toneless, terse remark over the intercom, and, at last, by the sobering pronouncement of the bombardier in each plane that they were at the I.P.,[11] and about to turn toward the target. There was always sunshine, always a tiny sticking in the throat from the rarefied air.

The B-25s they flew in were stable, dependable, dull-green ships with twin rudders and engines and wide wings. Their single fault, from where Yossarian sat as a bombardier, was the tight crawlway separating the bombardier's compartment in the plexiglass nose from the nearest escape hatch. The crawlway was a narrow, square, cold tunnel hollowed out beneath the flight controls, and a large man like Yossarian could squeeze through only with difficulty. A chubby, moon-faced navigator with little reptilian eyes and a pipe like Aarfy's[12] had trouble, too, and Yossarian used to chase him back from the nose as they turned toward the target, now minutes away. There was a time of tension then, a time of waiting with nothing to hear and nothing to see and nothing to do but wait as the antiaircraft guns below took aim and made ready to knock them all sprawling into infinite sleep if they could.

The crawlway was Yossarian's lifeline to outside from a plane about to fall, but Yossarian swore at it with seething antagonism, reviled it as an obstacle put there by providence as part of the plot that would destroy him. There was room for an additional escape hatch right there in the nose of B-25, but there was no escape hatch. Instead there was the crawlway, and since the mess on the mission over Avignon he had learned to detest every mammoth inch[13] of it, for it slung him seconds and seconds away from his parachute, which was too bulky to be taken up front with him, and seconds and seconds more after that away from the escape hatch on the floor between the rear of the elevated flight deck and the feet of the faceless top turret gunner mounted high above. Yossarian longed to be where Aarfy could be once Yossarian had chased him back from the nose; Yossarian longed to sit on the floor in a huddled ball right on top of the escape hatch inside a sheltering igloo of extra flask suits that he would have been happy to carry along with him, his parachute already hooked to his harness where it belonged, one fist clenching the red-handled rip cord, one fist gripping the emergency hatch release that would spill him earthward into air at the first dreadful squeal of destruction. That was where he wanted to be if he had to be there at all, instead of hung out there in front like some goddam cantilevered goldfish in some goddam cantilevered goldfish bowl[14] while the goddam foul black tiers of flak were bursting and booming and billowing all around and above and below him in a climbing, cracking, staggered, banging, phantasmagorical, cosmological wickedness that jarred and tossed and shivered, clattered and pieced, and threatened to annihilate them all in one splinter of a second in one vast flash of fire.

Aarfy had been no use to Yossarian as a navigator or as anything else, and Yossarian drove him back from the nose vehemently each time so that they would not clutter up each other's way if they had to scramble suddenly for safety. Once Yossarian had driven him back from the nose, Aarfy was free to cower on the floor where Yossarian longed to cower, but he stood bolt upright instead with his stumpy arms resting comfortably on the backs of the pilot's and co-pilot's seats, pipe in hand, making affable small talk to McWatt[15] and whoever happened to be co-pilot and pointing out amusing trivia in the sky to the two men, who were too busy to be interested. McWatt was too busy responding at the controls to Yossarian's strident instructions as Yossarian slipped the plane in on the bomb run and then whipped them all away violently around the ravenous pillars of exploding shells with curt, shrill, obscene commands to McWatt that were much like the anguished, entreating nightmare yelpings of Hungry Joe[16] in the dark. Aarfy would puff reflectively on his pipe throughout the whole chaotic clash, gazing with unruffled curiosity at the war through McWatt's window as though it were a remote disturbance that could not affect him. Aarfy was a dedicated fraternity man who loved cheerleading and class reunions and did not have brains enough to be afraid. Yossarian did have brains enough and was, and the only thing that stopped him from abandoning his post under fire and scurrying back through the crawlway like a yellow-bellied rat was his unwillingness to entrust the evasive action out of the target area to anybody else. There was nobody else in the world he would honor with so great a responsibility. There was nobody else he knew who was as big a coward. Yossarian was the best man in the group at evasive action, but had no idea why.

There was no established procedure for evasive action. All you needed was fear, and Yossarian had plenty of that, more fear than Orr or Hungry Joe, more fear even than Dunbar, who had resigned himself submissively to the idea that he must die someday. Yossarian had not resigned himself to that idea, and he bolted for his life wildly on each mission the instant his bombs were away, hollering, "Hard, hard, hard, hard, you bastard, hard !" at McWatt and hating McWatt viciously all the time as though McWatt were to blame for their being up there at all to be rubbed out by strangers[17], and everybody else in the plane kept off the intercom, except for the pitiful time of the mess[18] on the mission to Avignon when Dobbs[19] went crazy in mid-air and began weeping pathetically for help.

"Help who? Help who?" called back Yossarian, once he had plugged his headset back into the intercom system, after it had been jerked out when Dobbs wrested the controls away from Huple[20] and hurled them all down suddenly into the deafening, paralyzing, horrifying dive which had plastered Yossarian helplessly to the ceiling of the plane by the top of his head and from which Huple had rescued them just in time by seizing the controls back from Dobbs and leveling the ship out almost as suddenly right back in the middle of the buffeting layer of cacophonous flak from which they had escaped successfully only a moment before. Oh, God! Oh, God, oh, God, Yossarian had been pleading wordlessly as he dangled from the ceiling of the nose of the ship by the top of his head, unable to move.

"The bombardier, the bombardier," Dobbs answered in a cry when Yossarian spoke. "He doesn't answer, he doesn't answer. Help the bombardier, help the bombardier.[21]"

"I'm the bombardier," Yossarian cried back at him. "I'm the bombardier. I'm all right. I'm all right."

"Then help him, help him," Dobbs begged. "Help him, help him."

And Snowden lay dying in back.

【注解】

1. Creek：克里克人，印第安人的一族。
2. Enid：俄克拉荷马中部城市，附近多油田。
3. Cathcart, Korn, Black：卡思卡特上校、康中校、布莱克上尉。前两位都是利欲熏心、不择手段往上爬的野心家；布莱克则是一名打入空军的特工，为了邀功，在飞行员中掀起所谓效忠宣誓运动，并常常捏造事实，诬陷好人。
4. Havermeyer：投弹手之一，执行轰炸任务时无所畏惧，与主人公 Yossarian 相反。
5. Yossarian：投弹手之一，本书的主人公。
6. Doc Daneeka：邓尼卡医生，Yossarian 所在飞行队的军医。
7. Clevinger：飞行员之一，在一次轰炸任务中阵亡。
8. Orr：飞行员之一。
9. Appleby：飞行员之一，对 Yossarian 相当敌视，所以有下文 Yossarian 与 Appleby 在军官俱乐部大打出手的情节。
10. leg：旅程或飞行中的一段行程。
11. I.P.：initial point，起始点。
12. Aarfy：与 Yossarian 同机的领航员。
13. every mammoth inch：每一巨大的英寸，意思是从驾驶舱到救生舱门的距离平常看起来很近，但到危急时刻就显得十分遥远。
14. like some goddam cantilevered goldfish in . . . bowl：这里 Yossarian 把透明的驾驶舱比作一个金鱼缸，把自己比作一条金鱼。
15. McWatt：与 Yossarian 同机的飞行员。
16. Hungry Joe：飞行员之一，在战斗中因过于紧张几乎精神崩溃。
17. as though McWatt were to blame for . . . by strangers：好像他们在天上被素不相识的人干掉都是麦克沃特的错。

18. mess：此处指在轰炸法国东南部城市 Avignon 时与 Yossarian 同机的飞行员 Snowden（见本章最后）被防空火炮击中，内脏流了一地之事。
19. Dobbs：飞行员之一。
20. Huple：飞行员之一，年仅 15 岁。
21. help the bombardier：慌乱之中，Dobbs 以为 Yossarian 被击中，而实际被击中的是 Snowden。

【思考题】

1. Why is Chief White Halfoat so hostile to the white men? What is the implied criticism, if there is any, of the white men in relation to the red men?
2. When Chief White Halfoat told Yossarian about his miserable life story and said it was the army that saved him, Yossarian knew he was lying. Was Chief White Halfoat lying? What was he lying about?
3. There is an obvious sample of "black humor" in Chief White Halfoat's account of his people keeping getting "kicked off". Point out places in his account and demonstrate how black humor is employed.
4. At the beginning of the chapter, Heller says that Chief White Halfoat "had made up his mind to die of pneumonia", and then later refers to Yossarian in a similar way by saying he "decided right then and there to go crazy." Is there anything unusual about the wording of these two sentences? Give your comment.
5. Study the dialogue between Yossarian and Doc Daneeka about the rule, or "the catch", concerning the grounding of any crew members, and discuss the crazy logic in view of authoritarianism of the military and society.
6. From the description of Yossarian's fuss with the crawlway, the escape hatch, the parachute, and the reactions of other crew members in the plane, how would you describe their psychology and morale in fighting the enemy?
7. How does the theme of individual integrity work in the novel? Consider the cases of Yossarian in this chapter, and the cases of Chaplain Tappman, and Milo Minderbinder in the whole novel.

【简评】

《第 22 条军规》所表现的荒诞的现实在很大程度上是通过荒诞的语言来实现的。小说多次使用了语言的循环 (circulation)，包括自我消解 (self-cancellation)、悖论 (paradox)、不连贯 (discontinuity) 等。邓尼卡医生对第 22 条军规的解释便是一个典型的例子：继续飞行者是发疯，发疯者可以停飞，停飞须自己提出，自己提出便说明没有发疯，没有发疯就要继续飞行，继续飞行就是发疯，发疯者可以停飞……类似的例子在作品中比比皆是，如哈尔福特声称种族歧视坏透了，但在表述这一观点的过程中，他却使用了种族歧视的语言。

作品还制造出许多情节上的悖论，如哈尔福特一家住在哪里，哪里就会开采出石油，因此石油公司会派出大批人马追随他们。一旦他们在哪里住下，便会立即被撵走，好让石油公司开采石油，于是便出现了这样一个悖论："石油工人等着我们往他们那里去好把我们撵走。"此外，当地豪华酒店因为哈尔福特一家给他们带来的巨大生意，纷纷邀请他们免费入住，但同时又规定恕不接待印第安人。

《第22条军规》语言的另一特点便是将恐怖和幽默并置，造成一种黑色幽默的效果。第五章中"That was where he wanted to be ... in one vast flash of fire"的长句便是用一种黑色幽默的方式来描述飞机被击中而不能逃生的灾难性后果。在阅读这个长句时，读者的注意力往往被幽默的语言本身所吸引，从而使语言所描写的恐怖场景，即所谓的黑色得到了一定缓解。

Flannery O'Connor
1925—1964

弗兰纳里·奥康纳是美国当代南方小说家，生于美国佐治亚州一个天主教家庭，1945年毕业于佐治亚女子学院，获文学学士学位。1947年获艾奥瓦大学艺术硕士学位。在奥康纳短暂的一生中，除两年求学期间，其余时间她均在家乡佐治亚州度过，故而对那里的生活非常熟悉，创作了很多精湛的作品。

奥康纳因家庭遗传，在生命最后十几年里，一直患血液病，行动不便。但她在上学期间，已开始发表作品。尽管被病痛折磨，她也笔耕不辍。奥康纳共发表了两部长篇小说，即1952年的《慧血》(Wise Blood)和1960年的《暴力得逞》(The Violent Bear It Away)。但奥康纳更以其短篇小说闻名，生前发表过一部短篇小说集《好人难寻及其他》(A Good Man Is Hard to Find and Other Stories, 1955)。1964年奥康纳去世后，另一部短篇小说集《水到渠成》(Everything That Rises Must Converge, 1965)出版。1971年出版的《奥康纳短篇小说全集》(The Complete Stories)收录了她创作的全部31篇短篇小说。

奥康纳的作品充满着浓厚的宗教气息和南方乡土气息。她的故事大都以美国南方原教旨主义流行的地区为背景，描述了这一地区乡下人无意义和琐碎的生活，以及迷信和宗教引起的混乱和堕落。她认为生活是人对上帝的渴求和对现实的不信任两方面之间不断的冲突；作家的责任是发掘并展现现实生活中令人厌恶的怪异、荒诞现象，以使对这些现象习以为常、见惯不惊的读者对此能有清楚的认识。

奥康纳擅长描绘畸人。她认为真正有缺陷的人是那些没有意识到自己的缺点和局限的人。奥康纳笔下的人物不是完人，他们缺少同情、爱、自信和自知之明。她常常通过人物生理上的残缺来象征他们性格上的局限。这些人物通常也很贫穷，是美国南方的下层人。奥康纳认为这代表了普通人的情况，因为"生存的谜总是通过普通的生活得以展现"，而穷人与生活的原始力量更接近。奥康纳揭露这些南方人的贫穷、愚昧、狭隘和偏拗，同时，通过深入他们的内心世界，对他们坎坷的生活和对精神生活的渴求寄予了深厚的同情。

奥康纳常常被视为"南方文艺复兴"的代表作家之一。她虽然属于南方，却又超越了狭隘的地域界线。像福克纳一样，她能使这一地区的生活成为全人类的共同体验，被誉为福克纳传统的优秀继承者。奥康纳文笔超群，想象奇特，风格怪诞，既有哥特式的神秘，又有漫画性的滑稽，是一个有厚重历史感、有深奥哲学头脑的作家。她触及的通常是人性最深层、最敏感的部分，让读者沉思良久。她的人物性格鲜明，对话栩栩如生。她常常通过巧妙严谨的结构，用冷静的笔触，把人物内心最奇特、激烈的渴求与挣扎不露声色地表现出来。故事常常看似轻松、幽默、夸张，实则有触目惊心、发人深省的震撼力。

A Good Man Is Hard to Find

【题解】

《好人难寻》是奥康纳第一部短篇小说集《好人难寻及其他》的标题作品。这部小说集共收入了她的 10 篇短篇小说。这些作品的主人公大都是一些遭社会遗弃的人，性情乖戾，言谈怪异。奥康纳在描述他们时，常常以轻松幽默的笔触揭示隐藏的悲剧故事，指出他们之所以与社会格格不入，除了社会和家庭的因素，更重要的是他们自身的性格缺陷。

《好人难寻》是奥康纳的代表作，展现了她一贯的写作手法。作者用看似漫不经心的笔法叙述日常琐事，使读者误以为故事会平淡地发展下去，不会起伏跌宕。但是，在接近结尾处，故事却出现惊心动魄的转折，以意想不到的方式结束，从而留下强烈的讽刺效果，促使读者对现代社会的畸形进行深刻的思考。

A Good Man Is Hard to Find

The grandmother didn't want to go to Florida. She wanted to visit some of her connections in east Tennessee and she was seizing at every chance to change Bailey's mind. Bailey was the son she lived with, her only boy. He was sitting on the edge of his chair at the table, bent over the orange sports section of the Journal. "Now look here, Bailey," she said, "see here, read this," and she stood with one hand on her thin hip and the other rattling the newspaper at his bald head. "Here this fellow that calls himself The Misfit is aloose from the Federal Pen[1] and headed toward Florida and you read here what it says he did to these people. Just you read it. I wouldn't take my children in any direction with a criminal like that aloose in it. I couldn't answer to my conscience if I did."

Bailey didn't look up from his reading so she wheeled around then and faced the children's mother, a young woman in slacks, whose face was as broad and innocent as a cabbage and was tied round with a green head-kerchief that had two points on the top like rabbit's ears. She was sitting on the sofa, feeding the baby his apricots out of a jar. "The children have been to Florida before," the old lady said. "You all ought to take them somewhere else for a change so they would see different parts of the world and be broad[2]. They never have been to east Tennessee."

The children's mother didn't seem to hear her but the eight-year-old boy, John Wesley, a stocky child with glasses, said, "If you don't want to go to Florida, why dont cha stay at home?" He and the little girl, June Star, were reading the funny papers on the floor.

"She wouldn't stay at home to be queen for a day[3]," June Star said without raising her yellow head.

"Yea and what would you do if this fellow, The Misfit, caught you?" the grandmother asked.

"I'd smack his face," John Wesley said.

"She wouldn't stay at home for a million bucks," June Star said. "Afraid she'd miss something. She has to go everywhere we go."

"All right, Miss," the grandmother said. "Just remember that the next time you want to curl your hair."

June Star said her hair was naturally curly.

The next morning the grandmother was the first one in the car, ready to go. She had her big black valise that looked like the head of a hippopotamus in one corner, and underneath it she was hiding a basket with Pitty Sing, the cat, in it. She didn't intend for the cat to be left alone in the house for three days because he would miss her too much and she was afraid he might brush against one of the gas burners and accidentally asphyxiate himself. Her son, Bailey, didn't like to arrive at a motel with a cat.

She sat in the middle of the back seat with John Wesley and June Star on either side of her. Bailey and the children's mother and the baby sat in the front and they left Atlanta at eight forty-five with the mileage on the car at 55890. The grandmother wrote this down because she thought it would be interesting to say how many miles they had been when they got back. It took them twenty minutes to reach the outskirts of the city.

The old lady settled herself comfortably, removing her white cotton gloves and putting them up with her purse on the shelf in front of the back window. The children's mother still had on slacks and still had her head tied up in a green kerchief, but the grandmother had on a navy blue straw sailor hat with a bunch of white violets on the brim and a navy blue dress with a small white dot in the print. Her collar and cuffs were white organdy trimmed with lace and at her neckline she had pinned a purple spray of cloth violets containing a sachet. In case of an accident, anyone seeing her dead on the highway would know at once that she was a lady.

She said she thought it was going to be a good day for driving, neither too hot nor too cold, and she cautioned Bailey that the speed limit was fifty-five miles an hour and that the patrolmen hid themselves behind billboards and small clumps of trees and sped out after you before you had a chance to slow down. She pointed out interesting details of the scenery: Stone Mountain; the blue granite that in some places came up to both sides of the highway; the brilliant red clay banks slightly streaked with purple; and the various crops that made rows of green lace-work on the ground. The trees were full of silver-white sunlight and the meanest of them sparkled. The children were reading comic magazines and their mother had gone back to sleep.

"Let's go through Georgia fast so we won't have to look at it much," John Wesley said.

"If I were a little boy," said the grandmother, "I wouldn't talk about my native state that way. Tennessee has the mountains and Georgia has the hills."

"Tennessee is just a hillbilly dumping ground," John Wesley said, "and Georgia is a lousy state too."

"You said it," June Star said.

"In my time," said the grandmother, folding her thin veined fingers, "Children were more respectful of their native states and their parents and everything else. People did right then. Oh look at the cute little pickaninny!" she said pointed to a Negro child standing in the door of a shack. "Wouldn't that make a picture, now?" she asked and they all turned and looked at the little Negro out of the back window. He waved.

"He didn't have any britches[4] on," June said.

"He probably didn't have any," the grandmother explained. "Little niggers in the country don't have things like we do. If I could paint, I'd paint that picture," she said.

The children exchanged comic books.

The grandmother offered to hold the baby and the children's mother passed him over the front seat to her. She set him on her knee and bounced him and told him about the things they were passing. She rolled her eyes and screwed up her mouth and stuck her leathery thin face into his smooth bland one. Occasionally he gave her a faraway smile. They passed a large cotton field with five or six graves fenced in the middle of it, like a small island. "Look at the graveyard!" the grandmother said, pointing it out. "That was the old family burying ground. That belonged to the plantation."

"Where's the plantation?" John Wesley asked.

"Gone With the Wind[5]," said the grandmother. "Ha. Ha."

When the children finished all the comic books they had brought, they opened the lunch and ate it. The grandmother ate a peanut butter sandwich and an olive and would not let the children throw the box and the paper napkins out the window. When there was nothing else to do they played a game by choosing a cloud and making the other two guess what shape it suggested. John Wesley took one the shape of a cow and June Star guessed a cow and John Wesley said, no, an automobile, and June Star said he didn't play fair, and they began to slap each other over the grandmother.

The grandmother said she would tell them a story if they would keep quiet. When she told a story, she rolled her eyes and waved her head and was very dramatic. She said once when she was a maiden lady she had been courted by a Mr. Edgar Atkins Teagarden from Jasper, Georgia. She said he was a very good-looking man and a gentleman and that he brought her a watermelon every Saturday afternoon with his initials cut in it, E. A. T. Well, one Saturday, she said, Mr. Teagarden brought the watermelon and there was nobody at home and he left in on the front porch and returned in his buggy to Jasper, but she never got the watermelon, she said, because a nigger boy ate it when he saw the initials, E. A. T.! This story tickled John Wesley's funny bone[6] and he giggled and giggled but June Star didn't think it was any good. She said she wouldn't marry a man that just brought her a watermelon on Saturday. The grandmother said she would have done well to marry Mr. Teagarden because he was a gentleman and had bought Coca-Cola stock[7] when it first came out and that he had died only a few years ago, a very wealthy man.

They stopped at The Tower for barbecued sandwiches. The Tower was a part stucco and part wood filling station and dance hall set in a clearing outside of Timothy. A fat man named Red Sammy Butts ran it and there were signs stuck here and there on the building and for miles up and down the highway saying, TRY RED SAMMY'S FAMOUS BARBECUE. NONE LIKE FAMOUS RED SAMMY'S! RED SAM! THE FAT BOY WITH THE HAPPY LAUGH. A VETERAN! SAMMY'S ROUR MAN!

Red Sammy was lying on the bare ground outside The Tower with his head under a truck[8] while a gray monkey about a foot high, chained to a small chinaberry tree, chattered nearby. The monkey sprang back into the tree and got on the highest limb as soon as he saw the children jump out of the car and run toward him.

Inside, The Tower was a long dark room with a counter at one end and tables at the other and dancing space in the middle. They all sat down at a broad table next to the nickelodeon and Red Sam's wife, a tall burnt-brown woman with hair and eyes lighter than her skin, came and took their order. The children's mother put a dime in the machine and played "The Tennessee Waltz," and the grandmother said that tune always made her want to dance. She asked Bailey if he would like to dance but he only glared at her. He didn't have a naturally sunny disposition like she did and trips made him nervous. The grandmother's brown eyes were very bright. She swayed her head from side to side and pretended she was dancing in her chair. June Star said play something she could tap to so the children's mother put in another dime and played a fast number and June Star stepped out onto the dance floor and did her tap routine.

"Ain't she cute?" Red Sam's wife said, leaning over the counter. "Would you like to come be my little girl[9]?"

"No I certainly wouldn't," June Star said. "I wouldn't live in a broken-down place like this for a million bucks!" and she ran back to the table.

"Ain't she cute?" the woman repeated, stretching her mouth politely.

"Aren't you ashamed?" hissed the grandmother.

Red Sam came in and told his wife to quit lounging on the counter and hurry with these people's order. His khaki trousers reached just to his hip bones and his stomach hung over them like a sack of meal swaying under his shirt. He came over and sat down at a table nearby and let out a combination sigh and yodel. "You can't win," he said. "You can't win," and he wiped his sweating red face off with a gray handkerchief. "These days you don't know who to trust," he said. "Ain't that the truth?"

"People are certainly not nice like they used to be," said the grandmother.

"Two fellers come in here last week," Red Sammy said, "Driving a Chrysler. It was an old beat-up car but it was a good one and these boys looked all right to me. Said they worked at the mill and you know I let them fellers charge the gas they bought[10]? Now why I do that?"

"Because you're a good man!" the grandmother said at once.

"Yes'm, I suppose so," Red Sam said as if he were struck with the answer.

His wife brought the orders, carrying the five plates all at once without a tray, two in each hand and one balanced on her arm. "It isn't a soul in this green world of God's[11] that you can trust," she said. "And I don't count anybody out of that, not nobody[12]," she repeated, looking at Red Sammy.

"Did you read about that criminal, The Misfit, that's escaped?" asked the grandmother.

"I wouldn't be a bit surprised if he didn't attact[13] this place right here," said the woman. "If he hears about it being here, I wouldn't be none surprised to see him. If he hears it's two cent in the cash register, I wouldn't be a tall[14] surprised if he . . . "

"That'll do," Red Sam said. "Go bring these people their Co'-colas," and the woman went off to get the rest of the order.

"A good man is hard to find," Red Sammy said. "Everything is getting terrible, I remember the day you could go off and leave your screen door unlatched. Not no more."

He and the grandmother discussed better times. The old lady said that in her opinion Europe was entirely to blame for the way things were now. She said the way Europe acted you would think we were made of money and Red Sam said it was no use talking about it, she was exactly right. The children ran outside into the white sunlight and looked at the monkey in the lacy chinaberry tree. He was busy catching fleas on himself and biting each one carefully between his teeth as if it were a delicacy.

They drove off again into the hot afternoon. The grandmother took cat naps and woke up every few minutes with her own snoring. Outside of Toombsboro she woke up and recalled an old plantation that she had visited in this neighborhood once when she was a young lady. She said the house had six white columns across the front and that there was an avenue of oaks leading up to it and two little wooden trellis arbors on either side in front where you sat down with your suitor after a stroll in the garden. She recalled exactly which road to turn off to get to it. She knew that Bailey would not be willing to lose any time looking at an old house, but the more she talked about it, the more she wanted to see it once again and find out if the little twin arbors were still standing. "There was a secret panel in this house," she said craftily, not telling the truth but wishing that she were, "and the story went that all the family silver was hidden in it when Sherman[15] came through but it was never found . . . "

"Hey!" John Wesley said. "Let's go see it! We'll find it! We'll poke all the woodwork and find it! Who lives there? Where do you turn off at? Hey Pop, can't we turn off there?"

"We never have seen a house with a secret panel!" June Star shrieked. "Let's go to the house with the secret panel! Hey, Pop, can't we go see the house with the secret panel!"

"It's not far from here, I know," the grandmother said. "It wouldn't take over twenty minutes."

Bailey was looking straight ahead. His jaw was as rigid as a horseshoe. "No," he said.

The children began to yell and scream that they wanted to see the house with the secret panel. John Wesley kicked the back of the front seat and June Star hung over her mother's shoulder and whined desperately into her ear that they never had any fun even on their vacation, and that they could never do what THEY wanted to do. The baby began to scream and John Wesley kicked the back of the seat so hard that his father could feel the blows in his kidney.

"All right!" he shouted, and drew the car to a stop at the side of the road. "Will you all shut up? Will you all just shut up for one second? If you don't shut up, we won't go anywhere."

"It would be very educational for them," the grandmother murmured.

"All right," Bailey said, "but get this: this is the only time we're going to stop for anything like this. This is the one and only time."

"The dirt road that you have to turn down is about a mile back," the grandmother directed. "I marked it when we passed."

"A dirt road," Bailey groaned.

After they had turned around and were headed toward the dirt road, the grandmother recalled other points about the house, the beautiful glass over the front doorway and the candle-lamp in the hall. John Wesley said that the secret panel was probably in the fireplace.

"You can't go inside this house," Bailey said. "You don't know who lives there."

"While you all talk to the people in front, I'll run around behind and get in a window," John Wesley suggested.

"We'll all stay in the car," his mother said.

They turned onto the dirt road and the car raced roughly along in a swirl of pink dust. The grandmother recalled the times when there were no paved roads and thirty miles was a day's journey. The dirt road was hilly and there were sudden washes in it and sharp curves on dangerous embankments. All at once thy would be on a hill, looking down over the blue tops of trees for miles around, then the next minute, they would be in a red depression with the dust-coated trees looking down on them.

"This place had better turn up in a minute," Bailey said, "or I'm going to turn around."

The road looked as if no one had traveled on it in months.

"It's not much farther," the grandmother said and just as she said it, a horrible thought came to her. The thought was so embarrassing that she turned red in the face and her eyes dilated and her feet jumped up, upsetting her valise in the corner. The instant the valise moved, the newspaper top she had over the basket under it rose with a snarl and Pitty Sing, the cat, sprang onto Bailey's shoulder.

The children were thrown to the floor and their mother, clutching the baby, was thrown out the door onto the ground, the old lady was thrown into the front seat. The car turned over once and landed right-side-up in a gulch on the side of the road. Bailey remained in the driver's seat with the cat—gray-striped with a broad white face and an orange nose—clinging to his neck like a caterpillar.

As soon as the children saw they could move their arms and legs, they scrambled out of the car, shouting, "We've had an ACCIDENT!" the grandmother was curled up under the dashboard, hoping she was injured so that Bailey's wrath would not come down on her all at once. The horrible thought she had had before the accident was that the house she had remembered so vividly was not in Georgia but in Tennessee.

Bailey removed the cat from his neck with both hands and flung it out the window against the side of a pine tree. Then he got out of the car and started looking for the children's mother. She was sitting against the side of the red gutted ditch, holding the screaming baby, but she only had a cut down her face and a broken shoulder. "We've had an ACCIDENT!" the children screamed in a frenzy of delight.

"But nobody's killed," June Star said with disappointment as the grandmother limped out of the car, her hat still pinned to her head but the broken front brim standing up at a jaunty angle and the violet spray hanging off the side. They all sat down in the ditch, except the children, to recover from the shock. They were all shaking.

"Maybe a car will come along," said the children's mother hoarsely.

"I believe I have injured an organ," said the grandmother, pressing her side, but no one answered her. Bailey's teeth were clattering. He had on a yellow sport shirt with bright blue parrots designed in it and his face was as yellow as the shirt. The grandmother decided that she would not mention that the house was in Tennessee.

The road was about ten feet above and they could see only the tops of the trees on the other side of it. Behind the ditch they were sitting in there were more woods, tall and dark and deep. In a few minutes they saw a car some distance away on top of a hill, coming slowly as if the occupants were watching them. The grandmother stood up and waved both arms dramatically to attract their attention. The car continued to come on slowly, disappeared around a bend and appeared again, moving even slower, on top of the hill they had gone over. It was a big black battered hearse-like automobile. There were three men in it.

It came to a stop just over them and for some minutes, the driver looked down with a steady expressionless gaze to where they were sitting, and didn't speak. Then he turned his head and muttered something to the other two and they got out. One was a fat boy in black trousers and a red sweatshirt with a silver stallion embossed on the front of it. He moved around on the right side of them and stood staring, his mouth partly open in a kind of loose grin. The other had on khaki pants and a blue striped coat and a gray hat pulled down very low, hiding most of his face. He came around slowly on the left side. Neither spoke.

The driver got out of the car and stood by the side of it, looking down at them. He was an older man than the other two. His hair was just beginning to gray and he wore silver rimmed spectacles that gave him a scholarly look. He had a long creased face and didn't have on any shirt or undershirt. He had on blue jeans that were too tight for him and was holding a black hat and a gun. The two boys also had guns.

"We've had an ACCIDENT!" the children screamed.

The grandmother had the peculiar feeling that the bespectacled man was someone she knew. His face was as familiar to her as if she had known him all her life but she could not recall who he was. He moved away from the car and began to come down the embankment, placing his feet carefully so that he wouldn't slip. He had on tan and white shoes and no socks, and his ankles were red and thin. "Good afternoon," he said. "I see you all had you a little spill."

"We turned over twice!" said the grandmother.

"Once," he corrected. "We seen it happen. Try their car and see will it run, Hiram," he said quietly to the boy with the gray hat.

"What you got that gun for?" John Wesley asked. "What cha gonna do with that gun[16]?"

"Lady," the man said to the children's mother, "would you mind calling them children to sit down by you? Children make me nervous. I want all you all to sit down right together there where you're at."

"What are you telling us what to do for?" June star asked.

Behind them the line of woods gaped like a dark open mouth. "Come here," said their mother.

"Look here now," Bailey began suddenly, "we're in a predicament! We're in . . . "

The grandmother shrieked. She scrambled to her feet and stood staring. "You're The Misfit!" she said. "I recognized you at once."

"Yes'm," the man said, smiling slightly as if he were pleased in spite of himself to be known, "but it would have been better for all of you, lady, if you hadn't of reckernized[17] me."

Bailey turned his head sharply and said something to his mother that shocked even the children. The old lady began to cry and The Misfit reddened.

"Lady," he said, "don't you get upset. Sometimes a man says things he don't mean. I don't reckon he meant to talk to you that way."

"You wouldn't shoot a lady, would you?" the grandmother said and removed a clean handkerchief from her cuff and began to slap at her eyes with it.

The Misfit pointed the toe of his shoe into the ground and made a little hole and then covered it up again. "I would hate to have to," he said.

"Listen," the grandmother almost screamed, "I know you're a good man. You don't look a bit like you have common blood[18]. I know you must come from nice people!"

"Yes, mam," he said, "finest people in the world." When he smiled he showed a row of strong white teeth. "God never make a finer woman than my mother and my daddy's heart was pure gold," he said. The boy with the red sweatshirt had come around behind them and was standing with his gun at his hip. The Misfit squatted down on the ground. "Watch them children, Bobby Lee," he said. "You know they make me nervous." He looked at the six of them huddled together in front of him and he seemed to be embarrassed as if he couldn't think of anything to say. "Ain't a cloud in the sky," he remarked, looking up at it. "Don't see no sun but don't see no cloud neither."

"Yes, it's a beautiful day," said the grandmother. "Listen," she said, "you shouldn't call yourself The Misfit because I know you're a good man at heart. I can just look at you and tell."

"Hush!" Bailey yelled. "Hush! Everybody shut up and let me handle this!" He was squatting in the position of a runner about to sprint forward but he didn't move.

"I pre-chate that[19], lady," The Misfit said and drew a little circle in the ground with the butt of his gun.

"It'll take a half a hour to fix this here car," Hiram called, looking over the raised hood of it.

"Well, first you and Bobby Lee get him and that little boy to step over yonder with you," The Misfit said, pointing to Bailey and John Wesley. "The boys want to ask you something," he said to Bailey. "Would you mind stepping back in them woods there with them?"

"Listen," Bailey began, "we're in a terrible predicament. Nobody realizes what this is," and his voice cracked. His eyes were as blue and intense as the parrots in his shirt and he remained perfectly still.

The grandmother reached up to adjust her hat brim as if she were going to the woods with him but it came off in her hand. She stood staring at it and after a second she let it fall on the ground. Hiram pulled Bailey up by the arm as if he were assisting an old man. John Wesley caught hold of his father's hand and Bobby Lee followed. They went off toward the woods and just as they reached the dark edge, Bailey turned and supporting himself against a gray naked pine trunk, he shouted, "I'll be back in a minute, mamma, wait on me[20] !"

"Come back this instant!" his mother shrilled but they all disappeared into the woods.

"Bailey Boy!" the grandmother called in a tragic voice but she found she was looking at The Misfit squatting on the ground in front of her. "I just know you're a good man," she said desperately. "You're not a bit common!"

"Nome, I ain't a good man," The Misfit said after a second as if he had considered her statement carefully, "but I ain't the worst in the world neither. My daddy said I was a different breed of dog from my brothers and sisters. 'You know,' Daddy said, 'it's some a that can live their whole life out without asking about it and it's others has to know why it is, and this boy is one of the latters. He's going to be into everything!'" He put on his black hat and looked up suddenly and then away deep into the woods as if he were embarrassed again. "I'm sorry I don't have on a shirt before you ladies," he said, hunching his shoulders slightly. "We buried our clothes that we had on when we escaped and we're just making do[21] until we can get better. We borrowed these from some folks we met," he explained.

"That's perfectly all right," the grandmother said. "Maybe Bailey has an extra shirt in his suitcase."

"I'll look and see terrectly[22]," The Misfit said.

"Where are they taking him?" the children's mother screamed.

"Daddy was a card[23] himself," The Misfit said. "You couldn't put anything over on him[24]. He never got in trouble with the Authorities though. Just had the knack of handling them."

"You could be honest too if you'd only try," said the grandmother. "Think how wonderful it would be to settle down and live a comfortable life and not have to think about somebody chasing you all the time."

The Misfit kept scratching in the ground with the butt of his gun as if he were thinking about it. "Yes'm, somebody is always after you," he murmured.

The grandmother noticed how thin his shoulder blades were just behind his hat because she was standing up looking down on him,"Do you ever pray?" she asked.

He shook his head. All she saw was the black hat wiggle between his shoulder blades."Nome," he said.

There was a pistol shot from the woods, followed closely by another. Then silence. The old lady's head jerked around. She could hear the wind move through the tree tops like a long satisfied insuck of breath. "Bailey Boy!" she called.

"I was a gospel singer for a while," The Misfit said. "I been most everything. Been in the arm service, both land and sea, at home and abroad, been twict married, been an undertaker, been with the railroads, plowed Mother Earth, been in a tornado, seen a man burnt alive once," and he looked up at the children's mother and the little girl who were sitting close together, their faces white and their eyes glassy; "I even seen a woman flogged," he said.

"Pray, pray," the grandmother began, "pray, pray . . ."

"I never was a bad boy that I remember of," The Misfit said in an almost dreamy voice, "but somewheres along the line I done something wrong and got sent to the penitentiary. I was buried alive," and he looked up and held her attention to him by a steady stare.

"That's when you should have started to pray," she said. "What did you do to get sent to the penitentiary that first time?"

"Turn to the right, it was a wall," the Misfit said, looking up again at the cludless sky. "Turn to the left, it was a wall. Look up it was a ceiling, look down it was a floor. I forgot what I done, lady. I set[25] there and set there, trying to remember what it was I done and I ain't recalled it to this day. Once in a while, I would think it was coming to me, but it never come."

"Maybe they put you in by mistake," the old lady said vaguely.

"Nome," he said. "it wasn't no mistake, they had the papers on me."

"You must have stolen something," she said.

The Misfit sneered slightly. "Nobody had nothing I wanted," he said. "It was a head-doctor at the penitentiary said what I had done was kill my daddy but I know that for a lie. My daddy died in nineteen ought nineteen of the epidemic flu[26] and I never had a thing to do with it. He was buried in the Mount Hopewell Baptist churchyard and you can go there and see for yourself."

"If you would pray," the old lady said. "Jesus would help you."

"That's right," the Misfit said.

"Well then, why don't you pray?" she asked trembling with delight suddenly.

"I don't want no hep," he said. "I'm doing all right by myself."

Bobby Lee and Hiram came ambling back from the woods. Bobby Lee was dragging a yellow shirt with bright blue parrots in it.

"Throw me that shirt, Bobby Lee," The Misfit said. The shirt came flying at him and landed on his shoulder and he put it on. The grandmother couldn't name what the shirt reminded her of. "No, lady," the Misfit said while he was buttoning it up. "I found out the crime don't matter. You can do one thing or you can do another, kill a man or take a tire off his car, because sooner or later you're going to forget what it was you done and just be punished for it."

The children's mother had begun to make heaving noises as if she couldn't get her breath. "Lady," he asked, "would you and that little girl like to step off yonder with Bobby Lee and Hiram and join your husband?"

"Yes, thank you," the mother said faintly. Her left arm dangled helplessly and she was holding the baby, who had gone to sleep, in the other. "Hep that lady up, Hiram," The Misfit said as she struggled to climb out of the ditch, "and Bobby Lee, you hold onto that little girl's hand."

"I don't want to hold hands with him," June Star said. "He reminds me of a pig."

The fat boy blushed and laughed and caught her by the arm and pulled her off into the woods after Hiram and her mother.

Alone with The Misfit, the grandmother found that she had lost her voice. There was not a cloud in the sky nor any sun. There was nothing around her but woods. She wanted to tell him that he must pray. She opened and closed her mouth several times before anything came out. Finally she found herself saying, "Jesus, Jesus," meaning Jesus will help you, but the way she was saying it, it sounded as if she might be cursing.

"Yes'm," The Misfit said as if he agreed. "Jesus thrown everything off balance. It was the same case with Him as with me except he hadn't committed any crime and they could prove I had committed one because they had the papers on me. Of course," he said, "they never shown me any papers. That's why I sign myself now. I said long ago, you get you a signature and sign everything you do and keep a copy of it. Then you'll know what you done and you can hold up the crime to; the punishment and see do they match and in the end you'll have something to prove you ain't been treated right. I call myself the Misfit," he said, "because I can't make what all I done wrong fit what all I gone through in punishment."

There was a piercing scream from the woods, followed closely by a pistol report.

"Does it seem right to you, lady, that one is punished a heap[27] and another ain't punished at all?"

"Jesus!" the old lady cried. "You've got good blood! I know you wouldn't shoot a lady! I know you come from nice people! Pray! Jesus, you ought not to shoot a lady. I'll give you all the money I've got!"

"Lady," The Misfit said, looking beyond her far into the woods, "there never was a body that give the undertaker a tip."

There were two more pistol reports and the grandmother raised her head like a parched old turkey hen crying for water and called, "Bailey Boy, Bailey Boy!" As if her heart would break.

"Jesus was the only one that ever raised the dead," The Misfit continued, "and He shouldn't have done it. He thrown everything off balance. If He did what He said, then it's nothing for you to do but throw away everything and follow Him, and if He didn't then it's nothing for you to do but enjoy the few minutes you got left the best way you can—by killing somebody or burning down his house or doing some other meanness to him. No pleasure but meanness," he said and his voice had become almost a snarl.

"Maybe He didn't raise the dead," the old lady mumbled, not knowing what she was saying and feeling so dizzy that she sank down in the ditch with her legs twisted under her.

"I wasn't there so I can't say He didn't," the Misfit said. "I wisht I had of been there[28]," He said, hitting the ground with his fist. "It ain't right I wasn't there because if I had of been there I would of known[29]. Listen lady," he said in a high voice, "if I had of been there I would of known and I wouldn't be like I am now." His voice seemed about to crack and the grandmother's head cleared for an instant. She saw the man's face twisted close to her own as if he were going to cry and she murmured, "Why you're one of my babies. You're one of my own children!" She reached out and touched him on the shoulder. The Misfit sprang back as if a snake had bitten him and shot her three times through the chest. Then he put his gun down on the ground and took off his glasses and began to clean them.

Hiram and Bobby Lee returned from the woods and stood over the ditch, looking down at the grandmother who half sat and half lay in a puddle of blood with her legs crossed under her like a child's and her face smiling up at the cloudless sky.

Without his glasses, The Misfit's eyes were red-rimmed and pale and defenseless-looking. "Take her off and throw her where you thrown the others," he said, picking up the cat that was rubbing itself against his leg.

"She was a talker, wasn't she?" Bobby Lee said, sliding down the ditch with a yodel.

"She would have been a good woman," The Misfit said, "if it had been somebody there to shoot her every minute of her life."

"Some fun!" Bobby Lee said.

"Shut up, Bobby Lee," The Misfit said. "It's no real pleasure in life."

【注解】

1. aloose from the Federal Pen: 从联邦监狱中逃出。"aloose"是在 loose(松开)前加前缀而成。"Pen"为 Penitentiary 的缩写。
2. be broad: 开阔眼界，增长见识。
3. She wouldn't stay at home to be queen for a day：让她在家当一天皇后，她也不会愿意。
4. britches：裤子，breeches 的变体。
5. Gone With the Wind: 老祖母借用美国女作家玛格丽特·米切尔 (Margaret Mitchell, 1900—1949) 的小说《飘》(*Gone With the Wind*, 1936)，指农场都随风而逝，不复存在。
6. The story tickled John Wesley's funny bone: 故事把约翰·韦斯勒逗笑了。
7. Coca-Cola stock：可口可乐公司股票。
8. with his head under a truck：躺在卡车下修车。
9. Would you like to come be my little girl?：你愿意来这儿当小舞星吗？
10. I let them fellers charge the gas they bought：那帮家伙买汽油时，我让他们赊账了。"fellers"相当于 fellows；"charge"此处指赊账。
11. It isn't a soul in this green world of God's . . . : "It isn't a soul"相当于 There isn't a soul; "green world"为爱尔兰方言，即 good world (奥康纳的祖辈为爱尔兰人，故对爱尔兰方言颇有了解)。
12. I don't count anybody out of that, not nobody: 世界上没有人是可靠的，谁也不可靠。正规语法中，"not nobody"应为 not anybody。这里的双重否定指说话人没有受过太多的教育。下文还有类似用法。
13. attact: attack。
14. a tall: not at all。
15. Sherman：William Tecumseh Sherman (1820—1891)，美国内战时期北部联邦军将领。
16. What cha gonna do with that gun?: What are you going to do with that gun?
17. if you hadn't of reckernized me: if you hadn't recognized me。
18. common blood：出身低微。
19. I pre-chate that: I appreciate that. 多谢称赞。
20. wait on: wait for。
21. We've just making do: 我们只是凑合着而已。
22. terrectly: directly。
23. a card：神通广大的人，精明的人。
24. You couldn't put anything over on him: 在他面前，你要不了花招。
25. set: sat。
26. in nineteen ought nineteen of the epidemic flu: 指 1919 年欧洲流行的瘟疫。
27. a heap: 作状语，意为"许多"。
28. I had of been there: I had been there。
29. I would of known: I would have known。

【思考题】

1. Viewed objectively, the story is about how a homicidal maniac slaughters an innocent, common family he happens to encounter on the road. What does the story seem to imply about the spiritual condition of modern man? How does the author interpret this special situation as a comment on general human values?

2. What is the character of the old lady? Pleasant or unpleasant? Admirable or unadmirable? Selfish or unselfish? What conventional social and religious values does the grandmother represent? How are they exposed in the course of the story? How does her character relate to the story's interpretation?

3. What is the significance of the scene at the highway restaurant? How do the early episode prepare for the meeting with the Misfit's?

4. Study carefully the dialogue between the old lady and the Misfit. Which of the two, the sane woman or the homicidal maniac, is the more deeply involved in the religious question? Which, do you think, has a deeper understanding about life, society and religion?

5. O'Connor herself says the story is a story of original sin and the characters have the moment of grace, or epiphany. So what is the significance of the old lady's last words to the Misfit?

解读举例

1. 《好人难寻》是针对美国南方社会的道德性寓言，描述了当时美国社会中骇人听闻的暴行，表现了社会的堕落，善良的人们随时都会遭到无辜杀害。

2. 《好人难寻》是对人生价值的思考。"不合时宜的人"的残暴行为是对不公平的社会的报复，他没有体验到人生真正的乐趣，因而生存对他毫无意义。

Allen Ginsberg
1926—1997

艾伦·金斯堡是20世纪50年代末美国垮掉派文学运动的中心人物，出生于美国新泽西州的诺瓦克市佩特逊镇。他的父亲是一位中学英语教师，也是当地小有名气的诗人。他的母亲因担心政治迫害而患上精神恐惧症，住进精神病院，直至去世。母亲的不幸遭遇在金斯堡幼小的心灵里留下了巨大的创伤，并极大地影响着他后来的生活与创作。

1943年，金斯堡进入纽约哥伦比亚大学，在莱昂内尔·屈林 (Lionel Trilling，1905—1075) 等著名文学教授影响下开始对文学产生浓厚兴趣。1945年，金斯堡应征入伍，在二战结束后重回哥伦比亚大学，开始练习写作。1955年，金斯堡开始创作一首长诗，完成后将手稿寄给旅居墨西哥的另一位垮掉派作家凯鲁亚克。后者对此大为赞赏，并将此题名《嚎叫》(Howl)，因为他深深地感受到诗中所表达的所有思想与情感全都发自人类的心灵深处。翌年，旧金山的城市之光出版社 (City Lights) 出版了诗集《嚎叫及其他》(Howl and Other Poems)，金斯堡一举成名。《嚎叫》真实记载了美国"垮掉的一代"的思想情感，出版后引起了极大的轰动。《嚎叫及其他》中的其他一些诗篇也和《嚎叫》在形式与内容上有着许多相同之处。《加利福尼亚的超市》("A Supermarket in California") 通过一系列感叹句和疑问句表达了金斯堡对美国自惠特曼时代以来物质极大丰裕和精神极度贫穷的悲叹。《向日葵箴言录》("Sunflower Sutra") 是与布莱克《啊，向日葵》("Ah, Sunflower") 的对话，赞扬了向日葵在美国工业"污染的皮肤"下的高风亮节。

《嚎叫》是一部桀骜不驯、惊世骇俗的作品，体现了古典与现当代文学对金斯堡文学创作的重要影响。英国浪漫主义诗人布莱克、雪莱、济慈，美国浪漫主义诗人惠特曼，美国现代派诗人庞德、艾略特、威廉·卡罗斯·威廉姆斯，以及垮掉派作家凯鲁亚克的思想都在诗中得以体现。威廉姆斯曾教导年轻的金斯堡如何用自己的声音和自然说话的节奏来表现普通美国人的生活，如何把重点放在给人印象强烈的视觉意象上。此外，麦尔维尔、陀思妥耶夫斯基、坡、迪金森等19世纪作家，日本的俳句 (haiku)、保罗·塞尚 (Paul Cézanne，1839—1906) 的绘画，以及宗教等也都不同程度地影响了金斯堡的诗歌创作。

1959 至 1960 年间，金斯堡创作完成了《哀悼祈祷文》的第一、二节，并于 1961 年出版诗集《哀悼祈祷文及其他》(*Kaddish and Other Poems*)。《哀悼祈祷文》是一首自传性长诗，共五节，题献给作者的母亲诺米·金斯堡。作品将诗歌、小说、历史记载糅为一体，表达了作者对患精神疾病的母亲深切的同情和对美国专制统治的极大愤慨。美国评论家认为《哀悼祈祷文》是"一个痛苦的呐喊，一个回忆的呼喊，一个爱的呼唤，也许是垮掉派最优秀的诗作"。

在 20 世纪 60 年代，金斯堡还创作出版了《空镜》(*Empty Mirror*, 1961)、《现实三明治》(*Reality Sandwiches*, 1963)、《星球消息》(*Planet News*, 1968) 等诗集，并先后访问了法国、摩洛哥、希腊等国。20 世纪 70 年代初，金斯堡出版了是继《嚎叫》以来最重要的诗集《美国的衰落》(*The Fall of America*, 1972)，并于 1974 年荣获全国图书奖 (National Book Award)，金斯堡本人也被选为美国文学艺术学院院士。金斯堡的文学生涯如同他的个人生活一样始终充满争议与分歧，但他狂放的思想、大胆的创新、不羁的诗句拓宽了读者的思维空间。

Howl

【题解】

在《嚎叫》的序言中，威廉姆斯这样写道："抓紧你们的裙子，女士们，我们开始下地狱啦。"金斯堡在诗中描写的地狱就是美国。《嚎叫》共分三节和一个"脚注"。诗的第一节由一系列人物传记拼贴而成，真实地记录了包括凯鲁亚克等垮掉派作家及金斯堡本人的生活。诗中，作者悲叹这些人是他"这一代人的精英"，却"被一种疯狂毁灭"。诗的第二节是金斯堡处于麻醉状态下创作的。据说金斯堡当时正凝视着旧金山的弗朗西斯·德雷克爵士旅馆。旅馆塔楼似笑非笑的正面让他想起了《圣经》中的凶神莫洛克。在诗中，金斯堡借用这一形象来比喻美国社会中的各种邪恶。金斯堡还将纽约的摩天大楼、工厂、银行等建筑与机构都比作莫洛克肢体的一部分，以隐喻这种邪恶势力无所不在。诗的第三节是诗人对关在精神病院的卡尔·所罗门表达的同情。在他看来，所罗门代表着美国理性主义的牺牲者，包括金斯堡的母亲诺米。"脚注"部分用一种近乎疯癫的状态发出强烈的呐喊：神圣、神圣、神圣……一切都是神圣！与《嚎叫》第二部分描述凶神莫洛克的内容形成鲜明对立。

《嚎叫》使用的是金斯堡独创的"长句"韵律，每个诗句的长度以一次自然呼吸的长度断句。金斯堡的呼吸很长，因此诗句也长。以下选自《嚎叫》的"脚注"部分。

Footnote to Howl

Holy! Holy! Holy! Holy! Holy! Holy! Holy! Holy! Holy! Holy! Holy! Holy! Holy! Holy! Holy!

The world is holy! The soul is holy! The skin is holy! The nose is holy! The tongue and cock and hand and asshole holy!

Everything is holy! Everybody's holy! Everywhere is holy! Everyday is in eternity! Everyman's an angel!

The bum's as holy as the seraphim! The madman is holy as you my soul are holy!

The typewriter is holy the poem is holy the voice is holy the hearers are holy the ecstasy is holy!

Holy Peter holy Allen holy Solomon holy Lucien holy Kerouac holy Huncke holy Burroughsholy Cassady[1] holy the unknown buggered and suffering beggars holy the hideous human angels!

Holy my mother in the insane asylum! Holy the cocks of the grandfathers of Kansas!

Holy the groaning saxophone! Holy the bop apocalypse! Holy the jazzbnads marijuana hipsters peace & peyote pipes & drums!

Holy the solitudes of skyscraper and pavements! Holy the cafeterias filled with the millions! Holy the mysterious rivers of tears under the streets!

Holy the lone juggernaut! Holy the vast lamb of the middleclass! Holy the crazy shepherds of rebellion! Who digs Los Angeles IS Los Angeless!

Holy New York holy San Francisco Holy Peoria & Seattle Holy Paris Holy Tangiers Holy Moscow Holy Istanbul!

Holy time in eternity holy eternity in time holy the clocks in space holy the fourth dimension holy the fifth international holy the Angel in Moloch!

Holy the sea holy the desert holy the railroad holy the locomotive holy the visions holy the hallucinations holy the miracles, holy the eyeball holy the abyss!

Holy forgiveness! mercy! charity! faith! Holy! Ours! bodies! suffering! magnanimity!

Holy the supernatural extra brilliant intelligent kindness of the soul!

【注解】

1. Holy Peter holy Allen . . . holy Cassady：这里列举的人物均是垮掉派的人物。

【思考题】

1. In the opening line of *Howl*, Ginsberg claimed that he saw "the best minds" of "his generation" destroyed. According to "Footnote", what kind of people does he refer to in the poem as "the best minds" of "his generation"?
2. Compare the poem with Whitman's "Song of Myself", or "Spontaneous Me". What are the similarities and dissimilarities?

解读举例

1. 《嚎叫》是一部不道德的作品(金斯堡曾因《嚎叫》被起诉)。金斯堡所谓的反叛实际是企图破坏和谐的社会秩序和优良的传统道德观。他所谓的诗歌充其量是一种疯狂的自白而已，毫无艺术可言。

2. 《嚎叫》是一部革命性的作品。作品中长而有力的句式、排比重复的手法、反抑扬格及反诗节的韵律、地道的美国口语、平民化的表现风格、发自肺腑的内心自白等完全继承了惠特曼作品中自由豪放、奔腾激昂、酣畅淋漓、贴近生活的特点。因此他是一个"城市惠特曼"(urban Whitman)。他在诗歌中描写的"劣迹"不仅是用反传统、反价值的方式向压抑人性、迫害自由的美国社会提出强烈抗议，也是尝试使用一种"新的身体语言"来唤醒"全体美国人民的潜意识"。

Toni Morrison
1931—2019

作者简介

1993年，托妮·莫里森荣获诺贝尔文学奖，成为获此殊荣的第一位美国黑人女作家。莫里森原名科洛·安东尼·沃福德(Chloe Ardelia Wofford)，1931年出生于俄亥俄州洛伦城。父亲是一家造船厂的电焊工，为了养家糊口曾经在十七年内兼职三份工作。在她的成长过程中，父母一直告诫她要坚信自己，不要对白人抱任何幻想。孩提时代的沃福德不仅喜欢听奶奶讲的鬼怪或神话故事，还钟情于阅读文学作品，这些都为她日后的文学创作打下了基础。中学毕业之后，沃福德进入霍华德大学主修英语，其间改名为托妮。大学四年期间她热衷于参加学校剧团的表演，并于暑期去南方巡回演出。南方之行使莫里森对种族问题有了更深刻的了解，这在她日后的作品中有所体现。例如她在《所罗门之歌》(Song of Solomon, 1975) 中为主人公"奶娃"安排了一次了解自己身世的南方之旅。1955 年，莫里森在康奈尔大学获英语硕士学位，毕业后她在得克萨斯南方大学教了两年的书，1957 年回到霍华德大学执教，并加入了学校的写作爱好者组织，开始尝试文学创作。1970 年，莫里森出版了第一部作品《最蓝的眼睛》(The Bluest Eye)。

《最蓝的眼睛》根据莫里森在写作爱好者组织里写的一篇小故事发展而来，讲述的是黑人女孩皮克拉梦想着拥有一双像秀兰·邓波儿那样的蓝眼睛，但最终发疯的悲剧故事。莫里森以蓝眼睛为象征指出皮克拉是白人价值观念的牺牲品。《最蓝的眼睛》出版后，莫里森搬到纽约的兰登书屋总部做编辑工作。这一时期她还是炙手可热的书评人。1971 至 1972 年间她为《纽约时报书评》写过二十八篇书评，并为《时代》周刊撰写文章《黑人妇女对妇女解放运动的看法》。她认为如果女权运动只关心一些观点和态度，那么该运动就与黑人妇女无关；如果它关心的是同工同酬问题，那么这与黑人妇女的利益还有一定的联系。

莫里森的第二部作品《秀拉》(Sula, 1973) 探讨了黑人妇女的身份和关系。莫里森对黑人文化和黑人历史也极有兴趣，这主要体现在她的第三部小说《所罗门之歌》中。作品出版当年即获全国图书奖，是莫里森早期的代表作。小说讲述了一个北方中产阶级黑人青年麦肯·戴德(绰号"奶娃")的成长过程。小说通过奶娃复杂的家庭和社会背景，表现了奶娃在现实生活中的困惑。小说后部分描写了奶娃到南方的一次旅行。通过这次南方之行奶娃意外地发现了家族的历史，从而找到了自己的身份。莫里森的第四部小说《柏油孩子》(Tar Baby, 1981) 的名字取材于传说故事。作品探讨了殖民主义中的各种关系，通过黑人文化和白人文化的对比，作者表达了自己对黑人文化的自豪之情。

自 20 世纪 80 年代，莫里森专注于梳理黑人百年历史的"三部曲"的创作。她相继发表了《宠儿》(Beloved, 1987)、《爵士乐》(Jazz, 1992) 和《乐园》(Paradise, 1998)。这三部小说表现了百余年来黑人生活的方方面面。《宠儿》表现了黑人在奴隶制下的苦难。《爵士乐》把背景转移到 20 世纪 20 年代纽约哈莱姆区，表现黑人从南方涌入北方，从乡村进入城市后面临的困惑。《乐园》的故事发生在 1976 年，一群黑人建立了一个封闭的、天堂般的小镇，排斥白人和浅肤色黑人，然而，黑人过去的历史、现实的封闭与一种"黑人至上"的种族主义却使小镇的人们难以真正幸福地生活。这几部小说一方面继续探讨现代美国社会中黑人的身份与地位等问题，另一方面则在表现形式上不断摸索、创新。例如在《爵士乐》中，同一情节反复出现，视角与焦点也不断变化，制造出一种独特的效果，如同爵士乐一样，同一曲调的每一次出现都有不同的表现特点。因此书名不仅给小说设置了背景，更预示了作品的结构。2003年，莫里森发表小说《爱》(Love)，讲述了与中产阶级黑人比尔·科塞密切相关的几名黑人女性对其财产的争夺及她们之间的爱恨情仇。小说还探讨了民权运动对黑人生活的改善状况。此后她笔耕不辍，继续发表了《慈悲》(A Mercy, 2008)、《家园》(Home, 2012) 和《上帝保佑孩子》(God Help the Child, 2015) 等作品。

1993年，因"在小说中以丰富的想象力和诗情画意的表达方式，写活了美国现实一个极其重要的方面"，莫里森获得了诺贝尔文学奖。在颁奖仪式上，莫里森发表了以"语言的剥夺"为题的简短演说，反映了莫里森对语言多重功能的认识。通过文学创作，莫里森为美国黑人重新撰写了属于自己的历史。莫里森是一个相对传统的作家，她的作品探讨的大多是人的自我了解和家庭、社区中的各种关系，但她用自己细腻优美的笔触和超凡卓越的想象力赋予了这些传统题材新的形式。

Beloved

【题解】

《宠儿》自1987年发表以来就广受好评，莫里森也因该作品荣获1988年的普利策奖。2006年，《纽约时报》召集125名知名作家、评论家、编辑选出自己心目中"25年来最佳美国小说"，《宠儿》名列榜首。莫里森的前四部小说关注的都是当代黑人的生活。在《宠儿》中，她开始反思黑人历史，把笔触伸向黑暗的奴隶制时期，描写"小说人物不愿回忆，作者本人不愿回忆，黑人不愿回忆，白人不愿回忆"的一段历史。

小说的创作源于黑奴反抗历史中一个真实事件：一个名叫玛格丽特·加纳的女黑奴在逃往北方的途中，遭遇奴隶主的追捕，为了不让自己的孩子再次沦为奴隶，她亲手杀死了自己的小女儿。《宠儿》将其作为小说的中心事件展开，生动刻画了黑奴母亲塞丝的内心活动，展现了这一事件对塞丝生活造成的重大影响。怀着身孕的塞丝与三个孩子从南方奴隶主庄园"甜蜜之家"逃到北方，因奴隶主的追杀，她亲手杀死了2岁的小女儿，这个死去的孩子被取名为"宠儿"。此后，两个儿子皆因难以承受这一事件的打击，先后离开。塞丝与女儿丹芙过着封闭的生活，与邻居鲜有来往。18年后，当年在"甜蜜之家"的奴隶保罗·D来到塞丝家，回忆再次涌入塞丝的脑海。宠儿的鬼魂化身为一个妙龄少女，出现在家中。塞丝为了弥补过去，无微不至地照料着宠儿,加倍地偿还母爱。但宠儿无休止地索取爱,终于让塞丝心力交瘁。在女儿丹芙、保罗·D和黑人邻居的帮助下,鬼魂被驱除,塞丝也从过去的阴影中走了出来。

在《宠儿》的扉页题词中,莫里森把小说献给"六千万甚至更多"的黑奴亡灵。小说真实地展现了奴隶制对黑人人性的摧残,强烈地凸现了母爱这一主题。

以下内容选自《宠儿》第五章第一部分,描述宠儿的鬼魂如何来到塞丝家里。

From Beloved

Chapter 5   Part I

A fully dressed woman walked out of the water. She barely gained the dry bank of the stream before she sat down and leaned against a mulberry tree. All day and all night she sat there, her head resting on the trunk in a position abandoned enough to crack the brim in her straw hat. Everything hurt but her lungs most of all. Stopping wet and breathing shallow she spent those hours trying to negotiate the weight of her eyelids. The day breeze blew her dress dry; the night wind wrinkled it. Nobody saw her emerge or came accidentally by. If they had, chances are they would have hesitated before approaching her. Not because she was wet, or dozing or had what sounded like asthma, but because amid all that she was smiling. It took her the whole of the next morning to lift herself from the ground and make her way through the woods past a giant temple of boxwood to the field and then the yard of the slate-gray house. Exhausted again, she sat down on the first handy place—a stump not far from the steps of 124[1]. By then keeping her eyes open was less of an effort. She could manage it for a full two minutes or more. Her neck, its circumference no wider than a parlor service saucer, kept bending and her chin brushed the bit of lace edging her dress.

Women who drink champagne when there is nothing to celebrate can look like that: their straw hats with broken brims are often askew; they nod in public places; their shoes are undone. But their skin is not like that of the woman breathing near the steps of 124. She had new skin, lineless and smooth, including the knuckles of her hands.

By late afternoon when the carnival[2] was over, and the Negroes were hitching rides home if they were lucky—walking if they were not—the woman had fallen asleep again. The rays of the sun struck her full in the face, so that when Sethe, Denver and Paul D rounded the curve in the road all they saw was a black dress, two unlaced shoes below it, and Here Boy[3] nowhere in sight.

"Look," said Denver. "What is that?"

And, for some reason she could not immediately account for, the moment she got close enough to see the face, Sethe's bladder filled to capacity. She said, "Oh, excuse me," and ran around to the back of 124. Not since she was a baby girl, being cared for by the eight-year-old girl who pointed out her mother to her, had she had an emergency that unmanageable. She never made the outhouse. Right in front of its door she had to lift her skirts, and the water she voided was endless. Like a horse, she thought, but as it went on and on she thought, No, more like flooding the boat when Denver was born[4]. So much water Amy said, "Hold on, Lu. You going to sink us you keep that up." But there was no stopping water breaking from a breaking womb and there was no stopping now. She hoped Paul D wouldn't take it upon himself to come looking for her and be obliged to see her squatting in front of her own privy making a mudhole too deep to be witnessed without shame. Just about the time she started wondering if the carnival would accept another freak, it stopped. She tidied herself and ran around to the porch. Not one was there. All three were inside—Paul D and Denver standing before the stranger, watching her drink cup after cup of water.

"She said she was thirsty," said Paul D. He took off his cap. "Mighty thirsty look like."

The woman gulped water from a speckled tin cup and held it out for more. Four times Denver filled it, and four times the woman drank as though she had crossed a desert. When she was finished a little water was on her chin, but she did not wipe it away. Instead she gazed at Sethe with sleepy eyes. Poorly fed, thought Sethe, and younger than her clothes suggested—good lace at the throat, and a rich woman's hat. Her skin was flawless except for three vertical scratches on her forehead so fine and thin they seemed at first like hair, baby hair before it bloomed and roped into the masses of black yarn under her hat.

"You from around here?" Sethe asked her.

She shook her head no and reached down to take off her shoes. She pulled her dress up to the knees and rolled down her stockings. When the hosiery was tucked into the shoes, Sethe saw that her feet were like her hands, soft and new. She must have hitched a wagon ride, thought Sethe. Probably one of those West Virginia girls looking for something to beat a life of tobacco and sorghum. Sethe bent to pick up the shoes.

"What might your name be?" asked Paul D.

"Beloved," she said, and her voice was so low and rough each one looked at the other two. They heard the voice first—later the name.

"Beloved. You use a last name, Beloved?" Paul D asked her.

"Last?" She seemed puzzled. Then "No," and she spelled it for them, slowly as though the letters were being formed as she spoke them.

Sethe dropped the shoes; Denver sat down and Paul D smiled. He recognized the careful enunciation of letters by those, like himself, who could not read but had memorized the letters of their name. He was about to ask who her people were but thought better of it. A young colored woman drifting was drifting from ruin. He had been in Rochester four years ago and seen five women arriving with fourteen female children. All their men—brother, uncles, fathers, husbands, sons—had been picked off one by one by one. They had a single piece of paper directing them to a preacher on De Vore Street. The War had been over four or five years then, but nobody white or black seemed to know it. Odd clusters and strays of Negroes wandered the back roads and cowpaths from Schenectady to Jackson. Dazed but insistent, they searched each other out for word of a cousin, an aunt, a friend who once said, "Call on me. Anytime you get near Chicago, just call on me." Some of them were running from family that could not support them, some to family; some were running from dead crops, dead kin, life threats, and took-over land. Boys younger than Buglar and Howard[5]; configurations and blends of families of women and children, while elsewhere, solitary, hunted and hunting for, were men, men, men. Forbidden public transportation, chased by debt and filthy "talking sheets[6]," they followed secondary routes, scanned the horizon for signs and counted heavily on each other. Silent, except for social courtesies, when they met one another they neither described nor asked about the sorrow that drove them from one place to another. The whites didn't bear speaking on. Everybody knew.

So he did not press the young woman with the broken hat about where from or how come. If she wanted them to know and was strong enough to get through the telling, she would. What occupied them at the moment was what it might be that she needed. Underneath the major question, each harbored another. Paul D wondered at the newness of her shoes. Sethe was deeply touched by her sweet name; the remembrance of glittering headstone made her feel especially kindly toward her[7]. Denver, however, was shaking. She looked at this sleepy beauty and wanted more.

Sethe hung her hat on a peg and turned graciously toward the girl. "That's a pretty name, Beloved. Take off your hat, why don't you, and I'll make us something. We just got back from the carnival over near Cincinnati. Everything in there is something to see."

Bolt upright in the chair, in the middle of Sethe's welcome, Beloved had fallen asleep again.

"Miss. Miss." Paul D shook her gently. "You want to lay down a spell?"

She opened her eyes to slits and stood up on her soft new feet which, barely capable of their job, slowly bore her to the keeping room. Once there, she collapsed on Baby Suggs' bed[8]. Denver removed her hat and put the quilt with two squares of color over her feet. She was breathing like a steam engine.

"Sounds like croup," said Paul D, closing the door.

"Is she feverish? Denver, could you tell?"

"No. She's cold."

"Then she is. Fever goes from hot to cold."

"Could have the cholera," said Paul D.

"Reckon?"

"All that water. Sure sign."

"Poor thing. And nothing in this house to give her for it. She'll just have to ride it out. That's hateful sickness if ever there was one."

"She's not sick!" said Denver, and the passion in her voice made them smile.

Four days she slept, waking and sitting up only for water. Denver tended her, watched her sound sleep, listened to her labored breathing and, out of love and a breakneck possessiveness that charged her, hid like a personal blemish Beloved's incontinence. She rinsed the sheets secretly, after Sethe went to the restaurant[9] and Paul D went scrounging for barges to help unload. She boiled the underwear and soaked it in bluing, praying the fever would pass without damage. So intent was her nursing, she forgot to eat or visit the emerald closet[10].

"Beloved?" Denver would whisper. "Beloved?" and when the black eyes opened a slice all she could say was "I'm here. I'm still here."

Sometimes, when Beloved lay dreamy eyed for a very long time, saying nothing, licking her lips and heaving deep sighs, Denver panicked. "What is it?" she would ask.

"Heavy," murmured Beloved. "This place is heavy."

"Would you like to sit up?"

"No," said the raspy voice. It took three days for Beloved to notice the orange patches in the darkness of the quilt. Denver was pleased because it kept her patient awake longer.

She seemed totally taken with those faded scraps of orange, even made the effort to lean on her elbow and stroke them. An effort that quickly exhausted her, so Denver rearranged the quilt so its cheeriest part was in the sick girl's sight line.

Patience, something Denver had never known, overtook her. As long as her mother did not interfere, she was a model of compassion, turning waspish, though, when Sethe tried to help.

"Did she take a spoonful of anything today?" Sethe inquired.

"She shouldn't eat with cholera."

"You sure that's it? Was just a hunch of Paul D's."

"I don't know, but she shouldn't eat anyway just yet."

"I think cholera people puke all the time."

"That's even more reason, ain't it?"

"Well she shouldn't starve to death either, Denver."

"Leave us alone, Ma'am. I'm taking care of her."

"She say anything?"

"I'd let you know if she did." Sethe looked at her daughter and thought, Yes, she has been lonesome. Very lonesome.

"Wonder where Here Boy got off to?" Sethe thought a change of subject was needed.

"He won't be back," said Denver.

"How you know?"

"I just know." Denver took a square of sweet bread off the plate.

Back in the keeping room, Denver was about to sit down when Beloved's eyes flew wide open. Denver felt her heart race. It wasn't that she was looking at that face for the first time with no trace of sleep in it, or that the eyes were big and black. Nor was it that the whites of them were much too white-blue-white. It was that deep down in those big black eyes there was no expression at all.

"Can I get you something?"

Beloved looked at the sweet bread in Denver's hands and Denver held it out to her. She smiled then and Denver's heart stopped bouncing and sat down—relieved and easeful like a traveler who had made it home.

From that moment and through everything that followed, sugar could always be counted on to please her. It was as though sweet things were what she was born for. Honey as well as the wax it came in, sugar sandwiches, the sludgy molasses gone hard and brutal in the can, lemonade, taffy and any type of dessert Sethe brought home from the restaurant. She gnawed a cane stick to flax and kept the strings in her mouth long after the syrup had been sucked away. Denver laughed, Sethe smiled and Paul D said it made him sick to his stomach.

Sethe believed it was a recovering body's need—after an illness—for quick strength. But it was a need that went on and on into glowing health because Beloved didn't go anywhere. There didn't seem anyplace for her to go. She didn't mention one, or have much of an idea of what she was doing in that part of the country or where she had been. They believed the fever had caused her memory to fail just as it kept her slow-moving. A young woman, about nineteen or twenty, and slender, she moved like a heavier one or an older one, holding on to furniture, resting her head in the palm of her hand as though it was too heavy for a neck alone.

"You just gonna feed her? From now on?" Paul D, feeling ungenerous, and surprised by it, heard the irritability in his voice.

"Denver likes her. She's no real trouble. I thought we'd wait till her breath was better. She still sounds a little lumbar to me."

"Something funny 'bout that gal," Paul D said, mostly to himself.

"Funny how?"

"Acts sick, sounds sick, but she don't look sick. Good skin, bright eyes and strong as a bull."

"She's not strong. She can hardly walk without holding on to something."

"That's what I mean. Can't walk, but I seen her pick up the rocker with one hand."

"You didn't."

"Don't tell me. Ask Denver. She was right there with her."

"Denver! Come in here a minute."

Denver stopped rinsing the porch and stuck her head in the window.

"Paul D says you and him saw Beloved pick up the rocking chair single-handed. That so?"

Long, heavy lashes made Denver's eyes seem busier than they were; deceptive, even when she held a steady gaze as she did now on Paul D. "No," she said. "I didn't see no such thing."

Paul D frowned but said nothing. If there had been an open latch between them, it would have closed.

【注解】

1. the steps of 124: 蓝石路124号是塞丝的家。十八年前，她曾在这里杀死了自己的女儿。多年来，人们一直回避这间闹鬼的凶宅。
2. the carnival: 在前一章里，塞丝、丹芙、保罗·D幸福和睦，就要开始新的生活。然而，宠儿的到来打乱了他们的生活。
3. Here Boy: 狗名。
4. more like flooding the boat when Denver was born: 塞丝在逃亡途中乘着一条满是窟窿的小船渡过俄亥俄河，奔向自由。在白人姑娘艾米·丹芙的帮助下，在河中央生下丹芙。当时，浸到船里的河水与分娩时的羊水汇合在了一起。"Lu"是塞丝当时的化名。此后，塞丝给女儿取名"丹芙"，以纪念这位帮助她的白人姑娘。
5. Buglar and Howard: 塞丝的两个儿子。在目睹母亲杀死两岁的妹妹后，她的两个儿子视母亲为嗜血的巫婆，从此拒绝她的爱抚，13岁时，他们离家出走，再也没有回来。
6. talking sheets: 记录着逃亡奴隶信息的罪犯档案。
7. the remembrance of glittering headstone made her feel especially kindly toward her: 塞丝杀死女儿后，以向刻字工出卖10分钟身体为代价，请他在墓碑上刻上女儿的名字——Beloved。
8. Baby Suggs：塞丝的婆婆，在塞丝两个儿子出走后不久去世。她临死前已对生活失去了希望，只能躺在床上琢磨颜色等死，她让塞丝找来各种明快的颜色，如淡紫色和橙色等，以驱赶屋里令人窒息的单调。后文中，宠儿也对被子上橙色的补丁表现出了兴趣。
9. Sethe went to the restaurant: 塞丝靠在饭店工作为生。
10. the emerald closet: 树林里由灌木形成的一个房间，丹芙经常光顾，这里成了她的避难所。

【思考题】

1. Why does not Paul D ask Beloved where she comes from and how she comes?
2. There are several signs that seem to indicate that the mysterious stranger who suddenly turns up at 124 Bluestone is the spirit of Sethe's daughter returning in flesh. Try to find out these signs.
3. When Denver shows unusual compassion for Beloved, what does Sethe think about it?
4. *Beloved* is full of images. Without imagery, *Beloved* would be a sterile ghost story, fit only for titillating audiences into a shiver and nervous giggle. Find the images in the selection and discuss the function of various images in this novel.

解读举例

1. 《宠儿》是对美国奴隶制的血泪控诉。莫里森将此书献给美国六千万黑奴，她用诗一般的语言，展现了这段让无数人失语的历史。奴隶制本身的残酷，一些奴隶主的残暴和种族歧视，使得黑奴们遭受精神和肉体的非人折磨。在黑人获得解放多年后，塞丝的房子仍然幽魂不散，说明奴隶制虽已随着内战结束被废除，但其伤害和阴影仍然对黑人的生活产生着深远的影响，黑人只有勇敢地回忆、面对这段痛苦的历史，才能获得新生。

2. 《宠儿》是对母爱的歌颂。塞丝的母爱通过弑婴这一"可怕的仁慈方式"展现出来，既凸显了奴隶制对黑奴的摧残和黑人对自由的向往，也表现了塞丝母爱的浓烈和伟大。十八年后，宠儿又回到她的身边，塞丝毫无保留地献出了所有的爱，直至自己奄奄一息。为了加倍给予女儿应有的爱，她愿倾其所有，甚至置自己的生命和幸福于不顾。

3. 《宠儿》是后现代主义的一个范本。小说大量运用多视角叙事、时空交错、意识流、拼贴、蒙太奇、倒叙、插叙等手法，将发生在二十余年里碎片般的事件和记忆一点点重现，过去与现在交织，真实与虚构重叠。小说碎片式的叙述模式更深刻地表现了黑人因奴隶制而遭受的精神创伤。

4. 《宠儿》是一部魔幻现实主义作品。小说扑朔迷离，打破了生与死之间的界限宠儿这个角色"亦人亦鬼"。一方面，她可能是塞丝十八年前所杀之女的魂魄；另一方面，她也可能是从海上贩奴者那里劫后余生的幸存者。但无论宠儿"是人是鬼"，小说都真实展现了黑奴们的悲惨遭遇。

Philip Roth
1933—2018

作者简介

菲利普·罗斯，美国当今文坛颇具影响力的作家之一，曾多次提名诺贝尔文学奖。1933 年，罗斯出生于美国新泽西州纽瓦克市的一个中产阶级犹太人家庭，1954 年毕业于宾夕法尼亚州巴克内尔大学，1955 年获芝加哥大学文学硕士学位后留校教英语，同时攻读博士学位，但在 1957 年放弃学位学习，专心写作，以短篇小说集《再见，哥伦布》(*Goodbye, Columbus*, 1959) 一举成名，翌年获全国图书奖。

1946 年到 1950 年间，罗斯在威考希克中学读高中。在此期间，他阅读了大量有关欧洲移民的史料，并且深入了解了哈德逊河两岸的移民情况，这为他后来在作品中写下许多栩栩如生的人物形象奠定了基础。1950 年，他在纽瓦克罗特格斯学院注册读大学。翌年，他为摆脱纽瓦克狭隘的地方主义和抱着去看看美国其他地方的心理，又转到位于宾夕法尼亚州的巴克内尔大学就读。在这所大学学习期间，他帮助创建并参与编辑了《其他等人》(Et Cetera) 杂志。罗斯的第一个短篇小说《哲学，或类似的东西》("Philosophy, Or Something Like That", 1952) 就发表在这份杂志上。1954 年，他以优异的成绩毕业并获得英语学士学位。

到 1957 年为止，罗斯一共发表了七篇短篇小说，其中有两篇获奖。随后，他获得霍顿·米夫林文学研究基金和古根海姆研究基金的资助，于 1959 年出版了第一部短篇小说集《再见，哥伦布》。

从 1960 年起，罗斯开始在艾奥瓦大学作家工作室任教。两年后，又到普林斯顿大学做住校作家。在这一年，他出版了自己的第一部长篇小说《随波逐流》(Letting Go，1962)。这部小说描写芝加哥和纽约等地年轻犹太知识分子的生活。此后，发表了共计三十余部作品，其中包括三大系列小说 ("朱克曼系列"、"罗斯系列"、"凯佩史系列") 和其他非系列小说。

进入 21 世纪以来，罗斯笔耕不辍，接连出版了多部长篇小说，如《人类的污点》(The Human Stain，2000)、《垂死的肉身》(The Dying Animal，2001)、《反美阴谋》(The Plot against America，2004)、《鬼魂退出》(Exit Ghost，2007)，以及 "报应系列" 的 "晚年四部曲"：《凡人》(Everyman，2006)、《愤怒》(Indignation，2008)、《羞辱》(The Humbling，2009)、《报应》(Nemesis，2010)。除小说以外，罗斯还出版了文集《阅读自己和他人》(Reading Myself and Others，1975)，以及其他许多评论文章和短篇小说。

罗斯获奖众多。《再见，哥伦布》和《安息日剧场》(Sabbath Theater, 1995) 获全国图书奖，1986 年的《反生活》(The Counterlife)、1991 年的《遗产》(Patrimony) 获全国书评家协会奖，1998 年的《美国牧歌》(American Pastoral) 获普利策奖，《夏洛克战争》(Operation Shylock，1991)、《人性的污点》和《凡人》获国际笔会 / 福克纳奖 (PEN/Faulkner Award for Fiction)，2011 年获 "曼·布克国际奖"(Man Booker International Prize)。此外，罗斯还获得大量其他奖项。

Everyman

【题解】

《凡人》是罗斯2006年创作的中篇小说。小说以主人公"凡人"的葬礼开头,以倒叙的方式写到他死于手术台结束,在回顾中反思主人公的一生。"凡人"一生共经历三次婚姻。第一次婚姻留下的两个儿子,他们一生都对父亲抛弃其母耿耿于怀。第二次婚姻留下的女儿南茜对父亲充满关爱。第三次离婚后,进入老年的"凡人"搬到了新泽西海滩的退休社区,一个人过着孤独的生活。他早年为了工作与家庭从事的广告行业让他有一定的绘画基础,在晚年他试图重拾绘画并教别人美术。小说以细腻的笔触追述主人公在逐渐变老、患病过程中的心路历程,以及他对自己过往人生的反思和对即将到来的死亡不断的思考。

"凡人"并不是人物的真实姓名,主人公与作者罗斯一样出生于1933年,都出生于犹太家庭,出生地离罗斯的故乡纽瓦克也很近,小说中所描述的病痛和住院经历与罗斯的个人经历也多吻合,因此该小说有一定的自传性质。

全书未分章节,所选部分是小说开头的葬礼情节。

From Everyman

Here, where men sit and hear each other groan;
Where palsy shakes a few, sad, last grey hairs,
Where youth grows pale, and spectre-thin, and dies;
Where but to think is to be full of sorrow . . .

—JOHN KEATS, "Ode to a Nightingale"

AROUND THE GRAVE in the rundown cemetery were a few of his former advertising colleagues from New York, who recalled his energy and originality and told his daughter, Nancy, what a pleasure it had been to work with him. There were also people who'd driven up from Starfish Beach, the residential retirement village at the Jersey Shore[1] where he'd been living since Thanksgiving of 2001—the elderly to whom only recently he'd been giving art classes[2]. And there were his two sons, Randy and Lonny, middle-aged men from his turbulent first marriage, very much their mother's children, who as a consequence knew little of him that was praiseworthy and much that was beastly and who were present out of duty and nothing more³. His older brother, Howie, and his sister-in-law were there, having flown in from California the night before, and there was one of his three ex-wives, the middle one, Nancy's mother, Phoebe, a tall, very thin white-haired woman whose right arm hung limply at her side. When asked by Nancy if she wanted to say anything, Phoebe shyly shook her head but then went ahead to speak in a soft voice, her speech faintly slurred. "It's just so hard to believe. I keep thinking of him swimming the bay—that's all. I just keep seeing him swimming the bay." And then Nancy, who had made her father's funeral arrangements and placed the phone calls to those who'd showed up so that the mourners wouldn't consist of just her mother, herself, and his brother and sister-in-law. There was only one person whose presence hadn't to do with having been invited, a heavyset woman with a pleasant round face and dyed red hair who had simply appeared at the cemetery and introduced herself as Maureen, the private duty nurse who had looked after him following his heart surgery years back. Howie remembered her and went up to kiss her cheek.

Nancy told everyone, "I can begin by saying something to you about this cemetery, because I've discovered that my father's grandfather, my great-grandfather, is not only buried in the original few acres alongside my great-grandmother but was one of its founders in 1888. The association that first financed and erected the cemetery was composed of the burial societies of Jewish benevolent organizations and congregations scattered across Union and Essex counties. My great-grandfather owned and ran a boarding house in Elizabeth that catered especially to newly arrived immigrants, and he was concerned with their well-being as more than a mere landlord. That's why he was among the original members who purchased the open field that was here and who themselves graded and landscaped it, and why he served as the first cemetery chairman. He was relatively young then but in his full vigor, and it's his name alone that is signed to the document specifying that the cemetery was for burying deceased members in accordance with Jewish law and ritual. As is all too obvious, the maintenance of individual plots and of the fencing and the gates is no longer what it should be. Things have rotted and toppled over, the gates are rusted, the locks are gone, there's been vandalism⁴. By now the place has become the butt end of the airport and what you're hearing from a few miles away is the steady din of the New Jersey Turnpike. Of course I thought first of the truly beautiful places where my father might be buried, the places where he and my mother used to swim together when they were young, and the places where he loved to swim at the shore. Yet despite the fact that looking around at the deterioration here breaks my heart—as it probably does yours, and perhaps even makes you wonder why we're assembled on grounds so badly scarred by time—I wanted him to lie close to those who loved him and from whom he descended. My father loved his parents and he should be near them. I didn't want him to be somewhere alone." She was silent for a moment to collect herself. A gentle-faced woman in her mid-thirties, plainly pretty as her mother had been, she looked all at once in no way authoritative or even brave but like a ten-year-old overwhelmed. Turning toward the coffin, she picked up a clod of dirt and, before dropping it onto the lid, said lightly, with the air still of a bewildered young girl, "Well, this is how it turns out. There's nothing more we can do, Dad." Then she remembered his own stoical maxim from decades back and began to cry. "There's no remaking reality," she told him. "Just take it as it comes. Hold your ground and take it as it comes."

The next to throw dirt onto the lid of the coffin was Howie, who'd been the object of his worship when they were children and in return had always treated him with gentleness and affection, patiently teaching him to ride a bike and to swim and to play all the sports in which Howie himself excelled. It still appeared as if he could run a football through the middle of the line, and he was seventy-seven years old. He'd never been hospitalized for anything and, though a sibling bred of the same stock, had remained triumphantly healthy all his life.

His voice was husky with emotion when he whispered to his wife, "My kid brother. It makes no sense." Then he too addressed everyone. "Let's see if I can do it. Now let's get to this guy. About my brother . . . " He paused to compose his thoughts so that he could speak sensibly. His way of talking and the pleasant pitch of his voice were so like his brother's that Phoebe began to cry, and, quickly, Nancy took her by the arm. "His last few years," he said, gazing toward the grave, "he had health problems, and there was also loneliness—no less a problem. We spoke on the phone whenever we could, though near the end of his life he cut himself off from me for reasons that were never clear. From the time he was in high school he had an irresistible urge to paint, and after he retired from advertising, where he'd made a considerable success first as an art director and then when he was promoted to be a creative director—after a life in advertising he painted practically every day of every year that was left to him. We can say of him what has doubtless been said by their loved ones about nearly everyone who is buried here: he should have lived longer. He should have indeed." Here, after a moment's silence, the resigned look of gloom on his face gave way to a sorrowful smile. "When I started high school and had team practice in the afternoons, he took over the errands that I used to run for my father after school. He loved being only nine years old and carrying the diamonds in an envelope in his jacket pocket onto the bus to Newark, where the setter and the sizer and the polisher and the watch repairman our father used each sat in acubbyhole of his own, tucked away on Frelinghuysen Avenue. Those trips gave that kid enormous pleasure. I think watching these artisans doing their lonely work in those tight little places gave him the idea for using his hands to make art. I think looking at the facets of the diamonds through my father's jewelry loupe is something else that fostered his desire to make art." A laugh suddenly got the upper hand with Howie, a little flurry of relief from his task, and he said, "I was the conventional brother. In me diamonds fostered a desire to make money." Then he resumed where he'd left off, looking through the large sunny window of their boyhood years. "Our father took a small ad in the Elizabeth Journal once a month. During the holiday season, between Thanksgiving and Christmas, he took the ad once a week. 'Trade in your old watch for a new one.' All these old watches that he accumulated—most of them beyond repair—were dumped in a drawer in the back of the store. My little brother could sit there for hours, spinning the hands and listening to the watches tick, if they still did, and studying what each face and what each case looked like. That's what made that boy tick. A hundred, two hundred trade-in watches, the entire drawerful probably worth no more than ten bucks, but to his budding artist's eye, that backroom watch drawer was a treasure chest. He used to take them and wear them—he always had a watch that was out of that drawer. One of the ones that worked. And the ones he tried to make work, whose looks he liked, he'd fiddle around with but to no avail—generally he'd only make them worse. Still, that was the beginning of his using his hands to perform meticulous tasks. My father always had two girls just out of high school, in their late teens or early twenties, helping him behind the counter in the store. Nice, sweet Elizabeth girls, well-mannered, clean-cut girls, always Christian, mainly Irish Catholic, whose fathers and brothers and uncles worked for Singer Sewing Machine or for the biscuit company or down at the port. He figured nice Christian girls would make the customers feel more at home. If asked to, the girls would try on the jewelry for the customers, model it for them, and if we were lucky, the women would wind up buying. As my father told us, when a pretty young woman wears a piece of jewelry, other women think that when they wear the piece of jewelry they'll look like that too. The guys off the docks at the port who came in looking for engagement rings and wedding rings for their girlfriends would sometimes have the temerity to take the salesgirl's hand in order to examine the stone up close. My brother liked to be around the girls too, and that was long before he could even begin to understand what it was he was enjoying so much. He would help the girls empty the window and the showcases at the end of the day. He'd do anything at all to help them. They'd empty the windows and cases of everything but the cheapest stuff, and just before closing time this little kid would open the big safe in the backroom with the combination my father had entrusted to him. I'd done all these jobs before him, including getting as close as I could to the girls, especially to two blond sisters named Harriet and May. Over the years there was Harriet, May, Annmarie, Jean, there was Myra, Mary, Patty, there was Kathleen and Corine, and every one of them took a shine to that kid. Corine, the great beauty, would sit at the workbench in the backroom in early November and she and my kid brother would address the catalogues the store printed up and sent to all the customers for the holiday buying season, when my father was open six nights a week and everybody worked like a dog. If you gave my brother a box of envelopes, he could count them faster than anybody because his fingers were so dexterous and because he counted the envelopes by fives. I'd look in and, sure enough, that's what he'd be doing—showing off with the envelopes for Corine. How that boy loved doing everything that went along with being the jeweler's reliable son! That was our father's favorite accolade—'reliable.' Over the years our father sold wedding rings to Elizabeth's Irish and Germans and Slovaks and Italians and Poles, most of them young working-class stiffs. Half the time, after he'd made the sale, we'd be invited, the whole family, to the wedding. People liked him—he had a sense of humor and he kept his prices low and he extended credit to everyone, so we'd go—first to the church, then on to the noisy festivities. There was the Depression, there was the war, but there were also the weddings, there were our salesgirls, there were the trips to Newark on the bus with hundreds of dollars' worth of diamonds stashed away in envelopes in the pockets of our mackinaws. On the outside of each envelope were the instructions for the setter or the sizer written by our father. There was the five-foot-high Mosley safe slotted for all the jewelry trays that we carefully put away every night and removed every morning . . . and all of this constituted the core of my brother's life as a good little boy." Howie's eyes rested on the coffin again. "And now what?" he asked. "I think this had better be all there is. Going on and on, remembering still more . . . but why not remember? What's another gallon of tears between family and friends? When our father died my brother asked me if I minded if he took our father's watch. It was a Hamilton, made in Lancaster, P-A[5], and according to the expert, the boss, the best watch this country ever produced. Whenever he sold one, our father never failed to assure the customer that he'd made no mistake. "See, I wear one myself. A very, very highly respected watch, the Hamilton. To my mind," he'd say, "the premier American-made watch, bar none." Seventy-nine fifty, if I remember correctly. Everything for sale in those days had to end in fifty. Hamilton had a great reputation. It was a classy watch, my dad did love his, and when my brother said he'd like to own it, I couldn't have been happier. He could have taken the jeweler's loupe and our father's diamond carrying case. That was the worn old leather case that he would always carry with him in his coat pocket whenever he went to do business outside the store: with the tweezers in it, and the tiny screwdrivers and the little ring of sizers that gauge the size of a round stone and the folded white papers for holding the loose diamonds. The beautiful, cherished little things he worked with, which he held in his hands and next to his heart, yet we decided to bury the loupe and the case and all its contents in his grave. He always kept the loupe in one pocket and his cigarettes in the other, so we stuck the loupe inside his shroud. I remember my brother saying, "By all rights we should put it in his eye." That's what grief can do to you. That's how thrown we were. We didn't know what else to do. Rightly or wrongly, there didn't seem to us anything but that to do. Because they were not just his—they were him . . . To finish up about the Hamilton, my father's old Hamilton with the crown that you would turn to wind it every morning and that you would pull out on its stem to turn to move the hands . . . except while he was in swimming, my brother wore it day and night. He took it off for good only forty-eight hours ago. He handed it to the nurse to lock away for safekeeping while he was having the surgery that killed him. In the car on the way to the cemetery this morning, my niece Nancy showed me that she'd put a new notch in the band and now it's she who's wearing the Hamilton to tell time by.

Then came the sons, men in their late forties and looking, with their glossy black hair and their eloquent dark eyes and the sensual fullness of their wide, identical mouths, just like their father (and like their uncle) at their age. Handsome men beginning to grow beefy and seemingly as closely linked with each other as they'd been irreconcilably alienated from the dead father. The younger, Lonny, stepped up to the grave first. But once he'd taken a clod of dirt in his hand, his entire body began to tremble and quake, and it looked as though he were on the edge of violently regurgitating. He was overcome with a feeling for his father that wasn't antagonism but that his antagonism denied him the means to release. When he opened his mouth, nothing emerged except a series of grotesque gasps, making it appear likely that whatever had him in its grip would never be finished with him. He was in so desperate a state that Randy, the older, more decisive son, the scolding son, came instantly to his rescue. He took the clod of dirt from the hand of the younger one and tossed it onto the casket for both of them. And he readily met with success when he went to speak. "Sleep easy, Pop," Randy said, but any note of tenderness, grief, love, or loss was terrifyingly absent from his voice.

The last to approach the coffin was the private duty nurse, Maureen, a battler from the look of her and no stranger to either life or death. When, with a smile, she let the dirt slip slowly across her curled palm and out the side of her hand onto the coffin, the gesture looked like the prelude to a carnal act. Clearly this was a man to whom she'd once given much thought.

That was the end. No special point had been made. Did they all say what they had to say? No, they didn't, and of course they did. Up and down the state that day, there'd been five hundred funerals like his, routine, ordinary, and except for the thirty wayward seconds furnished by the sons—and Howie's resurrecting with such painstaking precision the world as it innocently existed before the invention of death, life perpetual in their father-created Eden, a paradise just fifteen feet wide by forty feet deep disguised as an old-style jewelry store—no more or less interesting than any of the others. But then it's the commonness that's most wrenching, the registering once more of the fact of death that overwhelms everything.

In a matter of minutes, everybody had walked away—wearily and tearfully walked away from our species' least favorite activity—and he was left behind. Of course, as when anyone dies, though many were grief-stricken, others remained unperturbed, or found themselves relieved, or, for reasons good or bad, were genuinely pleased.

Though he had grown accustomed to being on his own and fending for himself since his last divorce ten years back, in his bed the night before the surgery he worked at remembering as exactly as he could each of the women who had been there waiting for him to rise out of the anesthetic in the recovery room, even remembering that most helpless of mates, the last wife, with whom recovering from quintuple bypass surgery had not been a sublime experience. The sublime experience had been the private nurse with the unassuming professional air who'd come home with him from the hospital and who tended him with a high-spirited devotion that promoted a slow, steady recovery and with whom, unknown to his wife, he conducted a sustained affair once he had recovered his sexual prowess. Maureen. Maureen Mrazek. He'd called all over trying to find Maureen. He'd wanted her to come and be his nurse, should he need a nurse, when he got home from the hospital this time. But sixteen years had passed, and the nursing agency at the hospital had lost track of her. She'd be forty-eight now, more than likely married and a mother, a shapely, energetic young woman grown into middle-aged stoutness while the battle to remain an unassailable man had by then been lost by him, time having transformed his own body into a storehouse for man-made contraptions designed to fend off collapse. Defusing thoughts of his own demise had never required more diligence and cunning.

A lifetime later, he remembered the trip to the hospital with his mother for his hernia[6] operation in the fall of 1942, a bus ride lasting no more than ten minutes. Usually if he was traveling somewhere with his mother, it was in the family car and his father was driving. But now there were just the two of them alone together on the bus, and they were headed for the hospital where he had been born, and she was what calmed his apprehension and allowed him to be brave. As a small child he'd had his tonsils removed at the hospital, but otherwise he'd never been back there. Now he was to stay for four days and four nights. He was a sensible boy of nine with no conspicuous problems, but on the bus he felt much younger and found that he required his mother's proximity in ways he thought he'd outgrown.

His brother, a high school freshman, was in class, and his father had driven the car to work well before he and his mother left for the hospital. A small overnight case rested on his mother's lap. In it were a toothbrush, pajamas, a bathrobe and slippers, and the books he'd brought with him to read. He could still remember which books they were. The hospital was around the corner from the local branch library, so his mother could replenish his reading material should he read through the books he'd brought for his hospital stay. He was to spend a week convalescing at home before returning to school, and he was more anxious about all the school he was missing than he was as yet about the ether mask that he knew they would clamp over his face to anesthetize him. In the early forties hospitals didn't as yet permit parents to stay overnight with their children, and so he'd be sleeping without his mother, his father, or his brother anywhere nearby. He was anxious about that, too.

His mother was well-spoken and mannerly, as, in turn, were the women who registered him at the admissions office and the nurses at the nurses' station when he and his mother made their way by elevator to the children's wing of the surgical floor. His mother took his overnight case because, small as it was, he wasn't supposed to carry anything until after his hernia was repaired and he had fully recuperated. He had discovered the swelling in his left groin a few months earlier and had told no one but just tried pressing it down with his fingers to make it go away. He did not know exactly what a hernia was or what significance to give to swelling located so close to his genitals.

In those days a doctor could prescribe a stiff corset with metal stays if the family didn't want the child to undergo surgery or if they couldn't afford it. He knew of a boy at school who wore such a corset, and one of the reasons he'd told no one about the swelling was his fear that he too would have to wear a corset and reveal it to the other boys when he changed into his shorts for gym class.

Once he had finally confessed to his parents, his father took him to the doctor's office. Quickly the doctor examined him and made the diagnosis and, after conversing with his father for a few minutes, arranged for the surgery. Everything was done with astonishing speed, and the doctor—the very one who had delivered him into the world—assured him that he was going to be fine and then went on to joke about the comic strip Li'l Abner, which the two of them enjoyed reading in the evening paper.

The surgeon, Dr. Smith, was said by his parents to be the best in the city. Like the boy's own father, Dr. Smith, born Solly Smulowitz, had grown up in the slums, the son of poor immigrants.

He was in bed in his room within an hour of arriving at the hospital, though the surgery was not scheduled until the following morning—that's how patients were tended to then.

In the bed next to his was a boy who'd had stomach surgery and wasn't allowed to get up and walk yet. The boy's mother sat beside the bed holding her son's hand. When the father came to visit after work, the parents spoke in Yiddish, which made him think that they were too worried to speak understandable English in their son's presence. The only place where he heard Yiddish spoken was at the jewelry store when the war refugees came in search of Schaffhausen watches, a hard-to-find brand that his father would call around to try to locate for them—"Schaffhausen—I want a Schaffhausen," that would be the extent of their English. Of course Yiddish was spoken all but exclusively when the Hasidic Jews from New York traveled to Elizabeth once or twice a month to replenish the store's diamond inventory—for his father to have maintained a large inventory in his own safe would have been too expensive. There were far fewer Hasidic diamond merchants in America before the war than after, but his father, from the very beginning, preferred to deal with them rather than with the big diamond houses. The diamond merchant who came most frequently—and whose migration route had carried him and his family in only a few years from Warsaw to Antwerp to New York—was an older man dressed in a large black hat and a long black coat of a kind that you never saw on anyone else in Elizabeth's streets, not even other Jews. He wore a beard and sidelocks and kept the waist pouch that held his diamonds secreted beneath fringed undergarments whose religious significance eluded the nascent secularist—that, in fact, seemed ludicrous to him—even after his father explained why the Hasidim still wore what their ancestors had worn in the old country two hundred years before and lived much as they did then, though, as he pointed out to his father again and again, they were now in America, free to dress and to shave and to behave as they wished. When one of the seven sons of the diamond merchant got married, the merchant invited their entire family to the wedding in Brooklyn. All the men there had beards and all the women wore wigs and the sexes sat on different sides of the synagogue, separated by a wall—afterward the men and the women did not even dance together—and everything about that wedding he and Howie hated. When the diamond merchant arrived at the store he would remove his coat but leave on his hat, and the two men would sit behind the showcase chatting amiably together in Yiddish, the language that his father's parents, his own grandparents, had continued to speak in their immigrant households with their American-born children for as long as they lived. But when it was time to look at the diamonds, the two went into the backroom, where there was a safe and a workbench and a brown linoleum floor and, jammed together behind a door that never shut completely even when you had successfully struggled to hook it from within, a toilet and a tiny sink. His father always paid on the spot with a check.

After closing the store with Howie's help—pulling the lattice gate with the padlocks across the shop's display window, switching on the burglar alarm, and throwing all the locks on the front door—his father showed up in his younger son's hospital room and gave him a hug.

He was there when Dr. Smith came around to introduce himself. The surgeon was wearing a business suit rather than a white coat, and his father jumped to his feet as soon as he saw him enter the room. "It's Dr. Smith!" his father cried.

"So this is my patient," Dr. Smith said. "Well," he told him, coming to the side of the bed to take him firmly by the shoulder, "we're going to fix that hernia tomorrow and you'll be as good as new. What position do you like to play?" he asked.

"End."

"Well, you're going to be back playing end before you know it. You're going to play anything you want. You get a good night's sleep and I'll see you in the morning."

Daring to joke with the eminent surgeon, his father said, "And you get a good night's sleep too." When his dinner came, his mother and father sat and talked to him as though they were all at home. They spoke quietly so as not to disturb the sick boy or his parents, who were silent now, the mother still seated beside him and the father incessantly pacing at the foot of the bed and then out into the corridor and back. The boy hadn't so much as stirred while they were there.

At five to eight a nurse stuck her head in to announce that visiting hours were over. The parents of the other boy again spoke together in Yiddish and, after the mother repeatedly kissed the boy's forehead, they left the room. The father had tears running down his face.

Then his own parents left to go home to his brother and eat a late dinner together in the kitchen without him. His mother kissed him and held him tightly to her. "You can do it, son," his father said, leaning over to kiss him as well. "It's like when I give you an errand to run on the bus or a job to do at the store. Whatever it is, you never let me down. Reliable—my two reliable boys! I pop my buttons when I think about my boys. Always, you do the work like the thorough, careful, hard-working boys you were brought up to be. Carrying precious jewels to Newark and back, quarter-carat, half-carat diamonds in your pocket, and at your age that doesn't faze you. You look to all the world like it's some junk you found in your Cracker Jacks. Well, if you can do that job, you can do this job. It's just another job of work as far as you're concerned. Do the work, finish the job, and by tomorrow the whole thing will be over. You hear the bell, you come out fighting. Right?"

"Right," the boy said.

"By the time I see you tomorrow, Dr. Smith will have fixed that thing, and that'll be the end of that."

"Right."

"My two terrific boys!"

Then they were gone and he was alone with the boy in the next bed. He reached over to his bedside table, where his mother had piled his books, and began to read *The Swiss*

Family Robinson. Then he tried Treasure Island. Then *Kim*. Then he put his hand under the covers to look for the hernia. The swelling was gone. He knew from past experience that there were days when the swelling would temporarily subside, but this time he was sure that it had subsided for good and that he no longer needed an operation. When a nurse came by to take his temperature, he didn't know how to tell her that the hernia had disappeared and that his parents should be called to come take him home. She looked approvingly at the titles of the books he'd brought and told him that he was free to get out of bed to use the bathroom but that otherwise he should make himself comfortable reading until she returned to put out the lights. She said nothing about the other boy, who he was sure was going to die.

At first he didn't fall asleep because of his waiting for the boy to die, and then he didn't because he couldn't stop thinking of the drowned body that had washed up on the beach that past summer. It was the body of a seaman whose tanker had been torpedoed by a German U-boat[7]. The Coast Guard beach patrol had found the body amid the oil scum and shattered cargo cases at the edge of the beach that was only a block away from the house where his family of four rented a room for a month each summer. Most days the water was clear and he didn't worry that a drowned man would collide with his bare legs as he stepped out into the low surf. But when oil from torpedoed tankers clotted the sand and caked the bottom of his feet as he crossed the beach, he was terrified of stumbling upon a corpse. Or stumbling upon a saboteur[8], coming ashore to work for Hitler. Armed with rifles or submachine guns and often accompanied by trained dogs, the Coast Guardsmen patrolled day and night to prevent saboteurs from landing on the miles of deserted beaches. Yet some sneaked through without detection and, along with native-born Nazi sympathizers, were known to be in ship-to-shore communication with the U-boats that prowled the East Coast shipping lanes and had been sinking ships off New Jersey since the war began. The war was closer than most people imagined, and so was the horror. His father had read that the waters of New Jersey were "the worst ship graveyard" along the entire U.S. coastline, and now, in the hospital, he couldn't get the word "graveyard" to stop tormenting him, nor could he erase from his mind that bloated dead body the Coast Guard had removed from the few inches of surf in which it lay, while he and his brother looked on from the boardwalk.

Sometime after he'd fallen asleep he heard noises in the room and awakened to see that the curtain between the two beds had been pulled to screen off the other bed and that there were doctors and nurses at work on the other side—he could see their forms moving and could hear them whispering. When one of the nurses emerged from behind the curtain, she realized that he was awake and came over to his bed and told him softly, "Go back to sleep. You have a big day tomorrow." "What's the matter?" he asked. "Nothing," she said, "We're changing his bandages. Close your eyes and go to sleep."

He was awakened early the next morning for the operation, and there was his mother, already at the hospital and smiling at him from the foot of the bed.

"Good morning, darling. How's my brave boy?"

Looking across at the other bed, he saw that it was stripped of its bedding. Nothing could have made clearer to him what had happened than the sight of the bare mattress ticking and the uncovered pillows piled in the middle of the empty bed.

"That boy died," he said. Memorable enough that he was in the hospital that young, but even more memorable that he had registered a death. The first was the bloated body, the second was this boy. During the night, when he had awakened to see the forms moving behind the curtain, he couldn't help but think, the doctors are killing him.

"I believe he was moved, sweetheart. He had to be moved to another floor."

Just then two orderlies appeared to take him to the operating room. When he was told by one of them to use the bathroom, the first thing he did when the door was closed was to check if the hernia was gone. But the swelling had come back. There was no way out of the operation now.

His mother was allowed to walk alongside the gurney only as far as the elevator that was to take him to the operating room. There the orderlies pushed him into the elevator, and it descended until it opened onto a shockingly ugly corridor that led to an operating room where Dr. Smith was wearing a surgical gown and a white mask that changed everything about him—he might not even have been Dr. Smith. He could have been someone else entirely, someone who had not grown up the son of poor immigrants named Smulowitz, someone his father knew nothing about, someone nobody knew, someone who had just wandered into the operating room and picked up a knife. In that moment of terror when they lowered the ether mask over his face as though to smother him, he could have sworn that the surgeon, whoever he was, had whispered, "Now I'm going to turn you into a girl."

The malaise began just days after his return home from a month long vacation as happy as any he'd known since the family vacations at the Jersey Shore before the war.

He'd spent August in a semi-furnished ramshackle house on an inland road on Martha's Vineyard with the woman whose constant lover he had been for two years. Until now they'd never dared to chance living together day in and day out, and the experiment had been a joyous success, a wonderful month of swimming and hiking and of easygoing sex at all times of the day. They'd swim across a bay to a ridge of dunes where they could lie out of sight and fuck in the sunshine and then rouse themselves to slip into their suits and swim back to the beach and collect clusters of mussels off the rocks to carry home for dinner in a pail full of seawater.

The only unsettling moments were at night, when they walked along the beach together. The dark sea rolling in with its momentous thud and the sky lavish with stars made Phoebe rapturous but frightened him. The profusion of stars told him unambiguously that he was doomed to die, and the thunder of the sea only yards away—and the nightmare of the blackest blackness beneath the frenzy of the water—made him want to run from the menace of oblivion to their cozy, lighted, underfurnished house. This was not the way he had experienced the vastness of the sea and the big night sky while he'd served manfully in the navy just after the Korean War—never were they the tolling bells. He could not understand where the fear was coming from and had to use all his strength to conceal it from Phoebe. Why must he mistrust his life just when he was more its master than he'd been in years? Why should he imagine himself on the edge of extinction when calm, straightforward thinking told him that there was so much more solid life to come? Yet it happened every night during their seaside walk beneath the stars. He was not flamboyant or deformed or extreme in any way, so why then, at his age, should he be haunted by thoughts of dying? He was reasonable and kindly, an amicable, moderate, industrious man, as everyone who knew him well would probably agree, except, of course, for the wife and two boys whose household he'd left and who, understandably, could not equate reasonableness and kindliness with his finally giving up on a failed marriage and looking elsewhere for the intimacy with a woman that he craved.

Most people, he believed, would have thought of him as square. As a young man, he'd thought of himself as square, so conventional and unadventurous that after art school, instead of striking out on his own to paint and to live on whatever money he could pick up at odd jobs—which was his secret ambition—he was too much the good boy, and, answering to his parents' wishes rather than his own, he married, had children, and went into advertising to make a secure living. He never thought of himself as anything more than an average human being, and one who would have given anything for his marriage to have lasted a lifetime. He had married with just that expectation. But instead marriage became his prison cell, and so, after much tortuous thinking that preoccupied him while he worked and when he should have been sleeping, he began fitfully, agonizingly, to tunnel his way out. Isn't that what an average human being would do? Isn't that what average human beings do every day? Contrary to what his wife told everyone, he hadn't hungered after the wanton freedom to do anything and everything. Far from it. He hungered for something stable all the while he detested what he had. He was not a man who wished to live two lives. He held no grudge against either the limitations or the comforts of conformity. He'd wanted merely to empty his mind of all the ugly thoughts spawned by the disgrace of prolonged marital warfare. He was not claiming to be exceptional. Only vulnerable and assailable and confused. And convinced of his right, as an average human being, to be pardoned ultimately for whatever deprivations he may have inflicted upon his innocent children in order not to live deranged half the time.

Terrifying encounters with the end? I'm thirty-four! Worry about oblivion, he told himself, when you're seventy-five! The remote future will be time enough to anguish over the ultimate catastrophe!

【注解】

1. Jersey Shore：地名，新泽西州的一处海滩。
2. art classes：指主人公生前在退休之后曾开过美术辅导班。
3. who were ... nothing more：指"凡人"第一次婚姻中所生、如今也人到中年的两个儿子仅仅是出于义务而出席父亲的葬礼，缺少儿子对父亲的敬爱之情。
4. vandalism：毁坏失修。
5. P-A：Pennsylvania 的缩写，美国宾夕法尼亚州。
6. hernia：疝气，脱肠。
7. U-boat：U 型潜水艇（德国的一种潜水艇）。
8. saboteur：怠工者，破坏者。

【思考题】

1. How does the beginning of the story illustrate the role that Death plays in the novel?
2. In the novel we read "the world as it innocently existed before the invention of death, life perpetual in their father-created Eden, a paradise just fifteen feet wide by forty feet deep disguised as an old-style jewelry store—no more or less interesting than any of the

others". What causes the protagonist's nostalgic memory of his childhood?
3. Some readers would read the Jewish identity out of Roth's characters, but there are also people who would believe they are non-Jewish Americans. Find evidences from the text to make an argument.
4. Philip Roth's *Everyman* takes its title from the medieval morality play in which an unprepared sinner is informed by Death of his imminent judgement day. With the loss of friends, family, wealth, strength, beauty and knowledge, Everyman finally learns that when one is brought to death and placed before God, all he is left with are his own good deeds. In light of this, what is the significance of Roth's allusion to this medieval morality play?

【简评】

　　在葬礼上，按照犹太人的习惯，送葬的亲友会在棺材上放上土块，以示对死者的差别与尊敬。对于"放土块"这个动作，作者对不同的角色用了不同的表述：女儿南茜是"drop"，他哥哥是"throw"，两个儿子是"toss"，护士莫琳则是"lets the dirt slip slowly across her curled palm and out the side of her hand onto the coffin"。一个几乎同样的简单动作却用到不同的动词表达，除了表示作者不希望措辞的重复之外，也体现了动作的发出者对逝者的不同情感与态度。

　　主人公是小说中唯一没有真实姓名的人物。根据书名，读者会习惯地将他理解为"凡人"(Everyman)。主人公本人对自己的"普通人"(average human being) 身份也有过思考 (见所选部分的倒数第二段)，这种刻意的去名化 (un-naming act) 叙述行为体现了作者希望展示人类普遍且普通的命运，而非特定情境下特殊人物的命运。

Raymond Carver
1938—1988

　　雷蒙·卡弗是美国当代优秀的短篇小说作家，也是 20 世纪 80 年代美国新现实主义运动的中心人物。他一生共发表了五部短篇小说集和三部诗集，尤以短篇小说创作而著称于世。

　　卡弗出生在俄勒冈州一个贫苦的家庭，高中毕业后便承担起了生活的重担。由于喜爱文学，卡弗在打工之余到加州州立大学契柯分校学习写作。1960 年秋，卡弗转学到加州的洪堡学院，翌年春，便在学院的《柳叶石楠》杂志上发表了一篇不到

500 字的微型小说《父亲》，通过父亲与女儿的对话揭示了蛰伏在父亲心灵深处的存在危机。作品虽短，却预示了卡弗后来创作的主要内容与特征。

1967 年，卡弗的短篇小说《请安静些，好吗？》("Will You Please Be Quiet, Please?") 被收入《1967 年美国最佳短篇小说集》。1971 年，卡弗的短篇小说《邻居》("Neighbors") 发表在美国著名杂志《士绅》上。1973 至 1975 年，他的短篇小说连年被欧·亨利短篇小说奖年刊选入《优秀短篇小说集》。卡弗开始引起评论家注意，一些大学也纷纷邀请他前去讲学。1976 年，以《请安静些，好吗？》冠名的短篇小说集出版。该集子由 22 个故事组成，包括了卡弗 1963 至 1975 年间创作的大部分短篇小说。作品通过对普通人和平凡生活细致入微和完全白描式的表现，重新审视了普通人的生活困境和情感危机，揭示了他们心中被平庸与习俗所掩盖的巨大压抑、恐惧与异化，因此一发表即获得各方好评，并在第二年获得全国图书奖提名。

1977 年末，卡弗发表第二部短篇小说集《愤怒的季节》(*Furious Season*)，共收入 8 个短篇，除同名故事《愤怒的季节》外，其余故事后来都经修改后易名或同名发表在其他集子中。1981 年，卡弗发表了他的第三部短篇小说集《我们谈论爱情时谈论什么》(*What We Talk about When We Talk about Love*)，受到评论界的高度赞扬，后来成为美国简约派的经典之作。在收入该小说集的 17 个故事中，卡弗充分调动故事省略或隐含部分来制造一种张力，让人在阅读之后感悟到一种文字以外的境界与深意。著名文学评论家弗兰克·科摩德 (Frank Kermode，1919—2010) 指出，"卡弗的作品形式是如此的节俭，以至于读者得在读完作品后好一会儿才能领悟到，作品中哪怕最不起眼的一笔也表现了整个文化和整个道德的状况。"但卡弗的"节俭"也招来了一些非议，有些评论家认为卡弗所代表的简约派创作手法过于"贫乏"，像是患了"厌食症"。卡弗显然接受了评论界的批评。在后来出版的短篇小说集《天主教堂》(*Cathedral*, 1983) 中，许多作品明显变得"更加慷慨"（卡弗语），更富人情味，也更体现了一种较为积极的人生态度。最能说明这一点的是一篇题为《一件小小的好事》("A Small Good Thing") 的短篇小说。该短篇曾以《洗澡》("Bath") 为名收录在《我们谈论爱情时谈论什么》中。1988 年，卡弗出版了他生前最后一部短篇小说集《我打电话的地方》(*Where I'm Calling from*)。

在他所有的短篇小说中，卡弗用心地编织一个又一个的"小人物的故事"。他的人物多属社会底层的体力劳动者，如侍者、技工、邮差、车夫等。他们的生活中总是蛰伏着各种各样的经济、情感、婚姻危机与无奈，他们的家庭也总是处于崩溃与解体的边缘。卡弗对这些人怀有深切的理解和同情,因为他对这些人非常熟悉。他自己就来自这些人,他们的生活也曾经是他自己的生活。因此,他写作的主要目的就是要给这些被社会忽视的、边缘化的"沉默一族"一个发言和被他人了解的机会。

在语言风格上,卡弗继承了克莱恩、海明威等人开创的简约文风。他的短篇小说一般只有两三千字,《我们谈论爱情时谈论什么》中《受欢迎的技工》("Popular Mechanics")甚至不到 300 字。此外,卡弗的句子主要由动词、名词、代词等实义词组成,副词、形容词大多局限于最基本的词汇,以模仿社会下层老百姓朴实无华的语言。在《国家》(*The Nation*) 杂志中,罗伯特·休斯顿认为,虽然 200 多年前华兹华斯和柯勒律治就已经在《抒情歌谣》序言中提出要以"真正老百姓用的语言来写作",但他们实际都未能真正做到这一点,而卡弗做到了。

So Much Water So Close to Home

【题解】

《这么多水,离家这么近》选自短篇小说集《我们谈论爱情时谈论什么》,通过男主人公 Stuart 和 Gordon Johnson 等人外出钓鱼时发生的事和他们处理此事的态度表现了人性的冷漠和道德的沦丧。作品情节简约,语言精练,是卡弗短篇小说的代表作之一。

From What We Talk About When We Talk About Love

So Much Water So Close to Home

My husband eats with a good appetite. But I don't think he's really hungry. He chews, arms on the table, and stares at something across the room. He looks at me and looks away. He wipes his mouth on the napkin. He shrugs, and goes on eating.

"What are you staring at me for?" he says.

"What is it?" he says and lays down his fork.

"Was I staring?" I say, and shake my head.

The telephone rings. "Don't answer it," he says.

"It might be your mother," I say.

"Watch and see," he says.

I pick up the receiver and listen. My husband stops eating.

"What did I tell you?" he says when I hang up. He starts to eat again. Then throws his napkin on his plate. He says, "Goddamn it, why can't people mind their own business? Tell me what I did wrong and I'll listen! I wasn't the only man there. We talked it over and we all decided. We couldn't just turn around. We were five miles from the car. I won't have you passing judgment. Do you hear?"

"You know," I say.

He says, "What do I know, Claire? Tell me what I'm supposed to know. I don't know anything except one thing." He gives me what he thinks is a meaningful look. "She was dead," he says, "And I'm as sorry as anyone else. But she was dead."

"That's the point," I say.

He raises his hands. He pushes his chair away from the table. He takes out his cigarettes and goes out to the back with a can of beer. I see him sit in the lawn chair and pick up the newspaper again.

His name is in there on the first page. Along with the names of his friends.

I close my eyes and hold on to the sink. Then I rake my arm across the drainboard and send the dishes to the floor.

He doesn't move. I know he's heard. He lifts his head as if still listening. But he doesn't move otherwise. He doesn't turn around.

He and Gordon Johnson and Mel Dorn and Vern Williams, they play poker and bowl and fish. They fish every spring and early summer before visiting relatives can get in the way. They are decent men, family men, men who take care of their jobs. They have sons and daughters who go to school with our son, Dean.

Last Friday these family men left for the Naches River. They parked the car in the mountains and hiked to where they wanted to fish. They carried their bedrolls, their food, their playing cards, their whiskey.

They saw the girl before they set up camp. Mel Dorn found her. No clothes on her at all. She was wedged into some branches that stuck out over the water.

He called the others and they came to look. They talked about what to do.

One of the men—my Stuart didn't say which—said they should start back at once. The others stirred the sand with their shoes, said they didn't feel inclined that way. They pleaded fatigue, the late hour, the fact that the girl wasn't going anywhere.

In the end they went ahead and set up the camp. They built a fire and drank their whiskey. When the moon came up, they talked about the girl. Someone said they should keep the body from drifting away. They took their flash-lights and went back to the river. One of the men—it might have been Stuart—waded in and got her. He took her by the fingers and pulled her into shore. He got some nylon cord and tied it to her wrist and then looped the rest around a tree.

The next morning they cooked breakfast, drank coffee, and drank whiskey, and then split up to fish. That night they cooked fish, cooked potatoes, drank coffee, drank whiskey, then took their cooking things and eating things back down to the river and washed them where the girl was.

They played some cards later on. Maybe they played until they couldn't see them anymore. Vern Williams went to sleep. But the others told stories. Gordon Johnson said the trout they'd caught were hard because of the terrible coldness of the water.

The next morning they got up late, drank whiskey, fished a little, took down their tents, rolled their sleeping bags, gathered their stuff, and hiked out. They drove until they got to a telephone. It was Stuart who made the call while the others stood around in the sun and listened. He gave the sheriff their names. They had nothing to hide. They weren't ashamed. They said they'd wait until someone could come for better directions and take down their statements.

I was asleep when he got home. But I woke up when I head him in the kitchen. I found him leaning against the refrigerator with a can of beer. He put his heavy arms around me and rubbed his big hands on my back. In bed he put his hands on me again and then waited as if thinking of something else. I turned and opened my legs. Afterwards, I think he stayed awake.

He was up that morning before I could get out of bed. To see if there was something in the paper, I suppose.

The telephone began ringing right after eight.

"Go to hell!" I heard him shout.

The telephone rang right again.

"I have nothing to add to what I already said to the sheriff!" He slammed the receiver down.

"What is going on?" I said.

It was then that he told me what I just told you.

I sweep up the broken dishes and go outside. He is lying on his back on the grass now, the newspaper and can of beer within reach.

"Stuart, could we go for a drive?" I say.

He rolls over and looks at me. "We'll pick up some beer," he says. He gets to his feet and touches me on the hip as he goes past. "Give me a minute," he says.

We drive through town without speaking. He stops at a roadside market for beer. I noticed a great stack of papers just inside the door. On the top step a fat woman in a print dress holds out a licorice stick to a little girl. Later on, we cross Everson Creek and turn into the picnic grounds. The creek runs under the bridge and into a large pond a few hundred yards away. I can see the men out there. I can see them out there fishing.

So much water so close to home.

I say, "Why did you have to go miles away?"

"Don't rile me," he says.

We sit on a bench in the sun. He opens us cans of beer. He says, "Relax, Claire."

"They said they were innocent. They said they were crazy."

He says, "Who?" He says, "What are you talking about?"

"The Maddox brothers. They killed a girl named Arlene Hubly where I grew up. They cut off her head and threw her into the Cle Elum River. It happened when I was a girl."

"You're going to get me riled," he says.

I look at the creek. I'm right in it, eyes open, face down, staring at the moss on the bottom, dead.

"I don't know what's wrong with you," he says on the way home. "You're getting me more riled by the minute."

There is nothing I can say to him.

He tries to concentrate on the road. But he keeps looking into the rear-view mirror.

He knows.

Stuart believes he is letting me sleep this morning. But I was awake long before the alarm went off. I was thinking, lying on the far side of the bed away from his hairy legs.

He gets Dean off for school, and then he shaves, dresses, and leaves for work. Twice he looks in and clears his throat. But I keep my eyes closed.

In the kitchen I find a note from him. It's signed "Love."

I sit in the breakfast nook[1] and drink coffee and leave a ring on the note. I look at the newspaper and turn it this way and that on the table. Then I skid it close and read what it says. The body has been identified, claimed. But it took some examining it, some putting things into it, some cutting, some weighing, some measuring, some putting things back again and sewing them in.

I sit for a long time holding the newspaper and thinking. Then I call up to get a chair at the hairdresser's[2].

I sit under the dryer with a magazine on my lap and let Marnie do my nails.

"I am going to a funeral tomorrow," I say.

"I'm sorry to hear that," Marnie says.

"It was a murder," I say.

"That's the worst kind," Marnie says.

"We weren't all that close," I say.

"But you know."

"We'll get you fixed up for it," Marnie says.

That night I make my bed on the sofa, and in the morning I get up first. I put on coffee and fix breakfast while he shaves.

He appears in the kitchen doorway, towel over his bare shoulder, appraising.

"Here's coffee," I say. "Eggs'll be ready in a minute."

I wake Dean, and the three of us eat. Whenever Stuart looks at me, I ask Dean if he wants more milk, more toast, etc.

"I'll call you today," Stuart says as he opens the door.

I say, "I don't think I'll be home today."

"All right," he says, "Sure."

I dress carefully. I try on a hat and look at myself in the mirror. I write out a note for Dean.

Honey, Mommy has things to do this afternoon, but will be back later. You stay in or be in the backyard until one of us comes home.

Love, Mommy.

I look at the word Love and then I underline it. Then I see the word backyard. Is it one word or two?

I drive through farm country, through fields of oats and sugar beets and past apple orchards, cattle grazing in pastures. Then everything changes, more like shacks than farmhouses and stands of timber instead of orchards. Then mountains, and on the right, far below, I sometimes see the Naches River.

A green pickup comes up behind me and stays behind me for miles. I keep slowing at the wrong times, hoping he will pass. Then I speed up. But this is at the wrong times, too. I grip the wheel until my fingers hurt.

On a long clear stretch he goes past. But he drives along beside for a bit, a crewcut man in a blue workshirt. We look each other over. Then he waves, toots his horn, and pulls on up ahead.

I slow down and find a place. I pull over and shut off the motor. I can hear the river down below the trees. Then I hear the pickup coming back.

I lock the doors and roll up the windows.

"You all right?" the man says. He raps on the glass. "You okay?" he leans his arms on the door and brings his face to the window.

I stare at him. I can't think what else to do.

"Is everything all right in there? How come you're all locked up?"

I shake my head.

"Roll down your window." He shakes his head and looks at the highway and then back at me. "Roll it down now."

"Please," I say, "I have to go."

"Open the door," he says as if he isn't listening. "You're going to choke in there."

He looks at my breasts, my legs. I can tell that's what he's doing.

"Hey, sugar," he says, "I'm just here to help is all."

The casket is closed and covered with floral sprays[3]. The organ starts up the minute I take a seat. People are coming in and find chairs. There's a boy in flared pants and a yellow short-sleeved shirt. A door opens and the family comes in in a group and moves over to a curtained place off to one side. Chairs creak as everybody gets settled. Directly, a nice blond man in a nice dark suit stands and asks us to bow our heads. He says a prayer for us, the living, and when he finishes, he says a prayer for the soul of the departed.

Along with the others I go past the casket. Then I move out onto the front steps and into the afternoon light. There's a woman who limps as she goes down the stairs ahead of me. On the sidewalk she looks around. "Well, they got him," she says. "If that's any consolation. They arrested him this morning. I heard it on the radio before I come. A boy right here in town."

We move a few steps down the hot sidewalk. People are starting cars. I put out my hand and hold on to a parking meter. Polished hoods and polished fenders. My head swims.

I say, "They have friends, these killers. You can't tell."

"I have known that child since she was a little girl," the woman says. "She used to come over and I'd bake cookies for her and let her eat them in front of the TV."

Back home, Stuart sits at the table with a drink of whiskey in front of him. For a crazy instant I think some thing's happened to Dean.

"Where is he?" I say. "Where is Dean?"

"Outside," my husband says.

He drains his glass and stands up. He says, "I think I know what you need."

He reaches an arm around my waist and with his other hand he begins to unbutton my jacket and then he goes on to the buttons of my blouse.

"First things first," he says.

He says something else. But I don't need to listen. I can't hear a thing with so much water going.

"That's right," I say, finishing the buttons myself. "Before Dean comes. Hurry."

【注解】

1. breakfast nook：早餐角，指厨房专用来吃早饭的角落。
2. Then I call up . . . hairdresser's：接着我打电话给美容院预约做头发。
3. floral sprays：洒落（在棺木上）的鲜花。

【思考题】

1. Stuart told his wife that he had done nothing wrong for not reporting to the police promptly about the dead girl because they were five miles from the car and the girl was dead anyway. Do you think Stuart's excuse can be justified? Why?
2. Notice how the narrator describes the fishers in the second section: "They are decent men, family men, men who take care of their jobs. They have sons and daughters . . ." What is the tone when the narrator says this?

3. In the sixth paragraph of the second section, Carver gives us many details of the fishers' cooking and eating and drinking activities. Why is he so particular about these details here?
4. At the hairdresser's, Claire says to Marnie, "We weren't all that close . . . But you know." And then Marnie replies, "We'll get you fixed up for it." What do they mean?
5. Why does the driver of the green pickup stay behind Claire for miles before passing, and why does he ask her to roll down the window? What kind of man is he anyway?
6. When in the last section of the story Claire describes Stuart's answer to her question about the whereabouts of their son, she uses "my husband says", rather than "he says" or "Stuart says". What possible explanation can you give for this? What's the difference between the use of "my husband" here and that at the very opening of the story?
7. What is Claire's attitude towards her husband's offer to make love to her at the end of the story? What does the last word "Hurry" imply?
8. Study the beginning and ending of the story, and state how they differ from more traditional ways of beginning and ending a story.
9. What is the implied meaning of the title "So Much Water So Close to Home"?

【简评】

　　海明威曾把小说创作比作漂浮在海面上的一座冰山，露在水面上的只是冰山的八分之一，其他的八分之七则全部没入水中，需要读者自己潜入水中去探寻、发现。卡弗的短篇小说就像这样一座冰山。在"So Much Water So Close to Home"中，作者探讨了在现代社会看似"正常"的生活下人心不古、情感冷漠、道德沦丧等深刻问题，但作者却从头到尾不发一句议论，不作任何修饰，全靠细节说话，即使细节也被删减到最基本的事实描述，致使一些本来应有的细节缺失，造成一些句子字面意义理解上的困难。然而在保留下来的细节与词句中，几乎每个"平凡"细节、每句"大白话"中都包含着丰富的潜台词，若不反复阅读，仔细琢磨，恐怕不能理解其深意。从故事开头描写"我丈夫"的好胃口，从妻子看着丈夫和后来丈夫看着妻子的细节对比，从丈夫留给妻子的便条和妻子留给儿子的便条中分别使用的"爱"字中，再到几个垂钓者在浸泡在水中的尸体边上若无其事地钓鱼、吃喝、玩牌等细节描述中，都可以深切体会到作品主要人物不同的道德观、复杂的内心感受和思想变化。从作品的字里行间，读者还可以清楚地体会到卡弗本人对主人公及所发生事件的基本态度和价值取向。

Maxine Hong Kingston
1940—

汤亭亭是当代著名的美籍华裔女作家。父亲早年是乡村教师，1924年离华赴美，母亲直到1939年才漂洋过海，与父亲在加利福尼亚以开洗衣坊为生。汤亭亭出生在加州的斯托克顿，小时候阅读了父亲从中国带去的大量文学经典，因而中国文化对汤亭亭产生了深远的影响。1962年，她从加州大学伯克利分校毕业，获得文学学士学位，随后在夏威夷中学任教十余年。1976年发表处女作《女勇士》(The Woman Warrior)，一举成名，并获得全国书评家协会奖。此后，她开始在大学教书，现任加州大学伯克利分校荣休教授。继《女勇士》之后，汤亭亭又发表了《中国佬》(China Men, 1980) 和《孙行者》(Tripmaster Monkey: His Fake Book, 1989)，前者获得全国图书奖，后者荣获西部国际笔会奖。2004年，她发表《第五和平书》(The Fifth Book of Peace)，同样将回忆、历史、文化、幻想和现实融为一体，描述她对和平的向往。2006年由她主编、历次战争老兵撰写的《战争的老兵，和平的老兵》(Veterans of War, Veterans of Peace) 出版。这两部作品标志着汤亭亭开始把目光越过华裔的主题，面向全人类共同关心的一些话题。2011年，汤亭亭出版了她的新作《我爱宽阔的生命留白》(I Love a Broad Margin to My Life)。

美国华裔文学虽然早在19世纪上半叶就已萌芽，但直到《女勇士》获奖后，才获得广大美国读者的重视。可以说，20世纪90年代以来华裔文学在美国声誉鹊起，与汤亭亭的创作成就密不可分。《女勇士》与《中国佬》分别描述了汤亭亭的女性亲属和男性亲属背井离乡、移民美国、艰苦创业的经历，以及他们的子女在两种文化的夹缝中成长的历程，表现了东西方文化的冲突和他们作为少数族裔所特有的孤独感和疏离感。《孙行者》则以20世纪60年代美国反文化运动和嬉皮士生活为背景，描写崇拜垮掉派作家的华裔青年惠特曼·阿新为寻求自由，摒弃传统观念，在旧金山流浪的生活。汤亭亭的作品表现了美国白人社会对华裔的歧视和误解，在一定程度上解构了人们对华裔的刻板印象，塑造了华裔的新形象。因其艺术创作上的成就，汤亭亭荣膺1997年度美国国家人文奖章。

贯穿汤亭亭所有作品的一个共同主题是华裔对其身份的认识和理解。华裔一方面从祖辈那里受到中国传统文化的熏陶，另一方面又不可避免地受到美国白人主流文化的影响，他们往往对自己的文化身份产生疑惑。她的作品表现了华裔在白人社会中的惶恐、疑惑和忐忑不安，他们在陌生的美国文化中，摸索着生活，试图寻找、确定自己的身份。汤亭亭在写作过程中，也实现了对自己文化身份的"对比—发现—创造"的建构过程。以父母为代表的第一代移民对中国文化极度留恋，以儿女为代表的第二代移民最初对中国文化极度排斥，竭力认同白人主流文化，最后却发现，他们既不能完全摒弃从父母那里继承来的中国传统文化，又不能完全融入白人主流文化。他们必须将两种文化融合起来，才能确立自己作为华裔美国人在美国白人主流社会中的地位。汤亭亭的作品表现了华裔美国人从分离和异化逐渐走向调和，最后为自己重新定位的转变，实现了肯定性的自我创造，而不仅仅是对自己的种族根源给予否定。这一自我和他者间创造性的沟通也使得处于美国社会边缘的华裔文化迈向多元化文化的舞台。在文化研究盛行的今天，汤亭亭的作品自然也备受关注。

汤亭亭常常把事实与幻想、神话与生活、历史与现在融为一体，作品联想丰富奇异，时序混乱颠倒，行文恣意流畅，读起来让人感到天马行空、酣畅淋漓，因而她的作品常被认为是魔幻现实主义作品。

The Woman Warrior

【题解】

《女勇士》通常被视为一部自传，但汤亭亭辩解说她写的是小说，因为她在写作时，视野远远超出了自己的身世和经历，着眼于移民的共同感受和情怀。小说通过一个华裔小女孩的视角，描述她从母亲那里听来的有关中国的故事和她熟悉的华人生活。书中现实与想象、事实与虚构相互融合。中国的神话传说、妈妈的鬼怪故事、美国华人的现实生活在小女孩的脑海中交织在一起，给读者展现了一个处于两种文化背景、两种民族精神影响下的小女孩的成长和反思，刻画了她处于华人家庭和白人社会中的多重自我，反映了她对种族和性别问题的思考。标题中的"女勇士"是在美国长大的小女孩把中国巾帼英雄花木兰加诸自己身上进行的丰富联想。

《女勇士》也深刻表现了在两种文化传统中成长的女孩的痛苦。她的痛苦源于她是两种文化的"他者"，很难找到完全属于自己的精神归宿。小说的主人公在美国出生长大，她对中国的概念完全建立在母亲絮叨的故事和她自己的幻想之上。小说以历史上蔡琰的故事为结尾。蔡琰最终回到了故里，回到她熟悉的文化中，而千千万万的华侨却只能终生漂泊他乡。他们会无限思念遥远的家乡，而他们的孩子们却难以理解父辈们的语言和情感。对他们来说，一切只是唱歌般的嬉戏，或只是一种漂泊无定的愁绪，难以捉摸。

《女勇士》的另一个重要主题是女性主义。如同美国其他少数族裔女性，华裔女性同样在种族主义和性别主义的双重压迫下生活。作品生动描述了两代华裔女性如何在男权和种族的双重压迫下寻求自我的解放。正因如此，作品主人公才想象自己是女勇士花木兰，能够在白人和男性主宰的美国社会中找到自己的位置，获得人们的尊重。

下文选自《女勇士》第一部分"无名女子"。

From The Woman Warrior

Part 1

No Name Woman

"You must not tell anyone," my mother said, "what I am about to tell you. In China your father had a sister who killed herself. She jumped into the family well. We say that your father has all brothers because it is as if she had never been born.

"In 1924 just a few days after our village celebrated seventeen hurry-up weddings—to make sure that every young man who went'out on the road'would responsibly come home—your father and his brothers and your grandfather and his brothers and your aunt's new husband sailed for America, the Gold Mountain. It was your grandfather's last trip. Those lucky enough to get contracts waved goodbye from the decks. They fed and guarded the stowaways and helped them off in Cuba, New York, Bali, Hawaii. 'We'll meet in California next year,' they said. All of them sent money home.

"I remember looking at your aunt one day when she and I were dressing; I had not noticed before that she had such a protruding melon of a stomach. But I did not think, 'She's pregnant,' until she began to look like other pregnant women, her shirt pulling and the white tops of her black pants showing. She could not have been pregnant, you see, because her husband had been gone for years. No one said anything. We did not discuss it. In early summer she was ready to have the child, long after the time when it could have been possible.

"The village had also been counting. On the night the baby was to be born the villagers raided our house. Some were crying. Like a great saw, teeth strung with lights, files of people walked zigzag across our land, tearing the rice. Their lanterns doubled in the disturbed black water, which drained away through the broken bunds. As the villagers closed in, we could see that some of them, probably men and women we knew well, wore white masks. The people with long hair hung it over their faces. Women with short hair made it stand up on end. Some had tied white bands around their foreheads, arms, and legs.

"At first they threw mud and rocks at the house. Then they threw eggs and began slaughtering our stock. We could hear the animals scream their deaths—the roosters, the pigs, a last great roar from the ox. Familiar wild heads flared in our night windows; the villagers encircled us. Some of the faces stopped to peer at us, their eyes rushing like searchlights. The hands flattened against the panes, framed heads, and left red prints.

"The Villagers broke in the front and the back doors at the same time, even though we had not locked the doors against them. Their knives dripped with the blood of our animals. They smeared blood on the doors and walls. One woman swung a chicken, whose throat she had slit, splattering blood in red arcs about her. We stood together in the middle of our house, in the family hall with the pictures and tables of the ancestors around us, and looked straight ahead.

"At that time the house had only two wings. When the men came back, we would build two more to enclose our courtyard and a third one to begin a second courtyard. The villagers pushed through both wings, even your grandparents' rooms, to find your aunt's, which was also mine until the men returned. From this room a new wing for one of the younger families would grow. They ripped up her clothes and shoes and broke her combs, grinding them underfoot. They tore her work from the loom. They scattered the cooking fire and rolled the new weaving in it. We could hear them in the kitchen breaking our bowls and banging the pots. They overturned the great waist-high earthenware jugs; duck eggs, pickled fruits, vegetables burst out and mixed in acrid torrents. The old woman from the next field swept a broom through the air and loosed the spirits-of-the-broom over our heads. 'Pig.' 'Ghost.' 'Pig,' they sobbed and scolded while they ruined our house.

"When they left, they took sugar and oranges to bless themselves. They cut pieces from the dead animals. Some of them took bowls that were not broken and clothes that were not torn. Afterward we swept up the rice and sewed it back up into sacks. But the smells from the spilled preserves lasted. Your aunt gave birth in the pigsty that night. The next morning when I went for the water, I found her and the baby plugging up the family well.

"Don't let your father know that I told you. He denies her. Now that you have started to menstruate, what happened to her could happen to you. Don't humiliate us. You wouldn't like to be forgotten as if you had never been born. The villagers are watchful."

Whenever she had to warn us about life, my mother told stories that ran like this one, a story to grow up on. She tested our strength to establish realities. Those in the emigrant generations who could not reassert brute survival died young and far from home. Those of us in the first American generations have had to figure out how the invisible world the emigrants built around our childhoods fits in solid America.

The emigrants confused the gods by diverting their curses, misleading them with crooked streets and false names. They must try to confuse their offspring as well, who, I suppose, threaten them in similar ways—always trying to get things straight, always trying to name the unspeakable. The Chinese I know hide their names; sojourners take new names when their lives change and guard their real names with silence.

Chinese-Americans, when you try to understand what things in you are Chinese, how do you separate what is peculiar to childhood, to poverty, insanities, one family, your mother who marked your growing with stories, from what is Chinese? What is Chinese tradition and what is the movies?

If I want to learn what clothes my aunt wore, whether flashy or ordinary, I would have to begin, "Remember Father's drowned-in-the-well sister?" I cannot ask that. My mother has told me once and for all the useful parts. She will add nothing unless powered by Necessity, a riverbank that guides her life. She plants vegetable gardens rather than lawns; she carried the odd-shaped tomatoes home from the fields and eats food left for the gods. Whenever we did frivolous things, we used up energy; we flew high kites. We children came up off the ground over the melting cones our parents brought home from work and the American movie on New Year's Day—*Oh, You Beautiful Doll* with Betty Grable one year, and *She Wore a Yellow Ribbon* with John Wayne another year. After the one carnival ride each, we paid in guilt; our tired father counted his change on the dark walk home.

Adultery is extravagance. Could people who hatch their own chicks and eat the embryos and the heads for delicacies and boil the feet in vinegar for party food, leaving only the gravel, eating even the gizzard lining—could such people engender a prodigal aunt? To be a woman, to have a daughter in starvation time was a waste enough. My aunt could not have been the lone romantic who gave up everything for sex. Women in the old

China did not choose. Some man had commanded her to lie with him and be his secret evil. I wonder whether he masked himself when he joined the raid on her family.

Perhaps she had encountered him in the fields or on the mountain where the daughters-in-law collected fuel. Or perhaps he first noticed her in the marketplace. He was not a stranger because the village housed no strangers. She had to have dealings with him other than sex. Perhaps he worked an adjoining field, or he sold her the cloth for the dress she sewed and wore. His demand must have surprised, then terrified her. She obeyed him; she always did as she was told.

When the family found a young man in the next village to be her husband, she had stood tractably beside the best rooster, his proxy, and promised before they met that she would be his for ever. She was lucky that he was her age and she would be the first wife, an advantage secure now. The night she first saw him, he had sex with her. Then he left for America. She had almost forgotten what he looked like. When she tried to envision him, she only saw the black and white face in the group photograph the men had had taken before leaving.

The other man was not, after all, much different from her husband. They both gave orders: she followed. "If you tell your family, I'll beat you. I'll kill you. Be here again next week." No one talked sex, ever. And she might have separated the rapes from the rest of living if only she did not have to buy her oil from him or gather wood in the same forest. I want her fear to have lasted just as long as rape lasted so that the fear could have been contained. No drawn-out fear. But women at sex hazarded birth and hence lifetimes. The fear did not stop but permeated everywhere. She told the man, "I think I'm pregnant." He organized the raid against her.

On nights when my mother and father talked about their life back home, sometimes they mentioned an "outcast table" whose business they still seemed to be settling, their voices tight. In a commensal tradition, where food is precious, the powerful older people made wrongdoers eat alone. Instead of letting them start separate new lives like the Japanese, who could become samurais and geishas, the Chinese family, faces averted but eyes glowering sideways, hung on to the offenders and fed them leftovers. My aunt must have lived in the same house as my parents and eaten at an outcast table. My mother spoke about the raid as if she had seen it, when she and my aunt, a daughter-in-law to a different household, should not have been living together at all. Daughters-in-law lived with their husbands' parents, not their own; a synonym for marriage in Chinese is "taking a daughter-in-law." Her husband's parents could have sold her, mortgaged her, stoned her. But they had sent her back to her own mother and father, a mysterious act hinting at disgraces not told me. Perhaps they had thrown her out to deflect the avengers.

She was the only daughter; her four brothers went with her father, husband, and uncles "out on the road" and for some years became western men. When the goods were divided among the family, three of the brothers took land, and the youngest, my father, chose an education. After my grandparents gave their daughter away to her husband's family, they dispensed all the adventure and all the property. They expected her alone to keep the traditional ways, which her brothers, now among the barbarians, could fumble without detection. The heavy, deep rooted women were to maintain the past against the flood, safe for returning. But the rare urge west had fixed upon our family, and so my aunt crossed boundaries not delineated in space.

The work of preservation demands that the feelings playing about in one's guts not be turned into action. Just watch their passing like cherry blossoms. But perhaps my aunt, my forerunner, caught in a slow life, let dreams grow and fade and after some months or years went toward what persisted. Fear at the enormities of the forbidden kept her desires delicate, wire and bone. She looked at a man because she liked the way the hair was tucked behind his ears, or she liked the question mark line of a long torso curving at the shoulder and straight at the hip. For warm eyes or a soft voice or a slow walk—that's all—a few hairs, a line, a brightness, a sound, a pace, she gave up family. She offered us up for a charm that vanished with tiredness, a pigtail that didn't toss when the wind died. Why, the wrong lighting could erase the dearest thing about him.

It could very well have been, however, that my aunt did not take subtle enjoyment of her friend, but a wild woman, kept rollicking company. Imaging her free with sex doesn't fit, though. I don't know any women like that, or men either. Unless I see her life branching into mine, she gives me no ancestral help.

To sustain her being in love, she often worked at herself in the mirror, guessing at the colors and shapes that would interest him, changing them frequently in order to hit on the right combination. She wanted him to look back.

On a farm near the sea, a woman who tended her appearance reaped a reputation for eccentricity. All the married women blunt-cut their hair in flaps about their ears or pulled it back in tight buns. No nonsense. Neither style blew easily into heart-catching tangles. And at their weddings they displayed themselves in their long hair for the last time. "It brushed the backs of my knees," MY mother tells me. "It was braided, and even so, it brushed the backs of my knees!"

At the mirror my aunt combed individuality into her bob. A bun could have been contrived to escape into black streamers blowing in the wind or in quiet wisps about her face, but only the older women in our picture album wear buns. She brushed her hair back from her forehead, tucking the flaps behind her ears. She looped a piece of thread, knotted into a circle between her index fingers and thumbs, and ran the double strand across her forehead. When she closed her fingers as if she were making a pair of shadow geese bite, the string twisted together catching the little hairs. Then she pulled the thread away from her skin, ripping the hairs out neatly, her eyes watering from the needles of pain. Opening her fingers, she cleaned the thread, then rolled it along her hairline and the tops of her eyebrows. My mother did the same to me and my sisters and herself. I used to believe that the expression "caught by the short hairs" meant a captive held with a depilatory string. It especially hurt at the temples, but my mother said we were lucky we didn't have to have our feet bound when we were seven. Sisters used to sit on their beds and cry together, she said, as their mothers or their slaves removed the bandages for a few minutes each night and let the blood gush back into their veins. I hope that the man my aunt loved appreciated a smooth brow, that he wasn't just a tits-and-ass man.

Once my aunt found a freckle on her chin, at a spot that the almanac said predestined her for unhappiness. She dug it out with a hot needle and washed the wound with peroxide.

More attention to her looks than these pullings of hairs and pickings at spots would have caused gossip among the villagers. They owned work clothes and good clothes, and they wore good clothes for feasting the new seasons. But since a woman combing her hair hexes beginnings, my aunt rarely found an occasion to look her best. Women looked like great sea snails—the corded wood, babies, and laundry they carried were the whorls on their backs. The Chinese did not admire a bent back; goddesses and warriors stood straight. Still there must have been a marvelous freeing of beauty when a worker laid down her burden and stretched and arched.

Such commonplace loveliness, however, was not enough for my aunt. She dreamed of a lover for the fifteen days of New Year's, the time for families to exchange visits, money, and food. She plied her secret comb. And sure enough she cursed the year, the family, the village, and herself.

Even as her hair lured her imminent lover, many other men looked at her. Uncles, cousins, nephews, brothers would have looked, too, had they been home between journeys. Perhaps they had already been restraining their curiosity, and they left, fearful that their glances, like a field of nesting birds, might be startled and caught. Poverty hurt, and that was their first reason for leaving. But another, final reason for leaving the crowded house was the never-said.

She may have been unusually beloved, the precious only daughter, spoiled and mirror gazing because of the affection the family lavished on her. When her husband left, they welcomed the chance to take her back from the in-laws; she could live like the little daughter for just a while longer. There are stories that my grandfather was different from other people, "crazy ever since the little Jap bayoneted him in the head." He used to put his naked penis on the dinner table, laughing. And one day he brought home a baby girl, wrapped up inside his brown western-style greatcoat. He had traded one of his sons, probably my father, the youngest, for her. My grandmother made him trade back. When he finally got a daughter of his own, he doted on her. They must have all loved her, except perhaps my father, the only brother who never went back to China, having once been traded for a girl.

Brothers and sisters, newly men and women, had to efface their sexual color and present plain miens. Disturbing hair and eyes, a smile like no other, threatened the ideal of five generations living under one roof. To focus blurs, people shouted face to face and yelled from room to room. The immigrants I know have loud voices, unmodulated to American tones even after years away from the village where they called their friendships out across the fields. I have not been able to stop my mother's screams in public libraries or over telephones. Walking erect (knees straight, toes pointed forward, not pigeon-toed, which is Chinese-feminine) and speaking in an inaudible voice, I have tried to turn myself American-feminine. Chinese communication was loud, public. Only sick people had to whisper. But at the dinner table, where the family members came nearest one another, no one could talk, not the outcasts nor any eaters. Every word that falls from the mouth is a coin lost. Silently they gave and accepted food with both hands. A preoccupied child who took his bowl with one hand got a sideways glare. A complete moment of total attention is due everyone alike. Children and lovers have no singularity here, but my aunt used a secret voice, a separate attentiveness.

She kept the man's name to herself throughout her labor and dying; she did not accuse him that he be punished with her. To save her inseminator's name she gave silent birth.

He may have been somebody in her own household, but intercourse with a man outside the family would have been no less abhorrent. All the village were kinsmen, and the titles shouted in loud country voices never let kinship be forgotten. Any man within visiting distance would have been neutralized as a lover—"brother," "younger brother," "older brother"—one hundred and fifteen relationship titles. Parents researched birth charts probably not so much to assure good fortune as to circumvent incest in a population that has but one hundred surnames. Everybody has eight million relatives. How useless then sexual mannerisms, how dangerous.

As if it came from an atavism deeper than fear, I used to add "brother" silently to boys' names. It hexed the boys, who would or would not ask me to dance, and made them less scary and as familiar and deserving of benevolence as girls.

But, of course, I hexed myself also—no dates. I should have stood up, both arms waving, and shouted out across libraries, "Hey, you! Love me back." I had no idea, though, how to make attraction selective, how to control its direction and magnitude. If I made myself American-pretty so that the five or six Chinese boys in the class fell in love with me, everyone else—the Caucasian, Negro, and Japanese boys—would too. Sisterliness, dignified and honorable, made much more sense.

Attraction eludes control so stubbornly that whole societies designed to organize relationships among people cannot keep order, not even when they bind people to one another from childhood and raise them together. Among the very poor and the wealthy, brothers married their adopted sisters, like doves. Our family allowed some romance, paying adult brides' prices and providing dowries so that their sons and daughters could marry strangers. Marriage promises to turn strangers into friendly relatives—a nation of siblings.

In the village structure, spirits shimmered among the live creatures, balanced and held inequilibrium by time and land. But one human being flaring up into violence could open up a black hole, a maelstrom that pulled in the sky. The frightened villagers, who depended on one another to maintain the real, went to my aunt to show her a personal, physical representation of the break she had made in the "roundness". Misallying couples snapped off the future, which was to be embodied in true offspring. The villagers punished her for acting as if she could have a private life, secret and apart from them.

If my aunt had betrayed the family at a time of large grain yields and peace, when many boys were born, and wings were being built on many houses, perhaps she might have escaped such severe punishment. But the men—hungry, greedy, tired of planting in dry soil—had been forced to leave the village in order to send food—money home. There were ghost plagues, bandit plagues, wars with the Japanese, floods. My Chinese brother and sister had died of an unknown sickness. Adultery, perhaps only a mistake during good times, became a crime when the village needed food.

The round moon cakes and round doorways, the round tables of graduated sizes that fit one roundness inside another, round window and rice bowls,—these talismans had lost their power to warn this family of the law: a family must be whole, faithfully keeping the descent line by having sons to feed the old and the dead, who in turn look after the family. The villagers came to show my aunt and her love-in-hiding a broken house. The villagers were speeding up the circling of events because she was too shortsighted to see that her infidelity had already harmed the village, that waves of consequences would return unpredictably, sometimes in disguise, as now, to hurt her. This roundness had to be made coin-sized so that she would see its circumference: punish her at the birth of her baby. Awaken her to the inexorable. People who refused fatalism because they could invent small resources insisted on culpability. Deny accidents and wrest fault from the stars.

After the villagers left, their lanterns now scattering in various directions toward home, the family broke their silence and cursed her. "Aiaa, we're going to die. Death is coming. Death is coming. Look what you've done. You've killed us. Ghost! Dead ghost! Ghost! You've never been born." She ran out into the fields, far enough from the house so that she could no longer hear their voices, and pressed herself against the earth, her own land no more. When she felt the birth coming, she thought that she had been hurt. Her body seized together. "They've hurt me too much," she thought. "This is gall, and it will kill me." With forehead and knees against the earth, her body convulsed and then relaxed. She turned on her back, lay on the ground. The black well of sky and stars went out and out and out forever; her body and her complexity seemed to disappear. She was one of the stars, a bright dot in blackness, without home, without a companion, in eternal cold and silence. An agoraphobia rose in her, speeding higher and higher, bigger and bigger; she would not be able to contain it; there would no end to fear.

Flayed, unprotected against space, she felt pain return, focusing her body. This pain chilled her—a cold, steady kind of surface pain. Inside, spasmodically, the other pain, the pain of the child, heated her. For hours she lay on the ground, alternately body and space. Sometimes a vision of normal comfort obliterated reality: she saw the family in the evening gambling at the dinner table, the young people massaging their elders' backs. She saw them congratulating one another, high joy on the mornings the rice shoots came up. When these pictures burst, the stars drew yet further apart. Black space opened.

She got to her feet to fight better and remembered that old-fashioned women gave birth in their pigsties to fool the jealous, pain-dealing gods, who do not snatch piglets. Before the next spasms could stop her, she ran to the pigsty, each step a rushing out into emptiness. She climbed over the fence and knelt in the dirt. It was good to have a fence enclosing her, a tribal person alone.

Laboring, this woman who had carried her child as a foreign growth that sickened her every day, expelled it at last. She reached down to touch the hot, wet, moving mass, surely smaller than anything human, and could feel that it was human after all—fingers, toes, nails, nose. She pulled it up on to her belly, and it lay curled there, butt in the air, feet precisely tucked one under the other. She opened her loose shirt and buttoned the child inside. After resting, it squirmed and thrashed and she pushed it up to her breast. It turned its head this way and that until it found her nipple. There, it made little snuffling noises. She clenched her teeth at its preciousness, lovely as a young calf, a piglet, a little dog.

She may have gone to the pigsty as a last act of responsibility: she would protect this child as she had protected its father. It would look after her soul, leaving supplies on her grave. But how would this tiny child without family find her grave when there would be no marker for her anywhere, neither in the earth nor the family hall? No one would give her a family hall name. She had taken the child with her into the wastes. At its birth the two of them had felt the same raw pain of separation, a wound that only the family pressing tight could close. A child with no descent line would not soften her life but only trail after her, ghostlike, begging her to give it purposes. At dawn the villagers on their way to the fields would stand around the fence and look.

Full of milk, the little ghost slept. When it awoke, she hardened her breasts against the milk that crying loosens. Toward morning she picked up the baby and walked to the well.

Carrying the baby to the well show loving. Otherwise abandon it. Turn its face into the mud. Mothers who love their children take them along. It was probably a girl; there is some hope of forgiveness for boys.

"Don't tell anyone you had an aunt. Your father does not want to hear her name.

She has never been born." I have believed that sex was unspeakable and words so strong and fathers so frail that "aunt" would do my father mysterious harm. I have thought that my family, having settled among immigrants who had also been their neighbors in the ancestral land, needed to clean their name, and a wrong word would incite the kinspeople even here. But there is more to this silence: they want me to participate in her punishment. And I have.

In the twenty years since I heard this story I have not asked for details nor said my aunt's names; I do not know it. People who can comfort the dead can also chase after them to hurt them further—a reverse ancestor worship. The real punishment was not the raid swiftly inflicted by the villagers, but the family's deliberately forgetting her. Her betrayal so maddened them, they saw to it that she would suffer forever, even after death. Always hungry, always needing, she would have to beg food from other ghosts, snatch and steal it from those whose living descendants give them gifts. She would have to fight the ghosts massed at crossroads for the buns a few thoughtful citizens leave to decoy her away from village and home so that the ancestral spirits could feast unharassed. At peace, they could act like gods, not ghosts, their descent lines providing them with paper suits and dresses, spirits money, paper houses, paper automobiles, chicken, meat, and rice into eternity—essences delivered up in smoke and flames, steam and incense rising from each rice bowl.

My aunt haunts me—her ghosts drawn to me because now, after fifty years of neglect, I alone devote pages of paper to her, though not origamied[1] into houses and clothes. I do not think she always means me well. I am telling on her, and she was a spite suicide, drowning herself in the drinking water. The Chinese are always very frightened of the drowned one, whose weeping ghost, wet hair hanging and skin bloated, waits silently by the water to pull down a substitutes.

【注解】

1. origami: 日本折纸。

【思考题】

1. Why does the narrator's mother tell her the story of her aunt? What message does it send? Why is the aunt a "No Name Woman"?
2. How does the narrator tell the story of her aunt? Why do you suppose she tells it this way?

3. What is the status of a woman in the Chinese culture the narrator describes? Defend your answer with examples from the book. Consider the importance of appearance, usefulness, and self-discipline.
4. What is more important in the Chinese culture the narrator describes, the individual or the community? Why might this question be particularly interesting to a woman who grows up in the United States?
5. Why does Kingston say that she has participated in her aunt's punishment?
6. Is Kingston's description of the Chinese Americans still relevant in today's America? Cite examples from the novel to demonstrate your view.

解读举例

1. 《女勇士》是汤亭亭家族的传记，记叙了移民在美国艰苦创业的经历，表现了中国移民在美国受歧视、受压制的遭遇，反映了他们贫困、漂泊、艰辛的移民生活。

2. 《女勇士》表现了一位华裔小女孩寻求其文化身份的艰难历程。小女孩作为第二代移民，一方面从父母那里接受传统中国文化的熏陶，另一方面受到美国主流文化的影响，难以确定自己的文化身份。她与母亲的冲突实际上折射了中美两种文化的冲突。

3. 《女勇士》反映了女性反抗男权、追求幸福的努力。当时男性至上的社会剥夺了女性表达意愿、追求自由和幸福的权利。因此，书中的小女孩才幻想能像花木兰一样英勇善战，追寻幸福。她就是一个反抗男权的女勇士。

Cormac McCarthy
1933—

作者简介

科马克·麦卡锡是美国当代重要的小说家之一，迄今为止，共创作了包括其代表作《血色子午线》（*Blood Meridian, or The Evening Redness in the West*, 1985）在内的10部小说、2部戏剧、4部电影剧本和2篇短篇小说。麦卡锡不是传统意义上的高产作家，但却因其作品中所展现出来的极其鲜明的个人特色和广泛深刻的思想内涵引起了国内外读者及评论界越来越多的重视，麦卡锡也因此多次获得了包括普利策小说奖、鹅毛笔奖、全国图书奖、全国书评家协会奖、英国布莱克纪念

奖等多项国内外文学大奖，并被视作诺贝尔文学奖的有力竞争者。

1933 年，麦卡锡出生于美国罗得岛州一个爱尔兰裔家庭。1937 年，年幼的麦卡锡随父母迁至田纳西州诺克斯维尔，并进入了当地的天主教学校接受教育。1953 年，他加入了美国空军，开始长达四年的军旅生涯。在部队期间，麦卡锡开始大量阅读文学及哲学相关书籍，而正是这一段经历激活了流淌在麦卡锡血液里的创作天赋，为其日后的创作生涯打下基础。服役期满后，麦卡锡于 1957 年重返田纳西大学，不久后就在校内刊物上发表了《苏珊醒了》("Wake for Susan", 1959）和《意外沉溺》("A Drowning Incident", 1960）两篇短篇小说，并由此开启了长达半个多世纪的创作生涯。1965 年，麦卡锡发表了自己的第一部小说《看果园的人》(The Orchard Keeper）。1966 年，麦卡锡环南欧旅游，登陆伊比沙岛，在那里，他写下了第二部小说《外围黑暗》(Outer Dark)，并在返回美国之后于 1968 年发表了这部小说。1969 年，麦卡锡和妻子迁至田纳西州路易斯维尔，并根据真实事件写下了另一部小说《神之子》(Child of God, 1973）。1979 年，麦卡锡发表了半自传体小说《沙特里》(Suttree）。值得注意的是，这四部小说均有明显的南方哥特式文学（southern gothic literature）的色彩，作品大多以作家的故乡田纳西州阿帕拉契亚山乡为创作背景，里面充满了大量的自然景观描写，又具有较为惊悚的故事情节，故事主人公大多在漂泊追寻之旅中完成自我精神救赎。遗憾的是，由于福克纳、奥康纳等前辈作家在这一时期已经享誉文坛，麦卡锡的作品在当时并没有引起人们太多关注。

进入 20 世纪 80 年代，麦卡锡一转之前的地方文学特色，开始以美国西南边境地区为创作背景，创作出了奠定其文坛地位的西部小说（western novel）。在 2006 年《纽约时报书评》评选"过去 25 年出版的美国最佳小说"时，麦卡锡 1985 年发表的代表性作品《血色子午线》(Blood Meridian, or The Evening Redness in the West) 名列第三，被誉为 20 世纪最出色的一百部英文小说之一。20 世纪 90 年代以来，麦卡锡更是进入其个人创作的高峰期，在短短几年之内接连出版了《天下骏马》(All the Pretty Horses, 1992）、《穿越》(The Crossing, 1994）和《平原上的城市》(Cities of the Plain, 1998），这三部作品构成了"边境三部曲"（trilogy of the border）。这些西部小说大多继承了美国传统西部小说中"漂泊 – 历险 – 归返"的牛仔文化书写范式，但又超越了这一范式，对人与自然关系、人性暴力源泉、西部神话等各类错综交杂的宏大主题进行了探寻，带有鲜明的个人烙印。其中，《天下骏马》一书还获得了全国图书奖及全国书评家协会奖两项大奖。

进入到21世纪后，麦卡锡又先后出版了两部小说，分别是《老无所依》（*No Country for Old Men*, 2005）和《路》（*The Road*, 2006）。《老无所依》依旧以作者熟悉的西部边境为创作主题，根据这部小说改编的同名电影一经上映就获得了热烈反响。《路》则标志着麦卡锡创作风格上的又一次重要转型，开启了麦卡锡"后启示录小说"（post-apocalyptic novel）阶段的创作。该书以核战后的虚构世界为背景，讲述了一对父子在苍茫荒芜的漫天雪境中历经艰难跋涉，寻求远方可能存在的一丝温暖之地的故事，揭示了作者对后9·11时代人类应如何重启朝圣之旅、完成自我救赎的人文主义思考。

麦卡锡的小说大多聚焦于美墨边境地区社会中下层人士的生活体验及生活感悟，但又超越了地域限制，探究了生与死、善与恶、真与假等宏大主题。小说中，惬意的田园风景和荒凉的不毛之地、令人惊悚的暴力谋杀和隐隐存在的人性温暖等各种描写相互交融，让读者在梦魇般的阅读过程中又能感受到一丝救赎式的欢愉和宁静。作品中随处可见各种宗教、神话及哲学元素，以及麦卡锡简洁明快却又晦涩崇高的语言风格，都为解读其作品提供了无限可能。尽管麦卡锡一直以来坚持简单朴实的生活方式和极其低调的处世哲学，几乎从不接受任何公众采访，也从来不公开谈论自己的任何作品及个人生活，但这并不影响大众对他的喜爱和评论界对他的高度赞誉。著名评论家哈罗德·布鲁姆就认为他是美国当代真正的一流小说家，并称其为当代美国文学界"福克纳和海明威唯一的合法继承人"。

Blood Meridian, or the Evening Redness in the West

【题解】

《血色子午线》以无名氏主人公在美国西南部美墨边境地区的流亡经历为主线，讲述了一场针对印第安人规模浩荡、异常残酷的连环追逐大屠杀。故事的主人公无名无姓，大多数时候以"少年"（the kid）代指，只是在小说开篇和结尾处分别被称为"孩子"（the child）和"男人"（the man）。主人公"少年"十几岁时，加入了由怀特上尉带领的军事阻挠武装队伍，前往墨西哥境内开疆辟土，却遭到了印第安人的攻击。机缘巧合下，"少年"又加入了由罪犯、无业游民、老兵等各色人等组成的赏金猎人队伍，该队伍受雇于墨西哥政府，通过杀害并割取当地印第安人的头皮来换取经济利益。队伍表面上的首领是美墨战争的老兵格兰顿，实际上则由法官霍尔顿所操控。这些亡命之徒在墨西哥境内烧杀抢掠，无恶不作，很快遭到了当地印第安人的疯狂报复，几乎全部丧命，只有霍尔顿和少年侥幸逃生。作者在书中用影像镜头式的白描手法描写了大量血腥场面，如挂满死婴的树枝，跪地求情却依然被砍死的村民们，上一秒还坐在霍尔顿法官腿上玩耍、下一秒就被法官割掉头皮的小男孩……这些无一不在揭示战争的血腥本质及其对人性的摧残。

主人公"少年"作为整个事件的参与者及见证者，不仅经历了一场亡命天涯的流浪之旅，更是在旅途中见证了人性的贪婪和残酷，认清了霍尔顿法官等一众人等的嗜血本性，从而开启了自我反思的精神救赎之旅。下文为小说最后一章的后半部分，描述了多年以后，作为战争幸存者、此时已成长为"男人"的主人公在得克萨斯州格里芬堡的蜂巢酒馆与同为幸存者的霍尔顿法官相遇的场景。法官认为曾经的"少年"是他们当年那支队伍的背叛者，将其杀害于旅店的厕所内。故事至此结束。

From Blood Meridian

XXIII

On the north Texas plains - An old buffalo hunter - The millennial herds - The bonepickers[1] - Night on the prairie - The callers - Apache[2] ears - Elrod takes a stand - A killing - Bearing off the dead - Fort Griffin[3] - The Beehive[4] - A stageshow - The judge - Killing a bear - The judge speaks of old times - In preparation for the dance - The judge on war, destiny, the supremacy of man - The dancehall - The whore - The jakes and what was encountered there - Sie müssen schlafen aber Ich muss tanzen[5].

IN THE AFTERNOON he rode through the McKenzie crossing of the Clear Fork of the Brazos River and he and the horse walked side by side down the twilight toward the town where in the long red dusk and in the darkness the random aggregate of the lamps formed slowly a false shore of hospice cradled on the low plain before them. They passed enormous ricks of bones, colossal dikes composed of horned skulls and the crescent ribs like old ivory bows heaped in the aftermath of some legendary battle, great levees of them curving away over the plain into the night.

They entered the town in a light rain falling. The horse nickered and snuffed shyly at the hocks of the other animals standing at stall before the lamplit bagnios they passed. Fiddle-music issued into the solitary mud street and lean dogs crossed before them from shadow to shadow. At the end of the town he led the horse to a rail and tied it among others and stepped up the low wooden stairs into the dim light that fell from the doorway there. He looked back a last time at the street and at the random windowlights let into the darkness and at the last pale light in the west and the low dark hills around. Then he pushed open the door and entered.

A dimly seething rabble had coagulated within. As if the raw board structure erected for their containment occupied some ultimate sink into which they had gravitated from off the surrounding flatlands. An old man in a tyrolean costume was shuffling among the rough tables with his hat outheld while a little girl in a smock cranked a barrel organ and a bear in a crinoline twirled strangely upon a board stage defined by a row of tallow candles that dripped and sputtered in their pools of grease.

He made his way through the crowd to the bar where several men in gaitered shirts were drawing beer or pouring whiskey. Young boys worked behind them fetching crates of bottles and racks of glasses steaming from the scullery to the rear. The bar was covered with zinc and he placed his elbows upon it and spun a silver coin before him and slapped it flat.

Speak or forever, said the barman.

A whiskey.

Whiskey it is. He set up a glass and uncorked a bottle and poured perhaps half a gill and took the coin.

He stood looking at the whiskey. Then he took his hat off and placed it on the bar and took up the glass and drank it very deliberately and set the empty glass down again. He wiped his mouth and turned around and placed his elbows on the bar behind him.

Watching him across the layered smoke in the yellow light was the judge.

He was sitting at one of the tables. He wore a round hat with a narrow brim and he was among every kind of man, herder and bullwhacker and drover and freighter and miner and hunter and soldier and pedlar and gambler and drifter and drunkard and thief and he was among the dregs of the earth in beggary a thousand years and he was among the scapegrace scions of eastern dynasties and in all that motley assemblage he sat by them and yet alone as if he were some other sort of man entire and he seemed little changed or none in all these years.

He turned away from those eyes and stood looking down at the empty tumbler between his fists. When he looked up the barman was watching him. He raised his forefinger and the barman brought the whiskey.

He paid, he lifted the glass and drank. There was a mirror along the backbar but it held only smoke and phantoms. The barrel organ was groaning and creaking and the bear with tongue aloll was revolving heavily on the boards.

When he turned the judge had risen and was speaking with other men. The showman made his way through the throng shaking the coins in his hat. Garishly clad whores were going out through a door at the rear of the premises and he watched them and he watched the bear and when he looked back across the room the judge was not there. The showman seemed to be in altercation with the men standing at the table. Another man rose. The showman gestured with his hat. One of them pointed toward the bar. He shook his head. Their voices were incoherent in the din. On the boards the bear was dancing for all that his heart was worth and the girl cranked the organ handle and the shadow of the act which the candlelight constructed upon the wall might have gone begging for referents in any daylight world. When he looked back the showman had donned the hat and he stood with his hands on his hips. One of the men had drawn a longbarreled cavalry pistol from his belt. He turned and leveled the pistol toward the stage.

Some dove for the floor, some reached for their own arms. The owner of the bear stood like a pitchman at a shooting gallery. The shot was thunderous and in the afterclap all sound in that room ceased. The bear had been shot through the mid-section. He let out a low moan and he began to dance faster, dancing in silence save for the slap of his great footpads on the planks. Blood was running down his groin. The little girl strapped into the barrel organ stood frozen, the crank at rest on the upswing. The man with the pistol fired again and the pistol bucked and roared and the black smoke rolled and the bear groaned and began to reel drunkenly. He was holding his chest and a thin foam of blood swung from his jaw and he began to totter and to cry like a child and he took a few last steps, dancing, and crashed to the boards.

Someone had seized the pistol arm of the man who'd done the shooting and the gun was waving aloft. The owner of the bear stood stunned, clutching the brim of his oldworld hat.

Shot the goddamned bear, said the barman.

The little girl had unbuckled herself out of the barrel organ and it clattered wheezing to the floor. She ran forward and knelt and gathered the great shaggy head up in her arms and began to rock back and forth sobbing. Most of the men in the room had risen and they stood in the smoky yellow space with their hands on their sidearms. Whole flocks of whores were scuttling toward the rear and a woman mounted to the boards and stepped past the bear and held out her hands.

It's all over, she said. It's all over.

Do you believe it's all over, son?

He turned. The judge was standing at the bar looking down at him. He smiled, he removed his hat. The great pale dome of his skull shone like an enormous phosphorescent egg in the lamplight.

The last of the true. The last of the true. I'd say they're all gone under now saving me and thee. Would you not?

He tried to see past him. That great corpus enshadowed him from all beyond. He could hear the woman announcing the commencement of dancing in the hall to the rear.

And some are not yet born who shall have cause to curse the Dauphin's soul[6], said the judge. He turned slightly. Plenty of time for the dance.

I aint studyin no dance.

The judge smiled.

The tyrolean and another man were bent over the bear. The girl was sobbing, the front of her dress dark with blood. The judge leaned across the bar and seized a bottle and snapped the cork out of it with his thumb. The cork whined off into the blackness above the lamps like a bullet. He rifled a great drink down his throat and leaned back against the bar. You're here for the dance, he said.

I got to go.

The judge looked aggrieved. Go? he said.

He nodded. He reached and took hold of his hat where it lay on the bar but he did not take it up and he did not move.

What man would not be a dancer if he could, said the judge. It's a great thing, the dance.

The woman was kneeling and had her arm around the little girl. The candles sputtered and the great hairy mound of the bear dead in its crinoline lay like some monster slain in the commission of unnatural acts. The judge poured the tumbler full where it stood empty alongside the hat and nudged it forward.

Drink up, he said. Drink up. This night thy soul may be required of thee.

He looked at the glass. The judge smiled and gestured with the bottle. He took up the glass and drank.

The judge watched him. Was it always your idea, he said, that if you did not speak you would not be recognized?

You seen me.

The judge ignored this. I recognized you when I first saw you and yet you were a disappointment to me. Then and now. Even so at the last I find you here with me.

I aint with you.

The judge raised his bald brow. Not? he said. He looked about him in a puzzled and artful way and he was a passable thespian.

I never come here huntin you.

What then? said the judge.

What would I want with you? I come here same reason as any man.

And what reason is that?

What reason is what?

That these men are here.

They come here to have a good time.

The judge watched him. He began to point out various men in the room and to ask if these men were here for a good time or if indeed they knew why they were here at all.

Everbody dont have to have a reason to be someplace.

That's so, said the judge. They do not have to have a reason. But order is not set aside because of their indifference.

He regarded the judge warily.

Let me put it this way, said the judge. If it is so that they themselves have no reason and yet are indeed here must they not be here by reason of some other? And if this is so can you guess who that other might be?

No. Can you?

I know him well.

He poured the tumbler full once more and he took a drink himself from the bottle and he wiped his mouth and turned to regard the room. This is an orchestration for an event. For a dance in fact. The participants will be apprised of their roles at the proper time. For now it is enough that they have arrived. As the dance is the thing with which we are concerned and contains complete within itself its own arrangement and history and finale there is no necessity that the dancers contain these things within themselves as well. In any event the history of all is not the history of each nor indeed the sum of those histories and none here can finally comprehend the reason for his presence for he has no way of knowing even in what the event consists. In fact, were he to know he might well absent himself and you can see that that cannot be any part of the plan if plan there be.

He smiled, his great teeth shone. He drank.

An event, a ceremony. The orchestration thereof. The overture carries certain marks of decisiveness. It includes the slaying of a large bear. The evening's progress will not appear strange or unusual even to those who question the Tightness of the events so ordered.

A ceremony then. One could well argue that there are not categories of no ceremony but only ceremonies of greater or lesser degree and deferring to this argument we will say that this is a ceremony of a certain magnitude perhaps more commonly called a ritual. A ritual includes the letting of blood. Rituals which fail in this requirement are but mock rituals. Here every man knows the false at once. Never doubt it. That feeling in the breast that evokes a child's memory of loneliness such as when the others have gone and only the game is left with its solitary participant. A solitary game, without opponent. Where only the rules are at hazard. Dont look away. We are not speaking in mysteries. You of all men are no stranger to that feeling, the emptiness and the despair. It is that which we take arms against, is it not? Is not blood the tempering agent in the mortar which bonds? The judge leaned closer. What do you think death is, man? Of whom do we speak when we speak of a man who was and is not? Are these blind riddles or are they not some part of every man's jurisdiction? What is death if not an agency? And whom does he intend toward? Look at me.

I dont like craziness.

Nor I. Nor I. Bear with me. Look at them now. Pick a man, any man. That man there. See him. That man hatless. You know his opinion of the world. You can read it in his face, in his stance. Yet his complaint that a man's life is no bargain masks the actual case with him. Which is that men will not do as he wishes them to. Have never done, never will do. That's the way of things with him and his life is so balked about by difficulty and become so altered of its intended architecture that he is little more than a walking hovel hardly fit to house the human spirit at all. Can he say, such a man, that there is no malign thing set against him? That there is no power and no force and no cause? What manner of heretic could doubt agency and claimant alike? Can he believe that the wreckage of his existence is unentailed? No liens, no creditors? That gods of vengeance and of compassion alike lie sleeping in their crypt and whether our cries are for an accounting or for the destruction of the ledgers altogether they must evoke only the same silence and that it is this silence which will prevail? To whom is he talking, man? Cant you see him?

The man was indeed muttering to himself and peering balefully about the room wherein it seemed there was no friend to him.

A man seeks his own destiny and no other, said the judge. Will or nill. Any man who could discover own fate and elect therefore some opposite course could only come at last to that selfsame reckoning at the same appointed time, for each man's destiny is as large as the world he inhabits and contains within it all opposites as well. This desert upon which so many have been broken is vast and calls for largeness of heart but it is also ultimately empty. It is hard, it is barren. Its very nature is stone.

He poured the tumbler full. Drink up, he said. The world goes on. We have dancing nightly and this night is no exception. The straight and the winding way are one and now that you are here what do the years count since last we two met together? Men's memories are uncertain and the past that was differs little from the past that was not.

He took up the tumbler the judge had poured and he drank and set it down again. He looked at the judge. I been everwhere, he said. This is just one more place.

The judge arched his brow. Did you post witnesses? he said. To report to you on the continuing existence of those places once you'd quit them?

That's crazy.

Is it? Where is yesterday? Where is Glanton[7] and Brown and where is the priest? He leaned closer. Where is Shelby, whom you left to the mercies of Elias in the desert, and where is Tate whom you abandoned in the mountains? Where are the ladies, ah the fair and tender ladies with whom you danced at the governor's ball when you were a hero anointed with the blood of the enemies of the republic you'd elected to defend? And where is the fiddler and where the dance?

I guess you can tell me.

I tell you this. As war becomes dishonored and its nobility called into question those honorable men who recognize the sanctity of blood will become excluded from the dance, which is the warrior's right, and thereby will the dance become a false dance and the dancers false dancers. And yet there will be one there always who is a true dancer and can you guess who that might be?

You aint nothin.

You speak truer than you know. But I will tell you. Only that man who has offered up himself entire to the blood of war, who has been to the floor of the pit and seen horror in the round and learned at last that it speaks to his inmost heart, only that man can dance.

Even a dumb animal can dance.

The judge set the bottle on the bar. Hear me, man, he said. There is room on the stage for one beast and one alone. All others are destined for a night that is eternal and without name. One by one they will step down into the darkness before the footlamps. Bears that dance, bears that dont.

HE DRIFTED WITH the crowd toward the door at the rear. In the anteroom sat men at cards, dim in the smoke. He moved on. A woman was taking chits from the men as they passed through to the shed at the rear of the building. She looked up at him. He had no chit. She directed him to a table where a woman was selling the chits and stuffing the money with a piece of shingle through a narrow slit into an iron strongbox. He paid his dollar and took the stamped brass token and rendered it up at the door and passed through.

He found himself in a large hall with a platform for the musicians at one end and a large homemade sheetiron stove at the other. Whole squadrons of whores were working the floor. In their stained peignoirs, in their green stockings and melon-colored drawers they drifted through the smoky oil light like makebelieve wantons, at once childlike and lewd. A dark little dwarf of a whore took his arm and smiled up at him.

I seen you right away, she said. I always pick the one I want.

She led him through a door where an old Mexican woman was handing out towels and candles and they ascended like refugees of some sordid disaster the darkened plankboard stairwell to the upper rooms.

Lying in the little cubicle with his trousers about his knees he watched her. He watched her take up her clothes and don them and he watched her hold the candle to the mirror and study her face there. She turned and looked at him.

Let's go, she said. I got to go.

Goon.

You cant lay there. Come on. I got to go.

He sat up and swung his legs over the edge of the little iron cot and stood and pulled his trousers up and buttoned them and buckled his belt. His hat was on the floor and he picked it up and slapped it against the side of his leg and put it on.

You need to get down there and get you a drink, she said. You'll be all right.

I'm all right now.

He went out. He turned at the end of the hallway and looked back. Then he went down the stairs. She had come to the door. She stood in the hallway holding the candle and brushing her hair back with one hand and she watched him descend into the dark of the stairwell and then she pulled the door shut behind her.

He stood at the edge of the dancefloor. A ring of people had taken the floor and were holding hands and grinning and calling out to one another. A fiddler sat on a stool on the stage and a man walked up and down calling out the order of the dance and gesturing and stepping in the way he wished them to go. Outside in the darkened lot groups of wretched Tonkawas stood in the mud with their faces composed in strange lost portraits within the sashwork of the windowlights. The fiddler rose and set the fiddle to his jaw. There was a shout and the music began and the ring of dancers began to rotate ponderously with a great shuffling. He went out the back.

The rain had stopped and the air was cold. He stood in the yard. Stars were falling across the sky myriad and random, speeding along brief vectors from their origins in night to their destinies in dust and nothingness. Within the hall the fiddle squealed and the dancers shuffled and stomped. In the street men were calling for the little girl whose bear was dead for she was lost. They went among the darkened lots with lanterns and torches calling out to her.

He went down the walkboard toward the jakes. He stood outside listening to the voices fading away and he looked again at the silent tracks of the stars where they died over the darkened hills. Then he opened the rough board door of the jakes and stepped in.

The judge was seated upon the closet. He was naked and he rose up smiling and gathered him in his arms against his immense and terrible flesh and shot the wooden barlatch home behind him.

In the saloon two men who wanted to buy the hide were looking for the owner of the bear. The bear lay on the stage in an immense pool of blood. All the candles had gone out save one and it guttered uneasily in its grease like a votive lamp. In the dancehall a young man had joined the fiddler and he kept the measure of the music with a pair of spoons which he clapped between his knees. The whores sashayed half naked, some with their breasts exposed. In the mudded dogyard behind the premises two men went down the boards toward the jakes. A third man was standing there urinating into the mud.

Is someone in there? the first man said.

The man who was relieving himself did not look up. I wouldnt go in there if I was you, he said.

Is there somebody in there?

I wouldnt go in.

He hitched himself up and buttoned his trousers and stepped past them and went up the walk toward the lights. The first man watched him go and then opened the door of the jakes.

Good God almighty, he said.

What is it?

He didnt answer. He stepped past the other and went back up the walk. The other man stood looking after him. Then he opened the door and looked in.

In the saloon they had rolled the dead bear onto a wagon-sheet and there was a general call for hands. In the anteroom the tobacco smoke circled the lamps like an evil fog and the men bid and dealt in a low mutter.

There was a lull in the dancing and a second fiddler took the stage and the two plucked their strings and turned the little hardwood pegs until they were satisfied. Many among the dancers were staggering drunk through the room and some had rid themselves of shirts and jackets and stood barechested and sweating even though the room was cold enough to cloud their breath. An enormous whore stood clapping her hands at the bandstand and calling drunkenly for the music. She wore nothing but a pair of men's drawers and some of her sisters were likewise clad in what appeared to be trophies—hats or pantaloons or blue twill cavalry jackets. As the music sawed up there was a lively cry from all and a caller stood to the front and called out the dance and the dancers stomped and hooted and lurched against one another.

And they are dancing, the board floor slamming under the jackboots and the fiddlers grinning hideously over their canted pieces. Towering over them all is the judge and he is naked dancing, his small feet lively and quick and now in doubletime and bowing to the ladies, huge and pale and hairless, like an enormous infant. He never sleeps, he says. He says he'll never die. He bows to the fiddlers and sashays backwards and throws back his head and laughs deep in his throat and he is a great favorite, the judge. He wafts his hat and the lunar dome of his skull passes palely under the lamps and he swings about and takes possession of one of the fiddles and he pirouettes and makes a pass, two passes, dancing and fiddling at once. His feet are light and nimble. He never sleeps. He says that he will never die. He dances in light and in shadow and he is a great favorite. He never sleeps, the judge. He is dancing, dancing. He says that he will never die.

THE END

【注解】

1. bonepicker：指19世纪美国西部地区的拾骨者。当时，随着工业革命的推进，为了得到皮革制造业所需的牛皮，人们增加了对西部地区野生牛群的猎杀。偶然间，人们发现牛骨磨碎后可以当作肥料使用，于是，由西部农场主和一大批无家可归的流浪汉组成的拾骨者队伍应运而生。
2. Apache：阿帕奇人，印第安种族的一个重要部落，在小说前面的章节中曾多次出现。
3. Fort Griffin：格里芬堡，19世纪中后期美国在西南边境地区建立的众多堡垒之一，用于保护当地居民免受印第安人的侵犯。
4. Beehive：蜂巢酒馆，是小说最后一章中，主人公和律师多年后再度相遇的场所。
5. Sie müssen schlafen aber Ich muss tanzen：此句是对19世纪德国诗人施托姆的诗句的模仿。原诗是"我想要沉睡，而你必须跳舞"。此处作者做了细微改动，意为"您必须沉睡而我必须跳舞"。
6. And some are not yet born who shall have cause to curse the Dauphin's soul：法官此处借用了莎士比亚戏剧《亨利五世》中的台词，原句为"有些还没有成胎，有些还没有降生，他们全有理由咒骂王子太轻狂。"
7. Glanton：格兰顿，主人公所加入的那支赏金猎人队伍的名义头领。该段中随后提到的几个人，如布朗、牧师、谢尔比、泰特等，都曾是那支队伍的成员。

【思考题】

1. Do you think there is a symbolic meaning of the bear dancing on the boards in the bar? If yes, elaborate on it.
2. What is the lawyer's attitude toward his past behavior of scalping the Indian? Find some evidence in this chapter to support your view.
3. The author McCarthy ends up the whole novel with the lawyer's killing of the protagonist. What kind of information is conveyed by such an arrangement?

解读举例

1. 霍尔顿法官的双重形象深刻揭示了美国文化的矛盾性。霍尔顿法官在书中一直以身影巨大、无毛无眉的形象示人，仿佛是一个基因突变的巨婴。他精通天文、地理，懂得制造火药，能讲五国语言，能歌善舞，还会画画，对各种古代事物了如指掌，且经常和周围人就生死、战争、存在意义等宏大主题展开长篇大论；但就是这样一个具有法官形象的人，却从事着头皮交易这种血腥至极的种族屠杀"事业"。他代表了人类灵魂深处最为邪恶的一面，也是美国工业文明试图灭绝印第安文明这一历史罪行的代言人，小说也由此揭露了美国西进运动过程中所犯下的滔天罪行，隐含了作者本人对"天定命运论"的修正和对美国神话的解构，以及对美国历史发展进程中民族心理层面所存在缺陷的深刻反思。

2. 《血色子午线》是一本成长小说。"少年"作为整个故事的见证者及参与者，在小说前半部分像身边其他队友一样，机械般地参与到这场杀人游戏当中，而队伍的首领霍尔顿法官因此也"像爱自己的儿子一样"对他寄予厚望。"少年"在全书出现的频率并不高，甚至连续几个章节都完全未出现，他的这种适度缺失正是出于他对法官淫威的默认和屈从。然而，随着故事情节发展，"少年"不断被一张张血淋淋的头皮所刺激，并逐渐意识到自己所参加的这种头皮交易的本质，他逐渐变得不再全身心投入到这场杀戮罪行中，也因此招致法官的不满。小说最后，"少年"被当作"叛徒"遭到了法官的处决，他并没有通过"弑父"这种传统手段完成自己的成人礼，但他所遭遇的处决恰恰标志了他与法官在精神层面上的彻底决裂，主人公的心路历程也由此得以圆满。

Don DeLillo
1936—

作者简介

唐·德里罗是美国当代著名作家，他的作品展示了当代美国日常图景，揭露存在的社会问题，探讨了当代美国各种社会危机产生的根源，思考可能的解决之道。他曾荣获全国图书奖、国际笔会/福克纳文学奖、耶路撒冷奖等重要奖项。他与托马斯·品钦（Thomas Pynchon）、科马克·麦卡锡（Cormac McCarthy）、菲利普·罗斯（Philip Roth）并称为"美国当代最重要的四位作家"。

1936 年，德里罗出生在纽约市布朗克斯区一个意大利裔工人家庭。童年时期，他随父母迁居宾夕法尼亚东部的波维尔市，后返回纽约市生活。1958 年，他在福特汉姆大学获交际艺术学士学位。1975 年，他与芭芭拉·本内特（Barbara Bennett）结婚。

德里罗的写作生涯分为四个主要阶段。第一阶段为 20 世纪 60 年代至 70 年代，是德里罗的"习作阶段"，也是德里罗的多产时期。1960 年，德里罗在文学期刊《纪元》上发表第一篇短篇小说《约旦河》（"The River Jordan"）。时隔十一年，他的第一部长篇小说《美国志》（*Americana*, 1971）出版。此后，德里罗又接连发表了《球门区》(*End Zone*, 1972)、《琼斯大街》(*Great Jones Street*, 1973)、《拉特纳之星》(*Ratner's Star*, 1976)、《玩家》(*Players*, 1977)和《走狗》(*Running Dog*, 1978)等小说。从《美国志》到《走狗》，每部小说的题材各不相同，但均是对美国社会本质的探索，反映现代人精神焦虑、消费主义膨胀等美国当代社会问题。

在德里罗创作的第二阶段（20世纪80年代），德里罗的创作水平迈上新的台阶。在《亚马逊》(*Amazons*, 1980)和《名字》(*The Names*, 1982)等作品中，他的创作手法日臻成熟。此后，随着《白噪音》(*White Noise*, 1985)和《天秤星座》(*Libra*, 1988)等重要作品的发表，德里罗声名鹊起，并在后现代主义小说作家中占据一席之地。1985年，《白噪音》一举获得全国图书奖，成为德里罗写作事业的重要转折点。《天秤星座》是他的另一部代表作，荣获《爱尔兰时报》国际小说奖。德里罗指出人类的本质是一头原始的野兽，生活在高科技时代的美国人比其他时代的人更脱离人性。

在创作的第三阶段（20世纪90年代），德里罗更加关注现实问题，文笔更为娴熟，其写作事业登上新的高度。《地下世界》(*Underworld*, 1998)被认为是德里罗最有影响力的小说，小说长达八百多页，故事跨度从20世纪50年代到90年代，以古巴导弹危机和核扩散等真实的历史事件为背景，描绘了人类制造的"超真实"世界，深刻讽刺了后现代社会中人类生活被自己所造之物侵占的可悲景象。

进入21世纪后，德里罗的创作进入第四阶段。这一阶段德里罗发表了五部小说，即《人体艺术家》(*The Body Artist*, 2001)、《大都会》(*Cosmopolis*, 2003)、《坠落的人》(*Falling Man*, 2007)、《欧米伽点》(*Point Omega*, 2010)和《K氏零度》(*Zero K*, 2016)。这些作品篇幅均不长，德里罗也更注重语言本身，而非语言外的华丽因素。他倾向于书写简短明确、朴实无华的句子。《人体艺术家》和《欧米伽点》被视为姊妹篇，都关注时间和失去等主题。《坠落的人》则聚集于"9·11"事件。

德里罗的作品多维度地呈现了现代主义和后现代主义文学的创作风格。他的作品聚焦消费主义、阴谋、家庭解体与重组、暴力重生、学术界乱象等后现代主题，注重把握语言节奏，有意将写作的视觉感受融入文本，以增强读者的阅读体验。他在作品中运用超现实式、理性化和直白散文式等不同的对话风格，塑造形象更加饱满、个性更加鲜明的人物。德里罗的作品真实描绘美国的社会现实，探讨恐怖分子给当代美国社会和文化带来的冲击，揭示大众媒体在现代生活中的重要作用，展现群体心理的形成和发展过程，反思个人向群体屈服等现象。

White Noise

【题解】

《白噪音》讲述了美国一个小镇发生的一起灾难事件。这一事件导致小镇居民生活在死亡的恐惧之中，反映了美国当代社会面临的日常生活困境。全书分为三个部分，共40章。第一部分"波与辐射"讽刺了大学教育。杰克·格拉迪尼（Jack Gladney）是一位因开创希特勒研究而声名鹊起的教授，但他不懂德语。小说中的一些奇异事件，如身穿米莱克斯服套装的男子神秘死亡，以及坠落的飞机上惊恐的幸存者，都预示着接下来要发生的灾难。在第二部分"空中毒雾事件"中，一辆运载尼奥丁衍生物的罐车发生泄漏，在小镇上空形成一团黑色毒雾，小镇居民在高度恐慌中纷纷逃离。受到毒雾的威胁，死亡阴影笼罩整个小镇，没有人确定尼奥丁衍生物会产生的后果。在第三部分"戴乐儿闹剧"中，杰克发现妻子芭比特（Babette）用身体换取一种名叫"戴乐儿"的治疗死亡恐惧的实验性药物。然而，戴乐儿不仅没有明显的治疗效果，还存在许多副作用。杰克决定枪杀利用药物引诱芭比特的格雷（Gray），在子弹击中格雷后，杰克感到后悔，于是将格雷送至由德国修女经营的医院。杰克在医院里听到修女说不相信上帝和来世，感到十分震惊，信仰危机更加重他了的恐惧感。

下文选自该书的第二部分"空中毒雾事件"，讲述一辆运载化学物质的罐车发生泄漏，在小镇上空形成一团黑色毒雾，造成居民严重的恐慌。

From White Noise

Part II: Airborne Toxic Event (Excerpt)

Small crowds collected around certain men. Here were the sources of information and rumor. One person worked in a chemical plant, another had overheard a remark, a third was related to a clerk in a state agency. True, false, and other kinds of news radiated through the dormitory from these dense clusters.

It was said that we would be allowed to go home first thing in the morning; that the government was engaged in a cover-up; that a helicopter had entered the toxic cloud and never reappeared; that the dogs had arrived from New Mexico, parachuting into a meadow in a daring night drop; that the town of Farmington would be uninhabitable for forty years.

Remarks existed in a state of permanent flotation. No one thing was either more or less plausible than any other thing. As people jolted out of reality, we were released from the need to distinguish.

Some families chose to sleep in their cars, others were forced to do so because there was no room for them in the seven or eight buildings on the grounds. We were in a large barracks, one of three such buildings at the camp, and with the generator now working we were fairly comfortable. The Red Cross had provided cots, portable heaters, sandwiches and coffee. There were kerosene lamps to supplement the existing overhead lights. Many people had radios, extra food to share with others, blankets, beach chairs, extra clothing. The place was crowded, still quite cold, but the sight of nurses and volunteer workers made us feel the children were safe, and the presence of other stranded souls, young women with infants, old and infirm people, gave us a certain staunchness and will, a selfless bent that was pronounced enough to function as a common identity. This large gray area, dank and bare and lost to history just a couple of hours ago, was an oddly agreeable place right now, filled with an eagerness of community and voice.

Seekers of news moved from one cluster of people to another, tending to linger at the larger groups. In this way I moved slowly through the barracks. There were nine evacuation centers, I learned, including this one and the Kung Fu Palace. Iron City had not been emptied out; nor had most of the other towns in the area. It was said that the governor was on his way from the capitol in an executive helicopter. It would probably set down in a bean field outside a deserted town, allowing the governor to emerge, square-jawed and confident, in a bush jacket, within camera range, for ten or fifteen seconds, as a demonstration of his imperishability.

What a surprise it was to ease my way between people at the outer edges of one of the largest clusters and discover that my own son was at the center of things, speaking in his new-found voice, his tone of enthusiasm for run-away calamity. He was talking about the airborne toxic event in a technical way, although his voice all but sang with prophetic disclosure. He pronounced the name itself, Nyodene Derivative[1], with an unseemly relish, taking morbid delight in the very sound. People listened attentively to this adolescent boy in a field jacket and cap, with binoculars strapped around his neck and an Instamatic[2] fastened to his belt. No doubt his listeners were influenced by his age. He would be truthful and earnest, serving no special interest; he would have an awareness of the environment; his knowledge of chemistry would be fresh and up-to-date.

I heard him say, "The stuff they sprayed on the big spill at the train yard was probably soda ash. But it was a case of too little too late. My guess is they'll get some crop dusters up in the air at daybreak and bombard the toxic cloud with lots more soda ash, which could break it up and scatter it into a million harmless puffs. Soda ash is the common name for sodium carbonate, which is used in the manufacture of glass, ceramics, detergents, and soaps. It's also what they use to make bicarbonate of soda, something a lot of you have probably guzzled after a night on the town."

People moved in closer, impressed by the boy's knowledgeability and wit. It was remarkable to hear him speak so easily to a crowd of strangers. Was he finding himself, learning how to determine his worth from the reactions of others? Was it possible that out of the turmoil and surge of this dreadful event he would learn to make his way in the world?

"What you're probably all wondering is what exactly is this Nyodene D. we keep hearing about? A good question. We studied it in school, we saw movies of rats having convulsions and so on. So, okay, it's basically simple. Nyodene D. is a whole bunch of things thrown together that are byproducts of the manufacture of insecticide. The original stuff kills roaches, the byproducts kill everything left over. A little joke our teacher made."

He snapped his fingers, let his left leg swing a bit.

"In powder form it's colorless, odorless, and very dangerous, except no one seems to know exactly what it causes in humans or in the offspring of humans. They tested for years and either they don't know for sure or they know and aren't saying. Some things are too awful to publicize."

He arched his brows and began to twitch comically, his tongue lolling in a corner of his mouth. I was astonished to hear people laugh.

"Once it seeps into the soil, it has a life span of forty years. This is longer than a lot of people. After five years you'll notice various kinds of fungi appearing between your regular windows and storm windows as well as in your clothes and food. After ten years your screens will turn rusty and begin to pit and rot. Siding will warp. There will be glass breakage and trauma to pets. After twenty years you'll probably have to seal yourself in the attic and just wait and see. I guess there's a lesson in all this. Get to know your chemicals."

I didn't want him to see me there. It would make him self-conscious, remind him of his former life as a gloomy and fugitive boy. Let him bloom, if that's what he was doing, in the name of mischance, dread, and random disaster. So I slipped away, passing a man who wore snow boots wrapped in plastic, and headed for the far end of the barracks, where we'd earlier made camp.

We were next to a black family of Jehovah's Witnesses. A man and woman with a boy about twelve. Father and son were handing out tracts to people nearby and seemed to have no trouble finding willing recipients and listeners.

The woman said to Babette, "Isn't this something?"

"Nothing surprises me anymore," Babette said.

"Isn't that the truth."

"What would surprise me would be if there were no surprises."

"That sounds about right."

"Or if there were little bitty surprises. That would be a surprise. Instead of things like this."

"God Jehovah's got a bigger surprise in store than this," the woman said.

"God Jehovah?"

"That's the one."

Steffie and Wilder were asleep in one of the cots. Denise sat at the other end engrossed in the Physicians' Desk Reference. Several air mattresses were stacked against the wall. There was a long line at the emergency telephone, people calling relatives or trying to reach the switchboard at one or another radio call-in show. The radios here were tuned mainly to just such shows. Babette sat in a camp chair, going through a canvas bag full of snack thins and other provisions. I noticed jars and cartons that had been sitting in the refrigerator or cabinet for months.

"I thought this would be a good time to cut down on fatty things," she said.

"Why now especially?"

"This is a time for discipline, mental toughness. We're practically at the edge."

"I think it's interesting that you regard a possible disaster for yourself, your family, and thousands of other people as an opportunity to cut down on fatty foods."

"You take discipline where you can find it," she said. "If I don't eat my yogurt now, I may as well stop buying the stuff forever. Except I think I'll skip the wheat germ."

The brand name was foreign-looking. I picked up the jar of wheat germ and examined the label closely.

"It's German," I told her. "Eat it."

There were people in pajamas and slippers. A man with a rifle slung over his shoulder. Kids crawling into sleeping bags. Babette gestured, wanting me to lean closer.

"Let's keep the radio turned off," she whispered. "So the girls can't hear. They haven't gotten beyond déjà vu[3]. I want to keep it that way."

"What if the symptoms are real?"

"How could they be real?"

"Why couldn't they be real?"

"They get them only when they're broadcast," she whispered. "Did Steffie hear about déjà vu on the radio?"

"She must have."

"How do you know? Were you with her when it was broadcast?"

"I'm not sure."

"Think hard."

"I can't remember."

"Do you remember telling her what déjà vu means?"

She spooned some yogurt out of the carton, seemed to pause, deep in thought.

"This happened before," she said finally.

"What happened before?"

"Eating yogurt, sitting here, talking about déjà vu."

"I don't want to hear this."

"The yogurt was on my spoon. I saw it in a flash. The whole experience. Natural, whole-milk, low-fat."

The yogurt was still on the spoon. I watched her put the spoon to her mouth, thoughtfully, trying to measure the action against the illusion of a matching original. From my squatting position I motioned her to lean closer.

【注解】

1. Nyodene Derivative: 尼奥丁–D/尼奥丁衍生物，虚构的有毒物质。在小说的其他地方，它被称为 "Nyodene D."，据说含有氯化物、苯、酚类和碳氢化合物。
2. Instamatic: 柯达公司1963年至1988年间制造的傻瓜相机。
3. déjà vu: 幻觉。

【思考题】

1. What is Nyodene D.? What are the features of Nyodene D.?
2. What consequences may Nyodene D. bring to mankind? What are people's reactions

towards Nyodene D.?
3. What is the reaction of the narrator, Jack Gladney, when he discovers his son is delivering a speech to the crowd? Why doesn't Jack want his son to see him there? What kind of relationship might be between father and son?

解读举例

1. 《白噪音》被喻为"美国的死亡之书",死亡主题贯穿全文。白噪音既是媒体发出的噪音,又是现代人对死亡的理解。对死亡的恐惧一直困扰着杰克和芭比特,他们竭尽所能消解死亡恐惧。杰克沉迷于对希特勒的研究事业中,他把对希特勒的研究当作灵魂避难所,而芭比特不惜用自己的身体交换治疗死亡恐惧的药物"戴乐儿"。种种荒诞的方式体现出后现代社会中人们的焦虑和无助。

---

2. 《白噪音》反映了后现代工业社会普遍存在的自然生态危机和精神生态危机。随着工业文明的发展,人类文明与自然生态间的矛盾愈演愈烈。自然生态平衡在工业发展进程中被打破,人类生存环境也因此受到严重威胁。不仅如此,工业文明也引发了人们严重的精神生态危机,焦虑、痛苦和孤独感无处不在。通过杰克和芭比特一家的生活可以看出美国普通民众虽然过着富裕的物质生活,但精神世界贫瘠。

---

3. 德里罗通过描述"空中毒雾事件"展现生态危机,并深刻反思技术对后现代社会的影响。现代人被无处不在的技术奴役,技术的过度发展困扰着人们的生活。技术在给人们提供愉悦和便利的同时,也威胁着人们的幸福感、自我意识、生存环境及真实的人类情感。

---

4. 《白噪音》勾勒了一个充满想象的超真实世界,图像、符号和符码吞噬了客观现实。在超真实世界,图像扮演着比语言更重要的角色,是"超现实"。作为图像表达的电视在家庭生活中扮演着重要角色,成为家庭成员之一。20世纪80年代,媒体力量甚至控制着人们的自然反应:当媒体公布人们受毒气影响可能出现的症状时,格拉德尼的女儿们也会出现这些症状。当媒体宣布出现新的症状时,她们又开始遭受新症状的折磨。